Handbook of
Cross-Cultural
Counseling and
Therapy

Handbook of Cross-Cultural Counseling and Therapy

Edited by
PAUL PEDERSEN

PRAEGER

New York
Westport, Connecticut
London

Library of Congress Cataloging-in-Publication Data

Handbook of cross-cultural counseling and therapy.

Includes bibliographies and index.
1. Cross-cultural counseling.   2. Psychotherapy—
Cross-cultural studies.   3. Minorities—Counseling of.
I. Pedersen, Paul, 1936-   .
[BF637.C6H317   1987]   158'.3   87-9337
ISBN 0-275-92713-X (pbk. : alk. paper)

A hardcover edition of *Handbook of Cross-Cultural Counseling and Therapy*
is available from Greenwood Press (ISBN 0-313-23914-2).

Library of Congress Catalog Card Number: 87-9337
ISBN: 0-275-92713-X

First published 1985

Paperback edition 1987

Praeger Publishers, One Madison Avenue, New York, NY 10010
A division of Greenwood Press, Inc.

Printed in the United States of America

The paper used in this book complies with the Permanent
Paper Standard issued by the National
Information Standards Organization (Z39.48-1984).

10 9 8 7 6 5 4

To my mother, Estelle Bennett

Contents

Preface

There is no well-defined constituency for cross-cultural counseling and therapy either as a field or as a discipline. Most counselors or therapists with interest in cross-cultural issues have had to develop their own programs from courses, mentors, and published resources scattered throughout the related disciplines. Many of these resources emphasize the specialized perspective of some ethnic group in relation to the dominant culture with less emphasis on the general skills for working in a multicultural population. Other special-interest groups emphasize age, gender, life-style or socioeconomic status as the important determinant of a person's ''cultural'' viewpoint. Most education and training programs have emphasized a disciplinary viewpoint rather than the complementarity of inter-disciplinary perspectives on the same cross-cultural issues. This book seeks to cross over many of these cultural boundaries of fields and disciplines.

We selected the more prominent authors on cross-cultural counseling and therapy and asked them to condense their most important message in twelve manuscript pages. By keeping the chapters short we were able to encourage tightly written perspectives from a wide range of applications within the cover of a single volume. Authors were asked to keep their references to a minimum and synthesize-summarize the most important insights about the chapter topic as much as possible. Each chapter contains carefully chosen references that will lead the reader to the most important published reference resources on essential aspects of the chapter theme.

Wherever possible the authors were asked to follow a similar chapter format on their special topic including: (1) history, (2) present status, (3) fundamental assumptions, (4) fundamental theories, and (5) future directions, although in some chapters it was important for authors to modify this structure. Some of the chapters did not follow that format because the best treatment of the chapter's subject required a different format. The history section provides background and development of the specific topic and identifies the mentors, the most significant events, and the most significant contributions. The present-status section identifies contemporary issues under discussion, the controversies, prevailing trends, and the most important questions being asked. Six to eight of the most fundamental assumptions about the topic are identified along with the degree of support for each assumption. The most popular theoretical concepts are also identified for each chapter topic. A final section on future directions projects a scenario for how the topic is likely to develop within the next ten years and into the future.

Each of the five sections in this book is briefly introduced in an overview of the conceptual framework for counseling and therapy perspectives, counseling and therapy methods, client populations, issues and research, and education and training. Perhaps these chapters will increase the communication between otherwise isolated constituencies for whom cross-cultural counseling and therapy are important.

The two most serious problems in the literature about cross-cultural counseling and therapy are (1) that the literature is widely distributed among thousands of journals and publications that are not frequently well known even by professional counselors and therapists; and (2) that the quality of available publications is extremely uneven with many publications concealing bad methodology behind the culturally exotic. This reference handbook on cross-cultural counseling and therapy provides access to the network of resources on cross-cultural counseling and therapy while guiding the reader toward the more substantial publications on the topic. It will serve as a reference to the major ideas of the fifty more prominent authors in the field as well, so that the reader can follow up with other publications by these authors. Even the cross-culturally sophisticated counselor and therapist will no doubt discover colleagues from other disciplines or perspectives who are working along parallel lines. This reference handbook seeks most of all to reduce the confusion in the literature about cross-cultural counseling and therapy by combining these different perspectives and topics within the same volume. Readers new to this field receive an introduction to the many aspects of the field, and readers familiar with the field discover how other disciplines maintain parallel interests in cross-cultural counseling and therapy to widen their cross-cultural horizons.

By including so many of the most prominent authors in one volume and by condensing their most important messages, the handbook becomes a new kind of "encyclopedia" for a rapidly changing field. The book defines *culture* to include variables beyond ethnicity and nationality and defines *counseling* to include nonformal as well as informal contexts for counseling and therapy. The book not only demonstrates the "complexity" of cross-cultural counseling and therapy, but it maintains that a complicated perspective is both *good* and necessary for *authenticity*. Culture can be perceived in a positive rather than a negative perspective.

The importance of interculturally skilled counseling is widely recognized in the priorities of the National Institute of Mental Health, the American Psychological Association's accreditation criteria, the 1979 President's Commission on Mental Health Needs Assessment, and numerous other professional and public organizations at the national as well as the international level. However, there are few degree-oriented academic programs at the university level to train counselors specifically in cross-cultural skills. This *Handbook of Cross-Cultural Counseling and Therapy* is an attempt to meet the needs of preservice and in-service training in cross-cultural counseling and therapy.

Cross-cultural counseling and therapy research in the United States has failed to develop a unified theoretical basis for several reasons. First, the emphasis of research has been on abnormal behavior, and only recently has research discovered a pancultural core and then only for the more serious categories of disturbance such as schizophrenia or effective psychoses. Second, the complexity of research on cross-cultural counseling and therapy has been so difficult to manage that most researchers have ignored the cultural variable. Third, the available research on cross-cultural counseling and therapy has not focused on the applied and practical concerns of program development, service delivery, and techniques of treatment. Fourth, there has not been enough interdisciplinary collaboration across psychology, psychiatry, anthropology, and the other disciplines related to cross-cultural counseling and therapy. Sixth, research has emphasized the symptom as a basic variable while neglecting the complex interaction of persons, professional perspectives, institutions, and community.

A pluralistic perspective is needed that will accommodate the range of differences across cultural boundaries. Becoming skilled in accommodating the more obviously recognized cultural differences of nationality and ethnicity can provide the opportunity to develop multiple perspectives that will increase our accuracy in dealing with the sometimes less obvious differences of age, gender, life-style, socioeconomic status, and affiliation. Until the issues of cross-cultural counseling and therapy are seen and described in terms of increasing accuracy for all counseling and therapy, rather than meeting the demands of some special-interest group, we are unlikely to see more than a token acknowledgement of cultural variables in definition of the mental health professions.

This handbook is a convenient reference book to review the history, present status, fundamental assumptions, fundamental theories, and future directions of forty specializations within the broad field of cross-cultural counseling. Each chapter is written by one of the leading authors in that specialty. The forty chapters are themselves divided into five evenly divided clusters of chapters on (1) counseling perspectives that take the larger conceptual view of cross-cultural elements of counseling; (2) counseling methods, which reviews a range of alternative counseling approaches for including cultural data; (3) client populations, which includes two perspectives on some of the more recognized ethnic groups of the United States; (4) key issues of controversy in the various culture-sensitive "pressure points" of counseling and therapy; and (5) guidelines for education and training across cultural boundaries of counseling and therapy.

This handbook as a reference seeks to reduce the confusion of those fields of counseling and therapy interested in cultural variables and substitute a more intricate complexity that is ordered and not random in the study of personal cultural orientation.

Acknowledgments

I want to thank the fifty authors in these handbook chapters who willingly (more or less) condensed their most important messages to the very brief and confining format required. I would also like to thank Pat Moran, who helped me type and assemble the many chapter manuscripts; Howard Kligerman, James Campbell, Bob Wilson, and Anne Pedersen, who read chapters and helped make suggestions for changes; Florence Mitchell, who worked on the index; and Cynthia Harris from Greenwood Press, who provided support, encouragement, and understanding throughout the book-making process.

1

COUNSELING AND THERAPY PERSPECTIVES

In the twenty years since C. Gilbert Wrenn wrote about the culturally encapsulated counselor many of us have been eagerly seeking a conceptual framework for cross-cultural counseling and therapy. Although there are thousands of publications telling us what is wrong, there are few guidelines for the right way to approach cultural differences and similarities in counseling and therapy. These seven conceptual chapters are intended to provide a balance of positive and negative guidelines.

Edwin L. Herr and Donald Super both describe the opportunities for an expansion of cross-cultural career counseling to meet the increased needs of a multicultural society. However, Harry Triandis points out the tenacity of individualistic assumptions even in the face of "collectivist" cultures. Otto Klineberg likewise points out the dangers of imposing the culturally unique perspective of a dominant culture as a general principle applied to all cultures. Ludwig F. Lowenstein describes how the ideas of counseling and therapy have applied to Great Britain, and Nathan Deen shows how these ideas have grown and developed on the European continent. Juris G. Draguns concludes this section with a perspective of cultural differences from the popular viewpoint of illness or pathology.

It is clear that the applications of counseling and therapy are expanding to include a balance of conceptual framework such as individualistic-collectivistic or universal-unique. It is also clear that the ideas of counseling and therapy represent many of the core values of the Western industrialized world of Europe and North America. Finally, it is clear that most references to cultural differences relative to counseling have emphasized the pathology of deviation from the cultural norms of a host culture.

These initial chapters on the conceptual framework are intended to prepare the reader for more specific thematic chapters to follow as we examine cross-cultural counseling and therapy from different viewpoints.

International Approaches to Career Counseling and Guidance

EDWIN L. HERR

HISTORY

Contemporary approaches to career counseling and guidance have evolved in many parts of the world roughly during the past 125 years. Undoubtedly, crude mechanisms of distributing persons among available occupations, whether or not with their conscious choice, planning, and preparation, have existed since the dawn of recorded history. E. G. Williamson (1965) and H. Borow (1964) among others have catalogued some of these early perspectives on "vocational guidance" as early as Greek and Roman civilization and as they have occurred in subsequent centuries. Whether these historical mechanisms should be described legitimately as approaches to career counseling and guidance is moot, but they served such goals, however primitively, in their time and place in history using the family, churches, and other social institutions as the principal settings.

Confining one's historical analysis of the profession's beginnings to the last century and a quarter suggests a number of major concepts and mentors on which present conceptions rest. Perhaps foremost among the concepts are those of individual differences, the implications of them for human performance in education and work, and the scientific measurement and application of such knowledge in choosing and adjusting to a vocation. During the period of 1850 to 1900 the prime historical figures in these emerging human schemes were Francis Galton in England, Wilhelm Wundt in Germany, G. Stanley Hall and James McKeen Cattell in the United States, and Alfred Binet and V. Henri in France.

Much of this early research on the measurement of human characteristics and their implications for work performance culminated early in the twentieth century in models of counseling and guidance in the United States and Europe that applied the growing knowledge of individual differences in the service of individuals actually seeking access to jobs. One of the most notable of such models is that of Parsons's three-step process leading to "True Reasoning," which included assessment of individual characteristics, acquiring knowledge of available occupational opportunities, and the merger of individual and occupational information into a plan of action. This model, with its emphases on the combined use of psychometric assessment of the individual, occupational information, and a decision-making strategy, has tended to appear in some variation as a major paradigm of the provisions of career counseling and guidance in many parts of the world.

PRESENT STATUS

The international reasons for and the approaches to providing career counseling and guidance are a mosaic. Since career counseling and guidance are shaped by the economic conditions and political belief systems that prevail in any nation, it is obvious that differences across nations in these characteristics will yield significant variations in the shape and substance of career counseling and guidance, in who provides such services, in who should receive such services, and in where they are located.

At present an overarching reason for intensified attention to career counseling and guidance is the high rate of youth unemployment in nations throughout the world. These rates tend to be two or more times that of adult unemployment rates and raise serious concerns about the mechanisms facilitating the transition to work for youth. For example, B. G. Reubens (1981) analyzed European perspectives on the transition from school to work as including:

1. The special transition problems of early school leavers
2. Inadequate preparation in the basic competencies required in working life
3. Insufficient acquaintance with structure and organization of the work world
4. Too little or overspecialized vocational training, whether supplied by the educational or employment systems
5. Faults in all of the social institutions responsible for easing the transition of young people from school to work. (p. 35)

To be overly simplistic, the level of industrial development of a nation affects the type of work-related questions its population is likely to be able or is encouraged to consider. Certainly, these questions differ among nations considered to be the least developed, developing, and developed in terms of their kinds and levels of industrial development available. It is the level and type of development that defines the diversity and character of the nation's occupational structure, the training required of workers, the amount and character of trade with other nations, and related phenomena affecting the kind of work available.

The national level of industrial development also suggests the timing of the emergence of organized programs of career counseling and guidance. If access to work opportunities and information about their differences can be conveyed adequately within a family or tribal unit and if training can be accomplished by passing occupational skills from father to son or mother to daughter, there is really no need for an organized program of career counseling and guidance. As information becomes complex, however, occupations become more diverse. Personal hopes and fears related to achievement, livelihood, mobility, and career are stimulated by a wide range of opportunities. A context is created for viable, organized programs and specialties in career counseling and guidance. Thus those nations in which the Industrial Revolution and the mechanization of work tended to occur first—for example, Western Europe and the United States—are also those in which models of career counseling and guidance tended to arise first. As nations become industrialized, some form of career guidance and counseling tends to follow.

Also of interest is how governments view career counseling and guidance: as sources of human capital, as instruments of personal choice and fulfillment, and as a combination of both. A. G. Watts and E. L. Herr (1976) suggested that societies vary on at least two dimensions in their approaches to helping youth and adults with work-related and career questions. The two dimensions can be distinguished by (a) whether the primary focus of the counseling or guidance mechanism is on the needs of the society or on the needs of the individual, and (b) whether the counseling and guidance approach basically accepts the social-industrial status quo or is concerned with changing it in some set of prescribed directions. Thus if a society is prescriptive about individual talents being used in behalf of the state, the career-counseling and guidance mechanisms available are likely to be considerably different from those in a society in which assumptions about the need for social control and freedom of individual choice are different.

D. E. Super (1974) contended that when one examines career-guidance practices among the developed nations, four conflicting trends are apparent.

1. *Manpower use versus human development.* This trend essentially parallels the notions of Watts and Herr (1976) in regard to social control, human capital, social change, or individual needs as the bases for approaches to career counseling and development. In the example of manpower use, counseling and guidance are viewed as sociopolitical processes designed to direct and train persons in areas reflecting national economic and social needs. Human development as an emphasis would stress the provision of opportunities for individuals to know about and choose in accordance with their aptitudes, values, needs, and interests.

2. *Occupational choice versus vocational development.* The conflict inherent in this trend is whether career counseling and guidance should focus upon immediate choice of available jobs or, in addition, upon "educating people to choose," taking into account how immediate choice will likely affect intermediate and future goals, life-style, use of discretionary time, and family and community roles. Nations concerned about short-term employability and the needs of the labor market are not likely to be concerned about flexible career goals that other nations take for granted.

3. *Information dissemination versus counseling*. At issue here is whether the provision of accurate and pertinent information about educational and occupational opportunities is the primary or, indeed, sole function of career counseling and guidance or whether the major role of the latter mechanisms is to help persons decide what information is relevant to them, acquire it, and use it effectively.

4. *Professional guidance versus lay guidance*. Of concern here is how much and what kind of training specialists in career counseling and guidance need to be effective and whether a particular nation can or wishes to provide the resources required to "professionalize" such specialists.

Given the variety of political and economic factors that contribute to the provision of career counseling and guidance from nation to nation, it is not surprising that the form and location of such provisions differ internationally. In addition to school-based programs, vocational-guidance centers in many nations occur outside the school to provide testing, counseling, and placement for youth leaving school or adults seeking work. These vocational-guidance centers are frequently under the control of ministries of labor or universities and may provide career guidance, job placement, testing, or interviews with youth and adults. In some nations, they may provide special services for physically disabled or other occupationally disadvantaged persons who need specific help directed toward physical and mental adjustment before returning to work.

FUNDAMENTAL ASSUMPTIONS

Although the career-counseling and guidance techniques used from nation to nation tend to be similar, the purposes for which they are used tend to differ. Therefore, compiling a set of assumptions that undergird the provision of career counseling and guidance across the world is difficult. Nevertheless, those that follow seem to be relevant to the topic.

1. Although comparative approaches in guidance or counseling tend to contrast nations as though they were separate, homogeneous units, they rarely are. Most nations embody some pluralism in their working populations that is based on racial, ethnic, gender, socioeconomic, religious, or other grounds. These characteristics tend to filter the types of encouragement or information about work access and opportunities that different groups receive. In some nations career-counseling and guidance mechanisms serve to neutralize the effects of these factors; in other nations they perpetuate class or caste distinctions in the distribution of information and support related to work choice and access.

2. National legislation is a major influence in most nations in defining what counseling and guidance services will be available, to whom they will be directed, and who will provide them. In virtually all nations the provision of career counseling and guidance occurs in educational or community settings funded fully or partially by government funds. Although other organizations and persons in private practice may also deliver such services on a fee basis, the major

provisions of guidance and counseling in vocational-guidance centers, schools, and universities tend to be a function of government policy and fiscal support.

3. Virtually all industrialized nations and most developing nations have introduced career-guidance and counseling provisions into schools or community units. The primary assumption is that information about work opportunities, labor-market needs, and industrial discipline is sufficiently complex that it deserves treatment in school curricula or as a systematic provision of a specialist.

4. Individual development and the talents that result reflect a complex blend of hereditary and environmental factors including those that are psychological, sociological, educational, political, economic, and physical. National systems of career counseling and guidance tend to differ on which of these factors is pre-eminent and, therefore, which should receive the most attention in individual assessment, counseling, and remediation.

5. Persons who are able to find commitment and purposefulness in life are more likely to be productive, respectful of others, and able to adjust to change. The issue from nation to nation is: to what does one owe commitment? Through what means is one to be purposeful? Answers to such questions reflect the kind of individual achievement images and goals to which different national systems of career counseling and guidance are oriented and in the service of which they use their techniques and processes. In this sense a fundamental assumption is that to view career-counseling and guidance concepts and practices outside the context of the political and economic realities of the society in which they operate is to miss the subtle but pervasive influences upon the freedom of action or the environmental determinism by which personal careers are forged (Herr, 1978).

FUNDAMENTAL THEORIES

The fundamental theories on which international approaches to career guidance and counseling are based differ somewhat from nation to nation as political and economic factors shape the psychological environments in which achievement images, choice options, and freedom of choice are forged. In general terms, however, there are two classes of theory of prime importance: psychological and sociological. Respectively, these theories tend to emphasize individual action in career behavior or the effects of the social structure upon choices available and which persons (by socioeconomic class or gender or race or ethnicity) are eligible for which choices.

A. G. Watts (1976), in comparing the evolution of career-development theory in England with that of the United States, suggested:

It is intriguing that theories of career development in the USA have been so heavily dominated by psychologists whereas in Britain the contributions of sociologists have been much more prominent. The dominant force in the USA has been on the actions of individuals, while in Britain indigenous theoretical work has been more preoccupied with the constraints of social structures. . . the failure of the American social-structure evidence to have much influence on career development theory seems to be due basically to cultural and historical factors. From the beginning of its independent existence, the USA has been formally committed to the proposition that all men are created equal...As a result, there is belief that the individual controls his own destiny; that if he has appropriate abilities, and if these can be appropriately developed, his fate lies in his own hands. (p. 3)

Although there are variations on the two classes of theory underlying international approaches to career guidance, the most influential tend to flow from either psychological or sociological roots. These disciplinary bases differ in application, for example, depending on whether the focus of concern is individual pathology or normal development, individual differences or class distinctions, choice-making styles or differences in opportunity by population group. Due to the intense contemporary concern about employment and unemployment, characteristics of labor markets, and changes in the technological content of occupational structure, increasing attention has been turning to economics as an additional class of theory necessary to the development of effective models of career guidance and counseling.

FUTURE DIRECTIONS

It seems inevitable that one of the future directions for international approaches to career guidance and counseling is expansion. The social, economic, and occupational conditions that give rise to formal guidance systems are now being experienced worldwide. High rates of youth and adult unemployment; the complexity of the choice of and preparation for occupational entry; concerns about worker productivity, adjustment, and the quality of work life; shifts in the demographics of the labor force; and the effects of adaptation of advanced technology on labor-intensive industries are only a few of the issues shared in nation after nation. In a collective sense, these factors push inexorably toward a larger role for career guidance and counseling in national development plans.

Beyond expansion per se, a second future direction of international approaches to career guidance and counseling is growth in professional maturity. The historic evolution of international approaches to career guidance and counseling has been characterized by the adoption in developing nations of approaches to career guidance and counseling used in the developed nations. In many instances such career-guidance and counseling approaches have not worked effectively because they have been insensitive to the cultural, political, and economic differences that prevail between the originating and the adopting nation.

It has become increasingly evident to guidance and counseling leaders, in both national and international agencies, that career guidance and counseling does not operate in a political, economic, or social vacuum. The state of a national economy, the achievement images or social metaphors important to that nation at its level of industrial development, and political views of individual freedom of choice are some of the factors that affect both the process and the substance of career guidance and counseling. Acknowledgment of such realities will continue to stimulate a search for those elements that are common and effective across national models of career guidance and counseling and those elements that must be considered indigenous to a particular nation or culture. Such insights will likely improve the quality and credibility of planning for international programs of career guidance and counseling in the future.

REFERENCES

Borow, H. (1964) Milestones: A chronology of notable events in the history of vocational guidance. In Borow, H. (Ed.), *Man in a world of work*. Boston: Houghton Mifflin.

Herr, E. L. (1978) Career development concepts and practices: Some international perspectives. *Counseling and Human Development*, *11*(1), 1–12.

Reubens, B. G. (1981) *From school to work: A European perspective*. Columbus, Ohio: The ERIC Clearinghouse on Adult, Career, and Vocational Education, Ohio State University.

Super, D. E. (1974) The broader context of career development and vocational guidance: American trends in world perspective. In Herr, E. L. (Ed.), *Vocational guidance and human development*. Boston: Houghton Mifflin.

Watts, A. G. (1976) Introduction. In Watts, A. G., Super, D. E., Kidd, J. M. (Eds.), *Career development in Britain*. Cambridge, England: Hobson's Press.

Watts, A. G., & Herr, E. L. (1976) Career(s) education in Britain and the USA. *British Journal of Guidance and Counselling*, *4*(2), 129–142.

Williamson, E. G. (1965) *Vocational counseling: Some historical, philosophical, and theoretical perspectives*. New York: McGraw-Hill.

Career Counseling across Cultures

DONALD SUPER

An American counselor, working in an office in the United States, helps a foreign student returning home think through career plans. The same American counselor is sought out by a colleague who, having married a foreigner, is contemplating moving to the spouse's country to pursue a career there. Another American counselor employed in an overseas setting counsels a local student about a career in that country. This same American counselor talks with a local adult about a possible career in the United States. All of these situations, and others such as those in which foreign counselors work in the United States, involve cross-cultural counseling.

As a teaching and researching professor in France, I found that despite my own six years of secondary education in French schools and despite so complete an assimilation of the French culture in my teens that I dream of my adolescence in French, I was hesitant to counsel students or adults who sought my advice or counsel in France later when I lived and worked there. Four years of higher education in England had done a good deal to Anglicize me. *Information* about my field of psychology in France, the United Kingdom, and certain other European countries as well as in North America seemed to me to be within my competencies. I had their journals, knew many of the relevant people in my specialty, had lectured in their universities, and was familiar with their languages. *Information* about careers in the United States, if emigration was being considered, was also my domain, for I had ample American experience and the usual American publications on careers. However, I believed that I did not know the current labor market well enough in Europe nor did I know enough about the occupational mores to *counsel* about career development in France or England. For example, it was well known that clinical psychologists in French hospitals worked only as psychological examiners under close medical supervision, and that there were many non-medical psychoanalysts and many graphologists who had substantial private practices, but I knew little about their training, their professional affiliations, and their career patterns. I knew that vocational counselors who took my courses in Paris had two years of professional postgraduate training but no training in interviewing and counseling except as learned by them in their internships. But I was not sure that I understood the fine points of counselor-pupil-parent relationships in a country in which parental roles in decision making were prepotent.

These personal experiences in England and France, supplemented by brief periods of consulting and lecturing in Asia, Africa, and South America, bring out the point that in career counseling across cultures a variety of considerations are important: the counselor's attitude toward the other culture, the nature of the culture itself and particularly the ways in which it differs from that of the counselor, the patterns and determinants of career development in the other culture, and the nature of the labor market in the country in question. It is with these topics that this chapter deals, closing with some thoughts on the implications for training in cross-cultural career counseling. Interest in these issues being new, most of what follows is based on experience and observation rather than on research. Perhaps this volume will inspire people to carry out the needed studies.

THE COUNSELOR'S ETHNOCENTRISM

Schoolchildren in the United States learn that the first steamboat was invented by Robert Fulton and steamed up the Hudson River; their peers in France learn that the first steamer was invented by Michel Papin and steamed down the Rhine one hundred years earlier. The French textbooks are correct (the sailors burned Papin's primitive steamer to prevent technological unemployment). French children, on the other hand, have traditionally been taught that French is the most precise language in the world, despite the fact that French editors of international educational and scientific journals recognize that in their bilingual publications it takes more words, with less precision, to state in French what is said more concisely and more precisely in English.

Thus biases are learned early in life, and they are not easily changed. Americans often fail to think of Italian immigrant laborers as potential Michelangelos or Da Vincis. They do not see a Polish immigrant applying for manual work as a possible Copernicus or Conrad. They do not imagine the Chinese who, with the Irish, laid the rails that spanned the continent as Confuciuses or Sun Yat Sens. The effects of the old biases can determine the counselor's approach to a client without awareness of what is happening. The biases need to be examined, and they apply to race and to gender as well as to national background.

THE DIMENSIONS OF CULTURE

The dimensions of culture are many. They include the nature and rigidity of the class and caste structure, the value system, the relationship of the individual to the group, and the nature of the enterprise system. They include also the subject of the next section of this chapter, the nature and traditions of career development itself.

The Class Structure and the Opportunity System

It is commonplace that America, as a new country, is the land of opportunity. People in most of the countries of Europe have long viewed this continent as one to which a person could come with few if any resources and make a way, if not to the top, at least to a much better place in life than had been occupied in the old country. Americans, each wave of newcomers as well as those already established in the United States, have expected to make a better life for themselves and for their children. One could go from log cabin to president, as Abraham Lincoln did; from repair shop to great manufacturer, as Henry Ford did; from apprentice to inventor, statesman, and the darling of the French salons, as Benjamin Franklin did—and the examples are not all from the eighteenth and nineteenth centuries as the Polaroid camera, Beatle music, and the late Grace Kelly have made clear.

Although the Beatles first achieved fame and wealth in Great Britain, and were British, their native country has had a different tradition of social mobility. It might have been written of England that "by their accents ye shall know them," for Britain has long had an upper-class accent that prevailed at that level across the country and regional accents that grow stronger as one descends the social scale. This fact worked against social and occupational mobility, for it combined with the fact that to learn to speak like "one's betters" was seen by one's family and friends as attempting to put on airs. A. B. Hollingshead (1949) documented the fact that, in the American Midwest where he did his study of growing up, the children of the poorest and least well educated tended automatically to be shunted, by teachers and by employers, into the lowest-level opportunities available, while the children of the better-established adults were similarly placed in the way of the best opportunities. The saying "they come from a fine (no 'count) family" is still heard in America, although less frequently. Similarly, labor-dominated British politics have still not eliminated such attitudes, even though they are now less often expressed publicly.

American counselors who are visiting, observing, lecturing, counseling, or researching in Great Britain often fail to take the importance of the class system in Britain sufficiently into account. Those who do are nonetheless impressed by the importance of class in that union-dominated country. Students going to universities from working-class families find themselves suffering from anxiety because of the severance of ties with their familial cultures. The sons of unskilled and semiskilled workers in industrial cities find themselves forced, by their peers, to choose between the subcultures of those who cherish the group and reject teachers and work and those who accept the goals set by their middle- or lower-middle-class teachers and work for grades and for advancement.

British sociologists have, for some decades, stressed, and in fact almost immortalized, social class and the opportunity structure as determinants of careers. K. Roberts (1981) in particular argued that the British counselors (careers officers and careers teachers) who have been influenced by American self-realization theories and practices are wasting their time and that they would be of more real help to students if they would bend their efforts to helping them make the most of what is available to them. For self-realization Roberts would substitute self- and social-acceptance. There would be, then, no William Morrises of motorcar fame and wealth (Lord Nuffield), and no Margaret Thatchers at 10 Downing Street (she would presumably have married another grocer's son or perhaps a pharmacist-chemist), unless, of course, they had been moved to rise, as did Lord Nuffield, by the practical route followed by some who did not, like Mrs. Thatcher, have good access to the educational ladder.

In France the class system works differently. The Revolution at the end of the eighteenth century cleared the way for many to rise from humble origins, although most of those who broke through the class barriers were, like Napoleon and Pasteur, from the middle class. What France substituted for the aristocracy of birth was an aristocracy of intelligence. The reformers opened up the schools to all who would and could use them and, using a system of competitive examinations at each level, took the ablest higher and higher and thus into the civil service, the educational network, the professions, or management. Although Britain also relied heavily on competition in education, there the class barriers had not fallen as they had in France, and the language was less standardized.

Illustrations could be drawn, too, from India with its caste system and its classes within castes, from Japan and China with their different cultures, and from Kenya with its yet different complex of tribal mores.

The Individual and the Group

People growing up in the United States are exposed from early childhood to the philosophy and practice of seeking self-actualization. This is not to imply that everyone experiences, in a significant degree, encouragement and opportunity for self-expression and for self-development. The opportunity structure is important here, too, and there are great differences between people, between families, and between subcultures in this country. But a tradition was started by the early settlers from England and France, settlers who sought in a developing land opportunities that they believed did not exist for them in their homelands. The opportunity structure was fed first by the German religious and political groups who came here in the late eighteenth and nineteenth centuries; then by the Irish seeking to escape the potato famine and by the Scots displaced from the highlands or seeking better conditions than they had found in Ulster, and then again by the Italian and Polish peasants who knew that farming and construction work in North America would offer them more opportunities than they could find in their more stagnant economies. Semiskilled factory workers in

Connecticut some years ago, asked what they wanted for their children, replied, "A better life than I've had," and when asked next, "What might that be?" the answer was, "I don't know—they'll have to decide that themselves."

The strength of this tradition is such that it is easy for Americans to assume that the same motivation exists, in about the same degree, in other cultures. But Americans, except for Native American Indians or the descendants of imported blacks, are descendants of people who had the initiative to leave what they had and to strive for something better. As one American who went back to the village from which his ancestors had come put it, "Thank heavens for John James, who got up and went!"

In some countries the interests of the individual are subordinate to those of the parents and the parental family. The occupations to be pursued by the children are determined by family needs as seen by the parents. This is often observed in African and Asian cultures. Even in France, whose culture was also the "born-free" culture of the Swiss Jean-Jacques Rousseau in neighboring Geneva, it is the family that plays the principal role in the educational and vocational counseling that is carried on by the school counselors. In some cultures, as in Japan, the parents play a key role up to a certain age, at which time the school, university, or company for which the individual works becomes the decision maker in the shaping of careers. In others, as in the communistic West African country of Benin, it is the state that opens or closes the doors of opportunity in the school system and in the world of work, using what is deemed to be the interest of the state in routing pupils and entrants into the labor force one way or another (Super, 1983).

CAREER DEVELOPMENT IN SELECTED COUNTRIES

An encyclopedia of career development in diverse cultures would be an interesting and instructive volume, for it would point up and document the important differences that cross-cultural career counselors should keep in mind or look up as needed. At present, however, the studies needed have not been made and published. In a chapter such as this, the writer can only rely on personal observation in the countries known from personal experience and from reading in sources such as the special issue of the *Personnel and Guidance Journal*, May 1983, edited by Bea Wehrly and Nathan Deen, and in the series of case studies analyzed by the writer for UNESCO (Super, 1983).

The United Kingdom

Even in that "tight little island" there are differences in the prevailing career-development patterns in England, Wales, and Scotland. The school and university traditions of the two (some would say three) countries differ. England has striven for decades to break the ties of social class, speech, and opportunity structure in democratizing education and employment, with limited results. Scotland, on the contrary, has an old democratic tradition of public education and, with limited opportunities in its national economy, a way of exporting people to the far corners of the earth that dates from at least the fifteenth century. Even in Scotland, however, there are social-class differences in speech that differentiate the Scots-speaking middle and working classes from the English-speaking upper classes. In England and Wales that mark of class is even greater, and "non-U" youths who learn, in some schools and universities, to speak with an upper-class accent and to use upper-class words soon find themselves alien in, if not alienated from, their middle- or lower-class families. Some youths actually reject educational opportunities out of family or class loyalty. Since education is an important determinant of entry into the professional and managerial occupations, and since speech is often viewed as a mark of education, class is, as Roberts (1981) has stressed, a determinant of careers in Great Britain and especially in England.

In what Americans would call public schools in a manufacturing city British working-class boys have been shown to choose between middle-class values and careers, on the one hand, and working-class values and careers, on the other hand. The former were, in this subculture and at the same time of the study, known to one group as the "ear 'oles," the boys who listened to the teachers, did their assignments, and strove to excel in school with occupational careers in mind. The latter were known to themselves as "the lads," "the fellows" of a vanished America, the "good guys" of recent date in this country. The lads valued the opinions of their peers, who balked at, if they did not rebel against, the school, its values, and its teachers; they rejected school learning; they rejected occupational careers. They aimed at low-level jobs that paid better than apprenticeships or clerical work at the start and that did not require training. These were jobs on which they could socialize with their peers while working. With them, they could support being in the audience at football games and sharing the talk over a mug of beer in the neighborhood pub.

In another way, at least, career development in Great Britain has proceeded differently from in the United States. Here, mobility has been viewed with favor, as people move to better jobs, with "better" organizations, in "better" parts of the country. Not so in Britain, where in the civil service tradition stability was long considered a virtue and occupational mobility was frowned upon. This has changed some in recent years, but stability in the organization and thus organizational careers with or without mobility are still considered desirable, except in some of the competitive businesses fostered by modern methods of production and distribution.

France

The French Revolution and the educational reforms of the Napoleonic era did much more to break down the class system in France than did the Industrial Revolution in Great Britain. The aristocracy that had flourished and then deteriorated at Court in Paris had been discredited, largely exiled or destroyed, or become pseudo-bourgeois to survive. Education and advancement had been opened up not only to the bourgeois but to anyone who showed in grade school and then in a lycee that he or she had academic ability. Educational achievement became the ladder for entry not only into prestigious governmental positions and advancement but into the technical and managerial careers that required mastery of technical or verbal skills. The aristocracy of merit in an educated society that Thomas Jefferson had advocated, partly as a result of his knowledge of what was happening there, came close to realization in nineteenth- and twentieth-century France.

The opportunity structure still played a part: children living in isolated areas might get to an elementary school and generally did. One result was the minimizing of class and even, to a lesser degree, of regional differences in speech. But those who were not encouraged to read by their families and who were not supported in studying at home had less opportunity to achieve in school than did those who had educationally supportive families. Abraham Lincoln was not kept from reading borrowed books by the light of the cabin fireplace and was not scolded for not finding household chores with which productively to occupy his evenings. French children who did, in isolated areas, do well in elementary school still found it difficult to leave home to go to a secondary school in a population center. It was verbal ability and geography that largely determined career development in France, as many studies made during the past half-century have shown.

One result of the relatively recent awareness of these facts has been an emphasis on diversity of programs and on facilitating mobility within the school system, together with an interest in "rattrappage," in making it possible for people to catch up and to make up for time spent in less self-realizing activities than might have been found with better guidance or with an earlier awakening. Schools and institutions of postsecondary education no longer fit the simple two-track pattern that existed before World War II. School counselors have been transformed from selectors of apprentices to career counselors well armed with information concerning the variety of opportunities that lies ahead, well equipped to help students understand themselves in relation to these possibilities. Universities and polytechnics now have their own counseling centers and psychologists trained in career counseling. Meritocracy now recognizes a variety of ways of being meritorious.

The French educational system has thus become more like the American system. But as noted in the introduction to this chapter, having spent six years in it as a student and two years in it as a professor, I would not consider myself ready to take over, on an exchange basis, the work of a French school, university, or adult counselor. Not only have vocabularies changed since the two different eras of living and studying (1922–28) or working (1958–60) in France, but much that is *not* shown about the educational structure in the helpful publications of the Organization Nationale pour l'Information Scolaire et Professionnelle needs to be assimilated by a working counselor in France. The informal organization and the mores need to be known, and that requires currentness in the culture. Such currentness can be acquired by studying the culture while working in it, but experience shows that it is only after about a year of immersing oneself in the culture that one can really function in it, and that therefore a three-year stint is necessary if one is to be effective. The same might be said of work with minority subcultures in one's own country.

THE LABOR MARKET

Aspects of the labor market that cross-cultural counselors need to know about include entry qualifications-means of entry, advancement and working conditions. These aspects are, in one's own country, part of the counselor's stock in trade. In working with members of minority groups in one's own country one can quickly acquire the needed knowledge. These matters are open and subtle effects of ethnic, sex, and religious "minority" status on employment opportunities and legal provisions for minimizing or accentuating discrimination and the attitudes of these minorities and of employers toward discrimination, whether positive or negative. For example, an American woman who had begun to make her mark in a major regional planning authority in one specialty was called in by her manager and told that since the organization needed a visible woman, she was going to be promoted to director of another specialty in which she had not been working: the upshot of the interview was that she resigned, with due notice, for she would not work in an organization that was run in such an authoritarian way, and she would not accept promotion on the grounds of sex.

In a foreign country one must know the peculiar requirements of "qualifications" for employment. In England and Wales, for example, a "school leaver" is not a dropout, as the term implies to most Americans, but the nearest equivalent to a high school graduate. School leavers are youths who have reached the age of sixteen and can legally leave school and who do not plan to go on to an advanced liberal, scientific, or technical education. To have educational qualifications for employment that are comparable to an American high school diploma they take a series of school-leaving examinations, choosing as many subjects as they and their advisers consider wise. They thus have evidence of having "completed" a basic educational program. If they stay in school they go on to specialize in an academic secondary school and after one or two years take a second-level series of examinations in what they have specialized in and thus have higher-level general employment qualifications or use them as university-entrance examinations.

Tradition in England and Wales has also led to higher education being viewed as liberal although specialized education. For generations the best route to higher-level civil service careers was the study of the Classics at Oxford or of mathematics or science at Cambridge, even though other such subjects made inroads at both institutions after World War I. Business and industry were considered beneath a good student or a person of "good" background. It is only really since World War II that universities have been offering degrees in business and industrial management and that managers and engineers have not traditionally come up from the ranks of junior white-collar workers employed after school-leaving or from those of skilled workers who have obtained through experience or through special courses the technical knowledge needed for advancement.

Career development in the working world was thus until recently a virtually unacknowledged phenomenon, unmanaged, self-managed, or the result of availability when there was an opening in the company. Today the large corporations such as British Petroleum, Cadbury's Imperial Chemistry, and Lockwood's have formal programs essentially similar to those in the United States. In some cases, especially in smaller organizations, career development is left to the individual pursuing the career. A few colleges at Oxford and Cambridge even go as far as to have special "industrial courses," programs to which managerial employees and middle- or higher-level civil servants go for a term of higher education. Thus at Wolfson College, Cambridge, there are always from six to twelve men and women in residence studying something of special interest to them that is *not* directly related to their work. For example, a middle-management man from a plastics manufacturing company in the Midlands spent his eight weeks studying the development of the British canal system during the Industrial Revolution.

French logic led to an earlier shift to the recognition of specialties and of specialty training, especially when the glut of graduates of the lycees and of the universities oriented only to literary and legal careers began to have impact on the economy and on social unrest. The American system of postsecondary educational institutions of lower and higher levels was studied and, with modifications, adopted in France. Schools of business management sprang up about the time they did in Great Britain, and the very high-level engineering schools, to which only the intellectual elite could hope to go, were supplemented by a number of "nuts-and-bolts" engineering colleges in an attempt to produce more trained personnel for business and industry. Louis L. Thurstone wrote half-seriously of American colleges after viewing the first scholastic aptitude test data that there was a college for every I.Q. The same became nearly as true for France. Counselors in France need to know the French Ivy League and the French Podunk Colleges.

The means of entry into the world of work also need to be known. Does one apply for a factory job "at the gate?" Does one write letters to personnel directors applying for a managerial training job? Or does one apply through the training institution's faculty or placement service? What sort of approach is considered appropriate in presenting oneself to an employer in Brazil, Britain, France, India, Japan, Kenya, Nigeria, or Venezuela? A busy month in Kenya did not teach me anything about these matters nor did two weeks in India or Brazil.

How does one stabilize in one's job and in one's occupation in the foreign country? Do the differences in advancement methods that exist between fields of work in North America hold in Europe, Asia, Africa, Australia, and South America? Is merit recognized or does one have to advertise it? Does one make one's merit visible subtly or obviously? Can one generalize on these matters, even in one country, in one type of enterprise or occupation, or in one organization? In Britain those pursuing advancement in the marketplace tend to move by applying for better positions when they are advertised, although there is some talent hunting, especially in the competitive businesses: by British standards Americans are "pushy" in their self-promotion. Yet these two are kindred cultures.

It is standard practice in the State Department, the Peace Corps, and many multinational corporations for staff members who are to be stationed overseas to devote a period to studying the language and the culture of the country to which they are being posted. The training may be part time and spread out over a longer period or full time and intense for a shorter period. It may be before transfer or after taking up residence in the country. This is, however, not the standard practice of American counselors planning to spend a few months or a year, rarely more, in another country. Such disregard for the culture of the country to which one is going is hardly consonant with the desire or the need to function well in cross-cultural career counseling.

Intensive study of a foreign country and its culture is still less common among American counselors who deal with foreign students on American campuses. With students from many countries coming from differing cultures and with different languages, the task of knowing them all well is too great: some reading, some learning from the foreign students themselves, is all that is possible. This is an indication of the need for even greater caution in such work.

REFERENCES

Hollingshead, A. B. (1949) *Elmtown's Youth*. New York: Wiley. *Personnel and Guidance Journal*. (1983) International perspectives on counseling. *61*, 451–514.

Roberts, K. (1981) The sociology of work entry and occupational choice. In Watts, A. G., Super, D. E., & Kidd, J. M. (Eds.), *Career development in Britain*. Cambridge, England: Hobson's Press.

Super, D. E. (1983) *Educational and vocational guidance as means of increasing mobility in the educational system*. Paris: UNESCO.

Some Major Dimensions of Cultural Variation in Client Populations

HARRY TRIANDIS

HISTORY

In more than a hundred years of serious study of cultural differences and their implications for psychological functioning by anthropologists and psychologists (See Klineberg, 1980, for an overview) a number of important phenomena have been studied. Cultures differ in innumerable ways, but there are also many psychological universals (Lonner, 1980). Although some of what we have learned in counseling and therapy may, as a result of these universals, transcend culture, a lot of what we have learned does not. The major problems of psychological adjustment, such as alienation, and some minor psychological disturbances of everyday life viewed in cross-cultural perspective have been reviewed by G. Guthrie and P. P. Tanco (1980) and by W. Tseng and J. Hsu (1980); more serious psychopathology and how it is affected by culture have been reviewed by J. Draguns (1980), V. D. Sanua (1980), and A. J. Marsella (1980). Variations in psychotherapeutic procedures have been examined by R. Prince (1980).

PRESENT STATUS

It is unclear at this time which of the dimensions of cultural variation are of the greatest significance. Nor do we know how these dimensions must be incorporated in our thinking about counseling and therapy. Much research remains to be done on these issues. In this chapter we present some of the dimensions that have been identified and suggest how they *may be* incorporated in the thinking of cross-cultural counselors.

FUNDAMENTAL ASSUMPTIONS AND THEORIES

Variations in ecology (physical environment, climate, resources) result in variations in contingencies of reinforcement (what behaviors are followed by desirable or undesirable consequences). These differential schedules of reinforcement result in cultural differences in perceptual selectivity, information-processing strategies, cognitive structures, and habits. The cognitive structures may best be summarized by different elements of subjective culture (Triandis, 1972) such as categorizations of experience, associations among the categories, attitudes, beliefs, behavioral intentions (self-instructions about how to behave), norms, roles, and values. H. C. Triandis (1980) described a model that links these elements of subjective culture to behavior and reviewed numerous studies that support the model.

Cross-cultural counselors should be sensitive to cultural variations in the entities just described.

Perceptual Selectivity

Cultures differ about whether they pay most attention to what people *do* or *who* people are. For example, if a mother beats a child, members of one culture may emphasize the mother-element, and hence justify the action, but members of another culture may emphasize the behavior (beats)-element and question the action. In general, collectivist cultures (Triandis, 1985) tend to emphasize who the person is and almost always assume that in-group members in authority do the right thing; but out-group authorities are generally viewed with suspicion. Individualistic cultures are more likely to focus on the behavior and hence to question the actions. Only in-group authorities are not questioned in collectivist cultures.

In-groups include those persons an individual trusts and is ready to collaborate with. In some cultures people do not trust many people; in others they trust a lot of people. In-groups (for example, nuclear family, extended family, band, tribe, nation) in some cultures affect many behaviors profoundly; in others they affect only a few behaviors. In general, in collectivist cultures many behaviors are under the influence of in-groups, but in individualist cultures each in-group affects only a few behaviors. Also, in collectivist cultures people are very responsive to norms and roles, and in individualist cultures they are more concerned with personal enjoyment. In individualist cultures people have many in-groups (for example, family, school, work group, church, clubs), and they join them or drop them to maximize their personal enjoyment.

In collectivist cultures there is often more differentiation among persons by age, sex, religion, language, race, tribe, or status. Individualist cultures tend to consider such differences of lesser importance than do collectivist cultures. Thus, for instance, in some parts of India even one day's difference in age requires more respect for the older person; one of the important transgressions that horrify some Indians is for a wife to ask her husband to rub her legs, although it is expected that husbands will ask their wives to rub their legs; religion is often the cause of communal violence; status differences are exaggerated (see Triandis, 1972).

Most Western cultures are individualistic. Individualism is most clear in the case of the United States, Britain, and the former British Empire (for example, Canada, Australia), but there is considerable collectivism in Southern Europe. The cultures of Northern Europe were collectivist a few hundred years ago, so cultures that have retained many traditional elements are extremely collectivist. South America and East Asia are among the most collectivist regions of the world. People who have migrated and children from small families (for example, only children) are likely to be individualistic, even if they come from collectivist cultures. People who are very modern (strongly influenced by Western culture), educated, and urban are likely to be more individualistic than people who are traditional, illiterate, and rural.

In collectivist cultures people are more sensitive to the views of others and conform to in-group norms more reliably than in individualistic cultures. However, in-group norms are often limited to behaviors of direct relevance to the in-group, so the person often has considerable latitude of action when dealing with situations that do not concern the in-group. It appears that when a person is strongly controlled in in-group situations, there is much deviant behavior in out-group situations. For example, although persons may conform completely to norms concerning whom to marry, they may not conform at all to laws concerning how to drive.

Cultures differ in the extent people conform to norms. In "tight" cultures people observe norms with great care. Life is regulated to a great extent, particularly in in-group situations. Japan is an example of a tight culture. People in loose cultures may conform in in-group situations, but there are a lot of other situations when they do not conform, and the culture is very tolerant of deviation from norms. India and Thailand are examples of cultures that allow considerable deviance from norms.

When the applicable norms are few and clear and the culture is homogeneous, tightness is likely. When the applicable norms are numerous and unclear and the culture heterogeneous, looseness is likely. When there are many relevant norms or roles, conflict among them is likely, and then people can follow one set of forms just as easily as another. The situation in India, where the complexity of norms is great, is thus likely to result in looseness.

Information-Processing Strategies

In some cultures all information must be packaged into a broad framework defined by the culture. The framework may have a religious (for example, Muslim) or political (for example, USSR) basis. Actions are "correct" to the extent that they conform to this ideology. There are "correct" and "incorrect" ways of thinking and processing information. By contrast, in pragmatist cultures (for example, the United States) information is processed with little reference to a broad framework. Frameworks shift, depending on the nature of the information. What is "relevant" and what "works" are the important criteria, not whether the information "fits" the ideological framework.

Furthermore, when deciding what information to consider, members of some cultures consider all information that is in any way related to the topic (associative cultures), but in other cultures they consider only those elements of information of direct relevance to the solution of a problem (abstractive cultures). In associative cultures (for example, Japan) there is much reliance on paralinguistic cues (posture, eye contact, position of body in relation to other, gestures) to interpret a message. In abstractive cultures (for example, the West) there is much reliance on definitions of terms, and only the entities that fall within the definition are used in further discussion.

Cognitive Structures

There are so many cognitive structures, attitudes, norms, and roles, and they are so specific to particular cultures-situations, that a brief discussion is impossible. Readers who want to explore this topic may find some of the material in D. Landis and R. W. Brislin (1983) helpful. R. D. Albert's (1983) chapter is particularly relevant.

There are a few structures, however, that are so important that they need to be mentioned. First, the *self-concept* is the individual's theory of who he or she is. There is evidence that self-concepts vary. In some collectivist cultures the self is merely a bundle of roles (Shweder & Bourne, 1982); in individualist cultures it is an entity totally distinct from the in-group. Furthermore, self-esteem (I am good-bad), sense of power (powerful versus impotent), and activity (active versus passive) vary across cultures (Osgood, May, & Miron, 1975). Some values are particularly important. Whether human nature is conceived as good (allowing people to trust others) or bad (leading to distrust) and changeable (leading to optimism about counseling and therapy) or immutable (leading to pessimism about counseling and therapy) is an obviously critical dimension. The perspective that humans can master, adapt, or be subjugated to nature is also an important dimension. Emphasis on the past-present-future is relevant for planning. Valuing doing versus being versus being-in-becoming (Kluckhohn & Strodtbeck, 1961) is also relevant for therapy.

Habits

Cultures differ in the habits that most members of the culture exhibit. Habits are related to customs. But more than that, they are characteristic behavior patterns. For example, in "contact" cultures people are more likely to touch each other, to look each other in the eye, to orient their bodies so they face each other, to use small interpersonal distances and to speak loudly; in "no-contact" cultures people speak less and less loudly, touch each other less, do not look each other in the eyes, and use large interpersonal distances. Although there is some tendency for these habits to be interrelated, there are also many exceptions, for example, people who touch but do not look in the eye. But, in general, it is helpful to keep in mind that many behavior patterns that appear "abnormal" may be typical of members of particular cultures.

FUTURE DIRECTIONS

The implications of the dimensions outlined above for counseling and psychotherapy will require extensive research in the future. At this point we can only speculate. Nevertheless, there are some logical connections between what we know about cultural differences and what we do in counseling and therapy.

In analyzing the behavior of a client it is important to keep in mind that although therapists (who usually have a Western perspective even when they come from a non-Western culture) focus on the behavior of the client and the client's significant others, the client may be focusing on who the other is. Behavioral intentions depend on the attributes of the target of behavior. However, the attributes that are emphasized are vastly different from culture to culture. Americans consider *race* and *ideology* (system of beliefs) as very important; in African cultures *tribal membership* is the important attribute. *Sex* is important in most cultures but more important in collectivist than in individualist cultures. *Age* is very important in collectivist cultures. *Religion* is a crucial attribute in Muslim cultures and very important in some segments of the population in Christian and Jewish subcultures. *Nationality* is very important to some people but not to others.

Clients with a minority background may be more likely to use associative information processing. Such information processing is very functional in face-to-face situations, where people have common backgrounds. For instance, people raised in the same small village may have had so many common experiences that a simple word, like *yes*, may communicate a very complex meaning. To people from a metropolitan area, a "yes" does not mean much, since they miss the context that makes it meaningful. They need a detailed and explicit explanation of the situation that calls for a "yes." This is further complicated by the habits of certain populations of not saying "no." The Japanese have dozens of ways of implying "no," but rarely say "no." One needs to understand that a "maybe" means "no." Some cultures depend on context much more than others.

A client may be more inclined to see the big picture (for example, put behavior in the context of religion) than is the therapist. If the therapist knows nothing about the client's religion the client's behavior may appear bizarre. Many behavior patterns that are totally appropriate in the client's culture (for example, overdependence on the parents) may shock the therapist. Communication between client and therapist may suffer if the client is associative-ideological and the therapist abstractive-pragmatic. The client will appear fuzzy thinking, immature, and impractical, and the therapist will appear to the client cold, over-practical, unimaginative, and narrow. A confrontation between these two styles of information processing is likely to result in miscommunication.

Differences in values are particularly problematic for the relationship. Clients whose environment is unpredictable are characterized by eco-system distrust (Triandis, 1976). They feel that there are very few people that can be trusted; the environment does not operate lawfully but capriciously; what one does has little to do with what one gets. Such a view of the world is actually justified if the environment is unpredictable, if the individual has little power and cannot control it. The gap between the middle-class therapist who comes from a highly predictable environment and the lower-class client who comes from an unpredictable one can be large. The therapist may find the lack of planning, the "random walk" that characterizes much of the client's behavior, and the distrust of people as symptomatic of a major disorder. Yet these behaviors are perfectly understandable from a cross-cultural perspective. If what you do results in success only one in a hundred times, why plan, why develop a systematic way of doing things? If the promises that people make are reliable only once in ten times, why trust people? Note that to keep promises one needs resources. A mother who promises a toy and is unable to deliver it loses trustworthiness. Middle-class therapists may be unable to get into their clients' shoes, because their environment is too predictable.

The wealthy strata of a society tend to see humans as good, trustworthy, and reliable. The poor are likely to see humans as bad, untrustworthy, and unreliable. One must learn that both views of humans are accurate—for their corresponding environments. People who have traveled a lot, who are educated and have seen many points of view, tend to think of humans as changeable; but people who have seen only one small neighborhood may think that humans are not changeable. "Human nature" dictates what to do, and the way *we* do things is the only "natural" and "correct" way of doing things. Such ethnocentric perceptions make change much more difficult. If counseling and therapy require change, it is less likely to happen among those who see their own behavior patterns as "natural." In short, the therapist's efforts may appear to the client as overoptimistic and based on the wrong assumptions.

The client's stoic acceptance of life as it is with little effort to change it is perfectly understandable given that a culture stresses subjugation to nature. But the therapist is likely to believe that nature can be mastered. Many clients have a *being* orientation, but the therapist is likely to have a *doing* orientation. Thus the therapist may wonder why the client does not do something to get out of the bad situation, and the client may consider it perfectly correct to accept life as it is. Furthermore, the therapist's overoptimism is not always realistic, and that further confirms the client's view that there is no point in attempting to change anything.

The therapist is likely to be future oriented, but the client may be past or, more likely, present oriented. Satisfaction of basic needs is often the most important concern of the client, and that has to be done *now*. Thus many plans proposed by the therapist may be seen as unrealistic by the client.

In many collectivist cultures there is much power distance. That is, people with power are seen as very different from people without power. This is likely to increase the distance between client and therapist. Efforts by the therapist to reduce the gap may be perceived by the client as "inappropriate behavior." In many cultures client participation in decisions may be inappropriate, since the therapist is expected to "tell" the client what to do.

In tight cultures people have a greater aversion to uncertainty than in loose cultures. Therapy is in some sense uncertain, requiring the client to change in ways that are unclear and to become somebody who is different. People from tight cultures may find such uncertainties difficult to accept.

Collectivists may find that changes proposed, suggested, or implied in the course of therapy are unacceptable because they clash with in-group norms. Furthermore, although individualist clients may accept the outcomes of therapy and modify their behavior, collectivists are more likely to consult, discuss, and test their in-group's acceptance of these outcomes before modifying their behavior. Thus therapists may find that dealing with individuals is not optimal, and group therapy, involving the whole in-group, may be more successful.

The dimensions of cultural variation outlined above thus appear relevant to a number of critical decisions usually made by therapists. It must be emphasized, however, that the requisite research linking these dimensions with the appropriate modifications of therapeutic practice remains to be done. The above discussion must be read as suggestive rather than as definitive.

REFERENCES

Albert, R. D. (1983) The intercultural sensitizer or culture assimilator: A cognitive approach. In Landis, D., & Brislin, R. W. (Eds.), *Handbook of intercultural training*, Vol. 2. Elmsford, N.Y.: Pergamon Press.

Draguns, J. (1980) Psychological disorders of clinical severity. In Triandis, H. C., & Draguns, J. (Eds.). *Handbook of cross-cultural psychology*, Vol. 6. Boston: Allyn & Bacon.

Guthrie, G., & Tanco, P. P. (1980) Alienation. In Triandis, H. C., & Draguns, J. (Eds.), *Handbook of cross-cultural psychology,* Vol. 6. Boston: Allyn & Bacon.

Klineberg, O. (1980) Historical perspectives: Cross-cultural psychology before 1960. In Triandis, H. C., & Lambert, W. W. (Eds.), *Handbook of cross-cultural psychology*, Vol. 1. Boston: Allyn & Bacon.

Kluckhohn, F., & Strodtbeck, F. (1961) *Variations in value orientations*. New York: Harper & Row.

Landis, D., & Brislin, R. W. (1983) *Handbook of intercultural training*. Elmsford, N.Y.: Pergamon Press, 3 vols.

Lonner, W. J. (1980) The search for psychological universals. In Triandis, H. C. &

Lambert, W. W. (Eds.), *Handbook of cross-cultural psychology*, Vol. 1. Boston: Allyn & Bacon.

Marsella, A. J. (1980) Depressive experience and disorders across cultures. In Triandis, H. C., & Draguns, J. (Eds.), *Handbook of cross-cultural psychology*, Vol. 6 Boston: Allyn & Bacon.

Osgood, C. E., May, W., & Miron, M. (1975) *Cross-cultural universals of affective meaning.* Champaign: University of Illinois Press.

Prince, R. (1980) Variations in psychotherapeutic procedures. In Triandis, H. C., and Draguns, J. (Eds.), *Handbook of cross-cultural psychology*, Vol. 6. Boston: Allyn & Bacon.

Sanua, V. D. (1980) Familial and sociocultural antecedents of psychopathology. In Triandis, H. C., and Draguns, J. (Eds.), *Handbook of cross-cultural psychology*, Vol. 6. Boston: Allyn & Bacon.

Shweder, R. A., & Bourne, E. J. (1982) Does the concept of person vary cross-culturally? In Marsella, A. J., & White, G. M. (Eds.), *Cultural conceptions of mental health and therapy.* Dordrecht, Holland: Reidel.

Triandis, H. C. (1972) *The analysis of subjective culture*, Wiley.

—— (1976) *Variations in black and white perceptions of the social environment.* Champaign: University of Illinois Press.

—— (1980) Values, attitudes, and interpersonal behavior. In Howe, H., & Page, M. (Eds.), *Nebraska symposium on motivation, 1979*, Vol. 27. Lincoln: University of Nebraska Press, pp. 195–260.

—— (1985) Collectivism vs. individualism: A reconceptualization of a basic concept in cross-cultural social psychology. In Bagley, C. & Verma, G. K. (Eds.), *Personality, cognition, and values: Cross-cultural perspectives of childhood and adolescence.* New York: Macmillan.

Tseng, W., & Hsu, J. (1980) Minor psychological disturbances of everday life. In Triandis, H. C., & Draguns, J. (Eds.), *Handbook of cross-cultural psychology*, Vol. 6. Boston: Allyn & Bacon.

The Social Psychology of Cross-Cultural Counseling

OTTO KLINEBERG

Recent years have been marked by a striking convergence in the concerns of social psychologists and counselors. On the one hand, counselors must confront the problems that arise when they attempt to be helpful to clients from different social and cultural backgrounds. Alternatively, social psychologists have for some time been interested in cross-cultural psychology, including its implications for the practical issues involved in many varieties of cross-cultural contact. As valuable publications in the first category I would list *Counseling across Cultures* edited by P. Pedersen and colleagues (1976 and 1981) and *Counseling the Culturally Different* by D. W. Sue (1981); in the second category I would mention particularly the six-volume *Handbook of Cross-Cultural Psychology* edited by H. C. Triandis and others (1980) and the three-volume *Handbook of Intercultural Training* edited by D. Landis and R. W. Brislin (1983). Using these publications as the major, though not the sole, background for my own analysis of the relationship between cross-cultural counseling and social psychology, I have attempted to identify some issues that deserve further consideration.

In an article in which I attempted to deal with some of the issues raised in cross-cultural counseling (Klineberg, 1983), I identified some of the personality variables that have been regarded as creating problems for the American counselor. They included the alleged unwillingness on the part of Native American Indians to verbalize their feelings and their tendency to withdraw and try to work out their own problems; the excessive (from our point of view) modesty on the part of Japanese-Americans and their awe of authority, which intrudes in the counseling relationship; the unwillingness on the part of Indians (from India) to make their own decisions and their reliance upon authority figures to make decisions for them; the alleged importance of *machismo*, the cult of masculinity among Hispanics; the fact that Chinese and Japanese clients find it difficult to discuss intimate relations or difficulties, since these matters may reflect not only on the individual but on the whole family; and so on.

Although this list of aspects of national or ethnic "character" could be extended considerably, one further example here concerns the black Americans, who have emphasized their view that for them self-identity is always a people identity; "I am because we are, and because we are, therefore I am." Edmund Glenn (1981) quoted an African ambassador in Washington as saying: "The source of the greatest misunderstanding between Americans and Africans is the positive value attached by the Americans to individualism, and the negative valued attached to it by Africans." A similar point was raised, in another ethnic context, by the Chinese anthropologist Francis Hsu (1971), who wrote that in all Western definitions of personality it is described as a separate entity, distinct from society and culture. D. R. Price-Williams (1975) raised the question of whether personality should be regarded as a separate construct or whether the fundamental unit should be that or the interpersonal structure (the group or the society) from which the separate personality structure is derived. The difference may be fundamental in the counseling situation.

There are a number of more specific problems that face counselors who are eager to pay adequate attention to the impact of culture on the individual. Although they may be attracted and even impressed by the kind of cultural varieties to which reference has just been made, they will soon have to face the issue of the extent to which a cultural pattern is universal within the society with which it is, or appears to be, associated. Social psychologists have frequently expressed their worry about the tendency found in many anthropological reports of personality and culture to generalize the formulation to a whole society without having the evidence to support such a generalization. In the examples cited above, questions can be raised regarding the regional and local variations in the ascribed characteristics, differences relating to educational level, to rural or urban residence, to occupation, to sex, and to majority or minority status. When these and other factors are kept in mind, it is not too difficult to accept the conclusion reached by the historian Jacques Barzun in his review of a book about British "personality." Barzun pointed out that books about national character are the most impossible to write of all books.

Many years ago the anthropologist Ralph Linton (1945) attempted to put some order into this chaotic situation. Since no culture is ever completely expressed in any one individual, Linton introduced the idea of *status* as a necessary bridge. Linton defined status as the place in a particular system occupied by an individual at a particular time. He added that *role* refers to the sum of the culture patterns associated with a particular status; it includes the attitudes, values, and behavior ascribed by the society to all persons occupying this status. Undoubtedly, Linton made a distinct step forward through his insistence on personality variations related to status and role. However, he left out two important variables: the variations among individuals even when they may be equated in status and role and the impact of social change in determining the nature of the culture as a whole, as well as its links to the different roles and statuses that the society recognized.

In at least one respect counselors appear to be in an excellent position to observe the effect on personality of social change. The foreign students whom they are called upon to advise are striking examples of individuals undergoing rapid and far-reaching changes in their cultural orientation. They are sometimes successful in incorporating welcome aspects of the new culture in a harmonious integration with the culture of origin. Sometimes, on the contrary, the process may be difficult and painful, constituting some form of culture shock.

This form of culture conflict may create a difficult situation not only within the individual student but within the mind and conscience of those responsible for programs facilitating the international exchange of students. Most of us are strongly in favor of contact among the peoples of the world and regard the encouragement of study abroad as one of the best ways of facilitating such contact. In some cases, however, it may become one of the forces antithetical to cultural preservation, acting as a vehicle for the uncritical diffusion of Western culture and therefore the erosion of non-Western life-styles (Bochner, 1981). The resulting conflict that may arise within the foreign student will sometimes be accompanied by feelings of guilt at having forsaken the old traditional ways; it may also result, especially at the moment of the return home, in a repudiation of all that is traditional and acceptance of all that is new, with a consequent alienation from the original culture and from those who do everything in their power to keep it alive and healthy. Bochner suggested that programs will have to shift their goals explicitly and self-consciously from the present purpose of producing cultural exporters to the air of training cultural mediators, that is, people who have been taught to interpret both cultures to both societies, in the country of sojourn and in the country of origin. This presents a challenge to counselors whose clients, in the case of foreign students, may need help precisely in this area.

This does not mean that all foreign students reject their previous cultural and national identity as the result of the foreign sojourn. In our own study (Klineberg & Hull, 1979), a substantial proportion of foreign students reported that they felt more positive about their own country after their experience abroad; those who felt more negative were in the minority. Clearly, not all individuals change to the same extent or in the same direction.

This brings us back to the issues of individual variations with regard to culture in general. Mention was made above of the tendency of East Indians to look for a great deal of guidance and direction from their counselor. This may be true for the majority of cases, but certainly not universally; there will be numerous exceptions. In general, there will usually, if not always, be overlapping in the distribution of a particular personality trait when two ethnic populations are compared. In 1946, for example, D. V. McGranahan (1946) published a report on the reactions of German and American boys of high school age to test the hypothesis of a German pattern of unquestioned paternal authority. This hypothesis was in a sense borne out. To the question: "Do you think a boy is justified in running away from home if his father is cruel or brutal?" 50 percent of the German sample and only 30 percent of the American sample said no. There were still 45 percent of the Germans, however, who said yes and a considerable minority of the Americans (30 percent) who said no. Here we have a situation in which the overlapping is considerable, and the most that we are entitled to say is that *at that time* there was a difference *in the probability* of one or the other answer being given to this particular question in the two national groups.

In 1979 my colleagues in Paris and I (Klineberg, Zavalloni, Louis-Guerin, & Ben Brika, 1979), published a volume devoted to a comparison of the reactions of students in eleven countries to certain values and attitudes related to the "student revolt" in the late sixties and early seventies. There were indeed national or ethnic differences in regard to major issues such as nationalism, capitalism, the use of drugs, participation in political activity, and the degree of satisfaction with universities and society in general. There was *never* unanimity in any national sample, however, and although some of the variance within any national group could be explained by the particular political position of the respondents, there were still unexplained variations among individuals of the same political standpoint. The finding that the plans of American students for the future were much more likely to be concerned with private issues, such as occupational careers and the family, rather than with public or political and national issues would fit in with other descriptions of American attitudes, but the large internal variations reinforce once again the conclusion that we have the right to speak only of the *probability* of a certain reaction and never of the certainty that it will appear in the particular individual with whom the counselor has to deal.

One important development in social psychology is represented by the work of David McClelland (1961) on the achievement motive or what was called by Henry Murray the "need for achievement." This has led to extensive research using many different techniques, including the Thematic Apperception Test, measures of fantasy in children's readers, child training, historical analysis, indices of economic development, changes over time, and other experimental techniques. There have been many cross-cultural applications of the concept of the achievement motive and the variations in its expression. In his study of the Japanese, both in Japan and in the United States, George De Vos (1968) reported that there is definite preoccupation with achievement and accomplishment, but even more important is the need for affiliation. A great deal of the Japanese achievement motivation can best be understood in terms of the need to belong and participate cooperatively with others. Japanese subjects find it difficult to conceive of letting down one's family, one's social group, or one's occupational superiors. It has also been suggested that in Japan a business enterprise, no matter how large, is seen in the image of a household, with the interdependence and loyalty characteristic of the family. For the counselor, who may encounter clients with weak or absent achievement motivation in the American sense, such cultural differences may at least suggest directions in which to look in order to give guidance to a client who is failing in his academic work. It is interesting to note that McClelland's (1963) own definition of the need for achievement includes the desire to do well, not only for social recognition and prestige, but to achieve a feeling of personal accomplishment. This appears to exclude the sense of group accomplishment, an exclusion that unduly neglects the achievement of people working together for a common goal.

It is not possible to give an adequate account in this chapter of the range of cultural variations explored by anthropologists and social psychologists that might be relevant to the concerns of the counselor. There is, however, one area in which the observations go beyond the limits of probability to which reference was made above and reach a degree of generality that apparently makes certain behavior more predictable. I refer to what might be called "bodily communication," to which the anthropologist Edward Hall (1969, 1975) gave the name *proxemics*: this includes among other things the use of space as an aspect of culture, expressed in "conversational distance" as well as in the wider areas of city planning, architectural layout, and so on. *Conversational distance* involves the amount of space that separates two people who are talking together and which varies considerably from one culture to another. Hall described cases in which an American would literally back away from the too-close proximity of a "foreign" interlocutor, who in turn would find such a reaction on the part of the American insulting. Another, related example is that of *intrusion distance*, which refers to the distance one has to maintain from two people who are already talking in order to get attention but not intrude. In these cases, "correct" behavior is regarded as being relatively standardized within a culture, although differences related to social class, education, and region cannot be entirely excluded.

Another aspect of bodily communication refers to the language of gestures, which may lead to misunderstandings between people of different cultural background, since the same gesture may have contrasting meanings. A raised thumb is a signal of approval in America and most of Europe, but in Greece it is employed as an insult. Even simple gestures such as nodding the head to signal yes and moving the head from side to side to mean no are by no means universal; in Greece, Turkey, and southern Italy the head is usually raised to signify no, and a downward movement means yes. (See Collett, 1982; Morris, Collet, Marsh, & O'Shaughnessy, 1979; and Argyle, 1982, for many examples.) At a more complex level, many years ago Lafcadio Hearn (1894), in his discussion of the meaning of the Japanese smile, pointed out that when a Japanese is scolded or criticized by a person of superior rank, a pleasant smile shows the proper degree of submission. This reaction may be infuriating to the "superior" if he is an European or American, who expects a scolding to be followed by a facial expression indicating contrition or regret, rather than apparent amusement. When I spent a year in China under the old regime, I encountered the same reaction on the part of a worker whom I had employed.

Two chapters in the *Handbook of Cross-Cultural Psychology* edited by Triandis and others merit consideration. The first is by M. Zavalloni (1981), "Values," and the second by V. D. Sanua (1981), "Psychopathology." Zavalloni described a variety of typologies of values or value emphasis in different cultures in the writings of philosophers, sociologists, anthropologists, and social psychologists. She then discussed the use of survey techniques, designed to give statistical support to the typologies; a series of cross-cultural studies on youth values; the application of psychometric scales; and so on and concluded with suggestions for the directions that should be followed in future research on values. Sanua's chapter emphasizes the possible contribution of sociocultural variables to the development of pathology in a large number of different societies. He dealt with research on a number of possible causal factors, including familial antecedents, social class, studies of differences between normal and deviant children, variations in the frequency of deviation in national and ethnic groups, the stresses caused by sociocultural change, problems arising from the contact of cultures, differences between men and women, and variations in the symptomology of mental illness. Both of these chapters contain especially rich bibliographies.

In summary, cultural factors are important to counselors, and they have the responsibility of learning all they can about the cultural background of their clients. It is too much to ask that they become specialists on all the cultures of the world; it should not be impossible for them, however, to become aware of the range of values and patterns of behavior of which human societies and individuals are capable and to learn as much as they can about the particular ethnic groups that constitute their clientele. Many counselors have asked themselves what there is in counseling that is universal and what aspects need tailoring to meet the specific needs of specific groups. I see no alternative to developing awareness of both the universals and the cultural particulars. Finally, counselors should never lose sight of the fact that no two individuals are fully identical in their needs, their problems, and their values and goals. We cannot remind ourselves too often that these three approaches—to human beings in general, to members of particular cultural groups, and to the individual in his or her uniqueness—all require our full attention.

REFERENCES

Argyle, M. (1982) Inter-cultural communication. In Bochner, S. (Ed.), *Cultures in contact*. Oxford: Pergamon Press.

Bochner, S. (Ed.). (1981) *The mediating person*. Boston: G. K. Hall.

Collett, P. (1982) Meetings and misunderstandings. In Bochner, S. (Ed.), *Cultures in contact*. Oxford: Pergamon Press.

De Vos, G. (1968) Achievement and innovation in culture and personality. In Norbeck, N., Price-Williams, D. R., & McCord, W. (Eds.), *The study of personality: An interdisciplinary appraisal*. New York: Holt, Rinehart & Winston.

Glenn, E. S., & Glenn, C. (1981) *Man and mankind: Conflict and communication between cultures*. Norwood, N.J.: Ablex.

Hall, E. T. (1969) *The silent language*. Garden City, N.Y.: Anchor Press.

——— (1975) *Beyond culture*. Garden City, N.Y.: Anchor Press.

Hearn, L. (1894) *Glimpses of unfamiliar Japan*. Boston: Houghton Mifflin.

Hsu, F. (1971) Psychosocial homeostasis and Jen. *American Anthropologist, 73*, 23–43.

Klineberg, O. (1983) Counseling in cross-cultural perspective. *International Journal for the Advancement of Counseling, 6*, 83–92.

Klineberg, O., & Hull, W. F. (1979) *At a foreign university*. New York: Praeger.

Klineberg, O., Zavalloni, M., Louis-Guerin, C., & Ben Brika, J. (1979) *Students, values, and politics*. New York: Free Press.

Landis, D., & Brislin, R. W. (Eds.). (1983) *Handbook of intercultural training*. New York: Pergamon Press, 3 vols.

Linton, R. (1945) *The cultural background of personality*. New York: Harper & Row.

McClelland, D. (1961) *The achieving society*. Princeton, N.J.: Van Nostrand.

———. (1963). The achievement motive in economic growth. In Hoselitz, B. F., & Moore, W. E. (Eds.), *Industrialization and society*. The Hague: Mouton.

McGranahan, D. V. (1946) A comparison of social attitudes among American and German youth. *Journal of Abnormal and Social Psychology, 41*, 245–257.

Morris, D., Collet, B., Marsh, P., & O'Shaughnessy, M. (1979) *Gestures: Their origin and distribution*. London: Cape.

Pedersen, P., Draguns, J., Lonner, W. J., & Trimble, J. (Eds.). (1981) *Counseling across cultures*, rev. ed. Honolulu: East West Center.

Price-Williams, D. R. (1975) *Exploration in cross-cultural psychology*. San Francisco: Chandler & Sharp.

Sanua, V. D. (1981). Psychopathology. In Triandis, H. C. et al. (Eds.), *Handbook of cross-cultural psychology*, Vol. 6. Boston: Allyn & Bacon.

Sue, D. W. (1981) *Counseling the culturally different: Theory and practice*. New York: Wiley.

Triandis, H. C., et al (Eds.). (1981) *Handbook of cross-cultural psychology*. Boston: Allyn & Bacon.

Zavalloni, M. (1981) Values. In Triandis, H. C., et al. (Eds.), *Handbook of cross-cultural psychology*, Vol. 5. Boston: Allyn & Bacon.

Cross-Cultural Research in Relation to Counseling in Great Britain

LUDWIG F. LOWENSTEIN

The impact of social and cultural changes in a society are important because in the extreme they are capable of causing a variety of disturbances, even mental illness. It must be remembered that the immigrants, just as the indigenous population, vary in their attitude to the new country. Pakistani immigrants in Britain maintain the myth that they will return to their homeland, which enables them to keep alive their social relationships (both in Britain and Pakistan) and also to withdraw from a commitment to the norms of the wider British society.

Bradford University has a section dealing with cross-cultural work and especially that related to education. R. Beard, G. Verma, and P. Sanderson (1980) have been working since 1977 on the subject of the vocational adaptation of immigrant children in Britain and the role of the school. The project concentrates on two geographical areas with major immigrant settlements, West Yorkshire and London. Within these areas, the objective is to delineate the relationships among educational experiences, family and cultural backgrounds, peer-group influence, and labor-market opportunities in the formulation of attitudes to work, that is, vocational aspirations and expectations. The methods used to assess this study are semi-structured questionnaires being applied to a variety of subjects, and prolonged periods of observation and information interviewing.

The correlation between educational attainment and social-class origin has been of some considerable importance to a number of researchers including M. Macey (1980). The correlation between educational attainment and social-class origin focuses attention on the environment (for example, home) factors rather than instigation of school processes. Attention has also been directed to the secondary school, where failure is almost necessarily cumulative.

One study at Brunel University attempted to evaluate courses in advanced general practice for doctors trained overseas. Immigrant doctors appeared to have a large failure rate in examinations set by various professional bodies in medicine. The courses were set to explore the reason for this failure rate, which could be connected with examination modes, languages, and cultural differences (Barry and Leonard, 1976).

THE ROLE OF EDUCATION IN A MULTI-CULTURAL SOCIETY

The education of children from different cultural backgrounds has long been seen as a primary problem in the assimilation or integration of minority groups. S.M.K. Barry and C. J. Vorhaus (1979) published research attempting to answer the question: "Do West Indian children have a language barrier?" This report went to the Tavistock Institute of Human Relations in 1979. West Indian children appeared to have a lower performance rate in school and made up a disproportionate number of the educationally subnormal school population or those entering lower streams at school. Unlike other minorities, West Indians receive no language assistance such as that given to Pakistanis or Indians.

A similar study was reported through the London Institute of Education where L. Ankrah-Dove, S. Fernando, D. Grant, and A. Wijesinghe (1980) studied the school adjustment and family culture among primary-school children of Caribbean origin. This study arose from the shared concerns about the difficulties apparently faced by children of Caribbean origin in adjustment to the English school system. The study combined educational and psychiatric approaches in attempting to identify a relationship, if any, between a child's perception of school culture and its congruence with selected items of family culture. The implication of this relationship was explored in connection with adjustment in school. It was initially a small-scale exploratory study of 100 children from schools in a working-class neighborhood in London. Depth interviewing and repertory grid techniques were used to tap into personal constructs of culture among young children.

Research by R.G.A. Hanna (1980) sought to investigate the predictive validity of a general culture test and the results of a group interview technique as part of a procedure used for selecting teachers and comparing this with more traditional techniques. The general culture test was used to predict academic achievement in final degree examinations and success in a classroom. U. Prasher and A. Matthews (1980) researched the role of advisers in multi-racial education. This research has encouraged a wider discussion about what is meant by multi-racial education.

Cultural differences implicit in multi-ethnic societies are now an established issue in educational and social policy. The book written by G. K. Verma (1983) and a number of international scholars describes recent research, conceptualization in the field of education, ethnicity and race-relation processes, and a variety of methodological approaches. The papers focus on the themes of education in a multi-cultural society, identity, self-esteem, inter-cultural awareness, and inter-racial interaction and discuss the present state of affairs, indicating strategies for action.

Many children in Great Britain are currently growing up in a multi-cultural society and hence are experiencing what is unusual for Great Britain, a multi-cultural childhood. Bagley and Verma (1983) examined childhood and adolescence in a multi-ethnic society and attempted to show how children see, relate to, and struggle with an ethnically complex world.

The authors focused on the effects of culture, migration, and race relations on children from Jamaica, Japan, and India, both in their original countries and after migration to Great Britain. The object of this book is to examine how English children perceive their world now that it is occupied by immigrants, how children from various ethnic groups evaluate themselves, and how adolescents in Leeds, Bradford, Amsterdam, and India cope with the transition from school to work. The book has been written against a climate of limited economic opportunities due to the recession. There is an interesting case study of Gujerati children in Britain, eastern United States, and India. Self-esteem, cognitive styles, and group independence in the case of ten year olds are of particular interest. Language, identity, transition from school to work, bilingualism, and academic attainment are important considerations. The book demonstrates the struggles and alienation that are faced by South Asian and black youth in British society.

An earlier book by Verma, Bagley, K. Mallick, and L. Young (1979) showed that racial hatred was experienced in most societies and led to acts of frightening brutality. The book presents an interesting study of the factors that fostered prejudiced attitudes in individuals. The conclusions reached were based on a seven-year research project involving 4,000 individuals in Britain and the Netherlands directed at assessing the relative importance of social, psychological, and cultural factors.

The results indicated that prejudice was not associated with the grosser forms of mental psychology; rather, it was the expression of a normative pattern by which individuals, in devaluing others, strived to enhance their feelings of self-esteem and defend themselves against anxiety. As a consequence, measures of anxiety, poor self-esteem, and neurosis were significant predictors of prejudiced attitudes.

Bagley and Verma (1979) attempted to study racial prejudice for the individual and society. The authors looked in detail at social factors specific to the expression of a prejudiced opinion and the actual activity of racism. These factors included age, education, social class, and additional influences of housing conditions, deprivation, community and social movement, and so on. Particular attention was paid to the role of the mass media in the development of prejudiced attitudes and to the problems of predicting behavior from attitudes.

Earlier education had been realized to be an important aspect of not merely reducing the level of prejudices between minority and majority populations but in the form of compensatory education for slow-learning children (Ntuk-Idem, 1978). For many years educationalists were extremely concerned about the failure of children from poor backgrounds, including immigrant populations, to do as well as their peers at school, even though the educational system gave them equal opportunities. In Britain and America compensatory programs were introduced in the belief that these children were disadvantaged by the fact that they came from homes where cultural values clashed with those of the school.

Considerable controversy had developed over the work of these programs. This book was the first to give an account of one such British program focusing on West Indian children. It showed the positive results that were attained and so established performance norms that could be used as a basis for future projects.

Verma and Bagley (1983) acted as editors for a number of essays on the subject of social psychology, sociology, and education, organized around the theme of education in a multi-cultural society. The majority of the papers concerned Britain, but American and Canadian case studies were also reported.

The book suggested that a multi-cultural education was one of the means by which the identity of all children might be fostered. Evidence was presented showing that although young black children had to battle with the racist stereotype of the black people inherent in British culture and language, nevertheless, as they grew older, they acquired a self-concept that was as adequate as that of white children. It was noted that the negative use of teachers was an important factor in the scholastic underachievement of ethnic minorities.

The fundamental values of society must be reflected by the education that children receive. The educational curriculum must therefore be aware that we are now living in a multi-cultural society in Great Britain. This results both in the possibility of conflicts between subgroups who seek to retain their identity and conflict with the dominant culture traditions.

It was expected that the new immigrants to Great Britain would accommodate themselves to or become integrated with the native population. Although this has occurred to some degree, there has also been a tendency for the immigrant populations to want to retain their own traditions, customs, and language. It is now necessary to develop harmonious relations and to eradicate such hostility and anxieties about each other's aims and activities. One of the principal and most serious fears is real or actual racism. Immigrant communities who are usually at the bottom of the economic pecking order tend to pose a threat to the existing work force, especially those at the unskilled or semi-skilled level. Members of the non-European populations are often considered by tradition to be inferior although there is no biological or other reason for thinking this. There is a "no win" situation among immigrants, since if they compete effectively with the indigenous population and capture their jobs, there is reason for grievance from that point of view; if they fail to work or find work because they are unable to compete with the indigenous population, they are labeled as lazy, inadequate, or parasites on the state. Obviously, during times of economic crises, this tension is exacerbated, and during times of economic boom, there is less likelihood of such competition and hence less conflict.

Schools in Great Britain are increasingly accepting their responsibility in viewing cultural diversity as something inevitable and something to be dealt with constructively. The role of education in schools could well be to develop mutual respect for one another's traditions and beliefs.

The precedent of Christian denominational schools led to the establishment of schools for Moslem children, Jewish children, and other denominations. The Adventist schools are those largely used by those of West Indian origin. This is by far the less desirable approach, however, since it leads to fragmentation educationally, socially, and ideologically.

INTER-CULTURAL COUNSELING IN GREAT BRITAIN

There has been virtually no research on the subject of inter-cultural counseling in Great Britain. The view has existed that counselors dealing with immigrants or minority groups should seek to adjust such individuals to the norm of the indigenous population, or to follow the values of the native population. In this way, through a process of virtual conformity, the individual would both fit into the society and develop self-esteem through academic and vocational achievement. This is not to say that the minority group and its own traditions were not respected and understood, but it was felt that anyone coming as an immigrant must eventually either assimilate to the existing norms of that society or be prepared to suffer the consequences of not being accepted in certain areas. Great Britain has a tradition of non-interference in what an individual does in his own private time or in his home, providing it does not affect his neighbors adversely. Counselors who work with clients who are suffering from a variety of problems other than purely psychological ones are therefore less likely to be concerned about the individual's traditions and how they affect his or her current behaviors and difficulties.

There are counselors who view the problems of individuals from the perspectives of the client's social and cultural backgrounds. Nevertheless, to succeed and be accepted by the predominant culture a certain degree of conformity, or understanding of the norms of that society, is required. When there are, however, conflicts between the expectations of the immigrant cultures and those of the indigenous one, a client-centered approach would undoubtedly emphasize that which the clients themselves feel is most important, and therapy would proceed along those lines.

There is also some evidence, although it has not been researched adequately, that minority groups such as West Indians, Pakistanis, and Hindus in Great Britain fail to use the counseling services that are available to the degree that this is required or in comparison with the indigenous population. This is borne out from evidence obtained from other cultures and other countries having a racially diverse population such as Chicanos or Mexican-Americans and the white American population (Ruiz, Padilla, & Alvarez, 1978). The answer may well lie in the eventual appointment of professional therapists and counselors from the minority groups. Those from the ethnic minorities are more likely to be able to understand the personal needs of their members. The appointment of minorities as counselors should also reduce the suspicion, although not totally, toward the network of the establishment for solving problems. At least in this way the counselor and the client will speak the same language, albeit the counselor may have been integrated to some degree into the expectations and norms of the indigenous population.

There is no reason to believe that the counseling relationship is enhanced when people come from the same background, rather than when they come from very different backgrounds culturally and otherwise (Abad, Ramos, & Boyce, 1974; Torrey, 1972). It is vital for the counselor to recognize the background of a client and to identify the client's values that are likely to counteract any efforts made by the counselor.

One cannot, however, forget that the "basic" skills of any counselor are to do this normally, whatever background he or she comes from. The insensitivity of culture-encapsulated counselors can do much to damage the relationship with a client, not only for themselves but for future counselors who may be involved and who may be much more aware. Counselors must be capable of adopting the same approach as many minorities who mix well with both the predominant and minority culture, by adopting certain attitudes and behavior when in the company of the different groups. Thus the West Indian in Great Britain will frequently seek to behave like the British when in their company but upon returning to his or her own ethnic group revert back to the same language and demeanor that is current there.

It would seem sensible for those who practice counseling or therapy with minority groups to know a great deal about the ways of life and thinking of the minority with whom they may have to deal. In addition to this, special training may be required in academic institutions to prepare counselors and psychologists for this type of work. It is especially important to determine any culture-specific definitions of deviancy and accepted norms of behavior (Higginbotham, 1979). It has been well established that no behavior is in itself deviant, only in relation to a particular social norm. The social norm of a minority group may be different in certain respects from that of the indigenous population.

Most societies have laws and rules of behavior; some are more harsh in punishment for transgressors, but on the whole, there is more agreement than disagreement among societies. Individuals, therefore, have a choice whether to conform to a particular norm or whether to retain their own personal norms and standards, although these standards may come into conflict with the minority population to which they belong as well as with the predominant one. The role of the counselor is to point out the possible repercussions to behavior and attitudes as displayed and to discuss them with the client. By being ignorant of another culture and its expectations, misunderstandings, resulting in conflict, may occur, and it is undoubtedly the counselor's responsibility to reduce or limit such conflicts. But little, if any, work of this kind is being carried out in Great Britain, and hence research is lacking. Fortunately, it is available from other countries such as the United States (Pedersen, Draguns, Lonner, & Trimble, 1981).

Counseling that involves cross-cultural populations must consider, therefore, a number of variables including those of the counselors themselves and their own sensitivities, expertise, art, or capacity. This is weighed with their knowledge of cultural differences and the ability to accept these differences as part of a multi-cultural society wherein a considerable degree of different behavior is acceptable. Above all, counselors or therapists must remember that they are treating human beings, and the orientation must, therefore, be individual rather than based on a stereotype of a minority or majority population.

REFERENCES

Abad, V., Ramos, J., & Boyce, E. (1974) A model for delivery of mental health services to Spanish speaking minorities. *American Journal of Orthopsychiatry*, No. 44, 584–595.

Ankrah-Dove, L., Fernando, S., Grant, D., & Wijesinghe, A. (1980) *School adjustment and family culture among primary school children of Caribbean origin*. London: University Institute of Education.

Bagley, C., & Verma, G. K. (1979) *Racial prejudices: The individual and society*. London: Gower Press.

———— (1983). *Multi-cultural childhood*. London: Gower Press.

Barry, J.J.K., & Vorhaus, G. (1979) Assessment of multi-cultural teaching programme for children of West Indian descent with special regard to language. Paper, Tavistock Institute of Human Relations, London.

Barry, S.M.K., & Leonard, C. J. (1976) The evaluation of courses in advanced general practice for doctors trained overseas. Ongoing Research, Department of Education, Uxbridge: Brunel University.

Beard, R., Verma, G., & Sanderson, P. (1980) *The vocational adaptation of "immigrant" children in Britain, and the role of the school*. London: Leverhulme Trust Fund.

Hanna, R.G.A. (1980) *The predictive validity of a general culture test and a group interview technique*. Nottingham-Trent Polytechnic.

Higginbotham, H. N. (1979) Culture and mental health services. In Marsella, A. J., Tharp, R., & Ciborowski, T. (Eds.), *Perspectives in cross-cultural psychology*. New York: Academic Press.

Macey, M. (1980) A study of the effects of "in-school factors on the primary school child's mastery of basic literacy and numeracy skills." Paper, London.

Ntuk-Idem. (1978) *Compensatory education—studies of disadvantaged groups*. London: Gower Press.

Pedersen, P. B., Draguns, J. G., Lonner, W. J., & Trimble, J. E. (1981) *Counseling across cultures*. Honolulu: University Press of Hawaii.

Prasher, U., & Matthews, A. (1980) Survey of role of advisory officers for multi-education in local education authorities. Thesis, Department of Education and Science, Uxbridge: Brunel University.

Ruiz, R., Padilla, A. M., & Alvarez, R. (1978) Issues in the counseling of Spanish speaking/surnamed clients: Recommendation for the therapeutic services. In Walz, G. R. & Benjamin, L. (Eds.), *Transcultural counseling: Needs, programmes, and techniques*. New York: Human Sciences Press.

Torrey, E. F. (1972) *The mind game: Witch doctors and psychiatrists*. New York: Emerson Hall.

Verma, G. K. (1983) *Race relations and cultural differences*. London: Croom Helm.

Verma, G. K., & Bagley, C. (1983) *Self-concept, achievement, and multi-cultural education*. New York: Macmillan.

Verma, G., Bagley, C., Mallick, K., & Young, L. (1979) *Personality, self-esteem, and prejudices*. London: Gower Press.

Cross-Cultural Counseling from a West-European Perspective

NATHAN DEEN

Since 1965 the industrial countries of Western Europe have participated in a rapid population change, mainly caused by a large immigration of laborers, who left their poverty-stricken homelands around the Mediterranean expecting to find wealth as part of the industrial labor force. After a more or less successful settlement, they started to bring into the new homelands their families, and so the first children of Moroccan and Turkish parents entered the schools. K. Sandfuchs (1981) presented a vivid description of the situation:

Near the end of the sixties I was a teacher in an elementary school in Braunschweig. At that time, the first foreign student, an eight year old Turkish boy, was enrolled in our school. We did not recognize the meaning of this event. We did not have the faintest idea what to do with him, how to motivate him and help him integrate into school life and the teaching process—most of the interventions we made proved to be wrong afterwards. In the meantime the proportion of immigrants in this same school has risen to 30–40 percent. (p. 1; translation by the author.)

With slight modifications similar stories can be told about France, Belgium, the Netherlands, Britain. Two trends have influenced the transition of mainly homogeneous countries into a heterogeneous, multicultural situation.

First is the dissolution of colonial power. The growing number of former colonies gaining independence gave rise to a large stream of people who decided to move to the former motherland, to profit from the better infrastructure there. As a result, large groups of Asians, Caribbeans, and Africans immigrate to the former power base: Britain, Belgium, France, and the Netherlands.

The second stream was migrant labor, caused by a need for unskilled or semiskilled workers in the industrial nations and an ample supply of this kind of people in the nations around the Mediterranean. Although the nationality may be different (Algerians in France, Turks in Germany, Turks and Moroccans in

Holland), the pattern in all of these countries is similar. Hence, although Holland is used as a sample country for this chapter, because of its familiarity to the author, the issues are representative of the situation in the industrial countries of Western Europe.

A third stream consists of refugees. Compared to the other groups, this one is very small, although very diverse. Among them are refugees from Vietnam, from Latin American dictatorships (Chile, Uruguay, and so on), and from Eastern Europe or South Africa. Because the education level of these groups tends to be higher than that of the migrant-worker families, their acculturation often is less problematic.

A LITTLE CATALOGUE OF PROBLEMS

If in a small country with a homogeneous culture, for a period of ten years or so, a population increase of some 5 percent occurs, of a diverse and culturally different nature, one might expect it to affect society to some extent. Add to this that the migration concentrates itself in the big cities—Amsterdam, The Hague, Rotterdam, Utrecht—for an estimated 70 percent, there can be no doubt about its impact on life in these cities. Actually, the industrial cities transformed themselves overnight into multicultural societies, a situation that caught government (both nationwide and local) and population largely unprepared. Add again a shortage of housing that after World War II never was adequately solved, the growing recession that causes a rising unemployment with a terribly bad perspective for youth, and it will be clear that there are some problems. Not all of them can be treated here, so I will restrict myself to those aspects that have to do with the transformation of a monocultural to a multicultural situation and try to indicate where guidance and counseling may come in.

Problems Relating to Education

It is generally considered that the school system has the key to the solution of the cultural lag that is faced by the immigrant groups. Nonetheless, there is a growing conviction that in most schools teachers are wandering through the dark in search of a keyhole. The most pertinent problem is that of language. The majority of the immigrant children enter school with little or no knowledge of the Dutch language, and in many cases (especially with Moroccan or Turkish children) their parents are even illiterate in their own vernacular. In some cases starting school in the native language might be a solution, but in practice this usually is impossible. The teachers mostly do not speak Arabic or Turkish and, moreover, most of the time will place those children together with native Dutch children. A recent survey of results concludes that language learning consumes so much energy and effort that a majority of the Moroccan and Turkish children are unable to learn anything else (de Vries 1981). Generally, it can be said that the educational policy of the government directs itself to the problems of recently immigrated children. Marlene de Vries (1981) suggested that the emphasis on personality development of the immigrant pupil at the same time may negatively influence its adjustment to the new environment. She identified two main problems that have to be solved to equalize the opportunities of the "second-generation migrant worker": raising their level of cognition and the acquisition of fluency in the Dutch language.

The last problem is a subject of controversy as to the way that the education system should deal with it. Some hold that a second language should not be introduced before the native language is fully mastered; otherwise the child will be inadequate in both (*semilinguism*). Others emphasize that such an approach is unrealistic; immigrant children will be exposed to the language of the host country anyway. Moreover, the socio-economic (low) status of the families may have a larger impact on the level of intellectual functioning than the language has. In general, the policy of the Dutch government now is to provide native-language education for recently arrived children at the elementary level, until they have learned to find their way in Dutch. At the secondary level no provision of this kind is made, and the adequacy of the provision is locally different anyway. For many children, since *native language* means *official language*, even the native language is a second one (for example, in the case of Moroccan children of Berber descent). As a consequence, educational achievement of immigrant children, especially if they are of migrant-worker status, lags behind the general achievement level. In secondary education they usually will be included in those streams that are least in need of verbal fluency and performance. Hence this offers only limited access to the labor market and a poor chance of employment at present.

Problems Relating to Acculturation

The general slogan is that we'll have to learn to live in a multicultural society. This requires, besides knowledge of which values determine the culture and life-style of different groups, a basic attitude of mutual respect and acceptance. This is at least one value of importance that ought to be shared by everyone to make an acculturation of this type possible. Also, there has to be some consensus about the right of immigrant groups to conserve their cultural identity. This problem is not at all simple. Even though hardly anyone would adopt a melting-pot ideology as normative, it is certain that the meeting of different cultural patterns will affect one another. Dutch society has become an open, flexible, and tolerant society that has achieved a good deal of equality among citizens of different groups and among women and men. Authoritarian power is seldom accepted, and interaction between old and young, male and female, both in and out of school tends to be open and informal. Most immigrant groups, however, come from traditional societies, where the roles of males and females are narrowly defined and traditional patterns of behavior and authority are common. Even if no one would want to interfere, the simple fact of being exposed to different ways of life may have the effect of making people question formerly never-questioned values and become discontented with their traditional role. This is particularly true for women in outside jobs (if they are allowed to work) and for children, particularly girls, in school.

Especially when the cultural pattern is backed by Moslem religion (which is the case for Moroccans, Turks, and part of Surinam people), severe tension inside the family circle may result. At the other end of the continuum patterns may be found that are common in the Caribbean (extended family, matrilineal structures) that are divergent from the nuclear-family structure that is dominant in Holland.

In overview: the Mediterranean people miss the traditional outside life and feel thrown into a permissive and sinful society, Latin Americans miss the warmth and the sharing in their homeland, and some of the Dutch experience the colorfulness of their present society sometimes as a threat to their own values, lifestyles, and work. Although they are on the whole willing to accept diversity, they tend to consider some of the differences as backwardness (for example, male-female relationships) or as unethical (for example, excessive corporal punishment).

This raises the issue of cultural identity: what should be its definition? The challenge for each group will be to develop a mode of existence that is sufficiently in line with its own background to safeguard their members' self-esteem and feeling of belonging and at the same time is open enough to adapt to the dynamics of a multicultural society. This probably is one of the areas where guidance and counseling may offer a helping hand.

Problems Relating to the Labor Market

Before the economic recession started, and industry in Holland was booming, foreign labor turned out to be an addition to the existing labor force, necessary to keep the process going. In the eighties, with unemployment growing and becoming structural, this will be less and less so. Nonetheless, these immigrant groups are there and bound to stay. Return to the homelands is no real possibility for most of them, and governmental policy toward these groups has realistically moved to a support of measures that may help the new citizens adjust to their future environment. Problems, however, are immense and will grow with the second generation entering the labor market now and in coming years. Because lack of a command of the language and limited achievement in education will impair their opportunities, unemployment will be disproportionately high in this group. This may turn them into a vulnerable group that has to rely on welfare and whose disappointment and feelings of discrimination may have undesirable consequences for everybody involved. Second-generation immigrants, especially if from North Africa or of Caribbean descent, may well develop into a high-risk group that will be in need of special provisions.

GOALS

In previous publications I considered the problem of a general and a more specific culture of groups in our society. In that article I proposed that a society can function thanks to a general basis of communication that can be called a general concept of culture. Because different groups in our society find a common ground in this general concept of culture, the basis for communication is given. However, in the problem of the integration of immigrant groups in Western European societies the question is legitimized of whether in this confrontation a minimal basis of communication is present, and my answer has been mainly negative. I suggested that for some groups in our Dutch schools the home culture is so different from the dominant culture in Western European society that this minimal basis of communication in many cases simply does not exist. That is why I want to suggest that the goal of intercultural education will have to be to develop a minimal basis of communication that is a primary condition for the living together of diverse groups in one society. Thus the primary goal for education in multicultural schools is to teach their students to communicate and live together and to offer them the basic instruments to do so. For the development toward multicultural education this will mean that it is up to the school to develop intercultural understanding as a basic instrument for intercultural communication. This is a general aim for education. It is obvious that to reach that aim important tasks have to be accomplished by counselors in schools. A large part of the problems that students from other cultures will have stems from this phenomenon of bad communication and misunderstanding, which will lead to conflicts among patterns of life in different groups and between norms and values of which diverse groups are insufficiently aware.

A comprehensive system for counseling in which the organization of the school and the counseling of the persons are integrated will be necessary. I hold that this is true generally but certainly so when we talk about counseling of children of ethnic minorities in our education system. Otherwise, the counselor would usurp the responsibility of the teachers. The teaching-learning process is a responsibility of the school as a whole, and counselors should not take it upon themselves to remove their colleagues from that responsibility. To reach such a point it is necessary to raise the level of cultural awareness of teachers and counselors. It is essential for schools to help people become independent and ready for a responsibility in society. Now children from ethnic minorities usually belong to groups in society who are in a situation of disadvantage and whose opportunities in society usually are worse than those of native-born people. They belong to the lowest strata in society, and their chances toward emancipation are the least. This means that counseling of ethnic minorities will have a special significance. An adequate guidance and counseling process will be necessary to help them to overcome the bad start that they already have in life.

MEANS

It has been said often that in many Western countries the usual Rogerian model of counseling has strong limitations when the counseling of students from all social levels in the schools is involved. These limitations stem from the fact that the Rogerian model was developed and is especially appropriate for clients with a reasonable amount of verbal fluency. Generalizing, the Rogerian model seems to be made for a middle-class culture in which people are accustomed to verbalizing feelings and exchanging them in a verbal way. Many subgroups in our society do not communicate in that way. Working classes in our society especially have, according to Bernstein, a less verbal culture and are more apt to communicate by gestures and symbols than by a balanced way of speech.

Students from different cultures and especially from an Islam background will moreover often be very unfamiliar with behavioral patterns that seem to be obvious and normal in our Western verbal culture. Most textbooks that teach counseling emphasize, for instance, the importance of eye contact to relate well with a client. This is an example of clear cultural difference. In many cultures outside Western Europe it is very impolite and unbecoming to look a teacher, who is an authority figure, in the eyes when the teacher is speaking to you. If a teacher or a counselor urges a student to have eye contact, this will be experienced as a rude way of intruding in what a student always has learned to be the decent attitude. In this way the rapport that counselors try to establish will be blocked by their very behavior. This is just one example; many others could be added. The essence of the message is that every counselor always will have to realize that the person coming in for counseling is determined to a large extent by life history.

Students who have been raised in a certain pattern of norms and values will not very easily be able to distance themselves from these norms and values. This is certainly the case if this pattern of norms and values is inculcated and reinforced daily. If someone neglects that pattern of values the student may become completely confused. Consequently, counselors will have to realize that the cultural framework of the student determines whether the counseling offered is understandable. This problem is unidentified in many of our schools, because for the majority of our clients this general cultural concept of communication is already there and has been established in those years that preceded our meeting.

Whenever a counselor has to deal with students who are still in need of acquiring that general concept of culture, anticipation of a not-yet-existing basis for communication is not allowed. One consequence is that the non-directive model of Rogerian counseling is not always desirable in counseling of the immigrant student. This student, who in general will be raised in an atmosphere in which the adult authority cannot be contradicted and has absolute validity, will not understand a non-directive approach and will not be helped by it. In such situations a counselor will probably have to make a bypass by using authority as a means to develop a structure for the counseling situation in which in the end the counselee will be able to take up his or her role. A consequence will be that counselors in many cases will have to distance themselves from those convictions that usually will determine counseling behavior with students.

The development of a multicultural school will also have an aspect of awareness of the limitations of the teacher as representing the dominant culture or of the limitations of the dominant culture as such. Values that seem to be absolute may in some cases turn out to be open for discussion. That is not to say that counselors should deny their own values. What it does say is that a situation of counseling presupposes that a counselor can develop an empathic understanding for the pattern of norms and values of the client, the student who is coming in for help. Perhaps we can indicate such an attitude as cultural empathy. To be a good helper it is fundamental that counselors develop an empathic understanding of the norms and values that are behind the helpee's question. Because of this, cultural empathy is an important means for the counselor who has to work in a multicultural school. It is a basis for the development of understanding and for the delivery of effective and adequate help.

Again, this does express the bridge function of the teacher-counselor. In a multicultural school teachers and teacher-counselors are people who build a bridge between the dominant culture that gave rise to the school and those subcultures that will be owned by the students who enter this school. If these subcultures that we have to work with do not originate from the dominant culture, the pressure on the teacher-counselor to reach a point in which the student will be enabled to live in this society here and now will be heavy. Nonetheless, this is what is asked of them on the basis of their responsibility to help the student emancipate. That can be supported by the means that have been mentioned, but there may be more.

To effect this bridge situation it may be important for counselors to develop simulation situations and to teach students to handle the expectancies of the dominant culture by practicing them, especially those that belong to what could be called the "minimal baggage for survival." In this way students also can be taught to handle these value conflicts that cannot be avoided when people have to interact with a different culture. In this conflict the counselor will have to respect the cultural identity of the student. At the same time an integration of cultures never will mean the abolition of one's own identity. What has to be reached is a synthesis on higher level.

The road to multicultural counseling in the schools of Western Europe will be hard and difficult in the years to come. But it is a challenge that has to be met and will prove to be worthwhile.

REFERENCES

Berg-Eldering, L., van de (1978) Hulpverlening volgens "mediterraan model"? *Tijdschrift voor Maatschappijvraagstukken en Welzijnswerk*, pp. 59–62.
——— (1978) *Marokkaanse gezinnen in Nederland*. Alphen a/d Rijn.

Deen, N. (1983) Intercultureel onderwijs als kader voor het bevorderen van begrip tussen verschillende culturen. *Gloria, 6* (3), 5–11.

Deen, N. (Ed.), (all back issues) *International Journal for the Advancement of Counseling*. The Hague: Martinus Nijhoff Publishers.

de Vries, Marlene H. (1981) *Waar komen zij terecht? De positie van jeugdige allochtonen in het onderwijs en op de arbeidsmarkt*. The Hague.

Eppink, A. (1975) Mediterraan kultuurpatroon en hulpverlening. *Tijdschrift voor Maatschappelijk Werk*, pp. 203–215.

———. (1977) De tweede generatie gastarbeiders 2. *Tijdschrift voor Maatschappelijk Werk*, pp. 271–275.

——— (1978) Een stereotyp beeld van en bij hulpverlening aan mediterranen. *Tijdschrift voor Maatschappelijk Werk*, pp. 337–343.

Esch, W., van, Moenivalam, H., & Gademann, B. (1983) *Allochtone leerlingen in het voortgezet onderwijs*. Harlingen.

Essinger, Helmut, Helmich, Achim, & Hoff, Gerhard (H539), (1981) *Auslanderkinder im Konflikt*. Konigstein.

Gilbert, M. A., & Nordlie, P. G. (1978) An analysis of race relations/equal opportunity training. In *USAREUR, ARI Technical Report TR-78-B10*. Alexandria, Va.: U.S. Army Research Institute for the Behavioral and Social Sciences.

Hasemann, K. (Spring 1984) Perspectives for counseling in education in the Federal Republic of Germany. *Internationally Speaking APGA International Relations Committee*, pp. 4–5.

Kramer, J. (1980) *Unsettling Europe*. New York: Random House.

Krupinski, J., Stoller, A., & Wallace, L. (1973) Psychiatric disorders in East European refugees now in Australia. *Social Science and Medicine, 7*, 31–49.

Littlewood, R., & Lipsedge, M. (1982) *Aliens and alienists: Ethnic minorities and psychiatry*. New York: Penguin Books.

Marsella, A., & White, G. (1981) *Cultural conceptions of mental health and therapy*. Dordrecht, Holland: Reidel.

Martin, L., & DeVolder, J. (1983) Guidance and counseling services in the Federal Republic of Germany. *The Personnel and Guidance Journal, 61* (8), 482–487.

McGoldrick, M., Pearce, J., & Giordano, J. (1982) *Ethnicity and family therapy*. New York: Guilford Press.

Megarry, Jacquetta, Nisbet, Stanley, & Hoyle, Eric (1981) Education of minorities. *World Yearbook of Education*. London/New York: Kogan Page.

Sandfuchs, K. (Ed.) (1981) *Lehren und Lernen mit Auslanderkindern*. Klinkhardt, Bad Heilbrun.

Sartorius, N. (1979) Cross cultural psychiatry. In Kiser, K., et al. (Eds.), *Psychiatry Der Gegenwart*. Berlin: Springer-Verlag, pp. 711–737.

Sartorius, N., Pedersen, P., & Marsella, A. (1984) Mental health services across cultures: Some concluding thoughts. In Pedersen, P., Sartorius, N., & Marsella, A. *Mental Health Services: The Cross Cultural Context*. Beverly Hills, Calif.: Sage.

Sluysman, A. (1978) *De buitenlandse client en de Nederlandse hulpverlening*. pp. 386–389.

van der Meer, Ph. (1978) Is het begrip "mediterrane cultuur" bruikbaar in de hulpverlening? *Tijdschrift voor Maatschappelijk Werk*, pp. 189–193.

van Keulen, A. (1977) De tweede generatie gastarbeiders, Vol. 1. *Tijdschrift voor Maatschappelijk Werk*, pp. 265–270.

Wittkower, E. D. (Ed.). (all back issues) *Transcultural Psychiatric Research Review*. Canada: McGill University.

Psychological Disorders across Cultures

JURIS G. DRAGUNS

Research on psychopathological manifestations in different cultural settings has yielded two kinds of general findings. On the one hand, large-scale multicultural investigations have demonstrated that the same major disorders occur in a variety of very different cultures (World Health Organization, 1973). On the other hand, a wealth of research reports have documented the operation of cultural influences upon the manifestations, course, and outcome of psychological disorder. Integrating these two divergent strands of research findings, one could say that the expressions of abnormal behavior across cultures are different, yet comparable. One could also say that cultural variations in psychopathology occur around a detectable common core of universal features of psychological disturbance.

The objective of this chapter is to justify and to elaborate on these two conclusions. Encompassed within this survey are patterns of behavior and experience characterized by distress and/or disability. Since the field of study of psychological disorder across cultures is vast and, moreover, has been amply reviewed by several authors (Draguns, 1973, 1984; Favazza, 1978; Leff, 1981; Marsella, 1979; Murphy, 1983; Triandis & Draguns, 1980), the focus of this chapter is upon a subcategory of all research attempting to relate culture and abnormal behavior. The review concentrates upon explicit empirical comparisons of psychopathological behavior in two or more cultural settings. The reader is introduced to the typical research approaches, the conceptual and methodological problems encountered in implementing them, the attempts to solve these problems, the findings obtained, and the meaning attributed to them. In particular, an attempt is made to relate this body of evidence to the concerns and operations of working counselors and psychotherapists.

Although the origin of comparative studies of mental disorder goes back to the beginnings of this century (Murphy, 1983), only in the last three decades has a cumulative body of evidence developed on the manifestations of psychopathology in several cultures. A major effort was undertaken at the Transcultural

Psychiatric Research Center in Montreal (Murphy, 1983) in collecting data from practicing psychiatrists in countries around the globe on symptoms encountered by their schizophrenic and depressive patients. The results of these inquiries highlighted both the culturally distinctive and the humanly universal features of these two disorders. The culturally differentiating symptoms, moreover, seemed to be characteristic of broad cultural regions and appeared to be readily interpretable in light of prevailing cultural values. Thus experiences of personal guilt in depression were predominant in countries with a Judeo-Christian heritage but infrequent or atypical in settings with other religious traditions. In schizophrenia, ideational and paranoid symptomatology was characteristic of countries at a higher level of economic development and high rates of literacy. Catatonic manifestations were prevalent in many traditional, rural, and non-industrialized settings. Regardless of culture, a limited number of symptoms were found to be present in each of these two disorders. In the case of depression, they were dejected or depressed mood, diurnal mood change, insomnia, and diminution of interest in the social environment. In the case of schizophrenia, the following universal symptoms were identified: social and emotional withdrawal, auditory hallucinations, general delusions, and flat affect. These studies were much criticized because their results confound the perceptions of the reporting clinicians with the behaviors of the patients. Certainly, it would be rash to equate their findings with the actual occurrence of the patients' symptoms. It would, however, be equally rash to conclude that they were unrelated to patients' symptom manifestations.

Although the Montreal researchers took a bird's-eye view of psychopathology around the world, M. K. Opler and J. L. Singer (Draguns, 1973) addressed themselves to cultural variations found within the pluralistic American society. They studied young schizophrenic males of Italian and Irish descent and identified a host of subtle differences both in the manifestations and the underlying psychodynamics of persons with an identical psychotic disorder, that is, paranoid schizophrenia. These differences were traced to culturally mediated patterns of parent-child relationship in the formative periods of these young schizophrenics' lives. They were also able to trace these differences to important features of southern Italian and Irish cultures as they were transplanted to the New World.

This work led to a number of extensions in which members of a number of different United States ethnic groups were compared. Their approach and findings also influenced the psychiatric census study of the multiethnic population of Midtown Manhattan (Dohrenwend & Dohrenwend, 1974), which identified many class-related and culturally and religiously based differences in psychiatric symptomatology. Ethnically comparative studies of abnormal behavior have also appeared in Australia, Canada, England, Israel, Singapore, and Taiwan, documenting in each case differences in psychiatric symptomatology among people who share a physical habitat but differ in cultural heritage.

These findings are paralleled by a growing number of studies in which patients are compared from two or more settings that are both culturally distinct and geographically removed. This research brings with it major conceptual and meth-odological problems and requires their provisional or definitive resolution. These problems boil down to combining cross-cultural comparability with cultural sen-sitivity. For behaviors to be compared, observations of them have to be stand-ardized. This recognition has led to the development and cultural adaptation of a great many symptom scales and other instruments. These instruments have, for the most part, originated in the West and, most frequently, in the United States. Their application across cultures has entailed translation and adaptation. The dilemma of people involved in such operations has been this: how far to adapt the instrument to increase its cultural sensitivity. If you do not go far enough in pursuit of this goal, the operations of a research project will be more standardized than culturally sensitive. In the obverse case, they will gain in sensitivity but lose in cross-cultural comparability.

Equivalence versus sensitivity of research instruments is only one of the issues facing the cross-cultural investigator. Another problem is the equivalence of populations to be compared. Early attempts to equate populations at different cultural sites took the form of individual matching on several relevant dimensions of comparison, such as socioeconomic status, educational level, age, and sex. More recent work has been influenced by the recognition that individual matching raises serious methodological problems and that the gains produced by this procedure are more apparent than real. Consequently, recent comparisons of psychological disorders across cultures have either restricted themselves to a reasonably homogeneous population of depressives or have encompassed the entire range of psychopathology without attempting to equate the groups com-pared in any sociological, demographic, or biographic parameters.

Finally, comparisons of psychopathology across culture lines have the potential of confounding the patient variance with that of observers. An example may illustrate this state of affairs. One of the best known cross-cultural studies of psychopathology has been the so-called U.S.–U.K. project (Cooper et al., 1972). The impetus for the design and implementation of this study was the dramatic contrast in apparent frequency of depression and schizophrenia between England and the United States. Upon the application of standardized instruments for the detection of psychiatric symptoms and a partial interchange of psychiatric ob-servers, it was found that the major share of increased frequency of depression in England and of schizophrenia in the United States was attributable to the diagnosticians in the two countries rather than to the patients. Only the greater incidence of depression in Britain remained significant, although at a much reduced level, upon the application of these methodological refinements.

What has been learned in the course of these cross-cultural comparisons? One finding that has recurred in a variety of contexts pertains to the relationship between modal and deviant behavior in a cultural setting. Although a definitive demonstration of this relationship is lacking, the results of several cross-cultural comparisons suggest that psychopathology represents an exaggeration of normal and adaptive patterns of behaviors that are characteristic of a given culture. Thus the results of several comparisons of psychopathology in North and Latin America have been interpreted on the basis of the concept of sociocultural premise of passive response to stress, which is supposedly deeply embedded in Latin American cultural experience. Other studies involving Japanese and Western psychiatric patients have brought to the fore the importance of direct, immediate experience in the expression of psychopathology in Japan and its greater cognitive structuring in Western countries such as Germany and the United States (see Draguns, 1973).

The results of these and other bicultural studies, however, have been overshadowed by some large-scale, multicultural investigations. Of these studies, the International Pilot Study of Schizophrenia (IPSS) conducted by the World Health Organization (1973, 1979) in nine countries around the world is most prominent. Early results of this research pointed to the existence of a core pattern of schizophrenic symptoms that was present in all of the nine centers. They also led to the identification of a set of symptoms on the basis of which schizophrenia could be diagnosed at all of the sites of the investigation. These symptoms include restricted affect, poor insight, thinking aloud, poor rapport, incoherent speech, unrealistic information, and bizarre and/or nihilistic delusions.

More recent phases of IPSS (World Health Organization, 1979) have highlighted important differences in the course and treatment of schizophrenia across cultures. Somewhat surprisingly, schizophrenia was found to have a more benign course and a more favorable outcome in several of the developing countries included in the comparison, such as Colombia, India, and Nigeria, than in some of the most advanced and prosperous countries of the industrial world, such as Denmark, Great Britain, and the United States. Moreover, high socioeconomic status tends generally to be associated with favorable prognosis in this country and in some other cultures (Dohrenwend & Dohrenwend, 1974). On the basis of the results of the IPSS, this finding does not hold and indeed is reversed in some of the developing countries. It is the literate, well-educated, high-status subjects who were found to progress toward chronicity. Early findings from the IPSS led the authors of the World Health Organization (WHO) research to expect that the patients presenting core symptoms of schizophrenia would show poor prognosis. Contrary to expectations, no such relationship was found. To sum up this complex pattern of results, schizophrenia appears as a recognizable and comparable entity in all of the nine very different cultures in which it was studied by the WHO. Although it is diagnosed differently, a detectable core pattern emerges at all of the different sites of observation. Culture, however, does appear to influence the course and outcome of this disorder and to some degree its manifestations, although this point has been somewhat underemphasized in the reports extant from the IPSS so far. J. E. Cooper and N. Sartorius (1977) have advanced speculations on reasons why schizophrenia in industrialized and developed cultures tends toward chronicity.

These conclusions are in part paralleled by the results of research on depression. Early studies of non-Western patient populations incautiously and hastily concluded that depression does not exist in these settings. Recent research, more sophisticated in methodology, has demonstrated that a common core of vegetative symptoms of depression is found in a wide range of cultural settings in North America as well as South America, Asia, and Africa. These symptoms appear to include vegetative symptoms of depression, such as loss of appetite, sleeplessness, and loss of interest in sexuality as well as inability to enjoy customary pleasurable activities. What is not universal is self-blame and feelings of guilt, although it would be an overgeneralization to state that guilt is uniformly absent from the experience of all non-Western depressives (Marsella & Pedersen, 1981; Triandis & Draguns, 1980). Moreover, depression is difficult to detect and easy to miss when it is observed across the culture gulf. Studies even within the United States (see Draguns, 1973) suggest that depressive manifestations are overlooked and instances of bizarre behavior magnified in black patients by white psychiatric observers. Depression, especially when it occurs without an overlay of guilt, is to a large extent manifested by subtraction rather than addition. Its positive manifestations are often subtle and inconspicuous and are easily missed when observed across a culture gulf.

Beyond these two major varieties of psychopathology, cross-cultural differences have been revealed in two conditions. One of them is hysteria, before World War I the principal manifestation of the neurosis in the West (Leff, 1981). On the basis of the data available, it continues to be prominent in Asia and Africa, while it has dramatically declined in incidence in the West. The other is an acute confusional psychotic state that is short in duration and spontaneously reversible. Described under several names such as "transient psychosis," "bouffée délirante aiguë," and "hysterical psychosis," it is prominent in locations as different as the Caribbean basin, West Africa, and the islands of the South Pacific. Several of the prominent culture-bound syndromes, such as *amok*, probably represent particular cultural crystallizations of this disorder. Although the current *Diagnostic and Statistical Manual*, third edition, recognizes the possibility of such temporary psychotic states occurring in the United States, they are a lot less prominent in their visibility and, presumably, in their incidence.

What can be concluded from this survey? Research to date has documented the presence of both the universal and the cultural components of psychopathology. Two extreme positions have been refuted in the process. One of them holds that psychopathology, across its entire range, is identical regardless of where it occurs. A diluted version of this view maintains that cultural differences are present, but that they are minor and trivial. The opposite formulation posits that each culture creates its own disorder and that these disorders are unique to each culture and incomparable. Instead, we have a recognizable core of psychopathology, molded into a variety of manifestations by local influences and conditions. We can safely conclude that the way a person expresses and experiences psychopathology is the joint result of the disorder in question, the person's personality, and the culture in which it occurs.

The most general conclusion to be drawn from this review is that culture impinges upon the expression and social presentation of symptoms, the course of the disorder, and the response to treatment. Various cultures could be thought of as facilitating or inhibiting the experience and social communication of symptoms. Cultures could be thought of possessing different thresholds for the subjective experience and social report of particular manifestations of disorder. The diagnostic value of hallucinations is not cross-culturally constant; rather, there are cultures that more readily accept these kinds of experiences and others that interpose a high barrier in the path of their subjective or social acceptance. H.B.M. Murphy (1983), referring primarily to Ireland, made a similar point about delusions; a widely cultivated and generally valued social skill in story-telling may facilitate the development and the elaboration of delusions. It is incumbent upon the culturally sensitive counselor or clinician to recognize cultural contexts of presentation and thresholds of appearance of various manifestations of disturbance and distress.

Other cultural determinants of psychopathology include the learned and socially transmitted roles involved in the expression of disturbance and distress and the socially shared conceptions of psychological disorder. It has been shown in comparisons of Germany and the United States that psychiatrists, psychiatric patients, and the lay public in these two countries share views and beliefs on the nature of mental illness (Triandis & Draguns, 1980).

The content of a psychological disturbance is culturally colored. We have seen that depression, for example, is differently expressed in various distinct cultural settings. A fairly obvious avenue of cultural shaping occurs on the plane of delusions and hallucinations; as has been amply demonstrated, the content of these experiences expresses the concerns and preoccupations of their place and time (Leff, 1981; Murphy, 1983).

In more general terms, psychopathology reflects in an exaggerated and caricatured fashion the prevailing adaptive patterns of behavior of a given milieu. Fears and concerns experienced by normal people are blown out of proportion. Characteristic modes of dealing with stress are magnified to the point of absurdity. Stoic acceptance of the immutable vicissitudes of life in normals gives way to withdrawal into passivity; attacking vigorously and energetically the sources of such stress is replaced by frantic and explosive bursts of activity. Adaptively assertive and aggressive behavior shades off into destructiveness and violence.

Although culture is reflected in psychopathology, these two concepts should not be confused. One of the major pitfalls that a working counselor or psychotherapist should guard against is assimilating behavior patterns that are strange, unfamiliar, and different into the category of psychological disturbance. The conspicuous and tragic instances of psychiatric hospitalization and treatment because of language barriers and cultural misunderstandings are the results of such confounding. The counselor or clinician cannot avoid evaluating the appropriateness of a client's behavior, but he or she should always do it from within the client's cultural or social frame of reference.

This consideration brings up the question of the sources of information on which counselors or psychotherapists could base such decisions. It is unrealistic to expect that a counselor or clinician would have expert knowledge of all cultures he or she is likely to encounter in a complex pluralistic society such as that of the United States or Canada. It is equally unrealistic to attempt matching every counselor and counselee in cultural experience or background. Yet a counselor can seek information from a number of sources. First, there is a rapidly increasing store of research reports, accounts of personal experiences, and reviews of evidence pertinent to psychopathology across cultures. Second, colleagues of a given cultural background or familiar with the culture in question can be consulted. Third, social scientists with expertise in a given cultural area could provide valuable information. Fourth, members of such a cultural group could be interviewed to answer questions that would otherwise remain unanswered. Finally, the client and his or her family could be enlisted to fill in gaps in information not otherwise available and to explain events and occurrences that would otherwise remain baffling. The limiting factor here is that the objectives of counseling and psychotherapy should remain paramount and the quest for cultural information subsidiary to these goals.

REFERENCES

Cooper, J. E., & Sartorius, N. (1977) Cultural and temporal variations in schizophrenia. *British Journal of Psychiatry, 130,* 50–55.

Cooper, J. E., Kendell, R. E., Gurland, B. J., Sharpe, L., Copeland, J.R.M., & Simon, R. (1972) *Psychiatric diagnosis in New York and London.* London: Oxford University Press.

Dohrenwend, B. P., & Dohrenwend, B. S. (1974) Social and cultural influences on psychopathology. *Annual Review of Psychology, 25,* 419–452.

Draguns, J. G. (1973) Comparisons of psychopathology across cultures: Issues, findings, directions. *Journal of Cross-Cultural Psychology, 4,* 9–47.

———. (1982) Methodology in cross-cultural psychopathology. In Al-Issa, I. (Ed.), *Culture and psychopathology.* Baltimore: University Park Press, pp. 33–70.

———. (1984) Assessment of mental health and disorder. In Pedersen, P. B., Sartorius, N., & Marsella, A. J. (Eds.), *Mental health services: The cross-cultural context.* Beverly Hills, Calif.: Sage, pp. 31–58.

Favazza, A. (1978) Overview: Foundations of cultural psychiatry. *American Journal of Psychiatry, 135,* 293–303.

Leff, J. (1981) *Psychiatry around the globe: A transcultural view,* New York: Marcel Dekker.

Marsella, A. J. (1979) Cross-cultural study of mental disorders. In Marsella, A. J., Tharp, R. G., & Ciborowski, T. J. (Eds.), *Perspectives on cross-cultural psychology.* New York: Academic Press, pp. 209–262.

Marsella, A., & Pedersen, P. (1981) *Cross-cultural counseling and therapy.* Elmsford, N.J.: Pergamon Press.

Murphy, H.B.M. (1983) *Comparative psychiatry.* Berlin: Springer-Verlag.

Triandis, H. C., & Draguns, J. G. (Eds.) (1980) *Handbook of cross-cultural psychology.*
    Volume VI: Psychopathology. Boston: Allyn & Bacon.
World Health Organization (1973) *The International Pilot Study of Schizophrenia.* Ge-
    neva: Author.
——— (1979) *Schizophrenia: An international follow-up study.* New York: Wiley.

II

COUNSELING METHODS

Each discipline has developed its own methods for counseling across cultures. In addition to adapting the content of culturally appropriate counseling it is also important to adapt the methods by which that content is conveyed. The eight methods described in this section approach the same basic problems from contrasting disciplines. Having a wider range of methodologies to choose from, the culturally appropriate counselor or therapist is better prepared to match the right method with the right context.

The discipline of anthropology contributes an "ethnographic" methodology as described by Bea Wehrly and Karen Watson-Gegeo. Robert Sprafkin, Arnold Goldstein, and Jane Gershaw apply the behavioral psychological perspectives of structured learning to age and socioeconomic status as culturally defined perspectives, and Raymond Lorion and Delores Parron apply the clinical psychological perspectives to the difficult problems of treating lower-income groups. Lawrence Brammer applies the counseling psychology perspective to nonformal support systems outside the structures of counseling and therapy. Wynette Devore describes the contributions of social work toward understanding cultural variables in counseling and therapy. Aaron Wolfgang takes the perspective of a linguist and examines nonverbal variables of communication in counseling and therapy across cultures. Madeleine Leininger describes how nursing has approached transcultural differences. In the concluding chapter Jonathan Freedman describes a new field of clinical sociology as it relates to cultural variables.

Sometimes the disciplines of study can be more resistant to harmony than the culturally different populations being served. By combining a selection of different disciplinary perspectives we hope to encourage members of each discipline to read the parallel literature in other disciplines and work together for more cross-disciplinary cooperation.

Ethnographic Methodologies as Applied to the Study of Cross-Cultural Counseling

BEA WEHRLY AND KAREN WATSON-GEGEO

The need to broaden contemporary counseling theories and techniques for use in cross-cultural helping relationships has been recognized since the early 1960s. Following Gilbert Wrenn's (1962) descriptions of the counselor as "culturally encapsulated," a slow but steadily growing literature has decried the culturally bound nature of contemporary, Western-based counseling theory and practice (Beauvais, 1977; Green, 1982; Pedersen, Draguns, Lonner, & Trimble, 1981; Stewart, 1983; Sue, 1981; Super, 1983; Wehrly & Deen, 1983). The need for broadening methods of researching the process of counseling across cultures has been recognized. The potential usefulness of ethnographic methodology as a format for conducting research to build new theory in cross-cultural counseling has rarely been recognized, however.

HISTORY AND RATIONALE

In the social science field, ethnographic methodologies for gathering information and building grounded theory have been developing for nearly a century. Anthropologists have helped professionals in other disciplines realize that through this method researchers can acquire information that is often not attainable through traditional descriptive methods of research and use this data to build new theory. James Spradley (1979) called this the "quiet revolution" in the social sciences and described *ethnography* as "a fundamental tool for understanding ourselves and the multicultural societies of the modern world" (p. iii).

In the field of counseling and psychotherapy, the use of ethnographic methods to understand the cultural meanings of interactions across cultures is very limited and of relatively recent origin. Research in counseling and psychotherapy has been dominated by the quantitative research methods of psychology, which, in turn, are patterned after methods of physical science research with roots in the philosophy of logical positivism. The hypothetico-deductive paradigm for deducing hypotheses from theory, defining variables operationally, quantifying observable behaviors, and using objective methods to generate data to test hypotheses has been seen as "the scientific method." Within this model, counseling research has been limited almost entirely to quantitative methods that assume it is possible to study objectively all variables in the helping relationships and to produce knowledge about the structure of reality.

Recognition of the need to revise and/or broaden research methodology for studying human interactions has been gathering momentum. In 1975 Lee Cronbach warned that the two scientific disciplines of experimental control and systematic correlation were limited to finding answers to questions that had been formulated in advance. He challenged researchers to go beyond the methods of physical science "to know man as he really is" (p. 126). Leo Goldman (1976) called for a revolution in counseling research after stating that published research in counseling had been of little value, because it had "focused too narrowly on the traditional standards and methods of physical science" (p. 545).

In *The Personnel and Guidance Journal* (1981) special issue on research in counseling, Mary Lee Smith reviewed the history of counseling research, discussing the heavy influence that had come from psychology's "mimicking" of the physical science research methods. She saw these methods as inadequate for counseling research and viewed the challenges for the researcher as those of getting close enough to the subjects to be able to grasp an understanding of their behavior in the total milieu in which it occurs as well as being able to interpret this behavior to the readers of research. Smith advocated the use of naturalistic inquiry ethnographic methods as an alternative to hypotheses-testing research methods for study of the counseling process.

The following year, 1982, saw the publication of *The Counseling Psychologist* special issue on research methodologies. In this issue the major-contribution article was entitled "Qualitative Strategies in Counseling Research" (Neimeyer & Resnikoff, 1982). The authors argued that "while useful, an exclusive reliance on quantitative methods may neglect much data that is meaningful to counseling researchers" (p. 75). Ethnographic methods of participant and non-participant observation were among qualitative research methods described and critiqued. The commitment of qualitative methodology to the comprehension of subjectivity in the counseling process was emphasized by these authors.

Although there is evidence of the need to broaden the base of contemporary cross-cultural counseling theory, there is little evidence of the adoption of ethnographic methodologies to build grounded theory. Frederick Erickson's (1975) research of gatekeeping functions employed by junior-college counselors working with minority students is one of a very limited number of studies relying on ethnographic methods to generate descriptive data about cross-cultural counseling. Factors that may be deterring the use of ethnography are:

1. The labor-intensive nature of ethnographic research
2. The intensive training needed to learn the implementation of ethnographic research

3. The dearth of counselor-preparation programs that offer courses in ethnographic methodology

4. The dependence on counseling research paradigms based on psychological models

ASSUMPTIONS AND THEORETICAL FRAMEWORK

Ethnographic research aims to describe and analyze the "ways of living" or culture of a social group, focusing on specific cultural patterns in behavior, interaction, and shared meaning (Heath, 1982, p. 34). The unit of analysis in ethnographic studies is a social group of variable size (for example, community, neighborhood, family, classroom, counseling office, peer group) defined as mutually interacting (directly and/or indirectly), bound together by relationships and action-interaction sequences, located in a given context or situation, having a describable social structure and organization, and self-recognized as a social unit.

The ethnographer's goal is to provide a description and an interpretive-explanatory account of the interactants, their behavior, and their culture, arriving at grounded theory (Glaser & Strauss, 1967) useful in cross-cultural comparison. Ethnographers therefore make a distinction between *emic* and *etic* meanings and languages (Pike, 1964; Hymes, 1982). *Emic* interpretations are presented in the language (that is, concepts and categories) and from the point of view of a cultural insider—that is, a member of the social group under investigation. General statements of emic meaning are necessarily consensual or statistical. Since there are ultimately as many emic perspectives in a group as there are group members, attention to differences and variation is crucial for arriving at a genuine understanding of a group's culture. *Etic* interpretations are based on or use concepts and categories from the analytic language of the social sciences, especially anthropology, and therefore allow for cross-cultural comparisons. An etic interpretation is always from an outsider's point of view, even when the researcher is a cultural insider.

The ethnographic researcher in cross-cultural counseling shares with anthropologists a set of basic assumptions about human behavior and how to study it. The ethnographic perspective is comparative and relational, focusing on human social processes and the nature of social relationships within and across cultures (Firth, 1961). At a macro-cultural level, the ethnographer is concerned with cultural worldview as the lens through which individuals perceive and understand themselves and others. At a micro-interactional level, behavior in groups is seen as ordered by socially shared, but often tacitly held, rules, values, and expectations for behavior, including a cultural definition of the situation, expectations about relationships and conversations, or rules for interpreting and drawing inferences from talk and behavior. When participants in an interaction do not share these understandings, as is usually the case in cross-cultural counseling encounters, communication may break down, mistrust and frustration may be felt, and the interaction may be terminated without a satisfactory outcome.

As a result, ethnographic research emphasizes a holistic approach to counseling problems and encounters. In ascertaining how individuals form relationships, and how social relations are reflected in or affect individuals in different cultures, the ethnographer is working back and forth between the individual (micro) and the cultural group (macro) as analytic levels. Here anthropology diverges from psychology, with its more exclusive focus on the individual or on small social units, especially the family, and its assumption of an essentially Western world-view. A finished ethnographic report is required to situate individuals and their behavior within the concentric spheres of context that constitute experience, including personal and cultural history, family, community, and society. Relationships, beliefs, meanings, and events are examined in both their immediate context of occurrence (micro) and in relevant sociocultural-historical contexts (macro). By relating an event, behavior, or meaning to all of its potential micro and macro contexts, the ethnographer attempts a holistic account of it and a realistic understanding of its development (Watson-Gegeo, Maldonado-Guzman, & Gleason, 1981).

Ethnographic methods of research parallel the goals of such study. The ethnographer becomes a participant-observer in the social group or setting, spending several months observing interactions as they naturally occur. As an observer in the group, the ethnographer records and describes the scenes, behaviors, and values overtly manifested in interaction, detailing them in field notes that keep descriptions separate from analytic interpretations. Emic meanings are elicited by in-depth, usually open-ended interviews conducted from time to time with group members and also through casual conversation on a day-to-day basis. As a participant living with the group for a long period, the ethnographer also gains insight into tacit, implicit patterns of behavior and meaning. Over time the ethnographer acquires a knowledge of the group's language and an understanding of its social structure, organization, and the associated functions of cultural components.

In contrast to psychology, then, which relies on testing to evaluate differences, an ethnographic approach to cross-cultural counseling starts with naturalistic studies of interaction and behavior. Interpretations of behavior are then made not on the basis of pre-set analytic categories, as in positivistic social science, but in terms of emic meanings shared or partially shared by members of a cultural group or society. In fact, rather than resembling a positivistic paradigm, ethnography may be said to most closely resemble the interpretive paradigm that has evolved from hermeneutics (Bredo & Feinberg, 1982; Geertz, 1979). Moreover, in contrast to other naturalistic forms of observation, ethnography does not use pre-set coding categories when observing behavior. When used, coding schemes are developed in the field to be congruent with characteristics of the culture and situation identified by the ethnographer through observation. Finally, ethnographers are always participants as well as observers, using their own socialization into the group as one lens on meanings, values, and social processes.

CONTRIBUTIONS TO CROSS-CULTURAL COUNSELING

Difficulties in cross-cultural counseling seem to arise in situations where the counselor and counselee do not share a cultural definition of the situation. The expectations brought to counseling by the two individuals may be widely disparate. Since the culture in which each individual is socialized shapes the subjective reality of that person, the perceptions of reality brought to counseling by counselors and counselees from different cultures may differ widely. As an example, "culturally encapsulated," Western-oriented counselors often view problems brought by clients in terms of linear cause-effect relationships. These traditional Western-acculturated counselors usually attempt to eradicate, or at least ameliorate, the underlying roots of these problems in working with their clients. The non-Western-socialized counselees may view problems or causal relationships through vastly divergent cultural lenses. Their subjective realities have been shaped by different cultural conditioning so that counselor and counselee interpretations of the situations are incongruent.

Ethnography has the potential to help the cross-cultural counselor understand the cultural meanings of behavior (both verbal and non-verbal) exhibited by counselees from other cultures. Through the intensive and long-term procedures of ethnography, it is possible to determine how the counselee from another culture views the world and how that person behaves in the various spheres of his or her daily interactions. To attain this holistic understanding, counselors must be willing to get out of their offices and go to the "real world" of their culturally different clients. As ethnographers, counselors will enter this world with an idea of a researchable question (or questions) but must be willing to modify or change these questions as they work as participant-observers in the field. Since the process of ethnography is open-ended, it is subject to self-correction at any time during the study.

This ethnographic study will combine both micro- and macro-level work to gain understanding of the individual perspectives of the counselees and the collective perspectives of the larger social systems in which the counselees function daily. Through constant comparative analysis of data obtained in the field, the counselor-researcher will be developing new perspectives of the perceptions of reality of counselees from different cultures. These broader understandings of the cultural meanings of behavior can be used to formulate new theories for helping and counseling individuals from different cultures.

Through the broader views of behaviors gained from ethnographic investigations, the cross-cultural counselor can, then, serve as the "bridge" between cultures needed by the culturally different client. Ethnography can help the cross-cultural counselor gain the phenomenological perspectives necessary to understand this client as well as provide the basis for helping the culturally different person gain the broader perspectives for functioning in the various worlds of his or her everyday existence.

Some words by James Spradley seem to summarize the potential of this process:

Ethnography offers all of us the chance to step outside our narrow cultural background, to set aside our socially inherited ethnocentrism, if only for a brief period, and to apprehend the world from the viewpoint of other human beings who live by different meaning systems.... It is a pathway into understanding the cultural differences that make us what we are as human beings. (Spradley, 1979, p. v)

REFERENCES

Beauvais, F. (1977) Counseling psychology in cross-cultural setting. *The Counseling Psychologist, 7* (2), 80–82.

Bredo, E., & Feinberg, W. (Eds.). (1982) *Knowledge and values in social and educational research*. Philadelphia: Temple University.

Cronbach, L. J. (1975) Beyond the two disciplines of scientific psychology. *American Psychologist, 30,* 116–127.

Erickson, F. (1975) Gatekeeping and the melting pot: Interaction in counseling encounters. *Harvard Educational Review, 45,* 44–70.

Firth, R. (1961) *Elements of social organization*. Boston: Beacon Press.

Geertz, C. (1979) Deep play: Notes on the Balinese cockfight. In Rabinow, P., & Sullivan, M. (Eds.), *Interpretive social science: A reader*. Berkeley: University of California.

Glaser, B. G., & Strauss, A. (1967) *The discovery of grounded theory strategies for qualitative research*. Chicago: Aldine.

Goldman, L. (1976) A revolution in counseling research. *Journal of Counseling Psychology, 23,* 543–552.

Green, J. W. (1982) *Cultural awareness in the human services*. Englewood Cliffs, N.J.: Prentice-Hall.

Heath, S. B. (1982) Ethnography in education: Defining the essentials. In Gilmore, P., & Glatthorn, A. A. (Eds.), *Children in and out of school: Ethnography and education*. Washington, D.C.: Center for Applied Linguistics.

Hymes, D. (1982) What is ethnography? In Gilmore, P., & Glatthorn, A. A. (Eds.), *Children in and out of school: Ethnography and education*. Washington, D.C.: Center for Applied Linguistics.

Neimeyer, G., & Resnikoff, A. (1982) Qualitative strategies in counseling research. *The Counseling Psychologist, 10* (4), 87–89.

Pedersen, P. B., Draguns, J. G., Lonner, W. J., & Trimble, J. E. (Eds.). (1981) *Counseling across cultures*. Honolulu: University Press of Hawaii.

Pike, K. L. (1964) Towards a theory of the structure of human behavior. In Hymes, D. (Ed.), *Language in culture and society*. New York: Harper & Row.

Smith, M. L. (1981) Naturalistic research. *The Personnel and Guidance Journal, 59,* 585–589.

Spradley, J. P. (1979) *The ethnographic interview*. New York: Holt, Rinehart & Winston.

Stewart, L. H. (1983) On borrowing guidance theory and practice: Some observations of an American participant in the British guidance movement. *The Personnel and Guidance Journal, 61,* 507–510.

Sue, D. W. (1981) *Counseling the culturally different: Theory and practice.* New York: Wiley.

Super, D. (1983) Synthesis: Or is it distillation? *The Personnel and Guidance Journal, 61,* 511–514.

Watson-Gegeo, K. A., Maldonado-Guzman, A. A., & Gleason, J. J. (1981) Establishing research goals: The ethnographer-practitioner dialectic. *Proceedings of the Theory and Research Division, Association for Educational Communications & Technology,* Cambridge, Mass., 670–714.

Wehrly, B., & Deen, N. (1983) Counseling and guidance issues from a worldwide perspective: An introduction. *The Personnel and Guidance Journal, 61,* 452.

Wrenn, C. G. (1962) *The counselor in a changing world.* Washington, D.C.: The American Personnel and Guidance Association.

Structured Learning: Its Cross-Cultural Roots and Implications

*ROBERT P. SPRAFKIN, ARNOLD P.
GOLDSTEIN, AND N. JANE GERSHAW*

HISTORY

The cultural chasm that often exists between the professional helper (counselor or therapist) and the helpee (client or patient) has been identified as one of the contexts of intercultural counseling and therapy. Likewise, the imposition of one approach to counseling or therapy upon recipients whose cultural membership does not typically incorporate those beliefs has been another (Pedersen, 1982). These two related issues were the major contributions to the development of Structured Learning to deal with differences of culture compounded by differences of age and socioeconomic status.

The specific social and historical context of Structured Learning's development was the *deinstitutionalization* movement in the United States. Beginning around 1955, a year usually identified with the large-scale introduction of psychotropic medications into psychiatric institutions in North America, there were approximately 550,000 psychiatric inpatients in those institutions. In the years following that date those hospitals were emptied rapidly of their long-term clientele, so that within a decade fewer than half that number remained as psychiatric inpatients. Most important for the development of Structured Learning, this legion of newly deinstitutionalized patients, thrown upon community-based mental-health resources, tended to come from lower socioeconomic backgrounds. However, the majority of available approaches and assumptions about psychological treatments, best exemplified by verbal, insight-oriented psychotherapy, tended to reflect middle-class values, attitudes, and philosophies of life. Such therapies were most often used by helpers coming from middle- or upper-middle-class backgrounds and were generally most successful with patients who also came from middle-class backgrounds and held values, expectations, and attitudes about their world and about psychological treatment similar to those held by their therapists. These values, attitudes, and expectations were generally not shared by patients coming from lower socioeconomic backgrounds. It is no wonder that so many attempts at psychological treatment, as traditionally conceived, failed so miserably with these recently deinstitutionalized, lower-class patients (cf. Myers & Bean, 1965; Goldstein, 1981).

Structured Learning was developed in an attempt to incorporate the preferred learning styles and treatment expectations of the lower- and working-class patient, rather than attempting to force the patient into inappropriate (middle-class-oriented) existing verbal, insight-oriented psychotherapies. That is, an effort was made to "make the therapy fit the patient" rather than to "make the patient fit the therapy" (cf. Goldstein, 1973; Goldstein, Sprafkin, & Gershaw, 1976). By combining elements from the behavioral psychology literature that reflect preferences for action-oriented, concrete, authoritative, immediate-focused learning, the components of *modeling, role playing, social reinforcement*, and *transfer of training* were integrated into a training-treatment package in which the goal was to teach specific interpersonal and coping skills necessary for independent living outside of institutions.

PRESENT STATUS

At present, Structured Learning has been in wide-scale use for more than a decade. Its components—modeling, role playing, social reinforcement, and transfer of training—have been incorporated in a highly teachable, highly structured, group approach to psychological treatment. In a typical Structured Learning group, five to eight "trainees," all sharing similar skill deficits, are exposed to the above-mentioned procedures. Specifically, two trainers introduce the notion of a particular "skill" (for example, "Starting a conversation," "Asking for help") as comprised of a number of behavioral steps that constitute the skill. For example, the skill of "Starting a conversation" consists of the following steps: (1) greet the other person; (2) make small talk; (3) decide if the other person is listening; and (4) bring up the main topic (Goldstein, Sprafkin, Gershaw, & Klein, 1980). The skill is illustrated via *modeling* displays that have live or recorded vignettes of actors using the skill successfully by following the steps of the skill. Modeling displays always depict one skill at a time, using situations familiar to the trainees as content, always working out successfully for the main actor. Following the presentation of a few modeled vignettes, a discussion of the skill is generated by the trainers. Efforts are made to identify situations in trainees' present lives in which the trainee is likely to have difficulty using the particular skill. After situations are identified through the discussions, *role playing* is attempted. Role playing is presented as behavioral rehearsal or practice for situations that are likely to occur in trainees' lives. A main actor is selected on the basis of material presented, and that trainee chooses appropriate co-actors who resemble his or her real-life contacts in as many ways as possible (for example, "Who in the group reminds you of your boss? Your teacher?"). After co-actors are chosen, the main actor describes the scene that will ensue, and the trainers attempt to "set the stage" to make the role-play enactment as realistic as possible. The main actor is instructed to follow the steps, and both actors are coached about what they might say and do. The rest of the group members are reminded to observe particular aspects of the role play so that they can provide appropriate feedback.

The role play is presented and monitored closely by the trainers. At its completion the trainers elicit social reinforcement ("feedback") from group members. Attempts are made to structure the feedback in concrete, constructive, positive terms. After the completion of a number of role plays and of social-reinforcement sequences, those trainees who were main actors are given homework assignments. These activities represent explicit efforts at transfer of training, to encourage trainees to use their newly learned skills in real-life application settings. Homework assignments are presented as specific contracts, identifying when, where, and with whom the skill will be used. Trainees are also instructed on ways of evaluating their performances. In addition to homework assignments, a number of other "transfer enhancers" are built into the Structured Learning process (cf. Goldstein, Sprafkin, Gershaw, & Klein, 1980).

As mentioned previously, Structured Learning was originally developed in an attempt to help bridge a therapeutic cultural chasm between mental-health professionals and deinstitutionalized, lower socioeconomic status psychiatric patients. It rapidly became evident that the method, as well as many of the skills, could be used in skill-enhancement efforts with a variety of other clinical and non-clinical populations. Thus Structured Learning has been used with adolescents (Goldstein, Sprafkin, Gershaw, & Klein, 1980), geriatric patients (Lopez, 1980), police (Goldstein, Monti, Sardino, & Green, 1979), the lay public (Goldstein, Sprafkin, & Gershaw, 1979), and a number of other groups (Goldstein, 1981). The note of caution that is sounded, however, is that the enthusiasm for applying Structured Learning and related techniques to new populations often fosters claims of success that overwhelm available empirical evidence.

FUNDAMENTAL ASSUMPTIONS

Structured Learning, as well as other related approaches to interpersonal skills training, holds a number of assumptions about behavior and behavior change. Although these assumptions are given more or less emphasis in different approaches, they would probably be endorsed by most interpersonal skills trainers.

1. It is possible to conceptualize important human activities, including both observable and cognitive behaviors, in terms of skill proficiencies and skill deficiencies. That is, people can be viewed as more or less skillful (competent) in performing a variety of important interpersonal or intrapersonal behaviors.

2. Problematic behaviors reflect skill deficiencies. Such deficiencies may be the result of the person never having learned certain important skills, or such skills may have been learned but are not presently available due to disuse or inhibitions.

3. Skills can be identified. That is, particular patterns of behaviors can be categorized based on reliable observations over time, place, and person.

4. Once identified, important skills can be taught. Initially, this involves the specification of the behavioral steps that constitute each skill. After the steps have been identified, appropriate techniques are used to facilitate the learning of the skill, which can then be used in various situations. That is, attempts are made to teach not only specific behaviors but also the principles for skill application and the behavioral steps for skill use.

5. Particular behavioral manifestations may differ according to factors such as group membership, but the principles and teaching techniques should be applicable cross-culturally.

6. Skill proficiency, as evidenced by the performance of particular behaviors, *may* affect the individual's feelings of worth, self-esteem, and so on. However, primary attention is paid to bringing about behavior change.

FUNDAMENTAL THEORIES

The enhancement of interpersonal skills has been both a primary and secondary goal of most psychologically oriented interventions. Such skill enhancement was viewed typically as a secondary aspect of insight-oriented, psychodynamically based psychotherapies. Within these approaches to treatment it is generally assumed that once the individual gains insight into his or her problem, the underlying conflicts will be resolved and problematic behaviors or relationships will be improved. However, such improvement is dependent upon the client's acquisition of insight or self-understanding.

By the early 1950s in the United States there appeared a major challenge to insight-oriented approaches to psychological treatment. The impact of American academic psychology began to be felt in the psychotherapeutic arena as practitioners and researchers alike came to view the treatment of problematic behaviors in learning-theory terms. This wedding of academic psychology's traditional concern with learning and clinicians' preoccupation with the amelioration of human problems gave birth to the behavior-modification movement, with its reliance on definable procedures and goals, laboratory-derived methods, and training emphasis.

The behavior-modification movement incorporated clinical approaches based on both operant and respondent conditioning models. An example of the former would be the use of *token economies* (Ayllon & Azrin, 1968) to control disturbed-disturbing behaviors in severely impaired patient populations. A widely used example of the latter would be *systematic desensitization* (Wolpe, 1958), a technique that has been used most widely to reduce phobic avoidances and inhibition, including interpersonal avoidances. The interesting distinction between the two behavioral approaches mentioned above and Structured Learning (and other skill training) is that the control of disruptive behavior (with token economies) or debilitating anxiety (with systematic desensitization) assumes implicitly that once the disruptive behavior or anxiety is eliminated or controlled, the appropriate behaviors will emerge and be used effectively. However, if the effective behavior has never been learned adequately it can hardly emerge! Thus the need arises for approaches such as Structured Learning that attempt to teach new behaviors or skills. That is, the beginning assumption made by Structured Learning is *skill deficit* rather than *skill inhibition*. This also suggests that Structured Learning could be used in conjunction with, or sequentially with, other (behavioral) approaches. For example, it may be necessary first or simultaneously to control disturbing behaviors, using a token economy, before new behaviors are taught, using Structured Learning.

FUTURE DIRECTIONS

At the onset it was mentioned that one of the major inspirations for the development of Structured Learning was the need to bridge the cultural gap between the traditional orientation of psychotherapists and the nontraditional demands of the newly deinstitutionalized, lower socioeconomic status, chronic psychiatric patient. Since that time, Structured Learning has been used with other clinical and nonclinical populations: aggressive and withdrawn adolescents, police, clergy, geriatric patients, and the lay public. It is likely that the near future will see Structured Learning applied within other cultural and intercultural contexts.

Such likely applications within other cultural settings will necessitate the testing and possible revision of the Structured Learning components. Will the same combination of modeling, role playing, social reinforcement, and transfer of training be equally effective when applied with persons representing different national origins? Will the same skills and/or behavioral steps be applicable across cultures? It appears unlikely, since even within North American society somewhat different skills have been identified and used (cf. Goldstein, Sprafkin, & Gershaw, 1976; Goldstein, Sprafkin, Gershaw, & Klein, 1980).

It has also been mentioned that Structured Learning is but one of a number of skills-training programs and shares many commonalities with these related approaches. It is likely that an increased degree of convergence of techniques will occur, as well as a convergence of nomenclature (cf. Curran, Wessberg, Farrell, Monti, Corriveau, & Coyne, 1982; Sprafkin, 1984). What seems clear, however, is that social skills training has established itself firmly within the domain of psychological and psychoeducational treatment and training efforts and is likely to survive and flourish in the future.

REFERENCES

Ayllon, T., and Azrin, N. H. (1968) *The token economy: A motivational system for therapy and rehabilitation.* New York: Appleton-Century-Crofts.
Curran, J. P., Wessberg, H. W., Farrell, A. D., Monti, P. H., Corriveau, D. P., & Coyne, N.A. (1982) Social skills and social anxiety: Are different laboratories

measuring the same construct? *Journal of Consulting and Clinical Psychology*, *50* (3), 396–406.

Goldstein, A. P. (1973) *Structured learning therapy: Toward a psychotherapy for the poor*. New York: Academic Press.

———— (1981) *Psychological skill training*. New York: Pergamon Press.

Goldstein, A. P., Sprafkin, R. P., & Gershaw, N. J. (1976) *Skill training for community: Applying structured learning therapy*. New York: Pergamon Press.

———— (1979) *I know what's wrong, but I don't know what to do about it*. Englewood Cliffs, N.J.: Prentice-Hall.

Goldstein, A. P., Monti, P. J., Sardino, T. J., & Green, D. J. (1979) *Police crisis intervention*. New York, Pergamon Press.

Goldstein, A. P., Sprafkin, R. P., Gershaw, N. J., & Klein, P. (1980) *Skillstreaming the adolescent*. Champaign, Ill: Research Press.

Lopez, M. A. (1980) Social skills training with institutionalized elderly: Effects of pre-counseling structuring and overlearning on skill acquisition and transfer. *Journal of Counseling Psychology, 27*, 286–293.

Myers, J. M., & Bean, L. L. (1965) *A decade later: A follow-up of social class and mental illness*. New York: Wiley.

Pedersen, P. (1982) The intercultural context of counseling and therapy. In Marsella, A. J., & White, G. M. (Eds.), *Cultural conceptions of mental health and therapy*. Dordrecht, Holland: Reidel, pp. 333–358.

Sprafkin, R. P. (1984) Social skills training. In Corsini, R. J. (Ed.), *Wiley encyclopedia of psychology*. New York: Wiley.

Wolpe, J. (1958) *Psychotherapy by reciprocal inhibition*. Stanford, Calif.: Stanford University Press.

Countering the Countertransference: A Strategy for Treating the Untreatable

RAYMOND P. LORION AND DELORES L. PARRON

BACKGROUND

Throughout our respective careers, we have been interested in understanding and responding to the mental health needs of cross-cultural groups, specifically the poor and minority persons. Three decades of epidemiologic research confirm the persistence of a negative relationship among economic disadvantage, minority status, and indices of mental disorders. Unfortunately, the following conclusion remains as true now as it was originally:

The evidence is unambiguous and powerful that the lowest social classes have the highest rates of severe psychiatric disorder in our society. Regardless of the measures employed for estimating severe psychiatric disorder and social class, regardless of the region or the date of study, and regardless of the method of study, the great majority of results all point clearly and strongly to the fact that the lowest social class has by far the greatest incidence of psychoses. (Fried, 1969, p. 113)

Yet these statistics barely begin to communicate the level of need associated with low-income and minority status. In a recent analysis J. T. Gibbs (1984) argued convincingly that black adolescents are an "endangered species." Characterized by epidemic rates of unemployment, substance abuse, illiteracy, teenage pregnancy, and mortality by suicide, homicide, or vehicle accidents, the problems of these young people will affect the nation's mental-health status for decades. Already, many represent the product of two or more generations of

This chapter was written while the senior author served as visiting scientist and acting associate administrator for prevention in the Alcohol, Drug Abuse, and Mental Health Administration. The views expressed are not necessarily those of the National Institute of Mental Health or the Alcohol, Drug Abuse, and Mental Health Administration.

dependency on social-service agencies. Unskilled, unemployed, and uneducated, they are entering adulthood with neither the academic skills nor occupational attitudes and experiences to enable them or their offspring to escape their current cycle of poverty and disenfranchisement. Moreover, current social attitudes and public policies make it unlikely that any domestic program for reversing these trends will appear for the rest of the decade.

Thus the mental-health professions must appreciate and be prepared to respond to the needs of significant segments of the population whose emotional and behavioral disorders will be confounded by economic hardship, discrimination, and almost constant environmental stress. Diagnostically, it must be understood that their anxieties and depressions will frequently reflect both neurotic *and* realistic responses, and the definitions of coping and adaptation will be distinct from those applied to the majority population. In essence, we must be prepared to provide prescriptive and relevant services in forms that are acceptable to individuals who have little basis for assuming that we truly want to or can help them.

Our argument simply stated is that the therapist's attitudes toward low-income and minority groups has, to date, been a major obstacle to the delivery of effective mental health services. Our concern is that, if unchanged, these attitudes will defeat any attempts to respond to the increasing and multiple needs of low-income minority people. Hopefully, our comments will help reverse a trend whereby generations of therapists have been trained and, in turn, trained others to assume that the poor, the uneducated, and the minority populations are unresponsive to contemporary treatment modalities.

THERAPISTS' ATTITUDES AND TREATMENT OUTCOME

A prior review examined in detail the link between therapists' attitudes and treatment outcome (Lorion, 1978). Documentation of such a relationship has been reported in the mental-health literature for more than three decades. Interview studies of therapists unsuccessful with low-income clients have revealed that these therapists interpreted the inability of these persons to verbalize feelings, unwillingness to defer gratification, refusal to cooperate with treatment practices and schedules, and insistence on immediate symptom change as evidence of "client failure" or "resistence to change." Therapists criticized these clients' styles of dress, language patterns, work attitudes, dependence on social services, and general life-styles. Prognoses of unsuccessful treatment outcomes were consistently related to such negative attitudes and to early attrition or therapeutic failure. Process studies have revealed that therapists with negative attitudes tend to speak less during their initial session with low-income clients. Frequently, therapist communications in such sessions are abrupt, critical, and distant. Reflecting on such findings, A. P. Goldstein (1971) questioned whether intake interviews so characterized should not be viewed as the termination rather than the onset of treatment.

Evidence has also been reported about the positive link between therapist attitudes and outcomes. Therapists described by their clients as warm retain significantly more low-income and minority clients in treatment than did their counterparts rated as cold or distant. Similarily, therapists indicating a priori a preference for low-income and minority clients proved to be equally successful with clients from all economic groups. Finally, a number of researchers have reported that treatment outcome with such clients is determined more by therapist factors than by treatment modality. Thus it appears that the outcome of psychotherapy with low-income and minority patients may be influenced positively or negatively by the pre-treatment attitudes and expectations of the therapist. Fortunately, research to date indicates that therapist attitudes can be modified and that such changes do alter the likelihood that a low-income or minority patient will remain in and complete treatment (for example, Jacobs, Charles, Jacobs, Weinstein, & Mann, 1972).

Two major strategies have been identified as effective in altering therapists' attitudes toward low-income and minority clients. V. W. Bernard (1965) argued that such attitudes should be treated as any other form of countertransference. She suggests that examination of such attitudes become an integral part of therapist training. Discussion of such attitudes during supervisory sessions may enable neophyte therapists to recognize in themselves stereotypic assumptions that interfere with therapeutic acceptance and understanding. Jacobs and associates (1972) proposed and systematically studied the advantage of providing the therapist with accurate information about the life-styles, therapeutic expectations, and needs of low-income and minority clients. The results of their research confirmed that providing therapists with such information influenced both the therapist's activity during treatment and the client's continuation in and response to treatment. This research also made evident the advantages of preparing the therapist rather than the client for treatment. Prepared therapists were themselves able and, perhaps most importantly, willing to assist their clients in understanding the goals and procedures of psychotherapy. Thus it appears that therapist preparation and supervision can increase significantly the likelihood of a low-income and minority client's successful completion of psychotherapy.

STEREOTYPES AND ASSUMPTIONS: COUNTERING THE COUNTERTRANSFERENCE

As noted, accurate information has proven to be an effective way to counter the negative influence of stereotypic assumption. The most pervasive and inaccurate stereotype about low-income and minority clients may be that "they" are a homogenous group. Until recently, mental-health literature has ignored the diversity that characterizes these people. First, it should be recognized that these two groups are *not* identical. Minority populations are represented at all economic levels. In absolute terms, whites outnumber non-whites among the poor. Although low-income status is disproportionately characteristic of minority populations, especially blacks and Hispanics, the social policies of the past two decades have gradually produced noticeable positive shifts in their economic and educational characteristics.

For a long time low-income status has been used generically to refer to both the working class and the poor. As argued elsewhere (Lorion, 1973, 1978), these two groups differ markedly in their lives and response to psychotherapy. Working-class clients tend to respond to mental-health treatments in ways similar to the middle- and upper-socioeconomic groups. Thus the subgroup to which the literature about the "untreatable" most directly applies is the poor. It is equally important to recognize the inherent diversity of this group. The "poor" include single mothers, the elderly, the unskilled and unemployed workers, the uneducated transients commonly referred to as "street people" and "bag ladies," and, unfortunately, significant numbers of the recently deinstitutionalized mental patients. The "poor" also include migrant farm workers and some handicapped persons. Some "poor" have always been without money, dependent on social services for food and shelter and educated, at most, to a minimal level of functional literacy. For these individuals the "cycle of poverty" is very real. For others poverty is a more recent phenomenon resulting from loss of a spouse, retirement on an inadequate pension, or an unanticipated illness or injury. Although not comprehensive, this list of those included among the "poor" should alert the reader to the heterogeneity within this group.

A second misconception about low-income and minority individuals is that their lives are continuously bleak without any positive moments. Without question, their lives are difficult, stressful, and demanding. They have few resources and frequently, move from one crisis to another. Yet like other persons they also experience humor, warmth, and enjoyment. In working therapeutically with low-income and minority clients, mental-health practitioners frequently ignore the positive aspects of their clients' lives. By itself this omission can limit the therapist perspective, replace empathy with pity, and inhibit the therapist from recognizing and mobilizing resources that can assist the client to respond to emotional difficulties. We do not intend to suggest that the therapist should glamorize the life of the poor or the experience of minorities, for that would also be a misrepresentation of their lives. Rather, we suggest that the therapist be as open to discussing how the client spends time and resolves problems as to what those problems are. The therapist can acquire considerable insight by asking about the people with whom the client interacts, how recreation is found, and what sources of comfort and assistance are (or have been) available. Unique insights can also be gained through a home visit early in treatment. Thus correcting misconceptions about the quality of a client's life requires that the therapist be willing to learn about that life by examining how days are spent; how joys, whatever their nature, are gained; and how problems are solved.

A third set of assumptions relates to assertions that the poor and minority segments of society are unreliable, impulsive, and irresponsible. Once again, the need to appreciate the heterogeneity of the population is essential. It is most important, however, that situational specificity of such assertions be examined. In many cases, unreliability refers to the frequency with which clients either miss appointments or arrive late. Two realities of poverty may explain, in part, such "unreliability." The poor are frequently dependent on public transportation or private vehicles in serious disrepair. In any large urban setting, either of these things can cause innumerable problems in arriving anywhere "on time." Moreover, careful observation of public health-care facilities makes evident that an "appointment" often refers to the time at which the waiting begins. Rarely are clients in such settings seen at the designated time. Why should a client to a mental-health facility expect anything different if not informed otherwise? Moreover, in medical clinics those who are late are served eventually. How then is a client to interpret the fact that in spite of every effort to arrive, appointments at a mental-health clinic cannot be made up for another week, and, worse yet, the specified fee is still to be paid? Interviews with low-income clients who dropped out of treatment have shown that such early experiences combined with the uncertainty of ever arriving "on time" led many to abandon their help-seeking efforts. Tardiness thus became equated with unreliability and, from the therapist's perspective, with "resistance" to treatment. Unfortunately, far too few therapists understood the amount of effort often required to arrive, albeit late, for a session. Appreciation of such effort may have produced a different response to the tardy or missing client that, in turn, may have increased rather than decreased the likelihood of subsequent arrivals.

Missed appointments in combination with client insistence that their symptoms be treated have often been reported as evidence of low-income and minority impulsiveness (referred to, at times, as "inability to delay gratification"). Once again, it is important to understand therapy from the client's perspective. Why else would anyone go to a "doctor" except to have what hurts made better? How is the new client to know that psychotherapy differs in numerous ways from other forms of medical treatment? Although mental-health practitioners may insist that their services are distinct from *medical* treatments, those differences are not obvious to the initiated.

Appreciation and acceptance of the distinction should not be a prerequisite for treatment. Moreover, given the growing evidence of the acceptability and effectiveness of brief, problem-oriented treatment approaches, therapists must begin to examine their insistence that symptoms cannot be addressed until a "therapeutic relationship" has developed. It now appears that such interventions can be a very important contributor to the establishment of the therapist-client rapport essential to long-term interventions when such interventions are, in fact, necessary.

Sociological studies of the lives of the poor make evident that these individuals are capable of deferring gratification, for they do so on an almost daily basis. Providing for the needs of oneself and one's family on the resources available from food stamps, welfare, unemployment insurance, or even minimum wage (if one is able to negotiate that "much" for the unskilled job available) represents accomplishment of a difficult but critical economic task. Poverty, if nothing else, is characterized by an endless series of unpredictable crises that demand constant reallocation of meager resources from one necessity to another. Everything one owns is always at risk for needing repair; credit, when available, is expensive and short term, and savings must always be diverted from what is desired to what is needed. The therapist who understands the daily decision making necessary to survive economic hardship is likely to appreciate both the client's resourcefulness and insistence that treatment be quick and that symptoms be addressed immediately. To learn of these things, the therapist must be open to the client's issues, the client's priorities, and most importantly, the realistic bases that determine them.

TREATING THE "UNTREATABLE"

Thus far we have questioned the accuracy of the presumption that an individual who approaches the mental-health system for help should be viewed as "untreatable." To characterize such individuals as "unmotivated for treatment" reflects a lack of understanding about their lives and the obstacles they must overcome in seeking and obtaining mental-health services.

It should be noted, at this point, that there is little scientific support for the view that minority therapists should treat minority clients. As noted previously, low-income and minority clients respond most positively to therapists, regardless of race, who are warm, open, and sensitive to the many demands that characterize the lives of their clients. There is some evidence in the literature that therapists from low-income backgrounds may be more adept at working with such clients than their upper-income counterparts. Nevertheless, the critical variable appears to be *openness*, that is, the willingness to learn about and understand (not pity) the realities of low-income and minority life-styles. If that element is present in the therapist-client relationship, any of a number of alternative treatment modalities may be applied prescriptively to the client's needs (Acosta, Yamamoto, & Evans, 1982).

As argued elsewhere (Lorion, 1973, 1974, 1978; Lerner, 1972), low-income and minority clients should not be assumed a priori as inappropriate candidates for dynamic psychotherapy. The literature documents the effectiveness of this treatment modality for some low-income clients. Careful preparation of these clients early in treatment appears to be an important contributor to treatment success as is willingness on the therapist's part to assume an active role during the initial months of treatment.

Recent developments in the refinement of time-limited, problem-oriented interventions can assist therapists who work with low-income and minority clients (Lorion, 1978). These approaches offer the structure and predictability that facilitate client cooperation and provide visible indices of therapeutic progress. Repeated demonstration of their effectiveness assure the therapist that delivery of such interventions serves the client. Because retention rates for clients in brief treatment regularly exceed those for clients in open-ended treatment, time-limited interventions also offer an efficient means of using scarce therapist resources.

Less is known about the specific effectiveness of behavioral, group, and marital interventions for low-income and minority clients. The absence of such information should not, however, be interpreted as evidence of negative effectiveness. Conceptually, it is difficult to identify any basis for assuming that such interventions would not be effective. Once explained to the client, behavioral strategies may have a face validity that facilitates client cooperation. The availability of reliable indices of progress, the rapid acquisition of relaxation strategies that can be readily applied to reducing felt anxiety, and the ability to "practice" therapy apart from the clinic are consistent with low-income and minority client needs and life-styles. In a similar fashion, interventions that assist clients in recognizing and resolving marital and family conflicts can provide an important source of immediate relief as well as insure the availability of critically needed social support. Exploratory studies have demonstrated the receptivity of low-income and minority clients to such interventions. Once again, the important first step appears to be the therapist's explanation of the reasons for and the nature of the intervention itself. If able to anticipate what will occur during the session and reassured that the therapist will maintain control over what occurs during the early sessions, low-income and minority clients will respond positively to marital and family interventions. It should be noted, however, that in conducting such sessions, the therapist should understand and, insofar as possible, respect the client's attitudes about what topics are not appropriate for offspring. Ignorance of such cultural views has sabotaged many a promising treatment.

CONCLUSION

It should be apparent to the reader that we do not consider low-income and minority clients as inappropriate for treatment or particular treatments as per se inappropriate for them. Statements to the contrary have not been supported by systematic research. What has been established is that low-income and minority clients tend to terminate psychotherapy earlier than their nonminority, upper-income counterparts. For the most part, this pattern has been attributed to client characteristics. Careful examination of therapist's practices, however, suggests an alternative explanation. Intentionally or not, therapists communicate through their words and behavior their views about a client's appropriateness for psychotherapy. In turn, such communications and the assumptions on which they are based determine in significant ways the likelihood that a client will remain in treatment long enough to benefit from it or to commit himself or herself to its processes. The intent of this chapter has been to examine support for this alternative explanation and propose strategies for avoiding what we believe to be a very negative self-fulfilling prophecy. Our suggestions can be consolidated in a paraphrase of Hippocrates exhortation to physicians, that is, "know thyself *and* know thy client!"

REFERENCES

Acosta, F. X., Yamamoto, J., & Evans, L. A. (1982) *Effective psychotherapy for low-income and minority patients*, New York: Pergamon Press.

Bernard, V. W. (1965) Some principles of dynamic psychiatry in relation to poverty. *American Journal of Psychiatry, 122*, 254–267.

Fried, M. (1969) Social differences in mental health. In Kosa, J., Antonovsky, A., & Zola, I. K. (Eds.) *Poverty and health: A sociological analysis*. Cambridge: Harvard University Press.

Gibbs, J. T. (1984) Black adolescents and youth: An endangered species. *American Journal of Orthopsychiatry, 54*, 6–20.

Goldstein, A. P. (1971) *Psychotherapeutic attraction*. New York: Pergamon Press.

Jacobs, D., Charles, E., Jacobs, T., Weinstein, H., & Mann, D. (1972) Preparation for treatment of the disadvantaged patient: Effects on disposition and outcome. *American Journal of Orthopsychiatry, 42*, 666–674.

Lerner, B. (1972) *Therapy in the ghetto*. Baltimore: Johns Hopkins University Press.

Lorion, R. P. (1973) Socioeconomic status and traditional treatment approaches. *Psychological Bulletin, 79*, 263–270.

———— (1974) Patient and therapist variables in the treatment of low-income patients. *Psychological Bulletin, 81*, 344–354.

———— (1978) Research on psychotherapy and behavior change with the disadvantaged: Past, present, and future directions. In Garfield, S. L., & Bergen, A. E., (Eds.), *Handbook of psychotherapy and behavior change: An empirical analysis*. New York: Wiley.

Nitzer, J. (1982) *Unclaimed children*. Washington, D.C.: Children's Defense Fund.

Nonformal Support in Cross-Cultural Counseling and Therapy

LAWRENCE M. BRAMMER

Most counseling around the world is performed through nonformal helping groups of friends and relatives in a support network. *Nonformal* means not advertised openly and not professionalized or institutionalized. Nonformal counseling and therapy are the normal spontaneous outreach of caring people to others in need.

BACKGROUND

Although nonformal networks have existed as family groups and tribes since early human presence, these groups have evolved into three basic forms: family and friends, community self-help programs, and occupational networks.

Family and Friendship Groups

Family and friendship groups have been the most enduring forms of nonformal support. In the context of nonformal counseling these networks perform primary prevention functions through enabling people to share their feelings and explore their problems with those they know and trust. In Middle Eastern and Eastern cultures these networks primarily involve the extended family. Among Hispanic cultures of the Western hemisphere, the concept of "La Familia" is a highly functional source of psychological help. Sports clubs in some countries, such as the Soviet Union and the Netherlands, offer widespread opportunities to develop a network of friends capable of providing emotional support. Throughout the world, churches, mosques, and temples provide a support base for large segments of the population. The people of the United States, with their diverse cultural backgrounds and high mobility, find their networks in a variety of settings. They depend heavily on their work groups to develop the nonformal networks most fulfilling to their emotional and social needs. Americans use their health-care system to help manage crises and chronic problems (Caplan and Killilea, 1976).

Community Nonformal Support Groups

Two basic models of nonformal community support have evolved—neighborhood networks and focused self-help groups. In the neighborhood model, the whole neighborhood is the support group. An example in Europe is the Netherlands model of government-initiated support groups translated as ''neighborship.'' Specially trained community workers developed neighborhood support networks in urban centers, since these city dwellers lost the networks that were once such a common part of rural Europe. The Dutch networks were designed to provide direct nonformal support, especially at times of illness and death. They were designed also to reestablish the helping neighborhood with its caring attitudes and willing volunteer help.

A model developed in the People's Republic of China has an urban neighborhood base for formal and nonformal helping services. It is the smallest political unit also and consists usually of no more than 2,000 people. For those working in farm or factory communes, there is the work group that functions like a neighborhood support network. These neighborhood groups perform many services for their members—primary health care, job finding, child care, old-age assistance, and community services such as teacher aides and auxiliary police. Embedded in these more structured services is a vast pool of nonformal help through the neighbor-to-neighbor concept. The local council is also the entry point to more extended services and privileges through district hospitals, holiday centers, and living quarters, for example. Because these neighborhood councils have so much power over the lives of individuals they have mixed blessings. On the one hand, they see to it that people's needs are met, but it is the political funnel through which people achieve access to the broader services and opportunities. In the context of this chapter, however, the China experience is a unique example of a vast network of community helping services, largely nonformal. The elderly, for example, have meaningful tasks such as child sitting, acting as aides to teachers and police, and working in community sanitation. Families also receive help from other community members when problems of child management or illness emerge.

Methods vary widely from understanding support and friendly admonitions to threats of political consequences for the family if the situation were not to change. Depressions, for example, may be tolerated for a while, but finally a neighbor might say, ''You've been depressed long enough now; I'll see you at work tomorrow.'' There is a mixture of concern for the worker's welfare and chagrin for his or her lost productivity.

Almost all counseling and psychotherapy, except for extremely pathological conditions, are handled through this nonformal neighborhood network. Except for a limited health-care system, a formal structure of counseling and psychotherapy does not exist in China.

Another example of nonformal community helping networks is the Samaritan movement in Britain. The Samaritan group was organized in 1953 as a voluntary nonformal helper program oriented largely around crises but not limited to them. This movement spread to other countries because of its effectiveness in dealing with human problems in a nonformal manner. The Samaritans are loosely organized with a low profile network of volunteers from all walks of life. They will respond at any hour of the day or night to a wide variety of human problems from suicide threats to loneliness and fear. As their name implies they offer help in the form of compassionate friendship to people unwilling or unable to seek professional counseling. Their effectiveness lies in the power of face-to-face contact with caring people (Good, 1977).

The second community model for providing nonformal counseling is the self-help support group. In the United States, for example, this effort has become a vast movement. The peer and self-help movement has a clearinghouse listing of more than 500,000 self-help support groups in the United States alone (Lieberman and Borman, 1979). These groups are designed to deal with a specific human problem. Examples of some older and better-known nonformal self-help groups are Alcoholics Anonymous, Divorce Lifeline, and Cancer Lifeline. Most of these self-help groups have a local community origin, but the needs usually are so great that they spread quickly to national prominence. An example is ASIST (Alzheimers Support and Information Service Team). It focuses on nonformal support for families with elderly relatives suffering severe dementia.

Peer and self-help groups have several nonformal helping characteristics in common. They arise spontaneously to a need, such as adjusting to loss of a spouse; they are organized and led by persons who have suffered from and have recovered from the malady, dysfunction, or problem; and finally, they emphasize nonformal helping through nonprofessional volunteers.

Business and Professional Networks and Mentors

A third general type of nonformal network is the mutual support group that grows up around work functions. Almost all professional groups in the United States, for example, have their "networks." Most recently, business and professional women have been effective in creating networks as counterparts of the "old boy networks" that have existed for years among men (Welch, 1981).

An aspect of nonformal career networks is the mentor role. One or two people emerge from the person's network as especially admired or helpful. This nonformal counselor often becomes the role model for the younger person in addition to providing nonformal instruction or guidance—hence the title "mentor." Elizabeth Alleman (1982), who has done some of the sparse research on cross-sex mentor roles, countered the insinuations around proteges and mentors that there are inevitably sexual improprieties. Alleman found no such impropriety or even sex bias in the twenty-nine professional pairs she studied.

Mentors perform vital roles for young workers as they find their way into the nonformal networks. The long history of businesspeople finding their careers assisted through their networks is supporting anecdotal evidence for the power of these networks.

ASSUMPTIONS

In the past five years considerable interest among helping professionals and research psychologists has been focused on the importance and effectiveness of support. The traditional assumptions about the healing power of nonformal groups is being reaffirmed in the laboratory. There were forty presentations related to support networks at the 1982 American Psychological Association national meeting in Washington, D.C. The 1963 meetings had twenty-eight such presentations. The growing number of articles on support in professional journals matches growing lay interest in self-help groups. Underlying this enthusiasm for the power of supportive relationships is the assumption that support is good for everyone under nearly all conditions. This writer's survey of the research literature of the past ten years indicates that support must be applied differentially, meaning that the helper must look at the effects on each individual of the particular kind of support being offered. Support could be noxious for some people if offered at the wrong time and place and by the wrong person. Support efforts have a long history of fostering dependency and making coping less effective for some people.

In a productive effort at conceptual clarity, Sally Shumaker and Arlene Brownell (1983) emphasized the contextual aspects of support and stressor characteristics and their interaction. In evaluating the assumption that support is good for everyone, it is important to realize also that using social support is only one of several coping skills available to the stressed person.

The assumption that the availability of interpersonal networks significantly reduces vulnerability to stressors has much confirmation in the research literature (Caplan & Killilea, 1976; Gottlieb, 1981). It is apparent from the numerous studies cited by these writers that a key buffer for stress is a positive relationship with at least one significant other person. On the other hand, Roger Mitchell, Andrew Billings, and Rudolph Moss (1982) asserted that their reviews of the later studies produced mixed results—some supporting the "stress-buffering" hypothesis and some showing no effects of support on stress reduction. These reviewers claimed that these contradictory findings are a result of variable types of stress and support.

The assumption that supportive relationships must be nurturant to be helpful is open to question. Although a caring and loving relationship is helpful to the person in distress, it is important to realize that support networks fulfill a variety of functions for the person. Some of these additional functions are information, guidance, feedback, and laughter. This discussion highlights the key deficiency in research on support in that studies would be more valuable if they were more specific about the nature of the support being studied.

An assumption held by counselors and psychotherapists is that nonformal support networking skills are teachable—either in interviews or, more systematically, in workshop settings. In a study of coping skills useful in managing life transitions, L. Brammer and P. Abrego (1981) confirmed the idea that coping skills could be taught effectively in short-term workshops. Building or maintaining support networks was one of these coping skills.

TEACHING NONFORMAL SUPPORT NETWORKING SKILLS

The macro-skill of support networking can be divided into four or more subskills for simplicity in teaching participants in a workshop how to build and maintain a personal support network. The first step is assessing the current structure and function of one's present network. A simple sociometric analysis is made of the structure of the current network. A series of circles is drawn to represent specific people with one's self at the center. The circles are produced with names placed in relation to one's self on the basis of closeness and intensity. Dark lines are used to indicate intensely supportive relationships and light lines for more tenuous contacts. Arrowheads can be used to indicate direction of the support, since sometimes support is unidirectional. The goal here is to obtain a clear picture of the extent, intensity, and directionality of one's support network.

The second skill is specifying the nature of the support being received and rating the current level of satisfaction on each function. A rating scale is constructed with the functions of support deemed important down one side and a scale from one to five across the top to indicate degrees of satisfaction with the listed functions.

The third skill is assessing the contributions of each person in the network in terms of specific support functions performed and an estimate of quality of their impact (based on time spent and a rating of impact). This kind of analysis shows clearly where gaps in support functions are occurring and where overlap exists. Some people in one's network may appear to have negative impact or to be making undesired demands on time and energy.

The final subskill required in network development is discriminate judgment about changes needed. Examination of the worksheets brings out implications for change. Some relationships may need strengthening through more time or frequency of contact. Others may need to be dropped because they are mutually nonfunctional. Some new sources may need to be cultivated to fill missing functions, and new social skills may need to be learned. The goal for this activity is to help people do their own network analysis in order to make them more functional.

FUTURE DIRECTIONS OF CROSS-CULTURAL SUPPORT RESEARCH

Research productivity on cross-cultural nonformal support is likely to increase at an even faster rate than at present. It will be more focused in terms of what kinds of support people with particular problems are likely to find. More systematic and effective interventions for nonformal and formal counselors will be possible when this research is disseminated and converted to useful procedures. Counselors are likely to be more aware also of why their efforts at giving support are ineffective. In addition, counselors will be able to diagnose skill deficiencies, such as social skills and assertiveness, that may be underlying deficiencies in nonformal support.

REFERENCES

Alleman, E. (1982) Follow-up report on results of mentoring research. Manuscript, Association of Counselor Educators and Supervisors, Falls Church, Virginia.

Brammer, L., & Abrego, P. (1981) Intervention strategies for coping with transitions. *The Counseling Psychologist, 9,* 19–35.

Caplan, G., & Killilea, M. (1976) *Support systems and mutual help.* New York: Grune & Stratton.

Collins, A., & Pancoast, D. (1976) *Natural helping networks: A strategy for prevention.* Washington, D.C.: National Association of Social Workers.

Good, R. (January 23, 1977) *Samaritans stop suicide.* Interview report in *Sacramento Union.*

Gottlieb, B. (1981) *Social networks and social support.* Beverly Hills: Sage.

Lieberman, M., & Borman, L. (1979) *Self-help groups for coping with crises.* San Francisco: Jossey-Bass.

Mitchell, R., Billings, A., & Moss, R. (1982) Social support and well being: Implications for prevention programs. *The Journal of Primary Prevention, 3,* 77–95.

Shumaker, S., & Brownell, A. (August 1983) A taxonomy of social support. Paper presented to the American Psychological Association Annual Meeting, Anaheim, California.

Welch, M. (1981) *Networking: The great new way for women to get ahead.* New York: Warner.

Developing Ethnic Sensitivity for the Counseling Process: A Social-Work Perspective

WYNETTA DEVORE

A HISTORICAL PERSPECTIVE

In 1917 Mary Richmond suggested that the caseworker who ignored national and racial characteristics of ethnic populations and tried to apply standard measures applied to fellow citizens was liable to find surprises. Similar surprises were possible if assumptions were made about fixed characteristics. Eventually, the caseworker would, she believed, learn that national characteristics could not be ignored. This recognition of the importance of ethnic sensitivity came early in the development of social-work practice. However, her directive was not followed with much commitment; instead, in the search for equality of all persons, distinctive ethnic characteristics were set aside in favor of a general understanding of human development. Many practitioners believed that attention to the relationship between ethnic heritage and behavior was somehow incongruent with the profession's commitment to equality and the uniqueness of the individual. So the profession continued to collect data about people and their lives, to make assessments, and to plan for change without giving more than passing attention to ethnicity.

When young blacks called attention to the beauty of their blackness in the sixties, the profession became more diligent in its efforts toward sensitivity and began to focus on minority populations who found themselves discriminated against: blacks, Puerto Ricans, Chicanos, Japanese, Chinese, American Indians—people of color. This commitment has continued to the present.

However, little attention is paid to other ethnic groups, particularly white European ethnics. White stands as an ethnic designation encompassing all persons of the race. Ethnic uniqueness is lost in the general category. It is as though Mary Richmond was speaking only to her contemporaries. To have forgotten her message is to have ignored the specialness of each person who becomes a recipient of social-work services.

THE PRESENT STATUS OF ETHNIC-SENSITIVE
PRACTICE

Leon Chestang (1982) accurately assessed social work's present stance when he stated that the issue of ethnicity has been and remains a much-debated subject generating untold opinions, speculations, and emotions "because the social meaning of differences based on ethnicity carries so much weight in shaping opinions, speculations and emotions" (p. 117). Despite Mary Richmond's early directive, the issue of ethnicity has not been resolved.

Primary focus remains on people of color, although attention begins to include white ethnics, recognizing that particular characteristics often have ethnic roots and that the life of an Italian-American is distinctly different from that of a Jewish American, although both are identified as white.

In 1981 *Ethnic Sensitive Social Work Practice* by Wynetta Devore and Elfriede G. Schlesinger presented a model for ethnic-sensitive practice that is presented later in this chapter. Rather than concentrate on minority groups only, examples have been drawn from the Eastern European experience including Poles, Slavics, Italians, and Jews.

James W. Green in his work *Cultural Awareness in the Human Services* (1982) argued "that social service can and should be provided to people in ways which are culturally acceptable to them and which enhance their sense of ethnic group participation and power" (p. 4). Examples, however, for the most part again come from the ethnic-minority experience: blacks, Asians, Pacific Americans, urban Indians, and Chicanos. The appendix of cross-cultural-learning activities provides avenues for the development of cultural awareness that Green defined as a kind of sensitivity or frame of mind in regard to cross-cultural understanding that has to do with important qualities for effective social work, openness, alertness, and, most particularly, flexibility in relations with others.

These two works begin to focus on the need for social workers to be sensitive to ethnic differences with the assurance that such sensitivity will enhance the professional relationship and affirm the social-work commitment to the recognition of the uniqueness of each individual.

The major contribution to the development of ethnic sensitivity in social work came in 1982 with the publication of *Ethnicity and Family Therapy* by Monica McGoldrick, John K. Pearce, and Joseph Giordano. The contributors to this anthology include members of a variety of helping disciplines including social work. Two of the editors, McGoldrick and Giordano, are social workers. All professionals who counsel will benefit from this work. Nineteen ethnic groups are presented with consideration of their historical background, the impact of immigration when appropriate, family characteristics, the source of problems, and, most importantly, therapeutic suggestions. Families included range from representatives of the earliest American settlers to the British to more recent arrivals, the Asians.

A MODEL FOR ETHNIC-SENSITIVE PRACTICE

There exists for the social worker an array of approaches to practice including the psychosocial approach, several problem-solving approaches, the ecological approach, and the structural approach. Each in some way responds to Joel Fischer's (1978) view that practical theory contains two elements, a systematic interpretation of principles that help to understand the phenomena of interest and a clear delineation of principles for change. None of these approaches, however, gives particular attention to ethnicity as a factor to be considered in the assessment and planning phase of the work with a client and therefore no clues to the development of ethnic sensitivity.

The model for ethnic-sensitive practice developed by Devore and Schlesinger (1981) seeks to provide a guide for those who would enhance their ethnic sensitivity while embracing any one of the approaches listed here or others that have proven to be effective. The model is built on established social-work values as well as what we deem to be basic assumptions and principles.

Assumptions

1. Individual and collective history have bearing on problem generation and solution—the collective history of a group that may include slavery, an immigrant experience, the Holocaust, or flight from the ravages of civil war or revolution affects each individual in that group differently. Personality and recent life experience serve as filters determining which facets of ethnic history and identity will remain an integral part of a person's functioning, which will be forgotten, which will be consciously rejected.

2. Ethnicity is a source of cohesion, identity, and strength as well as a source of strain, discordance, and strife—the family, rituals and celebrations, language, and ethnic institutions all provide a source of comfort for many members of ethnic groups. The family gives the ethnic message and transmits its values. Rituals and celebrations reaffirm the value of ethnicity. Coming together, a group is able to give tribute to the past and assurances of continuity. Language may serve a self- and group-affirming function by continuing a comforting sound from the past. Institutions such as the church and ethnic school programs are a mechanism for the preservation of language, rituals, and traditions. But family, ritual, language, and institutions may be a source of strain, discord, and strife. As young members of the family move out into the mainstream they often begin to question the "old ways," and tension enters into the family. They may question the value of rituals and celebrations that call them home, away from a new life with diminishing ethnic identity. Language, so dearly cherished, becomes a burden when used by others as a tool of discrimination and ridicule. Even though ethnic school programs and the church may maintain values and traditions of a group, there are those who see little need for such efforts, which

often draw children away from activities in the community. Parents' efforts to assure a continuance of ethnic consciousness meet with resistance.

3. Social work pays major attention to problems as manifested in the present. The past, including ethnic history, affects and gives shape to problems presented in the present. Although it is important to recognize the value of history, customs, and beliefs at the individual and institutional level, it is important to realize that racism exists in the present and influences the daily life of ethnic-minority populations. An Italian family that carries on a tradition of "caring for our own" may in the present resist treatment for a seriously ill family member. Tradition generates a problem in the present that must be addressed in the present if the family member is to return to good health.

Principles

1. Social work is a problem-solving endeavor that attends to individuals' systematic concerns as they emerge out of client need and professional assessment—ethnic-sensitive practice is not limited to the concerns of individuals and families in interpersonal difficulties; it must reach out and attend to the individual consequences of racism, poverty, and discrimination. Individuals often internalize the negative images society holds of them with results that hamper their view of themselves as well as the quality of interpersonal relationships. The ethnic-sensitive practitioner does not "blame the victim" but seeks to address those institutions that perpetuate racism, poverty, and discrimination.

2. Skills must be adapted in accord with the particular needs and dispositions of various ethnic groups. Although there is a body of literature developing that pays attention to the skills for social-work practice, little attention has been paid by social workers to how skills and techniques may be modified to conform to cultural and ethnic dispositions. The ethnic-sensitive worker has available all of the skills and techniques learned and developed in the educational experience and through years in practice. It is necessary to make adaptations in those basic skills to respond to the ethnic dispositions that are determined to be an integral part of a client's life.

Tuning in, the development of preparatory empathy (Shulman, 1979), requires an awareness of the ethnic experience and its potential effect on the client with particular emphasis upon social-class position. The low-income black experience is not like the middle-income black experience. Both groups are victims of racism, but social-class position will significantly influence the impact.

When a counselor is attending, that purposeful behavior that conveys a message of respect must be reconsidered in the light of ethnicity. The counselor who is attending well presents an open posture, has good eye contact, and leans toward the client (Egan, 1975). These postures are designed to elicit a positive response and thereby an atmosphere in which problems may be resolved. There are, however, ethnic groups whose members find it hard to respond as anticipated. Asians and American Indians may view direct eye contact as shameful or a sign of disrespect. The client who avoids eye contact and resists the invitation of the attending posture must not be accused immediately of resisting or labeled pathological. Ethnic sensitivity requires an examination of the personal data or questioning to determine ethnic dispositions.

There are unnumbered other skills and techniques that require adaptation by the ethnic-sensitive social worker. These are but examples to serve as guides in further adaptations.

3. The "Route to the Social Worker" affects problem definition and intervention. The paths that lead to the social worker are varied, and it is these variations that affect problem definition and intervention. Routes may be viewed along a continuum from totally coercive, when clients are assigned by the courts, to totally voluntary, when individuals decide for themselves that there is a need for professional assistance with a problem. In between are highly and somewhat coercive designations as well as highly and somewhat voluntary ones. Persons in the coercive end of the continuum are more likely to have their problems defined for them by social institutions and will be members of ethnic-minority groups with low incomes. Voluntary clients are more likely to be of middle income and members of more acceptable mainstream ethnic groups. The ethnic-sensitive worker is obliged to be aware of the route taken in order to respond in an appropriate manner.

Layers of Understanding

Values, principles, and assumptions grow from layers of understanding essential for ethnic-sensitive practice. These layers include the knowledge, attitude, and skills discussed earlier as well as the following:

1. Basic knowledge about human behavior in the social environment, including knowledge about personality, life-cycle development, and the functioning of social institutions.
2. Self-awareness, including insights into one's own ethnicity, and how that influences practice. Ethnic-sensitive workers must ask who am I in the ethnic sense and become comfortable with the answer.
3. Knowledge about the impact of ethnicity and social class upon the daily life of individuals.

The model for ethnic-sensitive practice does not seek to replace any valid method for practice; it encourages practitioners to be aware of ethnicity and to begin to incorporate that awareness into practice.

THE FUTURE OF ETHNIC-SENSITIVE SOCIAL-WORK PRACTICE

The editors' request for a consideration of the future allows for the presentation of a dream. My dream is for a greater sensitivity to ethnicity that would recognize the ethnic groups within all races. Social workers' continual focus of race—people of color—cannot be stopped, for it challenges the profession to combat institutional racism in all of its overt and covert forms. The task for the future is to recognize that although white ethnics do not suffer from racism, they may well suffer in other ways because of their ethnic history.

Works such as the *Harvard Encyclopedia of American Ethnic Groups* (Thernstrom, 1981) tell us that there are possibly 106 separate groups in this country. Although the editors' methods and conclusions may well be questioned, it is the numbers that are of concern here. The future requires attention to these numbers. But as a social-work educator I hear few messages that encourage me and my colleagues to place increased emphasis upon ethnicity as a factor in the teaching of practice, human behavior, social policy, or research. Race continues to be the major thrust.

But this is a dream, and so I see a curriculum that in ten years will encourage and support ethnic-sensitive social-work practice as a matter of educational policy and social-work practitioners who respond to all facets of the individual including the ethnic dispositions.

REFERENCES

Chestang, Leon (January 1982) "Book Review." *Social Casework*, 27 (1), 117.

Devore, Wynetta, & Schlesinger, Elfriede G. (1981) *Ethnic sensitive social work practice*, St. Louis: Mosby.

Egan, Gerard (1975) *The skilled helper: A model for systematic helping and interpersonal relating*. Monterey, Calif.: Brooks/Cole.

Fischer, Joel (1978) *Effective casework practice: An eclectic approach*. New York: McGraw-Hill.

Green, James W. (1982) *Cultural awareness in the human services*. Englewood Cliffs, N.J.: Prentice-Hall.

McGoldrick, Monica, Pearce, John K., & Giordano, Joseph (Eds.). (1982) *Ethnicity and family therapy*. New York: Guilford Press.

Richmond, Mary (1917) *Social diagnosis*. New York: Russell Sage Foundation.

Shulman, Lawrence (1979) *The skills of helping individuals and groups*. Itasca, Ill.: Peacock.

Thernstrom, Stephan (Ed.). (1981) *Harvard Encyclopedia of American Ethnic Groups*. Cambridge, Mass.: Harvard University Press.

The Function and Importance of Nonverbal Behavior in Intercultural Counseling

AARON WOLFGANG

PRESENT STATUS

The study of nonverbal behavior is still at the embryonic stage in terms of research, theory, and practice. For instance, there is still no unified theory of nonverbal behavior; the research tends to focus on particular areas or single channels of nonverbal behavior (for example, facial expressions, gestures, interpersonal distance), and there are still questions of how the information gained from the research can be applied by the practitioner or for that matter in the training of practitioners (Wolfgang, 1983, in preparation; Wolfgang & Waxer, in press). At this time there are even questions by those well known in the field of how to define *nonverbal behavior* or whether there should be a field of nonverbal behavior (Harrison, 1983). Often the terms *nonverbal behavior*, *nonlinguistic behavior*, and *nonverbal communication* are used interchangeably. I prefer to use the term *nonverbal behavior*, because it does not carry with it the assumption that two or more people are necessarily communicating with one another when expressing nonverbal behavior in the other's presence. That is, some people are treated as nonpersons in our society, and their behaviors are often not attended to or even ignored.

For purposes of this chapter I prefer to define *nonverbal behavior* in the broad sense as behavior that transcends the written and spoken word (Harrison, 1974). I divide the study of nonverbal behavior into three areas: proxemics, kinesics, and paralanguage, because these three areas have received a great deal of attention in the research literature and have some practical implications for intercultural counseling. In brief, research in proxemics has shown that conversational distances vary with the cultural and racial background of the conversants (Susman & Rosenfeld, 1982; Willis, 1969). E. T. Hall (1969) found that interpersonal threat or uneasiness results in increased spatial distance. In the area of kinesics it has been shown that people can read more accurately the nonverbal behavior of others (for example, facial expression, body movement) who are more culturally, linguistically, and racially similar (Bhardwaj & Wolfgang, in preparation; Rosenthal, Hall, Archer, Dimatteo, & Rogers, 1979). Finally, the third area of nonverbal behavior is paralanguage. It refers to the extra-verbal elements that are associated with speech (for example, tone and loudness of voice, pauses and hesitations in speech, pitch, rate of speech). D. Crystal (1975) noted in reviewing paralinguistic effects in cross-cultural studies that it can be difficult to know when someone from another culture is upset or embarrassed, and the paralanguage can be misinterpreted as being rude or sarcastic by the tone of voice.

This brings us to another important question in this field and that is: how are verbal and nonverbal behaviors related? Few would dispute the notion that verbal and nonverbal behavior are highly interrelated. However, nonverbal behavior can replace, contradict, modify, and underscore speech, but unlike speech there is no common dictionary where you can look up the meaning of a particular gesture, posture, or frown that would necessarily have worldwide acceptance.

Thus it can be seen that it is important for the counselor to be aware of how nonverbal behavior functions in the intercultural counseling situation in the three areas described (proxemics, kinesics, and paralanguage) and to be sensitive to the cultural background of the client to reduce the probability of miscommunication, misdiagnoses, and misinterpretation of behavior. For a fuller treatment of this subject, see A. Wolfgang (1983, in press).

FUNDAMENTAL FUNCTIONS AND ASSUMPTIONS

There is a growing list of functions of nonverbal behavior. It has been shown that nonverbal behavior has an important function in the following ways: for social control (for example, impression management in counseling), in determining patterns of nonverbal involvement (for example, intimacy, attraction), in reflecting attitudes (for example, like/dislike, status, and degree of responsiveness), in revealing affect or emotional states, as sustaining or replacing verbal behavior, for self-presentation, in identifying the presence and intensity of anxiety, for communicating empathy, and for respect in the counseling situation (Argyle, 1975; Edinger & Patterson, 1983; Ekman, Sorenson, & Friesen, 1969; Mehrabian, 1972; Tepper & Hasse, 1978; Waxer, 1977).

Noting the various functions of nonverbal behavior helps make the intercultural counselor sensitive to the importance of nonverbal behavior and its analysis more manageable in the total communication process. These nonverbal functions can help reflect the nature of the relationship between the counselor and client and the amount of progress made. Since the total communication process involves, in addition to nonverbal and verbal behavior, cultural variables (Wolfgang, 1979), it is important for the intercultural counselor to be aware of how and in what ways cultural differences may impede communication. D. W. Sue (1977) reported that 50 percent of those from ethnic-minority groups drop out from counseling after the first session. It is also important for counselors to be aware that most of the research reported related to functions as well as to assumptions of nonverbal behavior is based primarily on white-middle-class participants. The results of this research can be misleading when used in counseling ethnic-minority clients. For instance, increased eye contact, smiling, and positive head nods have been cited as being most effective as positive nonverbal reinforcers resulting in improved test performance, increased counselor effectiveness, and so on. There is some evidence that some ethnic minorities do not appreciate prolonged eye contact and may consider it confrontive (for example, Erickson, 1979).

In addition to functions there are some commonly held basic assumptions of nonverbal behavior in human communication. Some of these assumptions are interrelated and have theoretical implications. One of the most commonly held assumptions is that nonverbal behavior operates primarily at the *unconscious* or *unawareness level* (Argyle, 1975), and therefore it is assumed that it is to be trusted more than words, because it is more spontaneous and difficult to censor or falsify (Mehrabian, 1972). Following these assumptions is the related assumption of *controllability*. Since nonverbal behavior is more primitive in the sense that it functions in revealing emotions, feelings, and so on, it is more difficult to control than words, and therefore it can be assumed that nonverbal behavior is more *powerful* than words in revealing emotions, attitudes, degrees of warmth-coldness and so on (Mehrabian, 1972).

The lack-of-awareness assumption is dealt with by Jerome Kagan's model (in Hansen, Stevic, & Warner, 1982) and M. Argyle (1975). Kagan's model deals with degrees of awareness of nonverbal action ranging from *awareness* where the client-counselor not only knows of the behavior but intends that it occur (for example, to demonstrate or portray what is meant by means of a gesture) to potential awareness (for example, facilitative gestures to increase clarification) where the client-counselor could be aware of the other's actions if it was brought to his or her attention to lack of awareness (for example, brief, forceful gestures of emphasis accompanying speech). Argyle (1975) like Kagan saw the distinction between conscious and unconscious nonverbal signals as a matter of degree. Argyle described situations where the sender-receiver of nonverbal signals is likely to be aware or unaware. He saw most nonverbal behaviors as being unaware to the sender but that both sender and receiver can become aware through training.

Related to the awareness assumption is the assumption of controllability and the notion that you can trust the nonverbal as being more truthful than the verbal. P. Ekman's model (in Hansen, Stevic, & Warner, 1982) deals with nonverbal leakage and clues to deception. His research shows that in deception the face is the best liar, the hands are next, and the legs are the poorest. Thus truth can better be differentiated by watching the clients' bodies than by watching only their faces. P. H. Waxer (1977) found that raters were able to identify the presence and intensity of anxiety on the basis of nonverbal cues alone, that is, without speech. Like Ekman, Waxer found the body and hand cues were most salient in communicating anxiety. D. Tepper and R. Hasse (1978) found that nonverbal cues were more powerful than speech in communicating empathy, respect, and genuineness.

In sum, these results show that these assumptions have limited support in that awareness is not a matter of either/or but a matter of degree, and the same holds true for the issue of truth and impact of nonverbal over verbal behavior. However, the research on the whole has only tested these assumptions indirectly because of the context in which they were carried out, that is, primarily laboratory, staged interactions among strangers. M. L. Knapp (1983), in discussing some common assumptions about the nature of human communication from which nonverbal behavior can be viewed, argued that the assumption likely to gain the widest acceptance among scholars and practitioners is the one that relates to the importance of the role of context for understanding verbal and nonverbal behavior. Thus research, to be generalizable to ongoing, dynamic, live, naturalistic, intercultural counseling situations, must be carried out in the future in that contextual frame of reference.

FUNDAMENTAL THEORIES OR MODELS

The equilibrium theory of intimacy proposed by Argyle and J. Dean (1965) is perhaps one of the most influential theories of nonverbal behavior in social interaction. This theory assumes that there is a definable level of intimacy that is appropriate in social interaction, and if it is disturbed, the interactants will show compensatory behaviors. For example, if an individual violates another individual's acceptable intimacy level and moves "too close," the amount of and frequency of eye contact would decrease to compensate for the closeness. In an intercultural counseling situation the typical counselor may not be generally aware of the appropriate intimacy levels of his or her intercultural clients, and all types of compensatory behaviors could occur that could be confusing to the client and counselor. For instance, in terms of cultural rules the Japanese do not ordinarily look higher-status people in the eye directly. What would be the reaction of the counselor? Would he or she move closer to try to establish eye contact? Would this threaten or confuse the client? Too much eye contact is considered threatening to the Japanese (Argyle, Furnham, & Graham, 1981). Argyle and his associates (1981) proposed a "games" model for understanding interaction in social situations. Just as you need to know the rules of a game (for example, tennis, cricket), you need to know the rules, goals, roles, and expectations of the client in the intercultural counseling situation. For instance, what nonverbal behaviors reflect positive intimacy, affiliation, confidence; are reinforcing; and reflect nonverbal involvement of clients from a West Indian, Japanese, or Latin culture? Unfortunately, we do not have a great deal of research information in these areas that deals directly with the intercultural counseling situation.

One model from anthropology postulates that people who speak Latin-derived languages are more contact oriented than those who speak Anglo-Saxon–derived languages (Montagu, 1971). That is, people from places such as Italy, France, South America, and Mexico may prefer to have more contact in their social interactions by coming closer, touching more, and using expressive gestures more than, say, English Canadians and Americans who tend in comparison to be more non–contact-oriented. The noncontact intercultural counselor may stereotype the client as being "too emotional," "too pushy," "too loud," and the client may find the white Anglo-Saxon counselor to be too "distant," too "cold," and too "unemotional." Counselors must be aware of these cultural differences but also must be careful not to stereotype nonverbally the people from different cultures into cultural slots.

Much of the research and many of the models in the past have focused on cultural differences rather than looked for universal behaviors. C. E. Vontress (1979) in his paper on the triadic view of existentialism in cross-cultural counseling cautioned the counselor not to look at clients only on the cultural level but also to try to understand them on the universal human levels.

What about the so-called popular broader psychological theories of counseling such as the nondirective and behavioristic approaches to counseling? How might they be characterized? Unfortunately, there is no one broad theoretical approach or model readily available to the intercultural counselor to guide him or her in the intercultural counseling situation to deal with personal-emotional problems of culturally diverse students (Wolfgang, in press). These theories say little about the role and function of nonverbal behavior and tend to be culture blind.

In the field of intercultural communications theories also suffer from some similar problems as the psychological theories in that they tend to be monocultural. W. S. Howell (1979) pointed out that the theories have been too analytic and not holistic enough. Intercultural communication, he argued, is not only analytic but also a "creative act" that requires insight and intuition. The intercultural communicator can prepare for the intercultural encounter by being analytical in the sense of obtaining knowledge and information to orient him or her to some extent for the coming event. However, the intercultural communicator cannot predict everything and must therefore be spontaneous and creative. For a more complete discussion on this topic see Wolfgang (1983, in press).

FUTURE DIRECTIONS

I see the study of nonverbal behavior gaining its rightful place in importance as an area of study for understanding more fully the nature of human communication. In view of the surge of research, books, and interest in nonverbal behavior in recent years showing its uses in a wide variety of social situations, it is likely that training of counselors in the use of nonverbal behavior for intercultural counseling will be more and more in vogue. Until now most training programs and writers in intercultural counseling have given only token or little recognition of the importance of nonverbal behavior (Wolfgang & Waxer, 1983).

In terms of theory we are likely to see emerging a more unified conception of intercultural communication that will clarify the role and importance of nonverbal behavior in intercultural encounters such as counseling. As practitioners, theoreticians, and researchers begin to work together from an interdisciplinary perspective we are more likely to obtain a more holistic, realistic view of the nature of human communication as a dynamic, ongoing process. In the future more research grants will be given to interdisciplinary teams of researchers. With the advent of improved technology in computers and videotaping we will be able to study peoples' nonverbal behaviors in more live, naturalistic, social situations such as intercultural counseling and study the nonverbal-verbal and cultural variables more comprehensively instead of using the more traditional, static, fragmented research approaches.

Considering the vitality and interdisciplinary nature in the study of nonverbal behavior where a variety of research and theoretical approaches are used, I am optimistic about the future of the field as one of the new frontiers of study.

REFERENCES

Argyle, M. (1975) *Bodily communication*. London: Methuen.

Argyle, M., & Dean, J. (1965) Eye contact, distance, and affiliation. *Sociometry, 28*, 289–304.

Argyle, M., Furnham, A., & Graham, J. A. (1981) *Social situations*. New York: Cambridge University Press.

Bhardwaj, A., & Wolfgang, A. (in preparation) *Nonverbal behavior: Face recognition and social distance of bilinguals and unilinguals*.

Crystal, D. (1975) Paralinguistics. In Benthall, J., & Polhemus, H. (Eds.), *The body as a medium of expression*. New York: Dutton.

Edinger, J. A., & Patterson, M. L. (1983) Nonverbal involvement and social control. *Psychological Bulletin, 93*, 30–56.

Ekman, P., Sorenson, L., & Friesen, W. V. (1969) Pan-cultural elements in facial displays of emotion. *Science, 164*, 86–88.

Erickson, F. (1979) Some cultural sources of miscommunication of interracial interviews. In Wolfgang, A. (Ed.), *Nonverbal behavior: Applications and cultural implications*. New York: Academic Press.

Hall, E. T. (1969) *The hidden dimension*. Garden City, N.Y.: Doubleday.

Hansen, J. C., Stevic, R. R., & Warner, R. W. (1982) *Counselling: Theory and process*, 3rd ed. Toronto: Allyn & Bacon.

Harrison, R. P. (1974) *Beyond words: An introduction to nonverbal communication*. Englewood Cliffs, N.J.: Prentice-Hall.

——— (May 1983) Past problems and future directions in nonverbal research. Paper presented at the Second International Conference in Nonverbal Behavior, Toronto.

Howell, W. S. (1979) Theoretical directions for intercultural communication. In Asante, A. K., Newmark, E., & Blake, C. A. (Eds.), *Handbook of intercultural communication*. Beverley Hills, Calif.: Sage.

Knapp, M. L. (May 1983) The study of nonverbal behavior vis-à-vis human communication theory. Paper presented to the Second International Conference on Non-verbal Behavior, Toronto.

Mehrabian, A. (1972) *Nonverbal communication*. New York: Aldine-Atherton.

Montagu, A. (1971) *Touching*. New York: Harper & Row.

Rosenthal, R., Hall, J. A., Archer, D., Dimatteo, R. M., & Rogers, P. L. (1979) Measuring sensitivity to nonverbal communication: The Pons test. In Wolfgang, A., (Ed.), *Nonverbal behavior: Applications and cultural implications*. New York: Academic Press.

Sue, D. W. (1977) Counseling the culturally different: A conceptual analysis. *Personnel and Guidance Journal*, *55*, 422–425.

Susman, N. M., & Rosenfeld, H. M. (1982) Influence of culture, language, and sex on conversation distance. *Journal of Personality and Social Psychology*, *42*, 66–74.

Tepper, D., & Haase, R. (1978) Verbal and nonverbal communication of facilitative conditions. *Journal of Counseling Psychology*, *25*, 35–44.

Vontress, C. E. (1979) Cross-cultural counselling: An existential approach. *Personnel and Guidance Journal*, *58*, 117–122.

Waxer, P. H. (1977) Nonverbal cues for anxiety: An examination of emotional leakage. *Journal of Abnormal Psychology*, *86*, 306–314.

Willis, F. N. (1966) Initial speaking distance as a function of speakers' relationship. *Psychonomic Science*, *5*, 221–222.

Wolfgang, A. (1983) Intercultural counseling: The state of the art. In Samuda, R., Berry, J., & Laferriere, M. (Eds.), *Multicultural education in Canada*. Toronto: Allyn & Bacon.

———— (in press) Intercultural counselling and nonverbal behavior: An overview. In Samuda, R., & Wolfgang, A. (Eds.), *Intercultural counselling and assessment*. Toronto: Hogrefe.

———— (in preparation) *Nonverbal behavior: Perspectives, applications, and intercultural insights*.

———— (Ed.). (1979) *Nonverbal behavior: Applications and cultural implications*. New York: Academic Press.

Wolfgang, A., & Waxer, P. (in press) Training counsellors to enhance their sensitivity to nonverbal behavior. In Samuda, R., & Wolfgang, A. (Eds.), *Intercultural counselling and assessment*. Toronto: Hogrefe.

Transcultural Caring: A Different Way to Help People

MADELEINE M. LEININGER

Our world of tomorrow is one of knowing how best to communicate, counsel, work with, and help people of different cultural backgrounds. It is a world that requires caring specialists to understand different values, beliefs, and responses to life situations, so that meaningful and satisfying relationships can occur. Achieving such goals requires the deliberate use of transcultural caring knowledge and skills.

Caring for people of different cultural backgrounds is essentially a new or different way for counseling and health personnel to assist people. It is a shift from a largely unicultural to a multicultural approach in human services. *Transcultural caring* means the deliberate and creative use of cultural-care knowledges and skills to assist people in attaining their well being and to help them live and survive in diverse and changing contexts (Leininger, 1981d). It means knowing explicitly cultural-care beliefs, values, and lifeways and using such knowledge in culturally specific ways to help people. Transcultural, therapeutic caring practices is one of the most important and satisfying challenges for counseling personnel today. It is a different and unique way to satisfy human cultural needs.

The thesis of this chapter is that transcultural-care/caring practices are not only a new or different way to help people but an essential need of humans to live and function in our multicultural world. Cultural caring is essential to human growth, interpersonal relationships, well being, and survival. Hence health-oriented personnel need to know cultural-care behaviors and processes to be effective in helping or counseling people. It is also my contention that care is one of the most elusive and "taken-for-granted" concepts of the helping professions; yet it is one of the most important means to help people in efficacious ways. Cultural care, therefore, must become an explicit and knowing way to serve people of different or similar cultural backgrounds. Hence this chapter explores the concept of cultural care as I have studied it for more than two decades (Leininger 1978, 1981d, 1983).

CARE: THE ELUSIVE AND "GOLD-MINE" CONCEPT

Care remains one of the most elusive and least-understood concepts in the helping professions; yet it appears to be one of the richest and most valuable "gold-mine" concepts to know and deliberately use in professional services. It has been difficult to understand why the concept of care has not been systematically studied until recently by the helping professions. The terms *care* and *caring* have been used in nursing for nearly a century in a general and "taken-for-granted" position. Other professions have used the term but with less frequency (Leininger, 1981b). The word *care* to both professional and lay people is used with different meanings and generally without knowledge of what care means to different cultural groups.

As a popular (lay) term, *care* is used to support better business practices such as the expressions "Caring is our business," "We care," "Caring is our service mode." These popular advertising phrases tend to increase business as a special and unique service to customers. In the health professions the term *care* as a noun, or *caring* as a verb, implies individualized or personalized professional practices but often without cognitive awareness of the nature, essence, components, and differential therapeutic or non-therapeutic outcomes (Leininger, 1981a; Gaut, 1981). Care tends to be a critical concept in the professional and non-professional world. Most assuredly, it is vaguely understood and explicitly used as a therapeutic treatment or healing practice.

Historical and Conceptual Aspects of Care

Aware of such ambiguities, I began in the mid-1950s to study care, using both a nursing and anthropological approach. I held that care was essential for human birth, growth, and survival through time. No human being as an infant or adult has survived without caring behaviors and processes, and care has been essential for the survival of *Homo sapiens* (Leininger, 1981c). But most importantly, care is culturally constituted and takes on meaning according to cultural beliefs, values, and practices of different cultures in the world. Cultural care becomes the blueprint for professional and therapeutic services to clients. I have hypothesized that cultural care is essential to promote human well being and recovery from life stresses, illness, and disabilities. Cultural care is the broadest and most comprehensive means to provide holistic services; yet it is also a means to provide very specific care. Indeed, the concept of care is figuratively like a rough diamond that has barely been discovered, let alone polished for its actual or potential therapeutic short- or long-range benefits to people. Cultural care and generic care remain the "gems" yet to be explicated, valued, and known in humanistic and scientific professional and lay human services. I have defined *generic care* as those assistive, supportive, or facilitative acts toward or for another individual or group with evident or anticipated needs to ameliorate or improve a human condition or lifeway (Leininger, 1981c). I have defined *profes-*

sional care as those cognitively and culturally learned action behaviors, techniques, processes, or patterns that enable (or help) an individual, family, or community to improve or maintain a favorable, healthy condition or lifeway (Leininger, 1981c). Also, *care* is the central, unique, unifying, and dominant factor that characterizes the nature of nursing (Leininger, 1980, 1981b). Since the mid-1950s I have been studying the care phenomenon with these definitions in mind and from a transcultural perspective of approximately forty cultures (Leininger, 1978).

Interestingly, from a historical, philosophical, and epistemological view, there had been limited study of the care phenomenon with nurses and other health professions until the late 1960s. M. Myeroff wrote about caring around 1971 as a process of helping others to grow and actualize themselves. W. Gaylin (1979) presented his ideas of care from a psychoanalytical viewpoint as a concept worthy of deliberation by health personnel. Along with my work and the thinking of John S. Hyde, care gradually became of more interest to nurses and other health-care professionals. Today, there are more articles on the subject of care and a beginning research focus on it (Leininger, 1983). I have also spearheaded national and international conferences on generic and transcultural care since the early 1970s (Leininger, 1979, 1981d). Today there are three major books published on the care phenomenon with a theoretical, research, and practice focus, namely, *Transcultural Nursing: Concepts, Theories, and Practices* (Leininger, 1978); *Caring: An Essential Human Need* (Leininger, 1981d); and *Care: The Essence of Nursing and Health* (Leininger, 1983). There have also been an increased number of scholarly and practice articles on care in nursing, which is helping care researchers and practitioners to discover and use care in an explicit way. Thus there is now more interest in studying care than ever before in the history of nursing and the health professions, and there is greater public awareness of the importance or value of care.

Theoretical and Cross-Cultural-Care Concepts

My theory of "Transcultural-Care, Diversity, and Universality" has been used to identify, document, and analyze care constructs of thirty-five Western and non-Western cultures. Only a brief explication of theory with a few findings is presented here to help the reader see how cross-cultural care might be used for counseling and therapy purposes. A full expose of the theory and research will soon be available in another publication (Leininger, in preparation).

Theoretically, I have postulated that care meanings, characteristics, and cultural manifestations differ among cultures primarily due to social structure, cultural values, beliefs, and environmental contexts (Leininger, 1984). But among the transcultural variations, there are some *universal* care attributes that transcend specific elements. It is the cultural-care *diversities* in relation to the similarities (or the universalities) that explain or predict the essential nature of care behaviors and therapy processes for human growth, well being, and survival. From documentation and explanation of the universal features of care will come principles and laws to govern life-care processes or the threats to such care processes and survival. Hence care diversities and universalities will be plain human behavior.

From the general theory of Transcultural-Care Diversity and Universality, several assumptions and postulates undergird the theory, such as the following:

1. Care is culturally defined and expressed with biological, social, religious, political, and economic factors that influence care diversity and variabilities among cultures.
2. Universal features of care exist among cultural groups in the world.
3. Care is the essential component for human growth, development, well being, and for recovery from illness and disabilities.
4. Care is an essential component of curing; however, care may be found without curing.
5. Folk and professional-care practices differ among human cultures.
6. Care components such as compassion, empathy, love, concern, presence, trust, support, succorance, nurturance, protection, and many others can be identified using an *emic* ethnographic study of cultures.
7. Marked differences between care giver and care receiver expectations lead to cultural stresses, burn-out, and/or interpersonal conflicts in counseling and therapy.
8. Therapeutic-care practices are contingent upon the conscious use of cultural-specific care constructs to fit particular culture lifeways.
9. Institutional cultural-care values, policies, and practices largely determine whether treatment and care practices are efficacious.
10. Transcultural-care concepts are essential for therapy and counseling practices.

As part of the theory, *three* major principles and modes of helping clients through counseling or in therapy were predicted to be therapeutic. The first is *culture-care preservation*, whereby the therapist recognizes a cultural-care construct to be desirable and helpful, and this cultural-care construct is retained to help the client. For example, the care construct of *sharing* and *generosity* are important to those of Polynesian heritage, and these concepts are preserved, valued, and retained in therapy and counseling. The second principle is *cultural-care accommodation*, in which the therapist or counselor makes special efforts to include old and new care features in full or part into the therapy. For example, the Sioux Indians value *respect* for elders, and the use of *silence* until the elder man has spoken. The therapist or counselor needs to accommodate these cultural-care attributes by acknowledging the elders, showing respect for them, and permitting them to speak first and may also include the Anglo greeting of "Hello."

The third principle of the theory to help clients of a different culture is *culture-care repatterning*. This principle means that once the care values are identified, the therapist works with the client to *repattern* or *restructure* care values so that the best of professional and folk lifeways fit together in a meaningful way. This is a creative principle but yet a more difficult one, since it requires an in-depth understanding of the cultural lifeways, the changes desired, and the specific care constructs the therapist is weaving into a new pattern for the client with the client's help and approval. These three principles become the therapy guidelines to operationalize culture-specific care for clients. If used effectively the theorist predicts evidence of client satisfaction and therapeutic outcomes. To date, these principles have led to therapeutic nursing practices.

Discovery and Use of Care Constructs in Therapy

From the study of thirty-five cultures and using an ethnocaring and minieth-nography research approach, forty-two care constructs have been identified to date. The *emic* approach was used to discover the local or native thoughts (ideas and meanings) and the uses of care in daily living. Some of the care constructs discovered were the following: comfort, compassion, concern for, empathy, helping, involvement, listening, loving, nurturance, presence, protection, respect, sharing, succorance, surveillance, tenderness, touch, trust, understanding, and others (Leininger, 1984). Each of these care constructs has several distinct attributes and characteristics. For example, there are different kinds of touch for different cultures, and there were a few cultures in which touch is a cultural taboo. Becoming aware of the qualitative aspects of care and the conditions for the uses of care has been a major discovery with care researchers.

It is of interest that the cultural informants interviewed and observed were able to identify the most important care constructs they would hope nurses and other health professionals would know and respect. Moreover, the informants were able to rank order the three most important care constructs. These constructs are now being used to guide transcultural nurse specialists and generalists in their work with clients. It has been encouraging to see the explicit use of care constructs being used as critical therapy guides and to see them become part of nursing-care plans and therapeutic interventions. Most importantly, these care constructs could be used by other therapists and counselors in a similar way and evaluated for their therapeutic aspects and for client satisfactions in helping people whose culture background varies from that of the therapist. Knowledge of the general lifeways of the culture and their cultural values and beliefs helps assure positive and meaningful therapy. Accordingly, some examples will be offered to show the specific uses of care constructs of different cultures studied.

With respect to specific cultural-care concepts for counselors and therapists, the following examples from my research findings may be useful; the care constructs are briefly discussed in order of importance with each culture (Leininger, in preparation).

Vietnamese and Care Constructs

The Vietnamese informants in the United States saw *family sharing* as the key concept of care. Sharing in material goods and non-material ideas with the family was extremely important to them. The Vietnamese expect that therapists and counselors will try to keep the family together so that sharing can occur, for without family sharing through communication about one another, caring cannot occur. When counselors use family sharing as caring, the clients are happy. The concept of *respect as caring* was the second highest care value. Respect for the family and for elders was extremely important and should be used as a guide for any therapy regimes. Signs of respect as a caring person are demonstrated by recognizing family members, listening to them, and valuing elders.

Appalachians and Care Constructs

The Appalachians in the United States saw care as *direct help* to their "hollow kinsmen." Professional persons were caring if they were "focused in" on helping them, trusting them, and understanding their needs. The concept of *trust* as care was closely linked to direct help in that you have to "check over" and trust a person who is helping you and especially strangers such as the government, intruders, and non-Appalachians. They said, "It took a while to *trust* outsiders since they seldom understand our ways." Hence the people watched for the care giver to be willing to "pitch in" and as someone who could be *trusted* as an outsider. A person who failed to meet these expectations was non-caring. They also wanted their special lifeways of how they dressed, talked, and looked to be respected. Hence respect and trust as caring were two dominant therapy concepts.

Southern Afro-American and Care Constructs

Caring to the southern Afro-American (black) meant "concern for my brothers and sisters." From my ethnocare study of the southern rural Afro-Americans for nearly a year, the dominant care construct was *concern for* one another and especially for their cultural-group members. *Concern for* was expressed by being attentive to their family needs, offering food to brothers and sisters, and coming together in all kinds of social and crisis situations. The second important care construct was *involvement*. Being a caring person meant "being involved" in helping or assisting others. The third care concept was *presence*. Being present was an indication that one cared for another. These three care constructs would be used in therapy.

Mexican-Americans and Care Constructs

For Mexican-Americans (whom I studied in two urban communities in the southern and western parts of the United States), care translated in meaning and importance as *succorance*. Succorance meant providing specific and/or direct help to one's family members in time of need or in usual daily life activities. This concept of care also meant being attentive and responsive to the "little things that count'' to the family members and others. A non-caring person would fail to give succorance. They believed professional health personnel needed to understand their concept of succorance to be helpful to them. Another care concept was *listening to* and *spending time* with the client. The current "rushing about" of nurses and physicians and not actively listening to Mexican-Americans were signs of non-caring behavior. *Involvement*, *loving*, and *empathy* were other care values of the Mexican-Americans with specific meanings.

Philippine-Americans and Care Constructs

For the Philippine-American, the major concept of care was *harmonious relationships* with others, especially among Philippine family members. One is perceived as a caring person when one maintains peaceful and harmonious relationships with others at home or at work. Disruptive and conflict situations are non-harmonious and reflect non-caring behaviors—all of much concern to observe with Anglo-American health personnel. A second important concept of care was *silence*. Silence as caring was congruent with harmonious relationships in that one needs to be quiet and reflect upon what is being felt and experienced. Silence is important to rest the mind and body and renew oneself. Allowing time to use silence and to listen are important caring considerations. Silence is important for healing and maintaining health. Another key caring concept was *respect for elders and those in authority*. Respect is a traditional Philippine value and linked with respect for people in authority. Several other care constructs were identified as *reciprocity* and *generosity* and would be used in therapy.

Anglo-American Caucasians and Care Constructs

For the middle-class Anglo-American Caucasians studied in several settings (within and outside hospitals), care means *alleviating stress*, *discomfort*, and *anxiety*. Anglo-Americans largely see a caring person as one who takes immediate action to relieve discomfort when well or ill and to prevent unnecessary anxieties. This was clearly evident when compared to other cultural groups. Another concept of care is providing *comfort to self* and *others*. Comfort measures are related to stress alleviation care value, but it is also important in non-stress situations. A non-caring person lets one suffer unduly and does not help a person to be self-reliant. Accordingly, *health instruction* or *providing information* was also an important sign of caring. To be self-reliant one has to control information and be self-sufficient and efficient. These care constructs were congruent with the American values of Anglo-Americans.

Although many other examples of transcultural caring could be offered with other cultures and subcultures in the world, the reader can study such care concepts in the forthcoming publication mentioned earlier (Leininger, in preparation).

The above examples point to the importance of identifying and using specific care constructs to counsel and provide therapy with different clients of diverse cultures. The use of care constructs identified and known by the people offers a rich and new approach in therapy and counseling. The use of specific culture-care concepts as treatment guides can be as powerful to help clients as most physiologically and technologically based treatments.

The idea of providing *cultural-specific care* that is tailored to meet the needs and expectations of clients from different cultures is essentially a new approach in the health field. This approach greatly increases the opportunity for client's cultural values, lifeways, and care patterns to be cognitively used and valued in treatment. As we know, clients from other cultures generally have to comply with the Anglo-American professional-treatment regimens, and there is often limited awareness of how health personnel (including physicians, social workers, and nurses) could use the client's care values as critical components of therapy or in counseling and interpersonal communication. A comparative awareness that there are different kinds of transcultural-care concepts for therapy and counseling is a different approach. It is a highly personalized and culturally based way to know, understand, and give assistance to people of different cultural and life orientations.

Most importantly, I contend that most people who come for professional health or counseling services are seeking care rather than specific treatment-curing regimens. Caring has healing, humanizing, and enabling power to one's self-esteem, growth, and actualization abilities. Care is a critical need today as people experience dehumanized services with the current rise in technology, scientist-ism, and the cult of efficiency in health services and with seeing violent crime and terrorism at an all-time high in human history.

One of the most important discoveries in my care research of thirty-five cultural informants was the heart-warming discovery that people value care and are aware of non-caring behaviors by health and other helping personnel. Care is, indeed, one of the most humanistic ingredients that characterizes human beings, and it is and has been the elusive ingredient in health and human services. Care must be recognized as a powerful healing, consoling, and assistive way to help others. Although it is one of the most difficult concepts (diamonds) to discover, its various and divergent components (facets) are the symbolically deep, brilliant, and resilient elements to be used in helping processes. Caring values are enduring therapy elements. Thus to help people of different cultures, caring must be incorporated into modern counseling and therapy practices. Transcultural caring is, indeed, a new, different, and unique way to help people.

REFERENCES

Gaut, D. (1981) Conceptual analysis of caring: Research method. In Leininger, M. (Ed.), *Caring: an essential human need.* Proceedings from the first two national caring research conferences. Thorofare, N.J.: Slack.
Gaylin, W. (1979) *Caring.* New York: Avon.

Leininger, M. (1978) *Transcultural nursing: Concepts, theories, and practices.* New York: Wiley.

—— (1979) *Transcultural nursing: Proceedings from four transcultural nursing conferences.* New York: Masson.

—— (October 1980) Caring: A central focus for nursing and health care services. *Nursing and Health Care, 1/3,* 135–143, 176.

—— (1981a) The phenomenon of caring: Importance, research questions, and theoretical considerations. In Leininger, M. (Ed.), *Caring: An essential human need.* Proceedings from the first two national caring research conferences. Thorofare, N.J.: Slack.

—— (1981b) Some philosophical, historical, and taxonomic aspects of nursing and caring in American culture. In Leininger, M. (Ed.), *Caring: An essential human need.* Proceedings from the first two national caring research conferences. Thorofare, N.J.: Slack.

—— (1981c) Cross-cultural hypothetical functions of caring and nursing care. In Leininger, M. (Ed.), *Caring: An essential human need.* Proceedings from the first two national caring research conferences. Thorofare, N.J.: Slack.

—— (1983) *Care: The essence of nursing and health.* Thorofare, N.J.: Slack.

—— (1984) *Qualitative research methods in nursing.* New York: Grune & Stratton.

—— (in preparation) *Transcultural care diversity and universality: A theory of care and nursing.*

—— (Ed.). (1981d) *Caring: An essential human need.* Proceedings from the first two national caring research conferences. Thorofare, N.J.: Slack.

Myeroff, M. (1971) *On caring.* New York: Harper & Row.

Clinical Sociology

JONATHAN A. FREEDMAN

The clinical sociologist uses insights derived from sociological theory, methods, and practice as the basis for either micro (groups, group members) or macro (organizations, communities, subcultures, societies) interventions. Although many practitioners from other disciplines use insights derived from sociology, a clinical sociologist tends to make such insight the cornerstone of practice (Swan, 1983; Straus, 1985; Fritz, 1982, 1984; Billson, 1983–84).

A clinical sociologist is likely to concentrate on discovering and working on issues involving the client's "socius" in relation to the psyche. C. Wright Mills's formulation in *The Sociological Imagination* (1959) powerfully gets at the relationship between one's personal autobiography and broad social trends, between personal troubles and social issues. This dualism can be the basis of imaginative strategies for intervention, for it grounds the issues of the person into the trends of the society.

The reemergence of clinical sociology as a viable subfield within sociology is one of the major directions in the development of sociology in the eighties. The Clinical Sociology Association of 400 members has existed only since 1978; yet already it has had considerable impact with its journal, ethics code, certification procedures, and conferences.[1] Sociologists are practicing in many states, are licensed in a few, and have begun to take part in state-level lobbying when other disciplines have attempted to exclude them. Clinical sociologists are working as clinicians in mental-health centers; are engaged in individual, group, and family therapy; run clinical units in general hospitals; direct training departments in the public and private sector; counsel clients on interactions with their pets, their finances, their addictions, and their stress; advise corporations on technology and the environment; research and recommend policy on voting rights and conflict

---

1. For information on the Clinical Sociology Association, write to Adrian R. Tiemann, Ph.D., Membership Coordinator, 2 Wilburn Avenue, Atherton, CA 94025.

resolution; run programs for immigrants; work in criminal justice; advise communities on their development; and teach and write so that others can use the power of sociological insights in their own work (Cohen, 1982).

Although this current movement is in part a response to the few academic job openings in sociology, no analyst of this subfield's development has been able to pinpoint the surprising convergences that have led to the acceptance of this professional identity. Although the field's traditional emphasis is teaching and research in academic settings, sociologists have been employed in non-academic settings for a long time. However, such practitioners have been frequently considered second-class (or corruptible) sociologists. Recent attempts that delineate the beginnings of the clinical-sociology tradition have gone beyond what many thought to be the initial point of demarcation—Louis Wirth's article in the *American Journal of Sociology* in 1931. It now appears that sociologists were doing clinical work in the first decade of the twentieth century.

Culture is an important concept within sociology, and comprehension of the social location of the client within culture is an important component of clinical sociological practice. In one of my clinical roles as a sociological consultant to clinicians from other disciplines, I find many clinicians who consider culture as a factor only if the person has roots in another country. Clients from the United States are seen as cultureless or as part of the broad melting pot. Sometimes blacks and Hispanics are acknowledged as having culture.

Clinical sociologists are adept at delineating particular cultural social locations (Glassner & Freedman, 1979). Is the client a third-generation Italian-American man living in a rural county miles away from any reminder of the ethnic neighborhood except for a mother visited once a year at Christmas? Her grandchildren have been taught by their father that her way of ethnic-centered life has little value. The grandmother has befriended a young immigrant family from Vietnam who has moved into a low-cost, vacated house down the block. She becomes a surrogate for their parents who are unable to leave Vietnam. They become a surrogate for her own children who are unable to relate to their own ethnicity. Or is the client a woman of seventy-five who has lived in institutions for forty years and whose current behavior of hoarding, attention-seeking through swearing, and frequent hallucinations of the presence of a powerful Satan is interpreted by staff as continuing mental illness keeping her from being deinstitutionalized? On review, these behaviors can be viewed as a competent response to what is possible in her learned role within the institutional culture and her acted-out wish, never verbalized, not to die among strangers. Or is the client a high-tech organization dependent on the insights of a once-youthful leadership that has lost its creativity with early success and now uses memoranda as a substitute? Or is it a community concerned about the impact of a new, nearby ski resort on the environment? There is a cultural dimension in each of these situations.

But to concentrate only on the cultural is insufficient. I see many levels of focus for a clinician from the intrapersonal through the broad societal in which the cultural component must be considered. A good clinical sociologist combines levels when engaging in diagnosis or treatment at any level. This is to discover the components of belief, for as W. I. Thomas (1928) stated, what people believe to be true will be true in its consequences. When you understand the components of those beliefs across levels of focus, you are prepared to diagnose, design, and deliver effective interventions individuated to the focus of the intervention, whether it be person, group, organization, community, sub-cultural group, or society.

At Hutchings Psychiatric Center, with the collaboration of the chief of social work, David Hoeldtke, I have been working on a checklist of questions that we have begun to use in our training of clinicians to make them sensitive to the levels at which private problems and socio-cultural issues interrelate. The Joint Commission on Accreditation of Hospitals (1983) now insists that the current environment and home situation be assessed including the "constellation of family and peer group, current living situation, and social, religious, ethnic, cultural, financial, emotional, and health factors and family expectations regarding the length and time of treatment" (Standards 17.5, p.65). The social assessment summarizes psychosocial problems, strengths, and disabilities and is completed by a clinician within 11 days of admission.

This checklist presents one way that a clinical sociologist could approach this assessment. Obviously, other discipline assessors ask some of these questions and then interpret them within their preferred framework of training. However, a skilled clinical sociologist can provide meaningful insights, since many of the questions on the checklist link to sociological theory and mid-range studies. These are not the only questions that can be asked, but they can act as a heuristic to aid in thinking about these issues, thereby generating additional questions. Think of these questions as possible markers for key places where the cultural system, social system, and personality system intersect. Innovative interventive strategies can develop at these crossroads.

Recognize that the level of intervention of the clinical sociologist can be at one or more of these levels of focus. However, one tries to briefly examine all levels to decide which are most relevant to the problem at hand.

LEVEL OF FOCUS

Intrapersonal

Explore recent dreams, current fears, and personal secrets.

Interpersonal

Who are significant others for this client? What does the client's support system look like? How are members of family and peers involved? What support is missing? What is the relationship of this client with his or her family? What major role does the client take within the family (sick role, troublemaker, center of attention, ignored as if dead)? Where are the boundaries for this family? Are they accepting of outside help or is it so enmeshed that it keeps strangers outside? Is spouse or child abuse an issue? Are there sexual issues for this client?

How concerned is the client about what others think of him or her? To what degree is the client's behavior adjusted to meet the demands of this "looking-glass" self? Has the client accepted a deviant label (mentally ill, juvenile delinquent, and so on), and does the client act as if all of his or her behavior must meet the image of the label? Does the client use the label as a way not to face the issues surrounding return to a "more acceptable" self-definition? Is the client an isolate or a marginal in relation to groups (Straus, 1982)?

Organizational

To what organizations does the client belong? How active is the participation? Is there a pattern of involvement with the organizations? If the client is not active now, was there a time when the client was active?

If the client works for an organization, explore the client's feelings about work in that setting. Explore the specific nature of the work, relationships with supervisor and subordinates, and plans about this work in the future. Explore the client's understanding about the culture of the organization.

If the client has been institutionalized for long periods, explore the feelings about institutionalization, the specific adjustments to that culture made by the client, which staff members were helpful and why, which staff members were difficult and why. Explore the person's position in the patient world within the institution.

Occupational

What type of work has the client done? Develop a career pattern with the client, paying particular attention to issues of career mobility. Did the client's occupation involve working alone or as a member of a team? How does the client's career pattern compare to a typical pattern within that field?

Community

What is the nature of the community in which the client lives? Is it a community with a sense of caring about those who live there? Are there community persons who give support to the client? Or is the community a place where urban gangrene has set in, where almost every resident is vulnerable to becoming a victim? If the community is not at either of these extremes, describe the social factors within the community that might be beneficial or detrimental to the client. Are there formal or informal social organizations to which the client might link? How familiar is the client with the community? How familiar are key members of the community with the client? Has the client a positive or negative reputation with the community, or is the client unknown?

Stratification Issues

What social class is the client? What social class are his or her parents? Is this a situation of upward or downward mobility or a static situation? Pay particular attention to downward mobility because of its relationship with a range of social problems. To what social class does the client aspire? Does the client try to reach this goal by hard work, by luck or magic, or has the client given up all reasonable hope of reaching this goal (Mancini, 1981)?

Ethnicity and Racial Issues

What ethnicity is the client? What race? How much is the client's sense of personal identity tied up with issues of race or ethnicity? Is the client preoccupied with these issues? Is there strong denial of such issues? Is there a theme central to the client's sense of identity? Have there been events deemed important by the client that shape the ethnicity or racial component of the client's identity? What involvement does the client have in organizations that are connected with ethnic or racial concerns? Are there other points of contact?

Religious Issues

What religion is the client? How does the client practice this religion? Is there a conflict between this client's personal belief system and that of the religion? Has the client attempted to resolve this difference? Have there been any significant shifts in religious practice over the years? What precipitated such change?

Issues of Aging

Does the client appear age-appropriate? Within a standard psychosocial framework, what appear to be the major development and moral issues for this client? Does the client think about death? Is the client "dying by inches" through heavy addictions?

Personal Belief Systems

How does the client explain this need for service? How does this explanation relate to a more general belief system? What features of the social landscape predominate in this belief system (ethnicity, race, community, social class, religion, organization, occupation, family, ethnicity, social change)?

Broad Societal Issues: Crime, Economy, Catastrophe

Is the client involved in the criminal justice system? As victim? As perpetrator? How fearful is the client about crime? Is this fear based on specific incidents?

What is the relationship of the client with the economy? Does the client have enough to live on? Is there a need for the development of benefits not in place?

Does the client have a sense of impending world catastrophe involving nuclear destruction or other forms of devastation? Is there a possibility that problems bothering the client could have a catastrophic component?

These questions and areas to probe cover the levels from individual through societal. I find them useful tools in developing the perspective of a client on his or her problems in relation to the world. If one's client is an organization or a community, these questions would have to be modified to reflect better a different level of focus.

Clinical sociology is an old subfield of sociology with a new lease on life. My fear is that some who read this article with a critical perspective of another profession or academic discipline will be able to discover with some ease that theorists or practitioners from that field have stated the same ideas or have been using a similar approach for years. There is so much overlap among fields— fields among fields within fields—and so much borrowing without acknowledgment that this would not be surprising. Sociological theory, methods, and practice in the mind and hands of a skilled clinical sociologist can be an important problem-solving tool as part of the coalition of those who work in the vineyard of culture.

REFERENCES

Billson, Janet Mancini (Ed.). (1983–84) *Clinical Sociology Review*, *2*.

Cohen, Harry (1982) *Connections: Understanding social relationships*. Ames: Iowa State University Press.

Fritz, Jan Marie (1984) *The clinical sociology handbook*. New York: Garland.

Fritz, Jan Marie (Ed.). (1982) *Clinical Sociology Review*, *1*.

Glassner, Barry, & Freedman, Jonathan A. (1979) *Clinical sociology*. New York: Longman.

Joint Commission on Accreditation of Hospitals (1983) *Consolidated standards manual/ 83 for child, adolescent, and adult psychiatric, alcoholism, and drug abuse facilities*. Chicago. See Standards 17.5 (p. 65) and 18.1.3.2 (p. 69).

Mancini, Janet K. (1981) *Strategic styles: Coping in the inner city*. Hanover, N.H.: University Press of New England.

Mills, C. Wright (1959) *The sociological imagination*. New York: Oxford University Press, pp. 3–8.

Straus, Roger A. (1982) *Strategic self-hypnosis*. Englewood Cliffs, N.J.: Prentice-Hall.

———— (1985) *Using sociology: An introduction from the clinical perspective*. New York: General Hall.

Swan, L. Alex (1983) *The practice of clinical sociology*. Cambridge, Mass.: Schenkman.

Thomas, W. I. (1928) *The child in America*. New York: Knopf. See also idem (1927) Situational analysis: The behavior pattern and the situation. Reprinted in Janowitz, M. (Ed.). (1966) *W. I. Thomas on social organization and social personality*. Chicago: University of Chicago Press.

Wirth, Louis (1931) Clinical sociology. *American Journal of Sociology*, *37*, 49–66. Reprinted in *Clinical Sociology Review*, *1* (1982).

III

CLIENT POPULATIONS

Frequently when people use the term *cross-cultural* they really mean cross-ethnic similarities or differences. Ethnic groups have been the most visible example of cross-cultural contact for most of us, and for that reason it is important to review the literature that has developed around some of the different ethnocultural groups. The several ethnic groups mentioned in this section illustrate examples that can be applied to a variety of other white or nonwhite ethnicities.

Joseph Trimble, Teresa LaFromboise, and Carolyn Attneave describe the rich variety of contrasting cultural viewpoints within the American Indian nations and communities. David Sue and Derald Sue point out the impact of inaccurate stereotypes being applied to the Asian-American client. Noreen Mokuau describes how difficult it is for Pacific Islanders to change their cultural values to fit other cultural demands. Amado Padilla and Nelly Salgado de Snyder project implications of working with the rapidly growing Hispanic community, and Oliva Espin describes the special role of Hispanic women within that community. Enrico Jones traces the source of ethnic awareness in the United States to leaders of the black community, and Elsie Smith describes the special role of black women in that movement.

There are probably more differences within any ethnic group than there are even between groups, given the rich variety of traditions and backgrounds of ethnicity. The collectivity of cultures outsiders describe within a single ethnic label provides an identity of membership for those within the system. The role of the cross-cultural counselor or therapist is neither to overemphasize nor to underemphasize the cultural labels of ethnicity in defining the needs of clients.

American Indians and the Counseling Process: Culture, Adaptation, and Style

JOSEPH E. TRIMBLE AND TERESA LAFROMBOISE

HISTORICAL PERSPECTIVE AND OVERVIEW

The counseling profession's legacy of interest in the nature of the counseling process and the responsiveness of American Indians to that process is rampant with controversy. A number of clinicians and counselors point to the incompatibility between the conventional counseling approach and the discrepant cultural background of many American Indians. A. Spang (1965) and J. F. Bryde (1971), for example, were among the few who early identified the inherent difficulties in counseling Indians. Bryde (1971) pointed to one problem when he maintained that the "counselor may unwittingly assume that the [Indian] accepts all the values of the dominant culture.... [the Indian], convinced that his way of life is best will listen to the counselor taking in only what he perceives will help him become a better Indian and filtering out any suggestions or innuendoes unconsciously designed to make him into a white man" (p. 3).

Another yet more fundamental problem occurs in the counseling process itself. S. Sue (1977) demonstrated that Indians, along with blacks and Asian-Americans, tend to underuse existing mental-health services; that is, the number of clients is significantly lower than the projected number who could partake of the services allegedly geared to meet their counseling needs. E. R. Barter and J. T. Barter (1974) attributed this underuse to the perceptions of certain urban Indians that the services are not responsive. S. Sue (1977); L. S. Schoenfeld, R. J. Lyerly, and S. I. Miller (1971); and S. Manson and J. E. Trimble (1982) added that underuse may be the result of Indian negative attitudes toward the presence of non-Indian counselors who are presumably insensitive to the cultural complexities of Indian problems.

Underuse of available services may also be attributable to a number of other considerations. According to a number of surveys, many reservation and urban Indians simply are not aware of the kinds of counseling services available. F.

C. Dukepoo (1980) and R. C. Cooley, D. Ostendorf, and D. Bickerton (1979) identified fear, mistrust, and insensitivity as major barriers to mental-health-service use in the Southwest. A. E. Hippler (1975) traced the underuse of services among several Alaska Native groups to a preference for more traditional forms of healing (counseling) lodged in magical beliefs about the spirit world. A number of researchers tie the problem of underuse directly to perceived differences in value orientations between non-Indian counselors and potential Indian clients (Trimble, 1981) and different beliefs about the etiology of the problems and the most effective way to deal with them (Trimble, Manson, Dinges, & Medicine, 1984; Dinges, Trimble, Manson, & Pasquale, 1981; Red Horse, Lewis, Feit, & Decker, 1978; cf. Kelso & Attneave, 1981). Whatever reasons are settled on to explain the underuse phenomenon, the point remains that counseling services for Indians are not being used to their fullest.

CURRENT STATUS

The problems of underuse and counselor incompatibility persist. At a much broader level there is an increasing need for more research in the area of Indian mental health, especially in counselor effectiveness and in prevention. The need also exists for more culturally appropriate counselor education and training.

Of all ethnic-minority groups in the United States, the American Indian has been most neglected in the mental-health field (Manson, 1982). One of the consequences of this benign neglect is the extreme scarcity of competent Indian mental-health practitioners and counselors. This scarcity is even more noticeable when one considers the insignificant numbers of non-Indians who are competent enough to work with Indian clients in counseling relationships (Trimble, 1981). The National Indian Counselors Association, itself a relatively new organization, for example, has a membership of some 150 Indians and non-Indians—many of the members themselves express some difficulty in counseling Indian clients, even those who may work with their own tribe.

In the past few decades scant progress has been made in the training of American Indians in the social and behavioral sciences in general and much less in counseling. Although exact figures are difficult to find, the best estimates indicate that there are no more than 80 American Indians and Alaska Natives with doctoral degrees in the social and behavioral sciences. Only a handful are actually working in positions where their efforts are being directed at impacting Indian mental-health programs. Moreover, because of the lack of graduate-level, trained, Indian mental-health professionals, many mental-health programs within the Indian Health Services (IHS) have become almost solely dependent on Indian paraprofessional counselors (Bergman, 1974; Manson & Trimble, 1982); the IHS preference, however, is for more trained Indian and Alaska Native professionals in psychology, psychiatry, and social work.

Mental-health research about American Indians has received considerable attention. In a review of the Indian mental-health literature D. R. Kelso and C.

L. Attneave (1981) remarked on the overwhelming but severely imbalanced amount of information; their review of almost 500 articles represents a small portion of the available literature. Although the literature on Indian mental health is extensive, the same cannot be said for the field of counseling and Indians. Most of the available material is commentary on the multitude of problems Indians experience when face to face with the counseling process and seemingly insensitive counselors. The research-oriented literature concerning the counseling process with Indians is extremely scanty and, at best, spotty. An overview of the Indian-counseling literature reveals enormous knowledge gaps and appears to raise far more questions than there are answers (Trimble & Hayes, 1984).

Research themes on the counseling process with American Indians tend to emphasize the salient differences between client and counselor regarding world-views and relevant problems for counseling, sources of social influence in counseling, and positive counselor attributes. Trimble (1981) illustrated that value differences between client and counselor need careful examination. In two related studies he found that (1) value preferences and differences among Indians can be as variable as they are among non-Indians; (2) value orientations and self-perceptions are uniquely correlated such that Indians with a weak value orientation are highly likely to have negative self-images (the opposite is equally true). P. Dauphinais, T. LaFromboise, & W. Rowe (1980) found similarities as well as differences in perceived problems of Oklahoma Indian high school students from diverse tribes and their non-Indian counterparts as did A. W. Blue (1977) with Canadian Indian college students. The social influence variables of counselor expertness, attractiveness, and trustworthiness, which are believed to affect the likelihood that clients would be willing to self-disclose problems and concerns or be influenced toward attitudinal and behavioral change, were manipulated in three studies of counselor style with American Indians. LaFromboise and D. Dixon (1981) verified the importance of counselor trustworthy behaviors and relative unimportance of counselor ethnicity on ratings of counselor effectiveness. J. Littrell and M. Littrell (1982) found that American Indian students' preferences for counselors varied with the counselor's sex, style of dress, and type of client problem. American Indians also rated counselors as more credible when they used a culturally relevant counseling style than when counselors used a directive or non-directive counseling style (Dauphinais, Dauphinais, & Rowe, 1981). In addition to evaluating counselor in-session behaviors and personal demographics (race and sex), Indian students rated the positive helper attributes of trustworthiness, knowledge of practical information, and willingness to engage in outreach activities as foremost qualities a counselor should possess.

FUNDAMENTAL APPROACHES

Is it conceivable that a traditional Indian, one steeped in the culture of the tribe, would respond to conventional counseling techniques regardless of the theoretical underpinnings? If not, is it possible to modify conventional techniques to render them appropriate for use with the traditional client? Is counseling, as currently conceptualized, totally ineffective for many would-be Indian clients? Answers to these questions are not straightforward, and if they were, the ability to generalize across Indian groups could be hampered by a multitude of conditions. More directly, Dinges and associates (1981) may be correct in their assertion that counseling "as currently practiced will very likely continue to be of limited significance for the overall emotional welfare of Indian peoples" (p. 245).

Yet one cannot deny the fact that many counselors have been effective in counseling American Indians. Although there is little data available to substantiate this claim and even less on the reasons for their effectiveness, an exploration of what seems to work may be useful.

Within the context of an Indian community there are a number of informal and formal resources that a resident can draw on to acquire some form of mental-health-related assistance. Family members and community-resource persons typically comprise the informal network, whereas services provided by their tribe, the Indian Health Service, and the Bureau of Indian Affairs comprise the formal network. Then, too, traditional healers, shaman or Indian "doctors," and extended families comprise yet another network that predates services provided by local, state, and federal governments. Each one of the service types meets local mental-health needs with varying degrees of efficiency and success (cf. Manson & Trimble, 1982). It is essential that a counselor understand the nature and complexity of the services, especially if one or any combination apparently is not generating positive outcomes for the client.

R. L. Bergman (1974), J. E. Trimble and S. A. Hayes (1984), and N. Dinges and associates (1981), among others, emphasized the importance of persistent forms of traditional healing approaches in providing a uniquely valuable form of intervention in matters involving emotional and behavioral disorders. Although the context and content of a shaman's ceremonial is typically guarded and cloaked in secrecy, the mere fact that they are successful with certain kinds of participants with well-defined problem disorders points up their perceived importance and persistence despite efforts on the part of missionaries and government representatives to eradicate them. In many Indian communities use of healers is a priority that supercedes by a wide margin considerations given to all other forms of clinical treatment.

There is a growing awareness in clinical and counseling psychology that an individual's problems are not solely attributed to the person. Emphasis is being placed on the context of the problem. Trimble and Hayes (1984) and Dinges and associates (1981), in keeping with this perspective, recommended that counselors attempt to understand the "cultural context" in which a client's problem may have occurred. Familial patterns, peer-group orientations, socialization emphases, tribal and ethnic identification are a few "social ecological" processes that should be understood to promote empathy effectively. In this vein, G. Youngman and M. Sadongei (1974) strongly recommended that counselors become familiar with traditional mannerisms and their role in the communication process.

The work of G. S. Goldstein (1974) and J. H. Shore and W. W. Nicholls (1977) illustrates the value of using the familiar orientation of many Indian youth in preventing emotional problems. In both studies houseparents, parents, and relatives were employed to work closely with students and juvenile offenders. Surrogate parents, actual parents, and relatives alike were taught parenting skills designed to promote positive forms of mental health. Results from both projects demonstrated the importance of using surrogate parents in tandem with counselors.

Client characteristics present a number of troublesome areas for many counselors regardless of the ethnic and cultural orientation of the client. With Indian clients the matter may be compounded even more by a host of personal orientations that are brought to the setting. Certainly, the counselor should be aware that many Indian clients simply do not know what is expected of them; the notion of what constitutes good client behavior may never have occurred to them. There are other factors too. Dinges and associates (1981) pointed out that Indian clients are likely to appear relatively passive, and the counselor may have to be creative in getting the client more actively involved in the counseling process. During the relationship the counselor may discover that the client's problem may well be a group problem; as a consequence, providing alternatives for individual change could be overshadowed by group preferences.

Effective counselors of Indian clients must be adaptive and fluid in their orientation. Knowledge of the cultural context and individual characteristics comes from an eager commitment to understand the essence of the social ecology of Indian communities—this involves extending oneself to go beyond the counseling setting and explore the context in which problems may occur. At a more specific level N. B. Miller (1982) presented nine strategies that could facilitate an effective counseling relationship with Indian clients. Among the strategies she recommended the following are most useful: (1) Personal ethnic identity in itself is hardly sufficient for understanding the influence of culture on the client. (2) The client's history contains a number of strengths that can promote and facilitate the counseling process. (3) A counselor should be aware of his or her own biases about cultural pluralism—they might interfere with the counseling relationship. (4) A counselor should encourage the client to become active in the process of identifying and learning the various elements associated with positive growth and development. (5) Most important are empathy, caring, and a sense for the importance of the human potential. In their own right, general counseling skills appear to be effective with Indian clients.

FUTURE DIRECTIONS

Interest in providing effective mental-health and counseling-related services for American Indians is rapidly increasing. Indian youth are beginning to explore seriously career opportunities in the mental-health fields. Despite the interest levels much remains to be accomplished to fill knowledge gaps and adequately staff counseling and community mental-health centers.

The future of the area largely rests with the responsiveness of training institutions. Presently, there are a handful of graduate training programs in counseling psychology that emphasize the unique training needs of Indians (for example, Western Washington University, University of South Dakota, University of Oklahoma, and, to an extent, Arizona State University). Institutions located in predominantly Indian areas need to explore curriculum-reform efforts and develop opportunities to provide culturally appropriate training opportunities.

Research is needed to identify a balance between the strengths and weaknesses of both indigenous and conventional counseling systems. Indians are not likely to absorb quietly "mainstream" life-style perspectives and certainly are not likely to accept the conventional wisdom of counseling-as-usual. Quite the contrary, many Indian communities are experiencing a renaissance and revitalization of traditional cultural styles. Yet the pressures of acculturation and accommodation will persist. The strains associated with marginality and cultural pluralism likely will continue to place additional burdens on many Indians. Counseling can be effective if counselors are equipped with the knowledge and skills required to understand the social ecology of Indian communities and the culture of origin that an Indian brings to the counseling setting.

REFERENCES

Barter, E. R., & Barter, J. T. (1974) Urban Indians and mental health problems. *Psychiatric Annals*, *4* (9), 37–43.

Bergman, R. L. (1974) Paraprofessionals in Indian mental health programs. *Psychiatric Annals*, *4* (9), 76–84.

Blue, A. W. (1977) A study of native elders and student needs. *BIA Education Research Bulletin*, *5*, 15–24.

Bryde, J. F. (1971) *Indian students and guidance*. Boston: Houghton-Mifflin.

Cooley, R. C., Ostendorf, D., & Bickerton, D. (1979) Outreach services for elderly Native Americans. *Social Work*, *29*, 151–153.

Dauphinais, P., Dauphinais, L., & Rowe, W. (1981) Effects of race and communication style on Indian perceptions of counselor effectiveness. *Counselor Education and Supervision*, *21*, 72–80.

Dauphinais, P., LaFromboise, T., & Rowe, W. (1980) Perceived problems and sources of help for American Indian students. *Counselor Education and Supervision*, *20*, 37–46.

Dinges, N., Trimble, J., Manson, S., & Pasquale, F. (1981). The social ecology of counseling and psychotherapy with American Indians and Alaska Natives. In Marsella, A., & Pedersen, P. (Eds.), *Cross-cultural counseling and psychotherapy: Foundations, evaluation, cultural considerations*. Elmsford, N.J.: Pergamon Press.

Dukepoo, F. C. (1980) *The elder American Indian*. San Diego: Campanile Press.

Goldstein, G. S. (1974) The model dormitory. *Psychiatric Annals*, *4* (11), 85–92.

Hippler, A. E. (1975) Thawing out some magic. *Mental Hygiene*, *59*, 20–24.

Kelso, D. R., & Attneave, C. L. (1981) *Bibliography of North American Indian mental health*. Westport, Conn.: Greenwood Press.

LaFromboise, T., & Dixon, D. (1981) American Indian perceptions of trustworthiness in a counseling interview. *Journal of Counseling Psychology, 28*, 135–139.

Littrell, J., & Littrell, M. (1982) American Indian and Caucasian students' preferences for counselors: Effects of counselor dress and sex. *Journal of Counseling Psychology, 29*, 48–57.

Manson, S. M. (Ed.). (1982) *Topics in American Indian mental health prevention*. Portland, Ore.: Oregon Health Sciences University Press.

Manson, S., & Trimble, J. E. (1982) Mental health services to American Indian and Alaska Native communities: Past efforts, future inquiry. In Snowden, L.R. (Ed.), *Services to the underserved: Historical and current issues*. Beverly Hills, Calif.: Sage.

Miller, N. B. (1982) Social work services to urban Indians. In Green, J. W. (Ed.), *Cultural awareness in the human services*. Englewood Cliffs, N.J.: Prentice-Hall.

Red Horse, J. G., Lewis, R. L., Feit, M., & Decker, J. (1978) Family behavior of urban American Indians. *Social Casework, 59*, 67–72.

Schoenfeld, L. S., Lyerly, R. J., & Miller, S. I. (1971) We like us. *Mental Hygiene, 55* (2), 171–173.

Shore, J. H., & Nicholls, W. W. (1977) Indian children and tribal group homes: New interpretations of the whipper man. In Unger, S. (Ed.), *The destruction of American Indian families*. New York: Association of American Indian Affairs.

Spang, A. (October 1965) Counseling the Indian. *Journal of American Indian Education*, 10–18.

Sue, S. (1977) Community mental health services to minority groups: Some optimism, some pessimism. *American Psychologist, 32*, 616–624.

Trimble, J. E. (1981) Value differentials and their importance in counseling American Indians. In Pedersen, P., Draguns, J., Lonner, W., & Trimble, J. (Eds.), *Counseling across cultures*, 2nd ed. Honolulu: University Press of Hawaii.

Trimble, J. E., & Hayes, S. A. (1984) Mental health intervention in the psychosocial contexts of American Indian communities. In O'Conner, W. A. & Lobin, B. (Eds.), *Ecological models: Applications to clinical and community mental health*. New York: Wiley.

Trimble, J. E., Manson, S. M., Dinges, N. G., &. Medicine, B. (1984) Towards an understanding of American Indian concepts of mental health: Some reflections and directions. In Pedersen, P., & Marsella, A. (Eds.), *Cross-cultural mental health services*. Beverly Hills, Calif.: Sage.

Youngman, G., & Sadongei, M. (1974) Counseling the American Indian child. *Elementary School Guidance and Counseling, 8*, 273–277.

Practical Counseling with American Indian and Alaska Native Clients

CAROLYN L. ATTNEAVE

HISTORY

The history of American Indian and Alaska Native relationships with European explorers, settlers, and eventual dominant societies in North America has been a long one and full of misunderstandings. Although a few early contacts were influenced by concepts of the "Noble Savage" and mistaken impressions of oriental splendors, the situation deteriorated rapidly as missionaries and economic competition for scarce resources dominated the relationships. Lack of resistance to European diseases, especially measles and smallpox, and unfamiliarity with distilled spirits and stimulants such as coffee soon facilitated the destruction of relationships and the decrease of the once-flourishing population of Native Americans to estimates of one-tenth of its original size by the end of the eighteenth century.

Attempts were made by humanitarian officials to "civilize" the tribal groups with whose welfare they were charged. With a few exceptions, however, this effort was dominated by the idea of extinguishing all native cultural traits. Until John Collier took over the Bureau of Indian Affairs under Franklin Roosevelt's presidency in the 1930s, the basic thrust was to remove the Indian children from the influence of their "pagan and primitive" parents and to rear and educate them solely in English-speaking boarding schools.

In this way, supposedly, the Indian problem would be solved in one, or at most two, generations. Counseling in these settings consisted of advising Indians how to be like the whites and to forget their Indian identity.

Although Collier was the first, and perhaps the only, anthropologist to have a serious impact on official Indian policy, his humane approach did not last long enough to reverse the trends, and until the 1970s the boarding-school policy was very much the same. However, local schools became available in many areas, and some more enlightened church-related schools were established as well, competing with the federal system. In the 1950s and 1960s, except for truly isolated tribal groups such as the Navajo or the Innuit (Eskimo) and other Alaska Natives, the federal boarding schools became the repositories of children too difficult to manage in local schools: delinquents for whom it was an alternative to reform schools, the retarded and educationally disabled, and probably a high percentage of the emotionally disturbed, abused, or neglected children of school age. The Bureau of Indian Affairs (BIA) used social workers to some extent and for a long period had medical responsibility as well, but the ratios of 200 children per each adult staff person (including dormitory representatives, teachers, counselors, social workers, and other mental-health resource persons) made any large-scale efforts at counseling and rehabilitation impractical.

In 1955 the Indian Health Service (IHS) was created and many of the human-services personnel transferred to it from the BIA. In 1969 the first Mental Health Services were formally established by the IHS, using psychiatric residents under supervision of personnel from the Menninger Clinic, the University of Washington, the University of Chicago, and other medical schools where an individual faculty member was interested. Local tribal persons who were natural counselors and leaders in their own communities were trained first as paraprofessionals and later as professionals in counseling and mental-health services. In the late 1970s and 1980s efforts to establish such services in urban settings, where by now more than half of the American Indian and Alaska Natives reside for large portions of their lives, have met with varying success, depending as much on skill in competing for funding and the goodwill of local professionals as upon the established need and desire for their services. A similar erratic course can be followed in tracing the development of tribal schools and adult-education programs conceived and operated by tribal people on reservations.

PRESENT STATUS

In 1978 there were 28 doctoral-level psychologists, about 12 psychiatrists, about 300 school counselors, and perhaps as many social workers of American Indian identification. The majority were involved with their own population, although many were not pursuing this as a full-time activity for economic reasons and because the settings were too isolated for professional growth. There are at least an equal number of each discipline "in the pipeline" as of 1980, and each year sees a considerable increase in trained native personnel available. In addition, medical schools and colleges in the areas near centers of Indian or Alaska Native populations often expose their students to field work with Indian populations as a part of their elective system. IHS now has well-established mental-health divisions in each of its jurisdictions, but many of them are operating on a regional rather than a local basis. Some tribes now contract for counseling and other mental-health services and cultivate a long relationship with local practitioners. However, when one considers the total population, estimated in the 1980 census as 1.8 million people, the number of indigenous persons trained in counseling is very small in proportion to need.

Dependence on non-Indian and non-local tribal counselors is a serious problem, since there are approximately 250 tribes, many of which have language, customs, history, and styles of relationship as different as those of people from Sweden, Italy, Turkey, and England—or any other combination of "civilized" countries.

Identity with tribe has not been erased, in spite of many efforts to do so, from Indian consciousness, nor has village and family life been removed from the Innuit memories. Where conscious recall of these elements of culture seems missing or full of lacunae, the unconscious persistence of tribal values, customs, and ways of relating are still very strong. In fact, confusions arising because of this very situation are often the source of problems referred for counseling or brought by tribal people themselves to professional resources for help.

Although a Pan-Indian movement has gathered some political strength, and there are efforts to distill common patterns that will be useful in understanding Indian clientele (Attneave, 1982), there is no substitute for learning about the local culture, customs, taboos, and history. Knowledge firsthand of the Navajo cannot be transferred without modification to the Sioux of South Dakota and of either to the Northwest Coastal tribes famous for their following of the sea and to whom horses were unknown until after 1900. This problem is even more complex in urban areas, where as many as 40 tribes may be substantially represented, especially in California, for instance, where most indigenous Indian peoples were exterminated purposely or by the misunderstandings that arose with early settlement of the region. In New York, Boston, and other urban centers, the indigenous natives of the state may be in the minority, and migratory groups may come from as far away as Nova Scotia and the Arctic Circle. The prairies of the Midwest and deserts of the Southwest contribute longer-term migrants, but in almost all cases travel "back home to the reservation" means a lack of continuity in residence over the years. For some exceptions to this trend one might consult Dorothy Miller's study of children in the San Francisco Bay area in the 1970s (Miller et al., 1974).

FUNDAMENTAL ASSUMPTIONS

Each of these tribes has a tradition of leaders, usually elders, both men and women, who have been delegated a role of advising, healing, and counseling. These persons are often very sophisticated in their psychological knowledge but may remain hidden to the non-Indian professional due to a long history of persecution and superstition by the dominant white society. Establishing a relationship on a peer or consultant level with these individuals, while not easy for an outsider, can be very helpful in developing understanding and gaining the confidence necessary for successful work with troubled individuals, families, or groups. Successful alcoholism counseling has almost always developed in settings where these individuals maintain an influence and where Indian ways of thinking and behaving can be incorporated with behavioral, chemical, and other forms of treatment. Alcoholics Anonymous is a similar indigenous method of treatment for the white population but seldom can be used without this kind of cultural modification and translation by Indians.

This example can be documented in a number of regions by consulting the Bibliographic Center now located at the University of South Dakota in Vermillion, where a computerized retrieval system makes more than 1,500 references relevant to American Indian mental health available. Subjects may be retrieved by tribe, by related tribes of similar cultural characteristics, or by geographic region in the United States and Canada. Topics in the index range from those by age group from infancy to old age and by type of problem, type of agency working with the problem, or tests and research tools used. A unique feature is the indexing of American Indian and Alaska Native values and cultural traits, particularly where they differ from mainstream population values and behaviors. D. Kelso and C. Attneave (1981) published the first 1,200 of these references, together with a system of indexing and directions for "being your own computer" that enables interested persons to locate the references germane to their interests no matter how narrowly or broadly defined.

Among traits fairly common to most American Indian persons is one that is widely misunderstood by Anglo-European persons. This appears to non-Indians as a lack of eye contact and is interpreted according to their own cultural norms as an indication of indifference at best and as "shifty-eyed" untrustworthiness at a more extreme level. However, the counselor should be aware that direct eye-to-eye gaze is most usually a sign of aggressiveness, often associated with a myth of "He who kills with his eyes." Equally likely in cross-gender encounters, it is a sexually aggressive gesture that can lead to embarrassing complications, with misunderstandings on both sides. Handshaking is a universal gesture, but among a majority of all Indians it is not the firm, energetic grasp. Rather, it is a feeling-touching of the other person, sensitive and gentle. To the uninitiated, this custom appears as though the Indian or Alaska Native is a cold fish or unresponsive. Like eye-contact habits, some adaptation to prevailing white-culture mannerisms has come about, but awareness and modification of behavior according to the cues of the client will help establish rapport and mutual understanding.

There will be many such behavioral idioms that will need to be understood locally. In Oklahoma a first contact with parents may be through an interpreter, as if the parents did not understand English, but the result is a necessarily more formal and respectful interaction at a slower pace than the usual, brisk American one. Later contacts may drop out the interpreter, unless he or she is also a family member concerned in solving the problem and therefore becomes a part of the active participants in sessions.

Family ties are usually strong and include extended family members. An aunt or uncle may be a functional parent when absence or alcoholism or other conditions make the biological parent unavailable. This is a carryover of the cultural trait that assigns sibling relationships to all cousins and where shared parenting is traditional. One psychiatric resident learned this to his dismay when he complained, "every time I want to talk about his mother, he starts in telling me about this aunt. I never encountered such resistance to therapy!" Fortunately, his supervisor recognized the trait for what it was and encouraged him to work with the material about the aunt, and therapy got back on an even keel.

A similar problem often arises when counselors discover that grandmothers are doing most of the child care, especially for young preschool and elementary-school children. While preserving the rights of parents, successful work with "parents" is usually not possible without winning the confidence of the grandmother and helping her—or in some cases the grandfather—as well. The elder is always respected, and often his or her accumulated experience has survival value for the counselor as well as the client.

It is interesting to note that most academic problems with younger Indian children are classified as learning disabilities, not mental retardation. Reading problems seem to be a combination of differences in assumed cultural background and real types of dyslexia and delayed eye-coordination maturation. Keenness of observation, ability to reason, and modal following of Piagetian cognitive stages seems well demonstrated when tests and assessments include material from the child's environment in the same fashion as tests constructed for English-speaking children. This is true whether or not the child actually is fluent in the tribal language. It often leads teachers to conclude that the child is lazy, uncooperative, or stubborn, rather than suggesting a change of teaching materials and techniques.

Other factors contributing to this pattern may be the widespread occurrence of mild to severe hearing loss due to the nearly epidemic proportions of respiratory infections. Although correctable, the surgery or other treatment of this problem is classified as elective and, often diagnosed at school entrance, is not tended to for years. Problems associated with learning by children with hearing loss are well known in the general population, but in remote and poverty-level areas where most Indian children attend school, there are simply not enough resources to care for these children, and the result is that they are ignored by all concerned. Parents probably also have hearing problems and consequently have no real appreciation of the advantages and behavior changes that could occur if this were corrected. As one grandmother put it to a school psychologist, "Joan ain't dumb. She just don't talk much," and suitable assessment techniques established that the grandmother was right, even though the girl had failed several grades.

Another way Indian children, youth, and adults get out of phase with their would-be helpers is a social-linguistic problem. In Anglo-European culture, the practice is for the teacher to question, listen to the student recite or read written work, and make corrections. The process is very public, and everyone expects that this is the way higher-status persons function, especially when teaching and learning are involved. In most Indian cultures, however, the expert does the talking and the pupil listens; applies the ideas, skills, or concepts privately; and performs for public viewing or for the teacher only when the material is mastered.

With these problems of cross-cultural communication, it is probably not surprising that there is a very high attrition rate in school with only a small percentage of American Indian children completing high school, since at adolescence the frustrations become intolerable for the youth, while physical energies are high and autonomy has often been achieved. An interesting phenomenon, now (1983–87) being investigated in both the United States and Canada, is the fact that most efforts to describe statistically the problems of Indian children list a few birth defects and then little or no service use until adolescence, when alcoholism, suicide, defiance of adults, and destruction of property bring the Indian and Alaska Native youth into contact with legal and medical facilities.

FUTURE DIRECTIONS

The future of work with these populations is an increasing challenge, an option. The total population has more than doubled in the past decade and continues to rise. The modal age is around 20 and will probably remain in the vicinity until the 1990s. Even at the present level of acceleration in the preparation and training of American Indian and Alaska Native professional and paraprofessional specialists in human services, there will not be enough of them to meet the needs of all Indian populations for the foreseeable years in the twentieth century. With half of the Indian and Alaska Native people living in large cities and centers of education and employment, the odds are good that they will be a part of the caseload of most professionals at some time in their careers.

With a status very much like that of immigrants, even though they are residing in their own indigenous homeland, there are many cross-cultural strains and many contributions to be made by the Indian and Eskimo to the dominant white culture—and to the culture of blacks and other minorities as well. It is to be hoped that a number of non-native counselors will find work with this population challenging and rewarding, and that they will be able to earn their welcome.

REFERENCES

Attneave, C. (1982) American Indian and Alaska Native families: Emigrants in their own homeland. In McGoldrick, M., Pearce, J., & Giordano, J. (Eds.) *Ethnicity and family therapy*. New York: Guilford, pp. 55–83.

Kelso, D., & Attneave, C. (1981) *Bibliography of North American Indian mental health*. Westport, Conn.: Greenwood Press.

Miller, D., et al. (1974) *American Indian socialization to urban life*. Final Report, NIMH Grant MH 2219. Washington, D.C.

Asian-Americans and Pacific Islanders

DERALD WING SUE AND DAVID SUE

Although Asian-Americans are often perceived as sharing the same or similar characteristics, it must be remembered that they are comprised of many diverse groups (Chinese, Japanese, Korean, Filipino, Guamians, Malays, Samoans, and Indochinese refugees). Each has its own language and cultural history. Consider also that there are very large differences within each Asian-American group in terms of acculturation, primary language, generational status (immigrants versus fourth- and fifth-generation Asian-Americans), and socioeconomic status.

The Asian-American population has doubled since 1970 and now comprises about 2 percent of the U.S. population (3.5 million), and the percentage continues to increase. Since 1975 about 300,000 Indochinese refugees have been admitted to the United States. Currently, the Asian-American category is comprised of approximately 806,000 Chinese-Americans, 775,000 Filipino-Americans, 701,000 Japanese-Americans, 355,000 Korean-Americans, 170,000 Hawaiian-Americans, 42,000 Samoan-Americans, 32,000 Guamian-Americans, and 400,000 of other Asian ancestry (Sue & Morishima, 1982). The Chinese, Filipino, and Korean communities are increasingly becoming composed to a greater extent of immigrants. Overall, with the continued admission of refugees from Indochina, the characteristics of the Asian-American population are changing.

The history of Asian-Americans in the United States indicates that they have been subjected to massive discrimination and prejudice. The Exclusion Act of 1882 against Chinese immigration and the Gentlemen's Agreement of 1907 limiting the immigration of Japanese, along with the relocation of more than 110,000 Japanese into detention camps during World War II, are examples of discrimination. Although Asian-Americans are considered "model" minorities, they still face discrimination and prejudice (Asian-American Advisory Council, 1973). Complaints of racial prejudice are also voiced by recent immigrants (Department of Health, Education, and Welfare, 1976; Kim, 1978). Asian-American behaviors, culture, and personality are a product of traditional cultural values, interaction with Western values, and responses to discrimination and prejudice.

The view that Asian-Americans are a successful minority is based mainly upon observations of well-educated and high-achieving members of this group. This belief has resulted in a general lack of interest and financial support. For example, at the White House Conference on Aging in 1971, Asian-Americans were not included (until a specific request by their representative was made) despite the fact that the incidence of poverty of aged Chinese is much higher than that for elderly black or Spanish-speaking populations (White House Conference on Aging, 1972). Similarly, Asian-Americans were initially not included in the National Institute for Mental Health Center for Minority Group Programs (Ochberg & Brown, 1973). In addition, Asian-Americans are often not considered eligible for affirmative-action programs because of the success image.

As a group, Asian-Americans show a bimodal distribution composed of a highly educated and successful group and a group characterized by low formal education and much less success. More than 40 percent of Chinese-Americans earn an annual income of less than $4,000, which is a higher percentage of poverty than average in the United States (Office of Special Concerns, 1974). In San Francisco and New York, half of the Chinese adult population have not gone beyond elementary school. Many of the new immigrants are also not "successful." A study of Southeast Asian refugees residing in Los Angeles County found that although the average family size was six, the average earned income was $370 a month. One-third of the families were on welfare. Of the adults, 41 percent had completed only an elementary-school education. Problems reported by the refugees included language difficulties, feelings of isolation, culture conflict, uncertainty about employment and the future, and the experiences of racism and discrimination (Department of Health, Education, and Welfare, 1976). Housing is also a problem for many Asian-Americans. Most of the Chinatowns, Manilatowns, Japantowns, in the United States are ghettos and severely overcrowded. Compounding the problem is the fact that most immigrants tend to migrate to these areas. Although language proficiency is a problem for immigrants, studies from the Office of Special Concerns (1974) predict that future generations of Asian-American children will speak their own language at home. Facility with English will continue to be a problem for future generations of Asian-Americans. At the University of California at Berkeley, more than 50 percent of students of Asian descent had to take remedial reading and composition courses, which is twice the rate for the general campus population (Sue, 1981).

Asian-Americans are also thought to suffer from few adjustment problems. Lower rates of admission for treatment among this group are often interpreted as lower rates of disturbance. The use of treated cases as a measure may be an underestimate, since Asian-Americans have strong cultural prohibitions against the admission of personal problems that reflect shame and stigma on the individual and the entire family. It would be difficult to believe that Asian-Americans are insulated against problems involving discrimination, culture conflicts, and generational conflicts between parents and children.

Several factors indicate that admissions statistics may underestimate the degree of mental disorders that exist in the Asian-American population. First, the results of several studies (Sue & McKinney, 1975; Sue & Sue, 1974) indicate that Asian-Americans seeking treatment were more severely disturbed than Caucasian youths (Okimoto, 1975). Second, more studies are indicating that problems such as juvenile delinquency, gang activity, and drug use are increasing (Lyman, 1973; Masuda, 1973). Third, as personality measures, Asian-Americans have indicated more feelings of isolation, loneliness, anxiety, and emotional distress than Caucasian students (Sue, Ino, & Sue, 1983; Sue & Kirk, 1972). These findings suggest that Asian-Americans do suffer a significant number of adjustment problems that are underestimated because of cultural prohibitions.

Asian-Americans face problems with culture conflict. P. G. Bourne (1975) found that young Chinese clients exhibited anxiety over the inability to reconcile the Western values of independence with concerns involving filial piety and family obligation. Asian-American students are under great pressure to succeed academically. They also reported feelings of social isolation and feelings of passivity in social relationships. Asian-American females reported feelings of guilt in establishing relationships with Caucasian males. Asian-Americans may develop several reference groups in the United States. Some may identify entirely with their Asian culture. Others may reject their Asian heritage and adopt the values of a larger society. Still others may become bicultural (Munoz, 1966; Sue & Sue, 1971; Yu & Kim, 1983). Each group will have its own unique set of problems that must be identified and dealt with. The increasingly growing number of immigrants with problems involving language proficiency, depression, and inability to gain employment or housing, will lead to the need to develop more resources to help these individuals adapt to their new environment.

Those Asian-Americans who do seek treatment are often described as the "most repressed of all clients," and in one study (Sue & McKinney, 1975) 52 percent of them dropped out of therapy after one session compared with 30 percent of the white clients. The same study also found that Asian-Americans average 2.35 treatment sessions versus 7.96 for white Americans. These statistics indicate some of the problems that occur when there is a clash in cultural values. Most counselors expect clients to exhibit psychological mindedness, to develop insight, to discuss intimate details of their lives, and to respond well to client-centered approaches.

Asian-Americans feel a great deal of stigma and shame in talking about personal problems. The terms *Haji* for the Japanese, *Hiji* for the Filipinos, *Mentz* for the Chinese, and *Chaemyum* for Korean-Americans indicate the shame and loss of face these Asian groups feel when talking about personal problems (Kim, 1978). This fact as well as the expectation of concrete direction (a study by D. R. Atkinson, M. Maruyama, and S. Matsui in 1978 found that Asians believed counseling was more credible when it was directive) and respect (silence) for authority often are responsible for the premature termination of treatment. Evaluating Asian clients as repressed or difficult to work with indicates a lack of knowledge of cultural differences and background and the inability to be flexible and to change the therapy to accommodate Asian clients.

There is also a widespread view that Asian-Americans are nonassertive and passive, and this view has been supported by results on paper and pencil tests indicating that Asian-Americans score lower than Caucasian students on dominance and aggression and higher on passivity and deference (Sue & Kirk, 1972). These characteristics are presumed to stem in part from cultural norms and values. R. E. Cambra, D. W. Klopf, and B. J. Oka (1978) believe that Asian-Americans are globally nonassertive and that this characteristic is associated with lower self-esteem, decreased social and employment opportunities, and less confidence. However, it is also possible that verbal inhibition may be situation-specific rather than a personality characteristic (Sue & Morishima, 1982; Tong, 1971). Asian-Americans may be assertive in some situations (with friends, in informal settings, or with members of their own racial group) and not in others (with authority figures, in classroom or counseling settings). A study by D. Sue, S. Ino, and D. M. Sue (1983) supported the situational hypothesis. In a series of role-playing situations, Asian-Americans were as assertive as their Caucasian counterparts; however, Asian-Americans did find it more difficult to be assertive with a professor than did Caucasian students. Thus the notion of global nonassertiveness was not supported. It is possible that Asian-Americans may be inhibited in more situations than Caucasians. If the results of this study are accurate, it would be important when working with Asian students to understand how their cultural values, such as deference to authority figures, may be appropriate with parents and relatives but counterproductive in interacting with professors, counselors, and other authority figures.

Reviewing the mental-health literature on Asian- and Pacific-Americans leads to the conclusion that there exists an adequate data base to move beyond mere descriptive studies. Within the next 10 to 15 years, the following trends in research and practice are foreseen.

1. Rather than focusing on general issues, greater and greater specificity is likely to result, especially in the area of treatment. For example, there is considerable movement among Asian-American mental-health professionals to develop culturally appropriate intervention strategies. Although it has been helpful to point out how traditional counseling-clinical practices may act as barriers to effective cross-cultural help, greater emphasis on culture-specific methods is likely to occur. Likewise, increasing concern is expected with specific issues-problems in respect to things such as alcoholism, drug abuse, juvenile delinquency, identity problems, and human sexuality.

2. Related to the first point is the need to identify the natural, help-giving networks present in Asian communities. The study of family and community resources to promote mental health and to deal with mental disorders has been

lacking. Yet an undertanding of these traditional resources (use of herbalists, respected elders, belief systems, and so on) may shed much light on the development of more appropriate mental-health practices.

3. The increasing diversity among the Asian population in the United States, especially with the large influx of the Indochinese, will create new problems and issues. Again, studies conducted in the past may not be as applicable to this new Asian group. Concepts of assimilation-acculturation and their effects on identity and language will become more complex. In this age of changing international relations and pressures in our society, it cannot be assumed that the experience of Asian immigrants in the late 1800s will be similar to that of the current immigrants. As a result, more and more importance will be given to the study of the Indochinese population.

4. Another major area that has recently attracted attention among Asian-American researchers and practitioners is the concept of assertiveness-nonassertiveness. It represents one of the most persistent topics of controversy among Asian-Americans. Not only that, but the notion of the nonassertive, passive, and inhibited Asian has major negative sociopolitical implications. It is expected that the study of global versus situational nonassertiveness will become an important topic of empirical research.

REFERENCES

Asian-American Advisory Council (1973) *Report to the governor on discrimination against Asians.* Seattle: State of Washington.

Atkinson, D. R., Maruyama, M., & Matsui, S. (1978) The effects of counselor race and counseling approach on Asian-Americans' perceptions of counselor credibility and utility. *Journal of Counseling Psychology, 25,* 76–83.

Bourne, P. G. (1975) The Chinese student—Acculturation and mental illness. *Psychiatry, 38,* 269–277.

Cambra, R. E., Klopf., D. W., & Oka, B. J. (1978) Communicative apprehension among University of Hawaii students. Dissertation, Department of Speech, University of Hawaii, Honolulu.

Department of Health, Education, and Welfare (1976) *Indo-Chinese refugee resettlement program.* Interagency Task Force Report. Washington, D.C.

Kim, B.L.C. (1978) *The Asian-Americans: Changing patterns, changing needs.* Montclair, N.J.: Association of Korean Christian Scholars in North America.

Lyman, S. (1973) Red Guard on Brant Avenue: The rise of youthful rebellion in Chinatown. In Sue, S., Wagner, N. N. (Eds.), *Asian-Americans: Psychological perspectives.* Bel Lomond, Calif. Science and Behavior Books.

Masuda, M. (1973) *Drug abuse in Seattle Asians.* Task Force Report of Seattle King County Drug Commission. Seattle, Wash.

Munoz, F. U. (1966) Family life patterns of Pacific Islanders: The insidious displacement of culture. In Meredith, G. M., & Meredith, C. W. Acculturation and personality among Japanese-American college students in Hawaii. *Journal of Social Psychology, 68,* 175–182.

Ochberg, F. M., & Brown, B. S. (1973) Key issues in developing a national minority mental health program at NIMH. In Willie, C. V., Kramer, B. M., & Brown, B. S. (Eds.), *Racism and mental health: Essays*. Pittsburgh: University of Pittsburgh Press.

Office of Special Concerns. (1974) *A selected socioeconomic characteristics of ethnic minorities based on 1970 census*, Vol. 2. Washington, D.C.: Department of Health, Education, and Welfare.

Okimoto, D. (1975) *Asian keyperson: Survey on drug abuse*. Task Force Report of Seattle King County Drug Commission. Seattle, Wash.

Sue, D., Ino, S., & Sue, D. M. (1983) Nonassertiveness of Asian-Americans: An inaccurate assumption? *Journal of Counseling Psychology, 30*, 581–588.

Sue, D. W. (1981) *Counseling the culturally different: Theory and practice*. New York: Wiley.

Sue, D. W., & Kirk, B. A. (1972) Psychological characteristics of Chinese-American students. *Journal of Counseling Psychology, 19*, 471–478.

Sue, S., & McKinney, H. (1975) Asian-Americans in the community mental health care system. *American Journal of Orthopsychiatry, 45*, 111–118.

Sue, S. & Morishima, J. K. (1982) *The mental health of Asian-Americans*. San Francisco: Jossey-Bass.

Sue, S., & Sue, D. W. (1971) Chinese-American personality and mental health. *Amerasia Journal. 1*, 36–49.

——— (1974) MMPI comparisons between Asian-American and non-Asian students utilizing a student health psychiatric clinic. *Journal of Counseling Psychology, 21*, 423–427.

Tong, B. R. (1971) The ghetto of the mind: Notes on the historical psychology of Chinese-Americans. *Amerasia Journal, 1*, 1–31.

White House Conference on Aging, 1971 (1972) *Asian-American elderly*. Washington, D.C.: U.S. Government Printing Office.

Yu, K. H., & Kim, L.I.C. (1983) The growth and development of Korean-American children. In Powell, G. J., Yamamoto, J., Romero, A., & Morales, A. (Eds.), *The psychosocial development of minority group children*. New York: Brunner/Mazel.

Counseling Pacific Islander–Americans

NOREEN MOKUAU

Counseling Americans of Pacific ancestry might best be understood by focusing on the individual in the context of culture. The term *Pacific Islanders* is a technical derivation from the United States Bureau of the Census classification of "Asian and Pacific Islanders." It is an ethno-cultural label for a heterogeneous constituency. This constituency is comprised of peoples from the Polynesia, Melanesia, and Micronesia island chains, with major attention being paid by the United States Bureau of the Census to the groups with the greatest recognition and numeric representation in the United States: Native Hawaiians (167,253), Samoans (42,050), and Guamanians (32,132) (U.S. Department of Commerce, 1981). This chapter addresses the mental-health and counseling concerns of these three major Pacific Islander groups.

Hawaiians, Samoans, and Guamanians represent a pluralistic population with distinctive histories, languages, systems of values and beliefs, and life experiences. Furthermore, within this general framework of heterogeneity, the reality of intragroup variance must also be acknowledged. All Hawaiians are not alike, nor are all Samoans or all Guamanians. Reasons for intragroup variance are multiple and complex and reflect differentiation in levels of acculturation, personality development, human nature, and so forth. The culturally responsive counselor in working with Pacific Islander–Americans will, therefore, predicate his or her practice on an informed understanding of the integration of individual and culture.

REVIEW OF THE LITERATURE

The literature on counseling Pacific Islanders has its origins in the proliferating conceptual and empirical research on counseling Asian-Americans. It is useful to review broadly three common thematic areas that do emerge in the Asian-American counseling literature. One common theme is the well-documented observation that Asian-Americans, in cities maintaining substantial numbers of these groups, tend to underuse mental-health services or tend to discontinue treatment after the initial visit (Hatanaka, Watanabe, & Ono, 1975; Sue & McKinney, 1975). A second area of commonality relates to the promotion of culture-specific or indigenous forms of helping within the different Asian-American groups. Various Asian authorities believe that the incorporation of culture-specific helping processes (for example, herbal medicines, folk healing, acupuncture, Morita and Naikan therapy) with contemporary Westernized models of treatment may lead to more effective outcomes (Egawa & Tashima, 1981). A third common theme in the literature has to do with the prescription of appropriate treatment styles and approaches based on the specification of various cultural values. For example, prescriptive claims for counselors to be active and directive (Sue & Sue, 1973; Atkinson, Maruyama, & Matsui, 1978), to focus on concrete services (Ho, 1976), to emphasize structure and a vertical working relationship (Yamamoto, 1978), and to minimize intrapsychic self-exploration (Tung, 1980) are linked with cultural factors such as emotional and verbal restraint, guilt and shame, and a desire for specificity and structure regarding role expectations and treatment process.

A major impetus for the current development of literature on counseling Pacific Islander-Americans per se derives from the increasing dissatisfaction among scholars and practitioners in attempting to extrapolate information on how to treat Pacific Islanders from studies done on Asian-Americans in general or from studies focusing on major Asian-American groups such as the Chinese, Japanese, and Filipinos. At its worst, the literature on Asian-Americans has created confusion based on overgeneralization. But at its best, it has increased public awareness and stimulated added investigation into the needs and concerns of the specific subcultural groups that comprise the "Asian and Pacific Islanders" category.

The literature on counseling Pacific Islanders is in an early stage of development and, as such, tends to be descriptive, fragmented, and incomplete. Interestingly, the little information that is available tends to parallel loosely the three thematic trends noted for the more generic Asian-American typology in the previous paragraphs. First, studies have been conducted that indicate that mental-health facilities are being underused by persons of Hawaiian, Samoan (Hawaii, Department of Health, 1982), and Guamanian (Shimizu, 1982) ancestry. Low use rates of facilities are not attributed to a lack of psychosocial problems among these Pacific Islander groups but are explained through a variety of factors such as lack of knowledge of existing mental-health services, language difficulties, stigma and shame, geographic or community inaccessibility, preference for helping sources other than Westernized mental-health facilities, and a values conflict between the philosophies underlying contemporary Westernized treatment models and those beliefs and traditions inherent in Pacific Islander cultures. Second, culture-specific conceptions of mental health, mental illness, and indigenous forms of helping are being rigorously advanced as a means of facilitating treatment for Pacific Islander clients (Markoff & Bond, 1980; Shimizu, 1982).

A specific example from Hawaiian culture is that of "talking story," a relaxed, undirected conversational exchange between worker and client that can create a familiar, personal kind of a relationship that will promote trust and rapport (Young, 1980). Third, and perhaps the area of weakest development, is the prescription of treatment styles and approaches based on perceived cultural values. For example, being supportive and directive may have greatest utility for working with Samoans who maintain traditional values (Markoff & Bond, 1980), or maintaining an informal and personal worker-client relationship may be facilitative in working with traditional, value-oriented Hawaiians (Young, 1980).

Native Hawaiians

Present-day Hawaiians are as diverse in their individual and collective character as any other ethnic population (Kanahele, 1982), but if there is one commonality that binds the Hawaiian community, it is the recognition of culture loss brought on by colonization intentions of "Western" culture since the arrival of Captain James Cook in 1778. Cultural, political, and economic change served to suppress many Hawaiian traditions associated with language, religion, crafts, values, and way of life. It has been hypothesized that it is this sense of culture loss and subsequent ethnic-identity confusion that has led to mental disorders characterized by feelings of inferiority, sadness, and depression (Thompson, cited in Kamehameha Schools/Bishop Estates, 1983) and that further underscore the negative social, economic, and educational statistics of Native Hawaiians.

Given the pervasiveness of the psychosocial fatigue and disorder that exists among Hawaiians today, it is also acknowledged that within recent years there has been the experience of a cultural renaissance. The parameters of a cultural renaissance include a longitudinal assessment and understanding of the problems that occurred as well as efforts to revive the currency of Hawaiian culture. Cultural renaissance refers to a search for a more developed higher sense of communal pride and identity as Hawaiians (Kanahele, 1982).

Samoans

Residents of American Samoa are U.S. territorial citizens who do not have full voting rights and representation but are able to travel freely between Samoa and all states of the Union. Since World War II, and more recently in the last few years, there has been increasing immigration because of association with military service and perceptions of improved economic and educational opportunities in the United States (Munoz, 1980).

The values of a traditional Samoan family emphasize communal property, an extended family network, strictly defined male-female roles and obligations, and physical child-rearing strategies. By contrast, the values of a white, middle-class, nuclear family lead to situations of culture conflict for Samoan Americans. Similar to Native Hawaiians, Samoans are overrepresented on social indicators such as crime, violence, low achievement in education, unemployment, and welfare rolls. Psychological problems such as alienation, loneliness, rootlessness, and low self-esteem exist among these islanders (Munoz, 1980).

Guamanians

Guamanians are territorial citizens of the United States and like American Samoans are able to travel freely between Guam and the United States. F. U. Munoz (1976) suggested that the 1960s was a peak immigration period for Guamanian-Americans and that reasons for immigration include military and educational and economic opportunities. The migration experience lends itself to social and cultural changes that precipitate psychosocial stresses related to economic insecurities and cultural shock (Shimizu, 1982). There is the adjustment from majority status to minority status, as well as the modification of values, beliefs, and life-styles. Traditional Guamanian (Chamorro) values such as interdependence, respect for nature, the supremacy of familial obligations, respect for old age, and respect for social position are in many ways contradictory to Western values, and Guamanian-Americans are placed in positions of cultural and ethnic-identity conflict.

ASSUMPTIONS OF TREATMENT

In an effort to facilitate the quality of treatment for Pacific Islander clients, several assumptions should be examined.

1. Treatment should be predicated on an understanding of the unique synthesis and impact of culture-general (etic) and culture-specific (emic) values of human functioning. These two contrasting orientations refer to the analysis of information that is either universal in applicability or unique to the culture in question. Literature on Pacific Islanders vigorously promotes an understanding of culture-specific values in working with this clientele and implicitly advances the integration of culture-general values. It is useful to remember that increasing acculturation to culture-general values and norms may not necessarily lead to a proportionate decrease in the influence of traditional values; a person may function satisfactorily in several, often contradictory cultural environments (Ishisaka & Takagi, 1982).

2. Treatment should accommodate the varying cultural perceptions and interpretations of psychopathology. The diagnosis of psychopathology in American society today is grounded in the medical model with its broad delineation of certain classes of behavior that are considered manifestations of emotional or psychiatric disorders. However, some of the behaviors perceived as pathological may indeed be considered culturally acceptable and valid in different ethnic groups. For example, in Hawaiian culture, a person who is emotionally close to his ethnic roots may have prolonged dreams or hallucinations about a beloved dead person. Depending on the content of the visions (*noho*), these experiences

may continue for years and still be considered normal manifestations of grieving (Pukui, Haertig, Lee, & McDermott, 1979). To attempt to substitute medical-model standards for alternative criteria more appropriate to the client's environment (Kanfer & Phillips, 1970) may result in the phenomena of encapsulation, whereby "normal" behavior for the subcultural group is mistakenly interpreted as pathological (Pedersen, 1976).

3. Contemporary or Western models of counseling and psychotherapy are inappropriate for Pacific Islander clients. An explanatory supposition for the underuse of mental-health facilities has been that Pacific Islanders' value systems conflict with the underlying philosophies and values of contemporary models of treatment. As a gross generalization, this is an inadequate explanation. If we classify models of treatment into three major schools of thought—psychodynamic, existential-humanistic, and cognitive-behavioral—and then examine the nature and scope of each school, we find great diversity of theoretical thought. There are some tenets of psychotherapeutic thought that may be appropriate and applicable to work with Pacific Islanders. For example, the acceptance in traditional Hawaiian and Samoan cultures of spirituality (Pukui, Haertig, & Lee, 1972; Markoff & Bond, 1980) may be understood within the existential framework. Another example is that active and directive techniques from the cognitive-behavioral school may be appropriate for Pacific Islanders who value structure and guidance. In essence, direct applications of contemporary models of treatment, without full consideration of cultural ramifications, may be inappropriate for Pacific Islander clients. However, there does appear to be cultural relevance for specified concepts and techniques from these various schools to Pacific Islander concerns. The key to the effective use of an eclectic treatment approach is to develop selection criteria and then systematically to draw out those concepts and techniques that best accommodate the needs of targeted clientele.

FAMILY THERAPY FROM A CULTURE-SPECIFIC AND CULTURE-GENERAL PERSPECTIVE

F. Barth's (1969) transactional model of ethnicity provides a conceptual framework from which to understand the role of the Pacific Islander family as the primary transmitter of values and beliefs and as a source of healing and treatment. The model emphasizes social boundaries and interpersonal relating as a means to examine values and behavioral signs that characterize cultural identity (Green, 1982). As the focal point of all life, the family unit in Hawaiian, Samoan, and Guamanian cultures is a sustaining force that defines and dictates values and culturally acceptable means of behavior. It is through this process of definition that cultural distinctiveness and social boundaries become important. When interpersonal conflict exists, and this distinctiveness is threatened, the family unit can also become a source of healing and treatment.

The most popular and advanced illustration of family therapy in Pacific Islander cultures is that of *ho'oponopono*, a healing method long used in Hawaiian culture.

Ho'oponopono is defined as "setting to right...to restore and maintain good relationships among family, and family and supernatural powers" (Pukui, Haertig, & Lee, 1972). L. Paglinawan (1983) outlined the steps of the *ho'oponopono* process. At the beginning and end of the session, prayers are offered as a means to strengthen spiritual and emotional commitment to the problem-solving process.

In the initial phase efforts are directed at identifying the general problem, and procedures for the problem-solving sequence are specified. Following this phase is a discussion phase in which only one problem or issue related to the general problem is dealt with at a time. All persons are allowed to speak, and confrontations and negative emotional expressions are minimized. As the dimensions of the problem are discussed, it often becomes evident how an initial act or the commission of wrongdoing could cause further misunderstandings and disruptive behaviors in the family. When the discussion phase is complete, the resolution phase takes place. This is the sincere confession of wrongdoing and the seeking of forgiveness by all members of each other. If restitution is necessary, appropriate arrangements are made. It is critical that mutual release between the person who has confessed and the person who has been forgiven be granted. The final phase of *ho'oponopono* includes a summary by the leader regarding the therapeutic process and a reaffirmation of the family's strengths and commitment to the basic unit. Once the closing prayer is given, food is offered to the gods, and then the family shares food together.

Although *ho'oponopono* was developed before the visit to the Hawaiian Islands by Captain Cook in 1778 and has been used in varying degrees during the past 200 years (Paglinawan, 1983), there is similarity in concepts and stage progression with contemporary models of family therapy that were developed in the United States beginning in the mid-1950s. One area of similarity refers to the definition of the family as an interacting, interdependent system forming a unified whole (Scherz, 1970). A second area of similarity is the view of therapy as the means to modify relationships in the family in an attempt to achieve harmony. The outcome of family therapy should be a simultaneous recognition of individualization as well as cohesion with the family unit. A third area of similarity relates to the identification of problem-solving stages. According to F. H. Scherz (1970) there is an initial phase in which trust and alliance are established, and the problem area is explored. In an assessment stage the problem is more specifically defined, and this leads to the formulation of a treatment plan with a goal and treatment methodology. At the next stage treatment principles and methods, active interventive measures, are undertaken to resolve the problem. Finally, there is a phase of termination and evaluation in which the problem has been resolved, the therapeutic group is terminated, and the process of therapy evaluated as to its effectiveness.

Although there is some similarity in basic conceptual definitions and stage delineation, there are differences regarding the content of interpersonal interaction. For example, the *ho'oponopono* strategy of discouraging the expression of negative feelings would conflict with the theoretical propositions of existential, gestalt, and person-centered therapies regarding transparency, congruency, and self-disclosures on matters of both positive and negative emotional impact. Minimizing confrontation in *ho'oponopono* is contradictory to rational-emotive therapy's emphasis on challenge and use of confrontation. In still another example, the *ho'oponopono* strategy of confession and forgiveness of wrongdoing is antithetical to the reality therapy supposition of responsibility of self. Finally, the acknowledgment of spiritual guidance in *ho'oponopono* is a mechanism not commonly recognized in most contemporary models of family therapy.

Whether from a culture-specific or culture-general framework, family therapy appears to be appropriate for work with Pacific Islander clients because of the cultural emphasis on the family unit. The determination of which framework, or which counseling theories, or which specific strategies-methods to use are contingent on the assessment of a multitude of factors including a family's cultural values orientation, presenting problem(s), identified client, and time contract.

FUTURE DIRECTIONS

Literature on counseling Pacific Islander-Americans is in an early stage of development. However, there appears to be momentum among scholars and practitioners qualitatively and quantitatively to improve and expand research studies and to increase application of research findings to practice. Future research should be broadly directed at understanding the interaction of individual and culture, especially since this interaction can facilitate development of effective and specific approaches to counseling and therapy.

Culture affects the development of individual personality and the individual in turn creates a living culture. Based on such an interactional model, the following research areas seem important for future investigations:

1. The identification of theories, concepts, and techniques of counseling and psychotherapy that may be appropriately linked with specified cultural values.

2. The degree of intragroup variance regarding cultural orientation and the effect of this variance on counseling process and outcome.

3. The exploration and descriptions of culture-specific or indigenous forms of helping.

4. A comparative evaluation of the appropriateness of therapeutic models with the different Pacific Islander groups.

These are just a few ideas on how best to enhance the knowledge base of intercultural counseling regarding Pacific Islander clientele. The optimism and conviction that I feel regarding the future of the field give strength to the promise that one day there will be culturally sensitive and relevant services for Pacific Islander–Americans.

REFERENCES

Atkinson, D. R., Maruyama, M., & Matsui, S. (1978) Effects of counselor race and counseling approach on Asian-Americans' perceptions of counselor credibility and utility. *Journal of Counseling Psychology*, *25*, 76–83.

Barth, F. (1969) *Ethnic groups and boundaries*. Boston: Little, Brown.

Egawa, J. & Tashima, N. (1981) Alternative service delivery models in Pacific/Asian communities. NIMH Grant No.1-Rol-MH32148, Pacific Asian Mental Health Research Project, San Francisco.

Green, J. W. (1982) *Cultural awareness in the human services*. Englewood Cliffs, N.J.: Prentice-Hall.

Hatanaka, H. K., Watanabe, B. Y., & Ono, S. (1975) The utilization of mental health services in the Los Angeles area. In Ishikawa, W., & Archer, N. (Eds.), *Service delivery in Pan Asian communities*. San Diego: Pacific Asian Coalition.

Hawaii, Department of Health (1982) Statistical report, 1981. Honolulu.

Ho, M. K. (1976) Social work with Asian Americans. *Social Casework*, *57*, 195–201.

Ishisaka, H. A., & Takagi, C. Y. (1982) Social work with Asian- and Pacific Americans. In Green, J. W. (Ed.), *Cultural awareness in the human services*. Englewood Cliffs, N.J.: Prentice-Hall.

Kamehameha Schools/Bishop Estates (1983) *Native Hawaiian educational assessment project*. Honolulu.

Kanahele, G. S. (1982) The new Hawaiians. *Social Process in Hawaii*, *29*, 21–31.

Kanfer, F. H., & Phillips, J. S. (1970) *Learning foundations of behavior therapy*. New York: Wiley.

Markoff, R. A., & Bond, J. R. (1980) The Samoans, In McDermott, J. F., Jr., Tseng, & Maretzki, T. W. (Eds.), *Peoples and cultures of Hawaii*. Honolulu: University Press of Hawaii.

Munoz, F. U. (1976) Pacific Islanders—a perpelexed, neglected minority. *Social Casework*, *57*, 179–184.

——— (1980) Pacific Islanders: Life patterns in a new land. In Endo, R., Sue, S., & Wagner, N. (Eds.), *Asian-Americans: Social and psychological perspectives*. Palo Alto, Calif.: Science & Behavior Books.

Paglinawan, L. (1983) Ho'oponopono. In Shook, E. V., *Ho'oponopono*. Honolulu: University of Hawaii, School of Social Work.

Pedersen, P. (1976) The field of intercultural counseling. In Pedersen, P., Lonner, W. J., & Draguns, J. G. (Eds.), *Counseling across cultures*. Honolulu: University Press of Hawaii.

Pukui, M. K., Haertig, E. W., & Lee, C. A. (1972) *Nana i ke kumu*. Honolulu: Hui Hana.

Pukui, M. K., Haertig, E. W., Lee, C. A., & McDermott, J. F. (1979) *Nana i ke kumu*, Vol. 2. Honolulu, Hui Hana.

Scherz, F. H. (1970) Theory and practice of family therapy. In Roberts, R., & Nee, R. H. (Eds.), *Theories of social casework*. Chicago: University of Chicago Press.

Shimizu, D.L.G. (1982) Mental health needs assessment: The Guamanians in California. NIMH Grant No. 1-R01-MH32148, Pacific Asian Mental Health Research Project, San Francisco.

Sue, S., & McKinney, H. (1975) Asian Americans in the community mental health care system. *American Journal of Orthopsychiatry*, *45*, 111–118.

Sue, S. & Sue, D. W. (1973) Chinese-American personality and mental health. In Sue, S., & Wagner, N. N. (Eds.), *Asian Americans: Psychological perspectives*. Palo Alto, Calif.: Science and Behavior Books.

Tung, T. M. (1980) Indochinese patients: Cultural aspects of the medical and psychiatric care of Indochinese refugees. Washington, D.C.: Action for Southeast Asians.

U.S. Department of Commerce, Bureau of the Census (1981) Census of the population. Washington, D.C.

Yamamoto, J. (1978) Therapy for Asian Americans. *Journal of the National Medical Association, 70,* 267–270.

Young, B.B.C. (1980) The Hawaiians. In McDermott, J. F., Jr., Tseng, W., & Maretzki, T. W. (Eds.), *People and cultures of Hawaii*. Honolulu: University Press of Hawaii.

Counseling Hispanics: Strategies for Effective Intervention

AMADO M. PADILLA AND NELLY SALGADO DE SNYDER

HISTORY

The importance of cultural considerations in the delivery of counseling and psychotherapy services to Hispanic Americans goes back only to about 1970. Before then little concern was given to the particular mental-health needs of Hispanics. Several factors can be identified as instrumental in the increased attention paid to Hispanics beginning in 1970: the community mental-health movement of the sixties and the focus on underserved populations; the dramatic increase in the Hispanic population during the past two decades, making them the fastest growing ethnic group in the United States today; and the ethnic mobilization of Hispanic professionals who began to advocate for relevant services for Hispanics.

Hispanic is a term used to designate those individuals who reside in the United States and whose cultural origins are in Mexico, Puerto Rico, Cuba, and other Latin American countries. As such the term *Hispanic* is not accepted by all individuals, and it is not uncommon to find reference to Latinos, or *La Raza* (literally meaning "the race"), in place of Hispanic in some communities. Similarly, within each specific subgroup there is some diversity of opinion about which label is most appropriate. For example, among Hispanics with ties to Mexico one is likely to find reference to *mexicano*, Mexican-American, Chicano, and even Spanish American as terms of self-identification used by various segments of the population.

According to census data there are now in excess of 15 million Hispanics in the United States. The majority are Mexican-Americans who reside primarily in the Southwest and West, followed by Puerto Ricans in the Northeast, and Cubans in the Southeast. Approximately 85 percent of Hispanics live in large urban centers and hold unskilled or semiskilled occupations. The median number of years of education is ten with between 25 and 40 percent dropping out of school before high school graduation. Family size is larger than it is for other American families (about three to four children on the average), but median household income is lower.

Overall, the Hispanic population is defined by a series of descriptors, all of which have come to designate a population at risk for mental-health problems and in need of special services. This is the reason why more relevant mental-health intervention strategies for Hispanics are called for.

PRESENT STATUS

The provision of adequate mental-health services to Hispanic populations is one of the areas that has received special attention from both service providers and researchers. Until recently, underuse of mental-health services was a particularly serious problem among Hispanics. L. H. Rogler and others (1983) summarized the findings of research studies on underuse in light of two theoretical perspectives: the *alternative-resource theory*, which explains underuse in terms of indigenous Hispanic social organizations that serve as therapeutic alternatives to the official mental-health agency system; and the *barrier theory*, which explains low use as a result of institutional and structural impediments inherent in the mental-health delivery system. Specifically, it is believed that failure to acknowledge Hispanic language and culture is a major factor in underuse of services by Hispanics.

Research on adequacy of mental-health services, although scarce, has shed light on some important issues. For example, language has been identified as one of the major factors that determine successful therapeutic intervention. It has been shown that dominant Spanish-speaking patients are more positive about their treatment experience when the therapist is bilingual or when trained bilingual interpreters are available. The importance of language is further demonstrated in studies that reveal that Spanish-speaking patients appear to be more disturbed when they are compelled to speak only in English, even if they are bilingual (Marcos, Urcuyo, Kesselman, & Alpert, 1973). Similarly, the concepts of mental health and illness vary among Hispanics depending on whether Spanish or English is spoken by the patient (Edgerton & Karno, 1971). Counselors must therefore recognize the importance of acculturative level of Hispanic clients and the need to be familiar with the Hispanic culture and knowledgeable of Spanish.

Another area currently undergoing much scrutiny by both psychotherapists and researchers alike is the relationship between acculturation and adjustment difficulties. Several investigators have independently developed scales to measure acculturation among various Hispanic subgroups (for example, Cuellar, Harris, & Jasso, 1980; Szapocznik, Scopetta, Kurtines, & Arnalde, 1978). The practical applications for the use of such a scale clinically in the diagnosis, psychodynamics, and treatment of Mexican-American psychiatric patients has been described by I. Cuellar, C. Martinez, R. Jimenez, & R. Gonzalez (1983).

F. X. Acosta and his colleagues (1982) made valuable contributions to the persistent problem of Hispanics dropping out from psychotherapy. Their findings reveal that the major reasons for discontinuation of treatment are unmet role expectations. Hispanic patients who hold negative attitudes toward the therapist and do not perceive psychotherapy as beneficial, even if the treatment modality and environment are culturally relevant, will tend to drop out from psychotherapy. The implications of the findings call for intervention before actual treatment. Pre-intervention in the form of information about the nature and process of therapy assists the client in understanding how best to participate in therapy. Orientation programs such as the one suggested by Acosta and others (1982) may help patients to be more self-disclosing and to express feelings, needs, and expectations of therapy in such a way that the benefits of counseling are maximized.

FUNDAMENTAL ASSUMPTIONS

Many assumptions have been made regarding the life conditions and mental-health needs of Hispanics. Since Hispanic counseling is a new, emerging field, research findings have only begun to refute and/or support such assumptions. A pluralistic counselor must be aware of these issues. The major assumptions are as follows:

1. *The prevalence and incidence of mental-illness problems among Hispanics is lower (or higher) than the general population.* Results from epidemiological studies regarding rates of incidence and prevalence of emotional problems among Hispanics are rare in spite of the size of this population, its cultural uniqueness, and disadvantaged status. The few available studies provide somewhat contradictory findings ranging from reporting higher rates of emotional problems (for example, Roberts, 1980) to similar incidence with other groups (for example, Keefe, Padilla, & Carlos, 1978) to fewer psychological problems (for example, Antunes, Gordon, Gaitz, & Scott, 1974). The only conclusion possible is that we do not have accurate prevalence and incidence information on psychological problems experienced by Hispanics, nor do we have good information on how psychological distress is manifested in this population.

2. *Hispanics suffering from emotional distress use folk-healing practitioners (curanderismo, santeria, espiritismo).* The extent to which Hispanics use folk-healing systems is unknown. The available literature indicates that differences in usage can be found among Hispanic subgroups and urban and rural populations. Recent studies indicate that although urban Mexican-Americans are familiar with folk illnesses such as *susto* (fright) and *mal de ojo* (evil eye), very infrequently do they practice folk healing (Van Oss Marin, Marin, Padilla, & De la Rocha, 1983; Keefe, Padilla, & Carlos 1978). Furthermore, Mexican-Americans tend to prefer and rely more on the help provided by physicians, relatives, or priests rather than *curanderos* (Karno & Edgerton, 1969; Keefe, Padilla, & Carlos, 1978). Among Puerto Ricans living in urban areas, as V. Garrison (1977) showed, *espiritismo* is relied on. For many, spiritism is primarily a crisis-healing cult

that attracts people in times of interpersonal stress and substitutes in many cases for professional mental-health care.

3. *Hispanic families provide their members with emotional support that lessens the impact of psychological stress.* Literature on Hispanic families indicates that both nuclear- and extended-family members are important sources of emotional support (Keefe, Padilla, & Carlos, 1978). Although it is true that the members of the extended family function as a natural, help-giving system, and the kinship seems to buffer the impact of certain stressors, the responsibilities, emotional involvement, and commitments with a large number of family members may also represent an additional source of stress. Much emphasis has been given to the positive aspects of the Hispanic family without evaluation of the negative consequences of large, extended families on the individual. The balance between number of family members available for support and quality of such support is still an issue to be dealt with by therapists working with Hispanics.

4. *Hispanic clients prefer a psychotherapist from their own ethnic group.* The varied information available about Hispanic attitudes toward therapist language and ethnicity suggests that biculturalism-bilingualism may be helpful, but not necessarily sufficient, to insure positive client attitude and therapeutic gain. Non-Hispanic therapists may be perceived positively in some cases (Acosta & Sheehan, 1976) and negatively in other cases (Furlong, Atkinson, & Casas, 1979). In at least one study less-acculturated clients were more likely to drop out of therapy, regardless of the therapist's background (Miranda, Andujo, Caballero, Guerrero, & Ramos, 1976). What is certain, though, is that therapists who do not appreciate Hispanic culture are unsuccessful with their Hispanic clients (LeVine & Padilla, 1980).

FUNDAMENTAL THEORIES

Concepts such as acculturation, marginality, and assimilation have been developed to explain from different theoretical perspectives the degree to which members of different cultures accommodate when they come into contact with one another. These concepts have become especially important in working with Hispanics and underlie many of the theoretical approaches taken in working with this population. For example, E. S. LeVine and A. M. Padilla (1980) proposed a pluralistic counseling approach in assisting Hispanic clients. *Pluralistic counseling* is defined as a therapeutic intervention that recognizes and understands a client's culturally based beliefs, values, and behaviors. This approach encompasses the client's personal and family history as well as social characteristics and cultural orientation in order to evaluate all of the ways in which culture affects the individual. The goal of pluralistic counseling is to help clients clarify their personal and cultural standards and to orient their behavior according to these standards.

Pluralistic counseling requires a number of skills from the therapist. The counselor must be knowledgeable and understanding of both minority and majority cultural values and beliefs as well as their behavioral manifestations. Objectivity and ability to integrate both sets of values within the client's presenting problem are also important. The counselor must be aware of the client's environmental conditions (that is, socio-economic level, education) that may be serving as mediators of positive or negative mental health. The acculturative level of the client and differences in acculturation between members of the same family must also be taken into account when working with Hispanics.

As in any other therapeutic approach, pluralistic counseling involves tasks such as goal setting, selection of therapeutic techniques, implementation, and evaluation. This process, however, is unique in that culture and environmental conditions remain as the central source for understanding the client's presenting problem. A good example of the implementation of this approach has been described by J. Szapocznik and his associates in their Bicultural Effectiveness Training (BET) intervention (Szapocznik, Santisteban, Kurtines, Perez-Vidal, & Hervis, 1983). BET was originally designed to ameliorate the acculturative stress observed in Cuban-American families, but the strategies can be used with other ethnic groups also undergoing acculturation. This culturally relevant treatment modality has proven efficient in reducing intergenerational conflicts and stress in families where problems stem from differences in acculturative level between parents and offspring. Based on a systems approach, the BET operates at three levels: Outcome (reducing intergenerational value-behavioral conflicts); Process (bringing structural changes in the family); and Content (focusing primarily on cultural issues). Basically, the BET consists of twelve lessons of two hours each presented to the family group in three phases. The first phase highlights the positive aspects of generational differences, and family conflicts are redefined from a cultural-conflict perspective. Phase two emphasizes areas in which cultural conflicts impact family interactions. The final phase consolidates the gains accomplished under the notion of biculturalism. The last session or termination of the intervention is also used to provide information on resources available in the community should new problems arise.

Another therapeutic approach that has become increasingly popular among therapists working with Hispanics is the family systems approach. Characteristics of the Hispanic family such as high degree of cohesion, hierarchical organization, exchange of emotional support, and interdependence make family therapy an exciting treatment intervention for Hispanics. S. Minuchin's structural-family-therapy approach is especially useful when working with Hispanics. Structural family therapy emphasizes the role of socio-economic and cultural factors as influential subsystems in the formation of the problem as well as in the process aimed at its solution. Emphasis is also placed on the moral and social codes that regulate the family dynamics within a specific social context. This approach has been used effectively with Puerto Rican families. It has also served as the basis for the development of other family-oriented interventions with Puerto Ricans (Canino & Canino, 1982).

Pluralistic interventions for children are even more novel than those for adults.

G. Costantino (1982) introduced the concept of folktale, or *cuento*, therapy. This strategy, originally developed with Puerto Rican children, incorporates three factors in the *cuento*: Puerto Rican cultural heritage, the mother figure, and the culture of the dominant society. The goal of *cuento* therapy is to bridge the gap between Puerto Rican and majority-group culture by having the mothers present narrative stories to their children with familiar characters and situations.

These examples are only a few of the newer approaches being taken for counseling Hispanics. Each is based on pluralistic principles of incorporating important cultural features in therapy. Practitioners engaged in providing services to Hispanics are hopeful that the inclusion of cultural themes in therapy will prove effective in assisting these culturally different clients.

FUTURE DIRECTIONS

Counseling interventions with Hispanics that attempt to make use of culture will continue to be developed. However, we do see an expansion of the types of problems that will be targeted for intervention. In the next decade we expect to see more interventions directed at abusing parents and their offspring, school programs for adolescents at risk of dropping out of school, adolescent sexual-counseling clinics, and services oriented to meeting the needs of Hispanic elderly.

There will be an increased effort to develop culturally relevant diagnostic instruments to assess the extent to which stressors impact on the psychological well being of Hispanics. These instruments, some of which are already being developed, will incorporate features to gauge acculturative level among Hispanics for the purpose of planning interventions that properly bring cultural content into focus when required. An essential element of these diagnostic instruments is also that they be compatible with the *Diagnostic and Statistical Manual*, third edition. Toward this end we envision greater effort to adapt, translate, and establish norms for instruments so that they will be more suitable for use with Hispanics. A good start in this direction has been made by M. Karno and his colleagues in their development of the Spanish-language version of the NIMH Diagnostic Interview Schedule (Karno, Burnam, Escobar, Hough, & Eaton, in press). There will also be much focused activity on obtaining good estimates of the incidence and prevalence of various psychiatric disorders among Hispanics.

Preventive services will continue to take on increased importance. The emphasis will be on mental-health education with a particular focus on the elimination of the stigma associated with emotional problems and mental illness, which often precludes or delays the use of counseling services. Interventions will also include training of clinicians in matters such as Hispanic culture and life-style, especially in those areas where many Hispanics reside.

REFERENCES

Acosta, F. X., & Sheehan, J. G. (1976) Psychotherapist ethnicity and expertise as determinants of self-disclosure. In Miranda, M. (Ed.), *Psychotherapy for the*

Spanish speaking. Monograph No. 3. Los Angeles: University of California, Spanish Speaking Mental Health Research Center.

Acosta, F. X., Yamamoto, J., & Evans, L. A. (1982) *Effective psychotherapy for low income minority patients*. New York: Plenum Press.

Antunes, G., Gordon, C., Gaitz, C. M., & Scott, J. (1974) Ethnicity, socioeconomic status, and the etiology of psychological distress. *Sociology and Social Research*, *58*, 361–368.

Canino, I., & Canino, G. (1982) Culturally syntonic family therapy for migrant Puerto Ricans. *Hospital and Community Psychiatry*, *33*, 299–303.

Costantino, G. (1982) *Cuentos Folkloricos*: A new therapy modality with Puerto Rican children. *Hispanic Research Center Bulletin*, *4*, 7–10.

Cuellar, I., Harris, L. C., & Jasso, R. (1980) An acculturation scale for Mexican American normal and clinical populations. *Hispanic Journal of Behavioral Sciences*, *2*, 199–217.

Cuellar, I., Martinez, C., Jimenez, R., & Gonzalez, R. (1983) Clinical psychiatric case presentation: Culturally responsive diagnostic formulation and treatment in an Hispanic female. *Hispanic Journal of Behavioral Sciences*, *5*, 93–103.

Edgerton, R. B. & Karno, M. (1971) Mexican American bilingualism and the perception of mental illness. *Archives of General Psychiatry*, *24*, 286–290.

Furlong, M. J., Atkinson, D. R., & Casas, J. M. (1979) Effects of counselor ethnicity and attitudinal similarity on Chicano students' perceptions of counselor credibility and attractiveness. *Hispanic Journal of Behavioral Sciences*, *1*, 41–53.

Garrison, V. (1977) The "Puerto Rican syndrome" in psychiatry and espiritismo. In Crapanzano, V., & Garrison, V. (Eds.), *Case studies in spirit possession*. New York: Wiley, pp. 383–449.

Karno, M., & Edgerton, R. B. (1969) Perceptions of mental illness in a Mexican American community. *Archives of General Psychiatry*, *20*, 233–238.

Karno, M., Burnam, M. A., Escobar, J. I., Hough, R. L., & Eaton, W. W. (in press) Development of the Spanish language version of the NIMH Diagnostic Interview Schedule. *Archives of General Psychiatry*.

Keefe, S. E., Padilla, A. M., & Carlos, M. L. (1978) The Mexican American extended family as an emotional support system. In Casas, J. M., & Keefe, S. E. (Eds.), *Family and mental health in the Mexican American community*. Monograph No. 7. Los Angeles: University of California, Spanish Speaking Mental Health Research Center.

LeVine, E.S., & Padilla, A. M. (1980) *Crossing cultures in therapy: Pluralistic counseling for the Hispanic*. Monterey, Calif.: Brooks/Cole.

Marcos, L. R., Urcuyo, L., Kesselman, M., & Alpert, M. (1973) The language barrier in evaluating Spanish American patients. *Archives of General Psychology*, *29*, 655–659.

Minuchin, S., Montalvo, B., Guerney, B., Rosman, B., & Shumer, F. (1967) *Families of the slums*. New York: Basic Books.

Miranda, M. R., Andujo, E., Caballero, I. L., Guerrero, C. C., & Ramos, R. A. (1976) Mexican American drop-outs in psychotherapy as related to level of acculturation. In Miranda, M. (Ed.), *Psychotherapy for the Spanish speaking*. Monograph No. 3. Los Angeles: University of California, Spanish Speaking Mental Health Research Center.

Roberts, R. (1980) Prevalence of psychological distress among Mexican Americans. *Journal of Health and Social Behavior*, 2, 134–145.

Rogler, L. H., et al. (1983) *A conceptual framework for mental health research on Hispanic populations*. Monograph No. 10. Bronx, N.Y.: Fordham University, Hispanic Research Center.

Szapocznik, J., Santisteban, D., Kurtines, W., Perez-Vidal, A., & Hervis, O. (1983) *Bicultural effectiveness training: A treatment intervention for enhancing intercultural adjustment in Cuban American families*. Paper presented at the conference Ethnicity, Acculturation, and Mental Health among Hispanics, Albuquerque, N.M.

Szapocznik, J., Scopetta, M. H., Kurtines, W., & Arnalde, M. A. (1978) Theory and measurement of acculturation. *Interamerican Journal of Psychology*, 12, 113–130.

Van Oss Marin, B., Marin, G., Padilla, A. M., & De la Rocha, C. (1983) Utilization of traditional and nontraditional sources of health care among Hispanics. *Hispanic Journal of Behavioral Sciences*, 5, 65–80.

Psychotherapy with Hispanic Women: Some Considerations

OLIVA M. ESPIN

Among Hispanics, as among other cultural and socioeconomic groups, women are more willing to seek psychotherapeutic help than men or at least to accept a recommendation to receive treatment more frequently than men. Although among Hispanics, as among other ethnic groups, males have higher rates of admission to mental hospitals (Bachrach, 1975), very few Hispanic males seem to seek psychotherapeutic treatment voluntarily (Abad, Ramos, & Boyce, 1974).

Most Hispanic women receive psychotherapeutic treatment at community mental-health centers or other agencies. Some are seen in private therapy, frequently with the assistance of Medicaid, student insurance, or other forms of third-party payments. Hispanic women who are involved in psychotherapy may be motivated by somatic complaints or because their children have been perceived to be ''at risk'' by schools or other institutions. In some cases Hispanic women may seek therapy for their own personal ''psychological'' reasons.

Those Latina women who seek therapy of their own accord may willingly engage in the therapy process as it is traditionally understood. However, for most Hispanic women, talking about their childhood feelings and experiences does not seem an effective means to cure persistent headaches or to understand why a child is misbehaving at school. Consequently, there is need for a therapeutic approach to work with Hispanic women that will address the special sociocultural circumstances in their lives, in addition to the intra-psychic components of the emotional conflicts they encounter. Although Hispanic women are not more prone to conflict than their white Anglo counterparts, they experience certain conditions that make them vulnerable to psychological stress. The minority status of Hispanics in general, rapid changes in the family, loss of support due to migration, contradictory expectations related to the role of women, high fertility, low income, single parenting, and other factors combine to create increased levels of stress for these women. A relevant therapeutic approach should take into consideration the unique strengths of Hispanic women and the stresses under which they function rather than operate on a set of a priori assumptions about psychotherapy. This chapter attempts to describe an understanding of Hispanic women's lives and its implications for psychotherapeutic treatment.

SIMILARITIES AND DIFFERENCES AMONG HISPANIC WOMEN

The experiental and emotional distance between an immigrant worker of peasant extraction who barely knows how to write her name in Spanish and a "Latin princess" who comes to the United States to study at a private educational institution with all expenses paid is enormous. If these two women met each other, they probably would not acknowledge any commonalities between them. Yet, as their therapist, I can recognize a common thread and historical background, a thread shared with daughters of immigrants born and raised in the streets of New York or in the rural areas of the Southwest.

The commonalities among Hispanic women that manifest themselves, in spite of enormous differences, are due to *historical influences* that have left their mark in cultural processes and class and race differentiation. Other commonalities have to do with the experience of *immigration*; with the cognitive and affective effects of *language*; and with the experience of *oppression*. Finally, their common experiences as *women* in Latin culture bond them together in spite of their diversity.

Historical and Cultural Influences on Hispanic Women

Trends created centuries ago in the relationships between men and women of different race, culture, and political status in Latin America persist today in Hispanic cultures. These historical and cultural influences have been modified, amplified, or otherwise distorted to give a certain character and tone to the lives of Hispanic women. The characteristics of the Spanish conquest and the influence of the Catholic church have had particular implications for these women.

Most Spanish "conquistadores" who came to the Americas were men without fortune, nobility, or other resources. The majority of them did not come with their wives or with any female relatives. They initially intended to return to Spain full of honors and riches in order to marry Spanish women of a higher class. However, the hardships of the enterprise delayed their return to Spain indefinitely, and many of them never returned. Thus what the conquerors believed to be the temporary sexual use of Indian women became their lifelong relationships. These relationships—some temporary, some stable—created the Mestizo population of Latin America. In spite of their known cruelties, many of the Spanish conquerors were willing legally to marry Indian or black women and to support and pass their inheritance to the children of those marriages (Boxer, 1975; Martinez-Alier, 1974). On the other hand, precisely because many of the conquerors' wives were not white, the lower status of all women was further compounded by racial factors in Latin America. European ancestry and "whiteness" were and still are highly respected among Latins. The non-white woman may be seen as not deserving the same respect as the white Latin woman, and she may not find, among Latinos and Anglos alike, the same protection accorded to her white Latin counterpart.

The Catholic church's insistence on the importance of virginity for all women, regardless of their race or social status, has been a challenge to a social system that otherwise could have been more oppressive to women. By emphasizing that all women, regardless of race and social class, held the duty and the right to remain virgins until marriage, and that all men were responsible to women whose honor they had "stained," the church discouraged consensual union and illegitimacy. However, by holding the standard of virginity as the proof of a woman's honorability, the church, and the culture in general, further lower the status of women who cannot or will not maintain virginity. This also fosters the perspective that once an unmarried woman is not a virgin, she is automatically promiscuous.

Other Common Experiences Relevant to Therapy with Hispanic Women

Although some Hispanic women are not immigrants, many of them come from immigrant families. Psychotherapists need to become familiar with the normal psychological processes and crises in the experiences of migration and acculturation as these things specifically affect Hispanic women. Successful adaptation after immigration involves resolution of feelings of loss and the development of decision-making skills, ego strength, and the ability to tolerate ambiguities, including sex-role ambiguities. Factors pertaining to the psychological makeup of the individual woman as well as specifics of the home subculture and social class interplay in unique ways with the characteristics of North American culture. The adoption of new ways of life may be associated with intense grief and feelings of guilt. Newly encountered patterns of sex roles combine with greater access to paid employment for women and may create an imbalance in the traditional power structure of the family.

One of the most prevalent myths encountered by Hispanic immigrants is that all American women are very "free" with sex. For the parents and the young women alike, "to become Americanized" may be equated with becoming sexually promiscuous. Thus in some cases dating and other behavior related to sex may become the focus of conflict among parents and daughters during the acculturation process.

Discussing the affective and cognitive implications of bilingualism and language is beyond the scope of this chapter. However, it is important to keep in mind that even for those Hispanic women who are fluent in English, Spanish may remain as the language of emotions, because it was usually the first language heard and learned and thus it is full of deep affective meaning. Psychotherapy relies too heavily on language to ignore its psychological implications in the therapeutic process, especially for persons who constantly change between two languages or who are participating in therapy in a second language.

The conditions of *oppression* under which most Hispanics live in the United States create certain psychological effects for both men and women. Hispanic women, oppressed both as women and as Latins, suffer from the physical and psychological consequences of oppression in a profound way. The conditions of oppression originating in the economic, political, and social structures of the world become psychological as the effects of these external circumstances become internalized (Freire, 1970). The external oppression of Hispanic women is expressed in political, educational, economic, and social discrimination. Psychologically, the oppression of Hispanic women develops through internalized attitudes that designate women as inferior to men, including Hispanic men; while designating all Hispanics as inferior to the white mainstream of North American Society.

There are specific forms in which the psychology of oppression affects Latin women. For example, as a reaction toward the oppression suffered by Hispanic men, Hispanic women may subordinate their needs even further to those of men. Women and children may be suitable recipients for the displaced anger of an oppressed man. It is not unusual to hear supposedly "enlightened" persons defending the violent behavior of men in oppressed groups on the grounds that their only outlet is to beat their wives and children. Even if the displacement can be understood in the case of each individual, to accept and justify it is to condone injustice under the guise of understanding.

If the role of women is currently beset with contradictions in the mainstream of American society, this is probably still more true for women in Hispanic groups. Despite shared features of history and culture, attitudes towards sex roles are extremely diverse among Hispanic women. For instance, some Latin women are willing to endorse "modern" and "liberated" sex roles concerning education and employment while maintaining very "traditional," "conservative" positions concerning sexual behaviors or personal relationships. Others are traditional in all respects, and still others reject all traditional beliefs concerning the roles of women.

Hispanic women experience a unique combination of power and powerlessness. The idea that personal problems are best discussed with women is very much part of the culture. There is a widespread belief among Latin women of all social classes that most men are undependable and are not to be trusted. At the same time, many of these women will put up with a man's abuses because having a man around is an important source of a woman's sense of self-worth. Middle-aged and elderly Hispanic women retain important roles in their families even after their sons and daughters are married. Grandmothers are ever present and highly vocal in family affairs. However, although Latin women have the opportunity to exercise their power in some areas, they also receive constant cultural messages that they should be submissive and subservient to males in order to be seen as "good women." Suffering and being a martyr are characteristics, of a "good woman." The high incidence of somatic complaints presented by low-income Hispanic women in psychotherapy might be a consequence of this emphasis on "martyrdom" and self-sacrifice as much as a somatic expression of needs and anxieties.

PSYCHOTHERAPY FOR HISPANIC WOMEN

What does therapy have to offer Hispanic women? Unfortunately, psychotherapy could be, and in fact has been in many instances, another instrument for the oppression of women and minorities. By helping them tolerate and adapt to established structures of oppression, psychotherapy can perpetuate the status quo. On the other hand, by increasing the individual's self-awareness and allowing a better perspective on the forces that impinge on the self, psychotherapy can become an instrument of growth and health.

Contrary to partisans of an exclusively intra-psychic or an exclusively social perspective, it is my professional observation that each woman who comes to therapy carries her own particular internalized combination of externally determined and intra-psychic conflicts. Thus it is essential to distinguish between those conflicts and suffering that have their source in socialization and oppression and those conflicts arising from intra-psychic sources.

This philosophy of therapy implies a commitment to the goal of making actual changes in the life situation of Latin women rather than simply attending to the alleviation of individual psychological symptoms. The commitment implied in this perspective on therapy does not detract from the therapist's professional seriousness and psychotherapeutic expertise. The therapist remains, as always, a professional with a given expertise. The desired outcome of this approach to therapy is the self-empowerment of Hispanic women. But precisely because of this perspective, therapy may be perceived as threatening by immediate members of the woman's family, who may not be ready to cope with changes she may make as the result of the therapy.

It is important for a psychotherapist to recognize that each Hispanic woman positions herself at some point along the range of behaviors allowed by the culture. Each woman's choice expresses something about who she is as an individual as well as what her cultural values are. Superficial knowledge of Hispanic culture may lead the therapist to accept as a cultural norm what might only be the client's expression of her individuality. Conversely, a behavior that conforms to strict cultural norms or violates them at a high personal cost can be interpreted by an unknowing therapist as strictly an individual choice with no cultural implications. Cultural norms may be used inaccurately by either client or therapist to explain or excuse a woman's restricted behavior and thus prevent the exploration of other factors in the individual's life history. Or culturally appropriate reactions to violation of norms can be interpreted by the unaware therapist as manifestations of personal neuroticism, thereby increasing the client's guilt and confusion. In short, although there is a danger of being insensitive to cultural differences, there is also the danger of accepting as "cultural" some behaviors or attitudes that might be self-defeating and damaging. Precisely because sex roles tend to be the last bastion of traditional values while all other norms may be changing under acculturative pressures, it is possible to support male-centered "cultural" values without considering their negative effects on women.

In therapy all life options, including an exploration of their ramifications, must be discussed to expand the range of possibilities available to the Hispanic woman and increase her sense of empowerment. Presumably, most of this exploration is conducted through a verbal interchange between therapist and client. In addition, the possibility of using other techniques in psychotherapeutic work with Hispanic women should be explored. Some techniques are particularly relevant for Hispanic women who typically present themselves as having somatic complaints rather than psychic conflicts. Examples of possible uses of these therapeutic modalities include progressive relaxation for general anxiety or phobias, the use of imagery and fantasy to treat "nervous" stomachs or ulcers, gestalt approaches that "give a voice" to headaches or to low-back pain, and the use of biofeedback and variations of meditation.

The recommendation that prescribed medication be taken with tea, which is generally considered to have soothing and curative powers, and the prescription of hot herbal baths for the general relief of tension are examples of an approach that would incorporate folk beliefs into treatment without interfering with the psychotherapy process. These activities are in harmony with Latin culture and may serve to give the Hispanic woman a feeling that some helpful action is being taken by her and her therapist, rather than "just talking" about some things that seem irrelevant to the presenting problem. The possible implications of "prescribing" anything in psychotherapy, however, cannot be ignored. A traditional therapist would probably see these procedures as "interfering with therapy" because of their important, but mostly unexamined, effects on the therapeutic relationship. However, for the therapist to seem to be "giving" to the women in culturally acceptable modes really serves to build the therapeutic alliance and thus increase the likelihood of successful therapy. In addition, some of these activities may constitute forms of self-care and self-help, sorely needed by many Hispanic women.

It was pointed out before that Hispanic women tend to rely on other women to discuss their personal problems, a fact that would suggest the development of women's groups as a viable form of therapy for Hispanic women (Hynes & Werbin, 1973; Olarte, 1983) not only for those who present mental-health problems but as a general form of primary prevention in places where women meet regularly in everyday life. As the group develops and grows it can become an important support system for women who may be leading very isolated lives, since in many cases they are separated geographically from their close relatives and childhood friends.

COMMENTS

In doing therapy with Latina women, as well as in any situation of cross-cultural psychotherapy, there is the question of what to do when the therapist's values, life experiences, and perspectives are drastically different from those of the client. An essential procedure sometimes is to make an appropriate referral. If this is not desired, it is important for the therapist to learn about the culture of the client from reliable sources. Finding a competent supervisor, knowledgeable and experienced in working with Hispanic women, is ideal. Although Hispanic therapists may not need these admonitions, the reality is that most therapists working with Hispanic women are not Latinos themselves. For those who are, it is important to be aware that their own loyaties to and conflicts with their background are, inevitably, part of what they bring to the psychotherapeutic relationship.

The brevity of this chapter does not allow for in-depth discussion of any of the points addressed. In spite of this strong limitation, the previous discussion has made evident that psychotherapeutic work with Hispanic women can be an exciting, innovative enterprise. It is also evident that this psychotherapeutic work is effective only when it takes into consideration the social, political, cultural, and historical contexts in which the lives of Hispanic women are immersed.

REFERENCES

Abad, V., Ramos, J., & Boyce, E. A. (1974) Model for delivery of mental health services to Spanish-speaking minorities. *American Journal of Orthopsychiatry*, *44*(4), 584–595.

Bachrach, L. L. (1975) *Utilization of state and county mental hospitals by Spanish Americans in 1972*. Rockville, Md.: National Institute of Mental Health, statistical note 116.

Boxer, C. R. (1975) *Women in Iberian expansion overseas, 1415–1815*. New York: Oxford University Press.

Freire, P. (1970) *Pedagogy of the oppressed*. New York: Salisbury Press.

Hynes, K., & Werbin, J. (1977) Group psychotherapy for Spanish speaking women. *Psychiatric Annuals*, *7*(12), 64–73.

Martinez-Alier, V. (1974) *Marriage, class, and colour in nineteenth century Cuba*. London: Cambridge University Press.

Olarte, S. (1983) Applications of Psychoanalytic Principles for the Treatment of Minority Women: Focus on the Hispanic Woman. Paper presented at the Twenty-Seventh Winter meeting of the American Academy of Psychoanalysis, Puerto Rico.

Psychotherapy and Counseling with Black Clients

ENRICO E. JONES

During the past fifteen or more years, in which blacks have been treated in psychotherapy in increasing numbers, questions about how therapy should be conducted with the black patient have often been raised. It is a difficult question to come to grips with cleanly, because among other complexities, it is embedded in the fluctuating nature of race relations in our society and hence in a continually evolving sociocultural context. At the heart of the issue is the contention that models of therapeutic intervention, as currently conceived and conducted, are inappropriate for the black population. Many ethnic-minority psychologists have maintained that because of important cultural differences between blacks and whites, traditional methods of psychotherapy are inadequate. Non-minority psychologists have not infrequently agreed with this conclusion, but for different reasons, calling for the development of new modes of intervention for minority clients who, according to this view, generally do not possess the attributes allegedly required for expressive psychotherapies. It pays to be wary here, since this is a controversial issue, and both of these points of view are not uninfluenced by ideological concerns. One cannot help but wonder whether those who continue to insist that it is only the rare black patient who is suitable for the psychological therapies remain under the spell of outmoded, stereotypic images, now rapidly being discarded. For their part, minority psychologists have sometimes emphasized the differences, cultural and otherwise, between blacks and whites, their motives influenced at least in part by their participation in the black social movement of the last decades that had as important themes racial identity, pride, and a renewed interest in cultural and historical roots. This social movement, which reached a peak in the 1960s, can itself be viewed as a kind of communal therapeutic, since not only was it a movement for social change, but it provided a context for the transformation of identity, the amelioration of alienation, and the enhancement of self-esteem.

Nevertheless, the assertion of differences has not helped to clarify how these differences specifically influence psychological intervention processes. Unquestionably, the recognition of cultural diversity has been terribly important. It has gone a long way in challenging, and correcting, the intolerable problems associated with the "deficit hypothesis," which derived from comparisons of blacks and whites on culturally loaded instruments, and from the assumption that black personality and social structure were primarily formed in response to the pathogenic experience of historical isolation and continued economic and cultural deprivation. The appreciation of diversity has led to a greater realization of how culture generates among individual members specific behaviors consonant with the main cultural themes and how these behaviors are comprehensible only if one understands, and understands sympathetically, the ethnic culture. It has led us to accept that without the understanding of the cross-cultural framework of individual behaviors—whether symptomatic, attitudinal, or treatment related—change-oriented interventions with ethnic populations will be of limited effectiveness. Finally, it has fostered a greater sensitivity to the role that values play in the study of ethnic people (Jones & Korchin, 1982).

But how has our acknowledgment of cultural differences helped to guide our conduct of psychotherapy with the black patient? So far it has helped very little. There has recently been a proliferation of books and articles on cross-cultural counseling and psychotherapy. One must applaud this development, since it reflects a growing awareness and sensitivity to minority issues in treatment situations. Still, little has been offered in terms of particular treatment strategies or techniques. Most of what has been proferred is in the way of generalities that can be summarized in a few phrases: (1) Develop a knowledge of the culture along with gaining experience in working with ethnic-minority clients. (2) Be prepared to adapt your techniques, especially the level of activity. (3) Communicate acceptance and respect for the client in terms that are intelligible and meaningful in his or her cultural frame of reference. (4) Be open to the possibility of more direct intervention in the life of the client than the traditional ethos of the psychological therapies might suggest (Draguns, 1981). Although this sort of counsel might not be completely self-evident to a therapist who has had no contact with black clients, it is a level of generality that is not particularly helpful. Certainly, the concepts and the research in the area appear insubstantial when contrasted to the extensive, detailed, and sophisticated literatures on other clinical topics, such as the uses of interpretation, the various approaches to dreamwork, or the problems of modifying psychological structure with borderline patients.

How can we account for this state of affairs, this relative feebleness of information about specifics of therapeutic strategy and technique with the black client? It is due to the fact that the concept of race, or the notion that the client is culturally different, is far too broad and indefinite. These concepts have some clinical utility, but the limits of their usefulness have not been acknowledged; they do not, for example, instruct us about patient characteristics and have little predictive value in terms of how therapy might evolve. The question "How to treat the black client?" is naively and simplistically phrased. It is as if one were asking how do we treat the narcissistic character disorder or the depressed patient. But black clients do not constitute a particular clinical or diagnostic type. Knowing that a patient is black fails to inform adequately about his views of psychotherapy, about his personality and psychological conflict, and about his aspirations and goals in therapy, let alone about educational level, social background, or environmental context. There is enormous within-group variability. The question is not how to treat *the* black client, but how to treat *this* black client.

These comments do not minimize the reality of cultural or ethnic differences. Certainly, it is true that if one were to take random samples of blacks and whites from, say, a local junior college and compare the two groups on any of a number of psychological dimensions, clear and replicable differences would likely emerge. Some of these differences will be the result of problems in psychometric instruments used, that is, their tendency to be culturally loaded. The emic (or cross-culturally invalid) nature of many psychological instruments has already been the subject of extended controversy (Butcher, 1982: Irvine & Carroll, 1980). However, other differences that emerge between the two groups will be more clearly related to differences in attitudes or social values; they are differences that make sense. But how will it help us in psychotherapy to know that, in general, blacks are likely to be more wary about self-disclosure or that they hold, for understandable reasons, less favorable attitudes toward the mental establishment and toward psychotherapy than do whites? Every psychologist is aware that moving from group data of this sort to applying it to an individual in a clinically useful way is problematic. Traits or attitudes that may be broadly characteristic of blacks may or may not be manifested by the individual who confronts the therapist in the consulting room, or at least they are likely to be exhibited in ways that are highly idiosyncratic or have strongly personalized meanings. It must be kept in mind, too, that black patients in psychotherapy may not be highly representative, since important self-selection factors enter into determining who seeks out psychotherapy. Indeed, there is evidence (Jones, 1982) that black and white patients in psychotherapy may be more alike than they are different. It is possible that the experience inherent in patient status (for example, psychological discomfort, motivation for change) may in fact override issues of cultural difference. The point is that the concept of race is far too general and is not tailor-made for what is idiographically more significant to the development of a particular person. The important causal chains that might be of prime interest to the psychotherapist involve whether the black patient is second-generation upper class, or the third child of parents who became anxious after the birth of the second oldest sibling, or the adolescent son of a man who became depressed after being laid off from work.

It is generally held that cultural differences have implications for all forms of intervention. Indeed, their consequences for family therapies, particularly those oriented toward change in family structure, may be more direct than for other treatment forms since we know from sociological research that important differences in family configurations among blacks and whites have been found with regularity (Myers, 1983). It has recently been pointed out, too, that cultural differences have import for behaviorally oriented treatments with black clients. In fact, it has been claimed that the behavioral approach within psychology has, more than other perspectives, properly recognized cultural differences in its assessment and intervention strategies, presumably because attention is paid to the specific response contingencies that are embedded in the culture-learning context (Jenkins et al., 1982). Although the behavioral literature offers innovative treatment procedures, especially for the treatment of alcohol and drug abuse, which continue to be important mental-health problems in the black community, precisely how cultural variables are apt to be employed to enhance the effectiveness and generalization of such treatments has by no means been spelled out and, in truth, is just beginning to be considered. The problem in the behavioral-treatment area corresponds to that fact when considering the impact of cultural difference in expressive therapies, that is, how, given the sheer number of culturally relevant variables, it can be determined which impinge on the behavior of a particular individual and through which set of (idiographic) mediating processes. An additional complication is the fact that most blacks live in two cultures, further obscuring the potential reinforcement value of any given cultural elements.

Any discussion of black patients in psychotherapy would be incomplete without some reference to socioeconomic status. In fact, the cultural factor requires discussion in conjunction with the socioeconomic variable, since it is not always made clear whether the characteristics presumed to be distinctive of the black client are attributable to cultural differences, or whether they can be accounted for by social status and educational level. There is an important literature on the treatment of underprivileged and lower-socioeconomic-status (SES) individuals, much of which has held that such clients are not sufficiently psychologically minded, are more fearful of therapy, are more pessimistic and passive, and want authoritarian direction and concrete results rather than introspective talk. These descriptions are similar, although not identical, to those that have been applied to (lower class?) black clients. For these and other reasons it has been commonly assumed that such clients achieve less successful outcomes in expressive therapies. This is true even if they manage to negotiate effectively the obstacles of lack of availability of treatments, expense, and negative therapist attitudes that frequently bar their entry into treatment.

The assumption that lower-SES clients have a particular and shared set of expectations and attitudes about psychotherapy has recently been challenged, and it has been suggested that lower-SES clients are better risks for the psychological therapies than commonly acknowledged and that treatment outcomes can be successful with such clients (Jones & Matsumoto, 1982). There are signs, too, of a gradual shift in therapists' attitudes toward the lower-SES client characterized by a reduction in unfavorable stereotypes, a greater willingness to treat such clients, and a new, if cautious, optimism about the potential effectiveness of psychotherapy with them. There is a growing realization that psychological stereotypes about the economically disadvantaged are highly unreliable predictors of patient characteristics and therapeutic outcome. Lower-SES clients, like the category "black clients," include individuals with a wide range of problems, personality types, and attitudes toward therapy. Socioeconomic status and culture (or race) have a similar status as concepts: they are poor psychological variables, especially in terms of human characteristics relevant for psychotherapy.

Case in point of the poor predictive value of client race is the entire literature on the effects of therapist-client racial similarity. The question of whether or not a white therapist can effectively treat a black patient (or whether it is preferable for black therapists to treat black patients) was once a seriously debated issue. Certainly, therapist race can be a consideration, since there are blacks who would not want to be seen by a white therapist, just as there are some women who would prefer a female therapist. It is usually recognized that a patient's choice of one kind of therapist indicates certain expectations, images, or the hope for, or avoidance of, a certain kind of relationship: that it has, in short, personalized meaning. Despite our understanding of this at the level of the individual, however, exhaustive reviews of diagnostic studies, preference studies, and analogue and field studies of individual and group therapy show few, if any, important effects of racial similarity in therapy (Sattler, 1977). It could be argued that the findings of psychotherapy research have in general been inconclusive about matters such as the influence of therapist characteristics on treatment processes and outcome and that the failure to find important race effects in psychotherapy reflects a larger problem with research in this field. I do not believe, however, that this is the case: the fact remains that patient race is an ambiguous, poorly defined independent variable from which we are hard pressed to draw anything like definitive conclusions.

Therapists who engage in treatment of people who are different from themselves in racial, ethnic, and social-class background realize that a shared system of ideas, or comprehensive cultural understanding, often does not exist. Other factors, such as gender, physical appearance, and personal experience, also influence cross-cultural or cross-racial intervention processes. The complexity and multiplicity of these several factors, and the processes through which they exert their influence during therapy, suggest that each therapist must discover how best to steer the course of therapy with a particular individual. Again, it is this kind of complexity that accounts for the generality of the usual recommendations, cited above, concerning treatment of the black, or other culturally or racially different, client.

At the risk of adding to the already existing list of only mildly helpful suggestions regarding psychotherapy with the black patient, I would like to underscore what are key elements in the treatment of ethnic-minority clients: empathy and countertransference. The appeal has frequently been made for new, more "culturally relevant" treatment programs in an attempt to accommodate to the perceived culturally different qualities of minority-patient populations. These changes in "service delivery" usually attempt to adapt to social customs or preferences, and such changes in style tend to be superficial and designed primarily to encourage the client's entry into treatment programs. They do not take into account what some have termed *deep culture*, that is, internalized cultural values and characteristic patterns of thinking. The concepts of empathy and countertransference take us beyond merely stylistic changes and begin to allow a greater specification of parameters more closely relevant to treatment.

It is generally held that in the act of empathy—the self-conscious awareness of the consciousness of others, or the sensitive perception of others' thoughts and feelings—one's own feelings are used as an index of what another is experiencing. Since you are judged by my perception of my own feelings, if we are too different, I cannot feel what you feel; empathy, then, depends on a bond based on the similarity of individuals. Cross-cultural psychotherapy, or therapy in racially dissimilar dyads, would necessarily be problematic, since *empathy* defined in terms of understanding others on the basis of shared qualities cannot occur. Attention has been drawn (Stewart, 1981) to the limits of the principle of similarity as the basis for establishing empathy and the need for an empathy based on differences. Empathy in this form would focus the imagination in a way that would transpose oneself into another, rather than upon one's own feelings, and in this way achieve a more complete understanding of culturally varied predispositions, personal constructs, and experience. This kind of outward movement of empathy, which actively attends to the subjective life of another, could lead to the clearer apperception of how a value orientation is reflected in the attitude of a particular client. The appearance of resignation and passivity in a patient, for example, may have to do with a cultural notion about the impossibility of change, an idea confirmed by the fact that real personal change has not been within his or her experience. Failures in empathy increase the likelihood of countertransference reactions, which might in this instance result in this client being viewed as "unmotivated for treatment" or in terms of another unhelpful stereotype.

Countertransference has been perhaps the most extensively addressed topic in discussions of the black patient. There are lengthy lists available describing a large variety of potential countertransference reactions, ranging from guilt and fear to a denial of differences. Any client can invoke in a therapist an unhelpful emotional response; what is noteworthy for this discussion is that it appears that black patients may evoke more complicated countertransference reactions and more frequently. The reason for this seems to be that social images of blacks still make them easier targets for therapists' projections and that the culturally different client provides more opportunities for empathic failures. A therapist's self-knowledge and continual self-awareness are the only means to prevent personal reactions from intruding in unhelpful ways. It is this therapist quality of *self-understanding*, as much as *cultural understanding*, that is of importance in treating the black client; and although culture and race clearly play a role, they should not be emphasized in a way that obscures the unique individuality of the person.

REFERENCES

Butcher, J. N. (1982) Cross-cultural research methods in clinical psychology. In Kendall, P. C. & Butcher, J. N. (Eds.), *Handbook of research methods in clinical psychology*, New York: Wiley.

Draguns, J. G. (1981) Counseling across cultures: Common themes and distinct approaches. In Pedersen, P. B., Draguns, J. G., Lonner, W. J., & Trimble, J. E. (Eds.), *Counseling across cultures*. Honolulu: University Press of Hawaii.

Irvine, S. H., & Carroll, W. K. (1980) Testing and assessment across cultures: Issues in methodology and theory. In Triandis, H. C., & Berry, J. W. (Eds.), *Handbook of cross-cultural psychology*. Vol. 2. Boston: Allyn & Bacon.

Jenkins, J. O., Rahaim, S., Kelly, L. M., & Payne, D. (1982) Substance abuse. In Turner, S. M., & Jones, R. T. (Eds.), *Behavior modification in black populations*. New York: Plenum.

Jones, E. E. (1982) Psychotherapists' impressions of treatment outcome as a function of race. *Journal of Clinical Psychology*, *38*, (4), 722–731.

Jones, E. E., & Korchin, S. J. (1982) Minority mental health: Perspectives. In Jones, E. E., & Korchin, S. J. (Eds.), *Minority mental health*. New York: Praeger.

Jones, E. E., & Matsumoto, D. R. (1982) Psychotherapy with the underserved: Recent developments. In Snowden, L. R., (Ed.), *Reaching the underserved: Mental health needs of neglected populations*. Beverly Hills, Calif: Sage.

Myers, H. F. (1983) Research on the Afro-American family: A critical review. In Bass, B. A., Wyatt, G. E., & Powell, G. J. (Eds.), *The Afro-American family: Assessment, treatment, and research issues*. New York: Grune & Stratton.

Sattler, J. M. (1977) The effects of the therapist-client racial similarity. In Gurman, A. S., & Razin, A. M. (Eds.), *Effective psychotherapy: A handbook for research*. New York: Pergamon Press.

Stewart, E. D. (1981) Cultural sensitivities in counseling. In Pedersen, P. B., Draguns, J. G., Lonner, W. J., & Trimble, J. E. (Eds.), *Counseling across cultures*. Honolulu: University of Hawaii.

Counseling Black Women

ELSIE M. J. SMITH

The recent professional efforts of white women to break away from the male-dominated views on psychology and to develop their own psychology of women have raised similar concerns among black women. Black women have begun to observe that their own unique situation has remained unexamined (Helms, 1979; Jeffries, 1976; Griscom, 1979). There are no texts on counseling minority or black women, whereas the opposite is true for white women. In this respect, there are no real mentors and most significant contributions. The topic of counseling black women is still in its infant stages.

Moreover, researchers have tended to submerge data on black women under topics such as counseling blacks or counseling women. As Walter Allen (1979) pointed out, the dual membership of black women in two special-interest groups, one black, the other white, has led to researchers' overlooking their unique psychosocial status.

As a result of their racial, historical, cultural, and structural position in American society, black women encounter, however, a number of mental-health-related issues. For instance, black women experience stress because of the multiple roles they assume (Reid, 1978).

ALCOHOLISM AND BLACK WOMEN

Clues to the mental-health status of black women can be found in the data on alcoholism, drug abuse, and suicide. According to Frederick Harper (1979), alcoholism constitutes an increasing menace to the mental health and well being of black communities; one-third of the scotch consumed in the United States is purchased by black Americans.

Alcoholism among black women has increased and, along with it, mortality rates for cirrhosis of the liver. In 1975 the mortality rate for cirrhosis of the liver for white women was 136 percent higher than in 1950, while the rate for minority females was 162 percent higher. The negative consequences of alcoholism among black Americans are many and perhaps exceed those for whites. Alcoholism not only contributes to violence against others and early death of its abusers, but it also has been linked to increased incidence of crime, child abuse, and unemployment. As Frederick Harper (1979) stated:

The negative consequences of alcohol use by blacks often exceed those for white Americans in terms of alcohol-related homicides, illnesses, accidents, family conflicts, assaults, and arrests. Among many blacks, the chemistry of psychological stress, racial problems, poverty, unstable employment, poor health care, and lack of education interacts with heavy drinking to cause explosive and detrimental consequences (p. i).

Overall, limited data exist on alcoholism and the black woman. What information is available does suggest that black women have different drinking patterns from white women. For instance, in a 1965 national survey of drinking practices among women, Don Cahalan and Ira Cisin (1965) found that black women differed from white women in that the former had a much higher proportion of abstainers and a higher rate of heavy drinkers. They concluded that black women's higher level of abstention might stem from such factors as lack of money to buy alcoholic beverages, religious beliefs, or a different life-style. On the other hand, the investigators conjectured that the higher proportion of heavy drinkers among black women who drink at all, compared to white women, might be related to their sense of greater alienation, their deprived economic state, and their more frequent filling of the role as head of household. Margaret Bailey, Paul Haberman, and Harold Alksne's (1965) study of black women in the Washington Heights District of New York attributed the high rates of drinking among black women to the fact that they carried major responsibilities as breadwinners, in addition to a more permissive drinking culture for black women than for white women.

Summarizing the data on alcoholism and black women, Frederick Harper (1979) concluded: (1) Black women are inclined to have higher rates of abstainers and also higher rates of heavy drinkers when compared with white women. (2) Black women demonstrate a stronger interest in treatment than black men, and the rate of treatment success is higher for black women. (3) Black female heavy drinkers in an urban environment are likely to be household heads, poor, and weekend drinkers.

SUICIDE AND BLACK FEMALES

Suicide is another indicator of stress among black females. Generally, researchers (Davis, 1975; Slater, 1973; Selden, 1976) have observed that suicide is increasing among young black males and females. Factors such as migration, rage and frustration, unemployment, racism, and the breakdown of traditional institutions have been associated with the high increase of suicide among blacks.

Although the suicide rate for black males is higher than that for black females, nonwhite female suicide rates (blacks comprised 90–94 percent of the nonwhite population from 1969 to 1975) increased 34 percent among the 19–24 age group and 14 percent for the 25–29 age group. Among blacks, suicide rates increase with the young, whereas among whites, suicide rates increase with advancing chronological age (Davis, 1978; *Vital Statistics, 1965–1975*).

Investigators (Bush, 1978; Pedersen, Awad, & Kinder, 1973) have reported differences between whites and blacks in the motivation for suicide, the age at which suicide occurs, and the techniques used to treat suicide attempts. A. M. Pedersen, G. A. Awad, and A. R. Kinder (1973) investigated the differences among 1,345 suicide attempters treated in the emergency department of a teaching hospital in Monroe County in New York State. The study took place during a three-year period. The investigators found that the rate of attempts by nonwhites was higher (160 per 100,000 per year) than that for whites (53 per 100,000). Most of the black suicide attempters were younger (in the 15–44 age group) than whites and were women. The ratio of women to men for nonwhites (primarily blacks) was 6 to 1, compared with a ratio of 3 to 1 for whites. Marital status distinguished the whites from the nonwhites. Nearly a third of the nonwhite women were either separated, divorced, or widowed, and more than half of the nonwhite men were single. Fewer blacks than whites had received psychiatric treatment before or after the suicide attempt. Pedersen, Awad, and Kinder (1973) further noted that nonwhites who commit suicide do not as often have a history of attempts and that attempts may not be as predictive of future suicides as they are for whites.

Studying 25 blacks and Anglos, James Bush (1978) found that all but two of the blacks related the precipitating events for suicide attempts as the recent loss or a threatened loss of a spouse or love. For whites, only three in the sample gave loss of lover as a precipitating event for suicide. Among black females, the loss or threatened loss of a significant loved one constituted the highest likelihood for precipitating a suicide attempt. According to James Bush (1978), young black females significantly more frequently "consider, plan, and attempt suicide around the loss or threatened loss of a love (spouse or boyfriend) relationship. The evidence does not show a similar degree of frequency or reliability for Anglo females'' (p. 9).

Beverly Howze (1977) reported a summary profile of 13 blacks, aged 18 to 34, who attempted suicide. Most of the women were usually married or involved in a long-standing relationship. Howze observed that all complained bitterly about continual states of severe frustration, their need to be loved, supported, and cared for; yet always feeling thwarted and rejected.

USE AND DELIVERY OF MENTAL-HEALTH SERVICES TO BLACK WOMEN

Black women and men differ from white women and men in their rates of admission to all psychiatric facilities and the types of mental-health facilities used. Mildred Cannon and Ben Locke's (1977) survey of national data revealed that in 1971 the rate of admissions among nonwhites to all psychiatric facilities in the United States exceeded that for whites by 45 percent. Nonwhite females accounted for 38 percent of this excess.

In addition, black females tend to experience patient-care episodes or admissions to mental treatment during the prime years of their lives, roughly from age 25 to age 44. Both black males and females have higher use of public rather than private mental-health facilities, whereas the opposite is true for white females (Rudov & Santangelo, 1978). Differences are found in the types of leading diagnoses made for black and white clients in treatment (Cannon & Locke, 1977). Nationally, black females are more likely to be diagnosed as schizophrenic and white females as depressive. The prognosis for schizophrenia is much less favorable than that of depression.

Julia Mayo's (1974) study showed that blacks have a traditional practice of "going to" the city hospital and that two-thirds of the people admitted to inpatient service of the community mental-health center under study came from outside the catchment area of the center. Differences in referral pathways to the community mental-health center were found for blacks and whites. Although more than half of the black clients were referred to the center by self or family, the remainder were brought in by the police or referred by a public health or welfare agency. In contrast, three-fourths of the white clients' path to the community mental-health center was through self, family, or private physician referral.

Richard Krebs (1971) studied the use and delivery of counseling services to 273 people who received treatment at an adult outpatient-service clinic. Krebs observed that therapists either consciously or unconsciously screen black women out of counseling treatment to protect themselves from these women's despair and anger and the therapist's own fear of failure. Krebs concluded: "From the therapist's side it would be understandable unconsciously to reject a black woman who was poor. If the therapist did not reject her on the basis of racial prejudice, he might well reject her to protect himself from the despair and anger of the patient" (p. 595).

Studies have tended to show that minority female clients have low levels of trust and self-disclosure in the counseling relationship (Wolkon, Moriwaki, & Williams, 1973). For example, in an early study, Sidney Jourard and Paul Lasakow (1958) found that even when socioeconomic factors were controlled, white females manifested the highest level of self-disclosure followed by white males, black females, and black males. A similar study by George Wolkon, Sharon Moriwaki, and Karen Williams (1973) found that lower- and middle-class, black female clients had lower self-disclosure scores (indicating a lower level of trust) than did white, middle-class females; black females preferred black therapists; and black females were more dissatisfied with treatment than were white females.

Jean Cole and Marc Pilisuk (1976) observed, however, that therapists prefer treating clients with whom they can identify and whom they consider good candidates for treatment. Clients who use an intrapsychic frame of reference (meaning focusing primarily on self) are generally preferred over those who see the causes of their difficulties resulting from a mixture of internal-intrapsychic and environmental-external conditions. Cole and Pilisuk found that black female clients may not be considered good candidates for counseling treatment because so many of their problems may be environmentally based. For example, when Cole and Pilisuk asked therapists: is there something about Third World people that makes it difficult to treat them, the therapists noted that they were uncomfortable dealing with problems that dealt with the clients' outside world, such as obtaining a job and financial difficulties. Hence when asked to describe her favorite case, one therapist responded that she preferred to deal with "intrapsychic problems that involve a minimum of environmental stress contributing to them" (p. 523).

Conversely, studies have indicated that the white female client is perhaps the most desirable of all racial and sex membership groups (Bergin & Garfield, 1971; Chesler, 1972). White female clients have traditionally been viewed as desirable, because they are more amenable to self-introspection, more docile, and more susceptible to the influence of male dominance (Chelser, 1972). White women have all of the language skills and the expectations of help and rescue that many therapists cherish. They have traditionally more readily assumed the posture of the helpee. Likewise, white women's assumed roles in life may evoke within counselors greater empathy than those black women have assumed. It is suggested that sex-role stereotypes of black women may have a different influence on the counseling relationship than do those of white women. Additional research is needed, however, to confirm or disconfirm this hypothesis.

FUTURE DIRECTIONS

Problems in counseling black women have been linked to counselors' lack of awareness, sensitivity, and knowledge of black women's history, culture, and life concerns. The life concerns of black women are both similar to and different from those of white women; thus the counselor should be cautious of overgeneralizing on the basis of sex. Strategies for psychotherapy with black women should focus on their strengths as well as their weaknesses. For instance, therapists may focus on minority women's positive coping skills and survival mechanisms.

REFERENCES

Allen, W. (1979) Family role, occupational statuses, and achievement orientations among black women in the United States. *Signs*, *4*, 670–686.

Bailey, M. B., Haberman, P. W., and Alksne, H. (1965) The epidemiology of alcoholism in an urban residential area. *Quarterly Journal of Studies on Alcohol*, *26*, 19–40.

Bergin, A. H., & Garfield, S. (1971) *Handbook of psychotherapy and behavior change: An empirical analysis.* New York: Wiley.

Bush, J. A. (1978) Similarities and differences in precipitating events between black and Anglo suicide attempts. ERIC Document Ed 159 570, pp. 1–15.

Cahalan, D., & Cisin, I. (1965) American drinking practices: Summary findings from a national probability sample. *Quarterly Journal of Studies on Alcohol*, *26*, 19–40.

Cannon, M. S., & Locke, B. Z. (1977) Being black is detrimental to one's mental health: Myth or reality? *Phylon*, 408–428.

Chesler, P. (1972) *Women and madness*. New York: Avon Books.

Cole, J., & Pilisuk, M. (1976) Differences in the provision of mental health services by race. *American Journal of Orthopsychiatry*, *46*, 510–525.

Davis, R. (1975) A statistical analysis of the current reported increase in black suicide rate. Ph.D. dissertation, Washington State University, Pullman.

——— (1978) Black suicide and the relational system: Theoretical and empirical implications of communal and familial ties. Discussion Papers 481–78, ERIC Document UD 018 390, pp. 1–29.

Griscom, J. (1979) Sex, race, and class: Three dimensions of women's experiences. *Counseling Psychologist*, *8*, 10–11.

Harper, F. (1979) *Alcoholism treatment and black Americans*. Washington, D.C.: U.S. Department of Health, Education, and Welfare.

Helms, J. E. (1979) Black women. *Counseling Psychologist*, *8*, 40–41.

Hendin, H. (1969) *Black suicide*. New York: Basic Books.

Howze, B. (1977) *Suicide*: Special references to black women. *Journal of Non-white Concerns in Personnel and Guidance*, *5*, (2), 65–72.

Jeffries, D. (1976) Counseling for the strengths of the black woman. *Counseling Psychologist*, *6*, 20–21.

Jourard, S. M., & Lasakow, P. (1958) Some factors in self-disclosure. *Journal of Abnormal and Social Psychology*, *56*, 91–98.

Krebs, R. C. (1971) Some effects of a white institution on black psychiatric outpatients. *American Journal of Orthopsychiatry*, *41*, 589–596.

Mayo, J. A. (1974) The significance of sociocultural variables in the psychiatric treatment of outpatients. *Comprehensive Psychiatry*, *15* (6), 471–482.

Pedersen, A. M., Awad, G. A., & Kinder, A. R. (1973) Epidemiological differences between white and non-white suicide attempters. *American Journal of Psychiatry*, *130*, (10), 1971–1976.

Reid, I. S. (1978) Health issues facing black women. *Conference on the educational and occupational needs of black women, Volume 2: Research reports*. Washington, D.C. The National Institute of Education, Women's Research Program, pp. 203–226.

Rudov, R., & Santangelo, A. (1978) *Health status of minorities and low-income groups*. DHW Publication (HRA) 79–627. Washington, D.C.: U.S. Department of Health, Education, and Welfare, Office of Health Resources Opportunity.

Seiden, R. (1976) Current trends in minority group suicidology. In Bush, J. (Ed.), *Suicide and blacks*. Los Angeles: Charles R. Drew Postgraduate Medical School.

Slater, J. (1973) Suicide: A growing menace to black women. *Ebony*, *33*, 153–160.

Smith, E. J. (1979) The stress resistant delivery (SRD) model: One approach for counseling minorities. In Parker, W. E. & Schauble, P. G. (Eds.), *Counseling blacks: Issues and strategies*. Monograph Series, Vol. 111, Gainesville: University of Florida, Psychological and Vocational Counseling Center.

Vital Statistics, 1965–1975, Volume 2: Mortality (1956–1975). Washington, D.C.

Wolkon, G. H., Moriwaki, S., & Williams, K. J. (1973) Race and social class as factors in the orientation toward psychotherapy. *Journal of Counseling Psychology, 20,* (4), 312–316.

IV

ISSUES AND RESEARCH

The complexity of cultural variables has discouraged research on the ways cultural differences affect counseling and therapy. Not only do the features of a personal cultural orientation include a wide range of demographic and ethnographic, status, and affiliation variables, but those variables continue to change, so the *salient* culture may be different from one moment to the next.

These eight chapters present a selection of issues and research findings to demonstrate how much more we need to know about culture. In the review of research Donald Atkinson shows how complicated it is to match the right client with the right counselor. Walter Lonner and Norman Sundberg point out the problems of accurate assessment and measurement appropriate to the cultural context. Clemmont Vontress takes an existential approach to counseling that transcends cultural boundaries. Sunny Sundal-Hansen identifies the ways in which gender differences overshadow other cultural differences and require special attention. Henry Borow and Chizuko Saeki describe the contrast between Eastern and Western assumptions in researching the issues of counseling and guidance. In the case of Afro-Americans, Gerald Jackson points out how a culture can derive its identity from outside, and Janet Helms describes how that cultural identity affects the treatment process. Leonore Adler reviews both how culture relates to social distances in counseling and how social distance relates to changing attitudes.

There is much research not included in this brief sample. The cross-cultural perspective is growing and changing rapidly as more is learned about the relationships between complex cultures. These several chapters describe part of the growing edge in that research.

Research on Cross-Cultural Counseling and Psychotherapy: A Review and Update of Reviews

DONALD R. ATKINSON

Research on cross-cultural counseling and psychotherapy in the United States has a relatively brief history. According to M. S. Griffith (1977), the role of racial differences in psychotherapy received some attention in the literature in the late 1940s, but no major empirical studies were generated at that time, and interest in this area faded by the 1950s. In 1970 J. M. Sattler reviewed research examining the racial experimenter effects in experimentation, testing, interviewing, and psychotherapy and found only three studies related to the latter category.

By the early 1970s, however, a growing number of studies examining the effects of race on counseling and psychotherapy began to appear in the professional literature. Four major reviews of this expanding body of research have appeared in the past ten years. D. K. Harrison's (1975) review of published and unpublished research examining the effects of race (black and white) on client- and counselor-related variables was the first to focus exclusively on the dynamics of cross-cultural counseling and psychotherapy. Sattler's (1977) classic review on the effects of therapist-client racial similarity (black and white) on counseling and psychotherapy covered published and unpublished research from the fields of counseling, psychotherapy, and social work. In 1983 two major reviews were published, one covering counseling, psychotherapy, and social work research but focusing predominantly on black-white dyads (Abramowitz & Murray, 1983) and one examining counseling research only but including studies in which American Indians, Asian Americans, and Hispanics as well as blacks served as subjects (Atkinson, 1983).

The purpose of this chapter is to update the seven categories of research examined collectively by the four earlier major reviews. Since no one reviewer employed all seven categories, it was often necessary in the current review to move conclusions reached by earlier reviewers to a different category in order to maintain overall consistency. The current review also attempts to examine factors other than inconsistent categorization that may account for the conflicting results obtained within and between earlier reviews. Thus, an attempt is made to examine research outcomes across ethnic groups, research designs, and research settings whenever possible.

CLIENT UTILIZATION OF MENTAL HEALTH SERVICES

The current review covers studies in which voluntary utilization patterns (for example, representation among client populations, differential dropout rates), usually taken from archival records, and attitudes toward utilization (for example, willingness to see a counselor, willingness to return to see a counselor), usually assessed in surveys or analogue studies, were examined. For the purposes of the present review involuntary use (for example, involuntary commitment to a state mental hospital) was judged to be evidence of differential treatment, not use.

Sattler (1977) reviewed archival studies of client use (under a section on differential treatment) and reached the conclusion that blacks are usually underrepresented as clients and are likely to have higher dropout rates than white clients in mental-health facilities. In reviewing and updating the Sattler article, S. I. Abramowitz and J. Murray (1983) left Sattler's conclusion regarding minority underrepresentation in mental-health facilities largely intact but suggested that more research on use does not support a tendency for blacks to terminate therapy earlier than whites.

On the surface it would appear that Sattler's (1977) strong conclusions about black underuse of mental-health facilities have not been substantiated by more recent research. However, it should be noted that his review covered archival studies primarily conducted in mental-health and psychiatric clinics and that the more recent research on use has employed predominantly a survey or analogue research design with college undergraduate populations. Thus both types of research design employed (archival versus survey and analogue) and type of population sampled (mental-health-clinic outpatients versus undergraduate college students) may account for differences between Sattler's conclusions and the outcomes of more recent studies, including the Abramowitz and Murray (1983) review.

The results of recent research also suggest that willingness to use counseling may be a function of within-group differences. For Asian-American subjects, D. R. Atkinson, M. Maruyama, and S. Matsui (1978) found that racial similarity affected willingness to return for counseling by members of an Asian-American rap group but not for members of the Young Buddhist Association. M. G. Haviland, R. K. Horswill, J. J. O'Connell, and V. V. Dynneson (1983) reported that a survey of Native American college students revealed a direct relationship between subject preference for an ethnically similar counselor and willingness to use a counseling center staffed by a Native American counselor. Thus use patterns appear to vary within ethnic groups, and general statements about minority use may not be warranted.

CLIENT PREFERENCES FOR COUNSELOR RACE-ETHNICITY

In his review of research involving black and white subjects, Harrison (1975) concluded that "counselees tend to prefer counselors of the same race" (p. 131). Sattler (1977) reviewed survey and analogue preference studies and reached the same conclusion. In updating the Harrison and Sattler reviews, Atkinson (1983) reported a fairly consistent preference by black subjects for counselors of their own race but found no documentation of a similar effect among other racial-ethnic groups.

Only three of the studies reviewed by Atkinson (1983) made any attempt to assess counselor preferences according to within-group differences. G. G. Jackson and S. A. Kirschner (1973) found that self-identified blacks, or Afro-Americans, expressed a stronger preference for racially similar counselors than did self-identified Negros. T. A. Parham and J. E. Helms (1981) reported that blacks who held "encounter," "immersion," and "internalization" identity attitudes were more likely to express a preference for a black counselor than were blacks who held a "pre-encounter" identity attitude. M. Gordon and R. J. Grantham (1979) found that black subjects preferred counselors of the same social-class background. A more recent study by A. R. Sanchez and Atkinson (1983) also found Mexican-American preference for counselor race-ethnicity to be a function of within-group differences. Thus these four studies confirm that within-group differences such as racial self-identification, racial-identity development, social-class background, and cultural commitment affect preference for counselor race-ethnicity.

EVIDENCE OF COUNSELOR PREJUDICE AND STEREOTYPING

Although a number of studies have attempted to assess the effects of counselor prejudice and stereotyping on differential diagnosis, treatment, and outcome, only a few studies have attempted to measure evidence of counselor prejudice and stereotyping directly. Harrison (1975) reviewed three studies in this area and concluded that although the findings tend to support prejudice on the part of white therapists, the data in this area are too limited to draw definitive conclusions. Atkinson (1983) updated the Harrison review and concluded that "research to date on counselor biases fails to offer conclusive evidence that minority clients are better served by minority counselors than by White counselors" (p. 83).

All studies examined by Harrison (1975) and Atkinson (1983), with the exception of one, employed either a survey or an analogue research design. Abramowitz and Murray (1983) delineated the shortcomings of analogue research, not the least of which is the high probability that subjects may "discern the true objectives of the study and adjust their responses so as to put themselves and their profession in a favorable light'' (p. 218). This problem is particularly acute when analogue (and survey) studies are used to assess directly counselor prejudices. The purpose of such a study is difficult to disguise, and participants are unlikely to reveal true prejudices given the profession's increasing concern for equality of treatment.

DIFFERENTIAL DIAGNOSIS OF CLIENT PROBLEMS

Sattler (1977) reviewed analogue, archival, and field research on differential diagnosis and concluded that ''the diagnostic judgements of clinicians (who in most of the studies were likely White) are not systematically biased in favor of or against Black clients'' (p. 260). Abramowitz and Murray (1983) updated Sattler's review and reached the same general conclusion for analogue studies. In reexamining the archival studies reviewed by Sattler and updating these results with more recent archival findings, however, they cautioned that it is premature to grant a blanket pardon to white practitioners at this time. To support their position, these authors cited recent evidence that: (a) more symptoms are ascribed to black than to white patients, (b) blacks receive more severe diagnostic labels than whites, and (c) blacks receive more than their share of schizophrenic and paranoid diagnoses.

Thus it appears that one can make a case for or against differential diagnosis due to race-ethnicity on the basis of research design employed. For the most part, analogue studies in which clinicians are exposed to contrived case records and then asked to make a diagnosis have failed to confirm an effect due to race-ethnicity of counselor or client. Archival studies based on actual case records, however, tend to support Abramowitz and Murray's (1983) conclusion that black clients are ascribed more symptoms and more severe diagnostic labels than are white clients.

DIFFERENTIAL COUNSELING PROCESS

By far the majority of studies on counseling process have employed an analogue design. Harrison (1975) reviewed research in this area and concluded that: (a) empathic understanding is directly related to depth of self-exploration by black clients, (b) black clients are more expressive with black counselors than with white counselors, and (c) research results on how client race affects the facilitative functioning of the counselor are mixed and inconclusive. Atkinson (1983) updated the Harrison review and found no consistent evidence of a counselor-client ethnic-similarity effect on counseling-process variables. Abramowitz and Murray (1983) reached a similar conclusion in their combined review of psychotherapeutic process and outcome research. These authors suggested that with the positive and negative split on the hypothesized race effect on counseling process (and outcome) has come a split along ethnic lines in reviewers' interpretation of these results; minority reviewers tend to see these findings as supportive of a differential process, and white reviewers tend to see the results as evidence that the white therapist is exonerated from a process bias.

In their analysis of the limitations of analogue research, Abramowitz and Murray (1983) suggested that most of the limitations would bias the results against race-ethnicity effect. In light of this point the fact that half of the studies examining race and counseling-process variables have found an effect may be viewed as more substantial than it might otherwise be. The fact that such a large number of studies have resulted in conflicting findings suggests that unassessed, uncontrolled variables (for example, subject characteristics) may account for varying outcomes.

DIFFERENTIAL TREATMENT STRATEGIES

Eight of 17 archival studies reviewed by Sattler (1977) under a category of differential treatment involved treatment strategies per se as a dependent variable; the other studies in this area employed dependent variables included in the present review as measures of client use. Six of the 8 studies on differential treatment strategies supported a therapist bias. Some of the findings were: (a) Blacks who were voluntary patients at a hospital-based, community mental-health center were more likely than whites to receive inpatient care. (b) Black women were more likely than white women to be assigned to crisis therapy rather than long-term therapy. (c) Black patients at an inpatient hospital were less likely than whites to receive individual psychotherapy and more likely to receive drugs as the only form of treatment. (d) Black clients in 17 community mental-health centers were more likely than whites to see a nonprofessional counselor. (e) Blacks attending an outpatient psychiatric clinic were less likely than whites to receive individual or group psychotherapy.

Abramowitz and Murray (1983) reviewed a number of archival studies on differential treatment and concluded that "the empirical case for race-differential assignment to drug, inpatient, and group treatment is decidedly mixed." They also pointed out that "scattered indications that Blacks sometimes are under-represented among those referred for individual and other intensive forms of therapy,... and more likely to be seen by a non-professional would appear to be cause for concern" (p. 233).

Although the results are not unequivocal, a number of major archival studies have documented that ethnic minorities receive not only different but less preferred forms of treatment than do whites.

DIFFERENTIAL OUTCOME OF COUNSELING AND PSYCHOTHERAPY

Treatment outcome is perhaps the most important measure of a racial effect in counseling and psychotherapy. Unfortunately, the lack of agreement regarding desirable treatment outcomes for psychology in general and the inability of present instruments to measure treatment effectiveness makes the assessment of outcome in cross-cultural counseling and psychotherapy almost impossible.

Harrison (1975) reviewed studies in which black subjects' satisfaction with counseling served as the dependent variable and found little evidence that same-race client-counselor pairings resulted in greater satisfaction. Sattler's (1977) review of field research on the effectiveness of therapy led to a similar conclusion. His often-quoted conclusion to this section of his review states that "Black clients report that they have benefited from treatment received from White therapists, who have used, as far as can be determined, traditional forms of therapy" (p. 276).

In a review of outcome variables that overlapped with the Harrison (1975) and Sattler (1977) reviews, Atkinson (1983) examined eight studies employing client reports of satisfaction as a dependent variable. Seven of the eight studies involved black subjects and one included American Indians as client subjects. Of these eight studies, three employing black subjects reported greater satisfaction when the subjects were seen by racially similar counselors.

Abramowitz and Murray (1983), in their combined review of process and outcome field research, found reason to disagree with Sattler's (1977) earlier conclusion that outcome research fails to substantiate an effect due to race. Reexamining and discounting some of the studies reviewed by Sattler (1977), Abramowitz and Murray (1983) argued that the effects of race on counseling remains a cloudy issue, clouded not only by conflicting research results but also by the research methodology employed by researchers. The current review leads to the same conclusion as that drawn earlier by Abramowitz and Murray (1983); the effects of race-ethnicity on counseling outcome remains unclear, clouded by conflicting results and the limitations inherent in all outcome research.

CONCLUDING STATEMENT

Two further observations regarding methodology need to be made about research examined in the current review. First, most of the research to date has involved an archival, survey, or analogue research design. In general, archival and survey research proved the greater protection against threats to ecological and external validity, and analogue research protects most effectively against threats to internal validity. However, in research that examines a politically sensitive issue like race-ethnicity, it seems very likely that subjects in analogue and survey studies are aware of the variables being studied. To the extent this is true, one might place greater credence on the results of archival studies where subjects generally do not know they are being studied.

Secondly, most of the research reviewed in this and earlier reviews has been carried out in one of three setting-subject combinations: college students, mental-health-agency outpatients, and psychiatric-hospital inpatients. Because of the high correlation between research design and setting-subject combination it is impossible to know if the differing outcomes of analogue and archival studies are due to research design or setting-subject combination. It is tempting to conclude that the problem of differential diagnosis and treatment exists only in mental-health agencies and psychiatric hospitals in which the predominant medical model places a heavy emphasis on differential diagnosis and treatment. However, it is equally plausible that differential diagnosis and treatment are accorded ethnic minorities in college settings as well, but the heavy reliance on analogue designs in the college setting precludes detection of this effect.

REFERENCES

Abramowitz, S. I., & Murray, J. (1983) Race effects in psychotherapy. In Murray, J., & Abramson, P. R. (Eds.), *Bias in psychotherapy.* New York: Praeger, pp. 215–255.

Atkinson, D. R. (1983) Ethnic similarity in counseling psychology: A review of research. *The Counseling Psychologist, 11* (3), 79–92.

Atkinson, D. R., Maruyama, M., & Matsui, S. (1978) The effects of counselor race and counseling approach on Asian Americans' perceptions of counselor credibility and utility. *Journal of Counseling Psychology, 25,* 76–83.

Gordon, M., & Grantham, R. J. (1979) Helper preference in disadvantaged students. *Journal of Counseling Psychology, 26,* 337–343.

Griffith, M. S. (1977) The influence of race on the psychotherapeutic relationship. *Psychiatry, 40,* 27–40.

Harrison, D. K. (1975). Race as a counselor-client variable in counseling and psychotherapy: A review of the research. *The Counseling Psychologist, 5,* 124–133.

Haviland, M. G., Horswill, R. K., O'Connell, J. J., & Dynneson, V. V. (1983) Native American college students' preference for counselor race and sex and the likelihood of their use of a counseling center. *Journal of Counseling Psychology, 30,* 267–270.

Jackson, G. G., & Kirschner, S. A. (1973) Racial self-designation and preference for a counselor. *Journal of Counseling Psychology, 20,* 560–564.

Parham, T. A., & Helms, J. E. (1981) The influence of Black students' racial identity attitudes on preferences for counselor's race. *Journal of Counseling Psychology, 28,* 250–257.

Sanchez, A. R., & Atkinson, D. R. (1983) Mexican-American cultural commitment, preference for counselor ethnicity, and willingness to use counseling. *Journal of Counseling Psychology, 30,* 215–220.

Sattler, J. M. (1970) Racial "experimenter effects" in experimentation, testing, interviewing, and psychotherapy. *Psychological Bulletin, 73,* 137–160.

———— (1977) The effects of therapist-client racial similarity. In Gurman, A. S., & Razin, A. M. (Eds.), *Effective psychotherapy: A handbook of research.* New York: Pergamon Press, pp. 252–290.

Assessment in Cross-Cultural Counseling and Therapy

WALTER J. LONNER AND NORMAN D. SUNDBERG

Readers of this chapter are probably professionals in the mental-health field who have limited familiarity with the general area of psychological assessment and the specialized area of cross-cultural testing. They likely work at least part of the time with clients or patients who are not members of the same culture. The counselor-client "mix" can be diverse. Most large countries are multi-racial and multi-ethnic. White Americans often work with blacks who speak a dialect and live in a special culture, but counseling and other human-service work also cuts across national boundaries. A Mexican therapist-in-training, for example, may work with a French Canadian client in a Montreal clinic, or a British psychiatrist whose patient is a recent immigrant from India could be working in a large clinic in Denmark. A therapist could also be working with a multi-ethnic group of clients or an entire family. In such situations the professional faces the problem of trying to assess others who have different living patterns, language usage, and values as well as different expectations and social supports with respect to solving personal problems or adjusting to situational problems. The overall goal in assessment, then, is for the counselor to minimize ethnocentrism and maximize useful and culturally appropriate information.

Assessment in counseling and psychotherapy includes interviewing, observing, testing, and analyzing documents. Assessment may apply to families, larger groups, and even communities. Here we will emphasize direct work with clients, particularly individuals, but we mention many research ideas and principles, particularly as they apply to psychological tests.

HISTORY

Psychological testing and assessment has a long history. Specialized texts (e.g., Cronbach, 1984; Sundberg, 1977) cover historical developments as well as specific tests and issues pertaining to their use. Although there is an almost equally long history in using tests developed in one culture to gather data in other cultures, only recently have there been attempts to take great pains in using tests fairly and accurately across cultures. General treatments of issues and problems in cross-cultural testing can be found in the work of Norman Sundberg and Linda Gonzales (1981) and Walter Lonner (1981). The book edited by S. H. Irvine and John Berry (1983) contains more than 40 chapters dealing with numerous topics in human assessment across cultures. The six-volume *Handbook of Cross-Cultural Psychology* (Triandis, 1980) is a valuable source of information.

PRESENT STATUS

Earlier attempts to develop a truly culture-fair test failed mainly because it is not likely that a test that has been effective in the originating culture can be equally effective elsewhere. Rather than attempting to develop a Rosetta Stone in cross-cultural assessment, test developers and users have become more interested in developing useful other-culture norms or developing tests that are to be used *only* among one group. Others may share a skepticism that since tests work imperfectly in the originating culture even under ideal conditions, they should surely not be used cross-culturally. This point of view may have some merit, especially if formal assessment is being contemplated for a client from another culture where tests are rarely, if ever, used. However, many believe that human beings are much more similar than they are different and therefore should be able to be assessed on the same dimensions with respectable accuracy.

Following are some of the more important of many issues in cross-cultural assessment. One of the dominant issues is whether (and, if so, which) psychological constructs or concepts are universally valid. For example, "intelligence" or "introversion" or "passive aggressiveness" may be *generally* understandable everywhere. But it is possible that there are as many variations of these and all other constructs as there are cultural groups, none of them matching perfectly the original intent underlying the construct. The problem in testing and assessment, then, is to solve various problems of *equivalence* (see Lonner, 1981), so that comparisons or accurate diagnosis can be made in terms that are fair and meaningful for each culture.

Diagnosis itself is an assessment issue. To test or assess usually means that the person being tested is put into a specific category, perhaps through the use of the American Psychiatric Association's *Diagnostic and Statistical Manual of Mental Disorders* (DSM:III). Since DSM-III and most other classification systems are products of Western-dominated psychology and psychiatry, the possibility of inaccurate diagnosis and the resulting potentially tragic consequences of such errors continue to concern methodologists. Once a false label is attached to an individual through improper use of tests, it may perpetuate stereotypes and encumber someone with an inaccurate attribution of a psychological deficit.

SOME ISSUES, PROBLEMS, AND ASSUMPTIONS

1. *What level and type of assessment is indicated?* In counseling and psychotherapy, assessment begins the instant that contact between counselor and client is first made. Much information from and about a client can result from dialogue and observation. The skilled cross-cultural counselor may not need to proceed beyond a strictly verbal level of assessment, but even at the interview level some basic principles of testing can be applied. A *test* is a standardized measure of a sample of behavior. Consistent with this definition, the counselor should be certain that the client's behavior has been sampled adequately through the use of standard questions so that generalizations may be made about future behavior. Subsequent interviews (different samples of behavior over time) will enhance one's confidence in making generalizations.

In many cases, however, one may need data that can only be provided by standardized tests. For instance, a client (or counselor) may want to get an index of intelligence or abilities or a better picture of a personality pattern. Thus although tests might be indicated and even encouraged, a general rule of thumb in using standardized testing as an adjunct to counseling is that the deeper a counselor wants to probe into the "psyche" or cognitions of a client from another culture, the more likely that errors will be made unwittingly. A corollary to this rule is: the less the counselor knows of the client's culture, the more errors one might expect.

2. *Which tests are most useful and why?* Another rule of thumb in cross-cultural assessment is that it may be wise to select from a small number of the older and more widely used tests. There is safety in tradition, experience, the existence of extensive norms, and a literature addressing the test's strengths and weaknesses. Standard testing books (Anastasi, 1982; Cronbach, 1984; Sattler, 1982) can be consulted for more details, but in the sphere of intelligence testing the Wechsler series or the System of Multicultural Pluralistic Assessment (SOMPA) should be considered. In the personality domain, for clients above age 16, the Minnesota Multiphasic Personality Inventory (MMPI) and the California Personality Inventory (CPI) are good candidates because they have been used so widely with diverse groups. Clients may need career or educational guidance, and thus the popular Strong-Campbell Interest Inventory might be useful. However, their frequent usage does not make them automatically reliable and valid for all groups. These tests have also been translated into many languages. Projective methods to assess personality, because they rely so heavily on clinical inferences, should probably be avoided by the cross-cultural therapist unless the therapist can justify and defend their use in specific cases.

The assessment of neurological deficit or central-nervous-system dysfunction usually extends beyond the training of the cross-cultural counselor, but several excellent tests are available. Texts cited earlier can be consulted for more information about such specialized tests.

3. *Problems associated with test administration.* Most psychological tests are

culturally isomorphic (that is, they are consistent with expectations, educational practices, and so on in the test-originating culture). A client who deviates from this isomorphism may present a host of possible problems. Unfamiliarity with the nature and purpose of tests can penalize someone from the outset. Different ways of responding (response sets) as a function of cultural style (for example, agreeing with nearly everything since it may be impolite to disagree) may contribute to unreliability and hence reduce validity. The unavailability of test norms would pose yet another problem. Differences in temporal values can pose difficulties as well, an obvious problem with timed tests.

4. *Assumptions about the role of measurement in cross-cultural assessment and research.* Joseph Trimble, Walter Lonner, and Jerry Boucher (1983) specified three assumptions that have been at the basis of most psychological measurement: that all individuals (1) can rank stimuli along a linearly constructed continuum (for example, rating the concept of "country" on a seven-point scale); (2) can generate psychosocial judgments about social and psychological stimuli by using two comparative and contrasting cognitive mechanisms; and (3) are capable of self-assessment by using evaluative and reflective cognitive processes. These assumptions may not be warranted in many cultural or ethnic groups; yet tradition guides researchers along these lines. For these reasons, Trimble and his associates recommended the encouragement of creative but carefully construed alternatives to standard-assessment procedures.

5. *What are the ethical and legal responsibilities associated with cross-cultural assessment?* Depending on the test, there are different levels of preparation and competence required of test users. These restrictions are both promoted and endorsed by professional organizations such as the American Psychological Association. Likewise, most test manuals will indicate the level of competence required to use the test. We recommend that test consumers take very seriously the published guidelines regarding competency levels.

Related to these caveats are several recommendations, which are modifications of similar recommendations made by Sundberg and Gonzales (1981):

a. Study the culture of the person being assessed. Try to appreciate the "worldview" of people from that culture and to understand their coping strategies, kinship patterns, modes of thinking, and so forth.

b. Be aware that when placed in a role of a cross-cultural assessor, you are a potential source of unreliability and even unintentional bias. Being aware of one's ethnocentrism and becoming dislodged from it would tend to promote more objective assessment.

c. Develop skills for dealing with common culture-related behavior patterns. Becoming increasingly familiar with, for example, communication styles, deference to authority, religious and spiritual beliefs, and beliefs about causality will pay great dividends in cross-cultural assessment.

d. Do not "overculturalize." Although "culture" is very important in understanding any individual, it is not the only variable that influences human behavior. Culture-transcending factors that all people experience and that often lead to counseling—economic deprivation, uncertainties about the future, loss of a significant other, a serious illness, rapidly changing world events—are important in assessing a person. Through a common core of genuinely human concerns, a counselor can develop immediate rapport.

e. Do not "overassess." Any assessment device has its limitations. The relative merits of any anticipated assessment technique should be weighed against its negative characteristics for the purpose of enhancing accuracy and meaningfulness of assessment. If time is limited for assessment, the available time may be better spent interviewing rather than administering tests, questionnaires, or other tools. On the other hand, interviewing, too, often done in the privacy of an office, is subject to many cultural problems. The skilled assessor balances all factors in obtaining the information needed to achieve the purposes of the assessment.

FUNDAMENTAL THEORIES

A cross-cultural counselor may adopt any theoretical background; there is no shortage of counseling theory. There are, however, only a few radically different modes of thought and theory concerning the nature of the therapeutic-change process, all of which have their own assessment procedures. These modes derive mainly from Western cultures. A summary of four of them follows:

1. *Psychoanalysis and its derivatives.* Although this approach is less influential today than it was during the first half of this century, it has left an enduring legacy. This legacy includes, among other assumptions, that unconscious determinants of behavior are extremely important and that psychologically troubled individuals need an analyst to help them understand the nature of "intrapsychic conflict," which has its origins during the first several years of life. Assessment procedures commonly used are depth interviews, dream interpretation, and projective methodology.

2. *Behavioral approaches.* The behavioral framework emphasizes the situational specificity of all behavior. Assessment is tied in with this emphasis. Using this approach, one must identify particular culture-specific stimuli and reinforcements that are associated with these stimuli. Since little or no abstraction of complex theoretical explanations is needed in such a framework, assessment usually involves procedures that are as close as possible to the actual troublesome behavior in question. Thus a behaviorally oriented counselor would likely not use standard psychological tests.

3. *Phenomenological, humanistic viewpoints.* This approach emphasizes the inevitable subjectivity of behavior and places great emphasis on the phenomenology of "selfness." This growth-oriented, forward-looking approach does not typically employ formal assessment procedures; any assessment that is done recognizes self-perception, non-verbal aspects of behavior, and social expectations.

4. *Information-oriented approaches.* This perspective cannot boast a heavy research tradition and is atheoretical. It is simply a practical approach that op-

erates on the simple premise that many problems in cross-cultural counseling stem from a client's temporary inability to cope with a new situation. Thus an informational and educational process, which may involve some assessment of abilities and interests and aptitudes, leading to an increasing awareness of one's place in the new culture is the primary goal.

Regardless of which theory of counseling or psychotherapy, and hence assessment mode, is adopted, one must be concerned about its appropriateness for each "other-culture" client. Although some may argue that the psychodynamic legacy is universally applicable, that the behavioral strategy is similarly pancultural in its simplicity, and that the phenomenological-humanistic perspective is more suited to cultural relativism, others would argue against such categorization.

FUTURE DIRECTIONS

In the next 10 to 20 years all countries will witness an increase in ethnic diversity, abandoning the once-held "ideal" of cultural homogenization. In a shrinking world and growing population, one of the last bastions of individuality is the freedom to belong to a certain ethnic or cultural group. Cultural reaffirmation will grow.

With respect to assessment in cross-cultural counseling, how this cultural diversity is handled in the future will follow one of two profiles. The first profile can be described as status quo and deterioration in cross-cultural contacts. Disturbed over failures in equal opportunities and affirmative-action legislation, minority groups everywhere may feel disenfranchised and alienated. A "we-they" mentality, similar to the polarized viewpoints in the debate over racial differences in intelligence, could thrive under such an atmosphere. Increasing social distances between those in power and those struggling as an "underclass" would set the stage for a different assessment mode than would the second profile. This profile would paint a picture of increasing understanding of all people in a pluralistic world. Different-but-certainly-equal would guide interpersonal, intercultural relations, policy making, and assessment. The discovery, acknowledgment, and nurturance of culture-specific talents through assessment would be a high priority, and there would be genuine concern about the welfare of ethnic groups in their own communities. Assessment under this prosocial environment would be qualitative and flexible. Ability, values, and personality patterns would be described in a "wheel" format rather than a "ladder" format, the latter describing or creating a hierarchy.

REFERENCES

American Psychiatric Association (1980) *Diagnostic and statistical manual of mental disorders*, 3rd ed. Washington, D.C..

Anastasi, Ann (1982) *Psychological testing*, 5th ed. New York: Macmillan.

Cronbach, Lee J. (1984) *Essentials of psychological testing*, 4th ed. New York: Harper & Row.

Irvine, S. H. & Berry, John W. (Eds.). (1983) *Human assessment and cultural factors*. New York: Plenum.

Lonner, Walter J. (1981) Psychological tests and intercultural counseling. In Pedersen, P., Draguns, J., Lonner, W., and Trimble, J. (Eds.), *Counseling across cultures*, rev. ed. Honolulu: University Press of Hawaii.

Sattler, Jerome M. (1982) *Assessment of children's intelligence and special abilities*, 2nd ed. Boston: Allyn & Bacon.

Sundberg, Norman D. (1977) *The assessment of persons*. Englewood Cliffs, N.J.: Prentice-Hall.

Sundberg, Norman D., & Gonzales, Linda R. (1981) Cross-cultural and cross-ethnic assessment. In McReynolds, P. (Ed.), *Advancement in psychological assessment*, Vol. 5. San Francisco: Jossey-Bass.

Triandis, Harry C. (Gen. Ed.). (1980) *Handbook of cross-cultural psychology*, Vols. 1–6. Rockleigh, N.J.: Allyn & Bacon.

Trimble, Joseph E., Lonner, Walter J., & Boucher, Jerry D. (1983) Stalking the wily emic: Alternatives to cross-cultural measurement. In Irvine, S. H., & Berry, J. W. (Eds.), *Human assessment and cultural factors*. New York: Plenum.

Existentialism as a Cross-Cultural Counseling Modality

CLEMMONT E. VONTRESS

Existentialism can be traced to Socrates, who counseled humans to know themselves; to the Stoics, who advised them to master themselves and to confront destiny; to the teachings of Blaise Pascal of the seventeenth century; Friedrich Nietzsche of the nineteenth century; and Martin Heidegger, Jean-Paul Sartre, and Martin Buber of the twentieth century; and to the insights of many other thinkers who devoted their lives to conceptualizing and explicating the human condition (Mounier, 1947). It is a philsophy, not a psychotherapeutic theory; as such, it is the oldest and most radical of the healing arts (Koestenbaum, 1971).

Existentialism is also global in its view of humanity. That is, it takes a perspective that transcends cultural and national boundaries. As members of Homo sapiens, all humans are in the same predicament, regardless of their racial, ethnic, or national identities (Vontress, 1979). They live perforce simultaneously in three interacting environments: the *Umwelt* (natural environment), the *Mitwelt* (interpersonal environment), and the *Eigenwelt* (private, personal environment) (Binswanger, 1962, 1963). The cross-cultural-counseling enterprise can be understood by examining significant existential themes suggested by the environments. Many of these concepts have direct implications for the nature and conduct of the counseling encounter, diagnosis, recommendation-prognosis, intervention, and follow-up.

THE ENCOUNTER

The counseling relationship is an existential encounter in which two or more individuals meet to talk about the difficulties of moving through life. At least one of the interactants, usually referred to as the "client," is in need of advice, direction, support, or interlocution; another, generally called the "counselor," provides the help seekers with whatever existential insight is possible or beneficial at the time. Two ideas—psychotherapeutic eros and death—illuminate the nature of the encounter. Psychotherapeutic eros implies that the counselors should have affection for their clients simply because they are human (Boss, 1963). Philosophically, they love their clients as they love themselves, and although they may be worlds apart in terms of geographical origin and native culture, their feeling of sameness constitutes a human bond that transcends geography and culture.

Death, a key existential concept, serves as a relationship beacon for counselors. Individuals who recognize and accept their ultimate nonbeing are generally authentic, transparent, and courageous in efforts to bridge human differences (Caponigri, 1971). They are not afraid to be themselves or to expose their humanity. Racial, ethnic, and national differences are not denied or avoided. Instead, they, like life itself, are a challenge. The fact of death is the strongest motive and requirement for learning to be one with fellow humans (May, 1967). All who live must die; those who must die should live cooperatively and supportively with others. This attitude is essential for counselors. Those who try to disguise their feelings of racial, ethnic, or national superiority under a cloak of psychological mumbo jumbo deceive themselves, not their clients.

DIAGNOSIS

In diagnosing cross-culturally, counselors may use five key existential concepts as guidelines in defining client problems, their manifestations, and etiology. The first one is *Dasein*, which connotes that each person is a unique entity posited in the world to imprint a special contribution. Counselors aid clients best by helping them to discover the essence of their individualities and to find the courage to allow themselves to unfold to completeness.

Human epigenetic (biological and social) development is facilitated by three interacting environments—the *Umwelt, Mitwelt,* and *Eigenwelt*—as discussed by Binswanger (1962, 1963). Out of the progressive unfolding comes a sense of responsibility to nature, others (usually to nurturers and socializers), and self—product of nature and nurture. Therefore, responsibility is the second concept useful in diagnosing across cultures, because an individual's degree of responsibility to others and self is a measure of personal *raison d'être*.

The third concept is authenticity, which, according to James Bugental (1965), is a person's being in-the-world in accordance to one's true self. Authentic people do not deceive themselves about who they are, that is, their likes and dislikes or strengths and weaknesses (Flam, 1970). Indeed, knowledge of self is requisite to meaningful existence regardless of one's native culture. It is the road map that, if read carefully, tells each person how to fulfill personal uniqueness in life.

The fourth concept is meaning in life. The search for purpose, even when frustrated, is psychotherapeutic because it provides the searcher a reason for being (Frankl, 1967). As Victor Frankl (1962) pointed out, meaning can make the difference between life and death in difficult situations. It is important to find out from clients whether they have meaning in life and can identify its source and how consumed they are by it.

The fifth concept is existential anxieties or the illusive fear of proceeding through life as nature insists. When infants tumble into the world, they are charged with sufficient energy to get them through life. As adults, they have no recourse but to move toward their ultimate destination—death. Life means death. Those who deny this basic reality are usually immobilized, stuck, or indecisive in life. Instead of making good use of their time on earth, they stop, cringe, or hide, hoping that destiny will somehow pass them by.

These, then, are diagnostic guidelines that existential counselors may use advantageously in counseling all clients. The guidelines should not be used as yardsticks to judge normality. They reflect the human condition in general, not requirements and expectations of a particular culture.

RECOMMENDATIONS-PROGNOSIS

After diagnosing client conditions, counselors usually decide what ought to be done, why, by whom, and to what extent; that is, they make recommendations. They also predict outcomes of anticipated interventions. These expectations are called "prognoses." In reality, the two procedures are inseparable, because the helper should not consider implementing a therapeutic idea without simultaneously considering its consequences (Vontress, 1982).

In deciding courses of action and probable outcomes, cross-cultural existential counselors draw upon insights implicit in the Binswangerian concepts *Umwelt*, *Mitwelt*, and *Eigenwelt* (Vontress, 1979). First, it is important that helpers consider how the natural environment and client beliefs about it impact on people who are cultural products of specific geocultural settings. Failure to weigh the value of what is "natural" and therefore important to the client often invalidates recommendations and reduces the accuracy of predictions about the outcome of psychotherapeutic applications (Vontress, in press).

Clients are simultaneously products of nature and nurture. Although they are each endowed with a culturally transcendent uniqueness, they need the counsel of conspecifics, especially those with heightened existential awareness. As philosophers, existential counselors are among those who see the wholeness and reality of human existence. In helping fellow human beings decide what to do in life, they serve best by engaging them in a Socratic dialogue. The intent should be to help clients discover themselves, to act upon the knowledge of their discoveries, and to anticipate the outcomes of their actions. Since each person is transculturally unique, counselors should resist temptations to impose counselor solutions on their clients.

Recommendations are most effective and predictions most accurate when clients understand their inner beings. However, counselors should not participate in the exploration of the *Eigenwelten* (private worlds) of their clients as if they were isolated entities. Instead, helpers assist best by encouraging clients to examine closely their total existence, which takes place in the vortex of the *Umwelt, Mitwelt,* and *Eigenwelt.* Individual actors are necessarily centerpieces of all conditions, circumstances, and influences surrounding and affecting them as living organisms. They, as long as they are conscious, are free to take a stand toward whatever (Frankl, 1967).

INTERVENTION

Intervention is any action taken by the counselor to modify the client's situation (English & English, 1958). This means that encounter, diagnosis, and recommendations-prognosis are also aspects of intervention. Even so, there are no specific rules of conduct for existential counseling because it is not a curative process in the usual sense; it is a philosophic venture (Bugental, 1965). Instead of controlling, manipulating, or professionally distancing themselves from clients, existential counselors are close, concerned, but nonpossessive friends and guides. They receive clients from all racial, ethnic, and national backgrounds with psychotherapeutic eros and provide them the beginnings of a new support system in unfamiliar cultural surroundings.

In general, the more socially different the client's native culture is from the unfamiliar culture, the more that counselor support is needed. For example, international students from non-English-speaking African countries are apt to encounter more problems adjusting to or otherwise negotiating the American environment than students from Europe generally. American Hispanics, all other things being equal, encounter fewer problems on North American campuses than do students from American Indian or Afro-American communities. The type of family from which people come affects the degree of support needed in a new culture. People from extended families are accustomed to the love, concern, and influence of many significant others, especially elders of the group. Away from such environment, they long for the psychological buoyancy of customary surroundings. On the other hand, those from nuclear families in which individualism and self-reliance are encouraged are apt to get along fairly well without great need for external support. In large measure, differences in family styles are cultural. However, in addition to recognizing cultural differences, counselors, in deciding how much intervention is needed to help clients become self-reliant, should consider primary the uniqueness of the individual.

FOLLOW-UP

Follow-up, the review of intervention effectiveness, is especially important in cross-cultural counseling, because most counselors operate perforce on untested grounds, culturally speaking. Taking stock of work frequently enables them to make procedural corrections in working with specific clients and to develop a more effective overall approach to helping culturally different clients in general.

In ongoing relationships, counselors may begin each interview with a brief inquiry into the efficacy of previously implemented decisions. When relationships are successfully terminated, counselors should encourage clients to stay in touch to report their progress. Sometimes this may take the form of a counseling session; however, it is often a letter, card, or telephone call to let the counselor know how things are going. In general, "graduates" of existential counseling are "loyal alumni," who are eager to share their feelings of courage, self-direction, and self-reliance with those who assisted them to find their way in life.

CONCLUSIONS

Existential counseling is not counseling as usual. It is not a psychological enterprise but a philosophical venture. As philosophers, counselors take a panoramic view of human beings in the world. Although it is important to consider specific cultures and their impact on individuals socialized in them, it is more useful to become fully aware of the human condition. As members of the same species, individual members of Homo sapiens face conspecific and culture-specific problems simultaneously.

REFERENCES

Binswanger, L. (1962) *Existential analysis and psychotherapy*. New York: Dutton.
————— (1963) *Being-in-the-world: Selected papers*. New York: Basic Books.
Boss, M. (1963) *Psychoanalysis and daseinanalysis* (L. B. Lefebre, trans.). New York: Basic Books.
Bugental, J.F.T. (1965) *The search for authenticity: An existential analytic approach to psychotherapy*. New York: Holt, Rinehart & Winston.
————— (1969) Someone needs to worry: The existential anxiety of responsibility and decision. *Journal of Contemporary Psychology*, 2, 41–53.
Caponigri, A. R. (1971) *A history of Western philosphy, Volume 5: Philosophy from the age of positivism to the age of analysis*. Notre Dame, Ind.: University Press of Notre Dame.
English, H. G., & English, A. C. (1958) *A comprehensive dictionary of psychological and psychoanalytic terms: A guide to usage*. New York: McKay.
Flam, L. (1970) *La philosophie au tournant de notre temps*. Paris: Presses Universitaires de France.
Frankl, V. E. (1962) *Man's search for meaning: An introduction to logotherapy* (I. Lasch, trans.; preface by G. W. Allport; a newly revised and enlarged edition of *From death-camp to existentialism*). New York: Touchstone/Simon & Schuster.
————— (1967) *Psychotherapy and existentialism: Selected papers on logotherapy* (with contributions by J. C. Crumbaugh, H. O. Gerz, & L. T. Maholick). New York: Touchstone/Simon & Schuster.
Koestenbaum, P. (1971) *The vitality of death: Essays in existential psychology and philosophy*. Westport, Conn.: Greenwood Press, 1971.
May, R. (1967) *Existential psychotherapy*. Toronto: CBC Publications.
Mounier, E. (1947) *Introduction aux existentialismes*. Paris: Société des Editions Denoël.

Vontress, C. E. (1979) Cross-cultural counseling: An existential approach. *Personnel and Guidance Journal, 58,* 117–122.

——— (1982) Social class influences on counseling. *Counseling and Human Development, 14,* 1–12.

——— (in press) An existential approach to cross-cultural counseling. *Counseling and Values.*

Sex-Role Issues in Counseling Women and Men

L. SUNNY SUNDAL-HANSEN

In examining sex-role issues in counseling across cultures, a caveat is in order. It should be apparent that one cannot address such issues without looking at the economic, social, and political structure and context of a nation; the distribution of women and men in education and work; the influence of religion and tradition on sex roles; the stage of development of a culture and where it is on a continuum of change; and the stage of development of counseling and guidance in each nation. Awareness of the forces for and against change is essential in examining issues of changing sex roles.

It should also be pointed out that although sex-role issues pervade many aspects of life in both industrialized and rural nations, most of the theory, research, and development has emerged from Western cultures. Nonetheless, issues of women in development in Third World nations are gaining increased attention from government and international agencies. Sex-role issues in counseling women and men are a growing concern across cultures, although they often have been neglected in the past.

HISTORICAL BACKGROUND

Recognition of the differential experiences of women and men has begun to appear in the counseling and psychological literature of Western nations in the past 20 years, much of it in the area of educational-vocational or career counseling. Although most of the earlier theories and studies were about men and created by men, especially in vocational psychology, there has developed a new psychology of women and, even more slowly, a new psychology of men. New knowledge is gradually finding its way into counseling psychology programs and professional practices in schools, colleges, and agencies.

Many developments in the profession have begun in the United States, an understandable fact, since counseling has strong roots here. But in Western

European and North American nations especially, societal developments have contributed to a growing awareness of the changing role and status of women and a beginning awareness of impacts on the role and status of men. Among them is the U.N. Decade for Women (1976–85), which has stimulated many publications and much action to develop women's potentials in both industrialized and Third World nations. Although cause-effect is not always clear, the international women's movement has affected women's opportunities across cultures. The movement of women into the labor force, with 46 percent of the world's women economically active, has been cited by many as one of the most dramatic changes of the century. Global progress toward literacy, population control (along with equal access and pay and opportunity for use of talent) as well as reduction of poverty, violence, rape, battering, and abuse have much to do with counselors as facilitators of human development.

Several societal changes in Western cultures particularly have contributed to the new possibilities for multiple roles for men and women. Changes brought about by technology, such as labor-saving appliances, have made housework easier. Development of the pill has made it possible for women and men to control the timing and number of children. The cross-cultural movement for human and civil rights has produced a call for reducing the barriers and increasing the opportunities for those limited by race, sex, age, ethnicity, or handicap. Legislation providing not only equal opportunity for women but "equal status of the sexes," such as in Scandinavia, has provided legal mandates affecting both women and men and the work of the counselor, especially in schools and colleges. The increasing diversity within cultures due to immigration has called attention to the need for multicultural counseling and to sex-role differences within these cultures (see Part III in this book, especially the chapters of Elsie Smith and Oliva Espin).

STATE OF THE ART

A growing body of literature exists, particularly in the United States, on the new psychology of women and men. Although much of the early literature focused on the vocational psychology of men, studies of women tended to focus on role conflicts: traditionals and pioneers, homemakers and innovators. In the 1970s the literature began to focus on women's career development, sex-role stereotyping and socialization, criticism of traditional psychology and therapy, and sex bias in counseling and education. It is significant that gender issues have been reported primarily from a female perspective, with relatively little emphasis on male role issues. A number of special issues of the *Counseling Psychologist* were developed in the United States in the 1970s dealing with counseling men and women. Creative thinkers and researchers such as Mary Sue Richardson (1981), Joseph Pleck (1981), James O'Neil (1981), Helen Farmer (1978), Tom Skovholt and James Morgan (1981), and others have begun to study women and men's lives from a more integrative perspective.

On the international level, the literature seems to have addressed more specifically the issues of sex-role stereotyping and socialization, especially in schools.
A report published by the Council of Europe (1982) presents studies from an
international workshop held at Hønefoss, Norway, in 1981. Educational researchers found considerable evidence, both subtle and blatant, of stereotyping
in Western European schools and provided a working statement on how to reduce
it. A comprehensive study by John Williams and Deborah Best (1982) examined
sex stereotyping in 30 Western and Third World nations. It should be pointed
out that the sex-role literature is interdisciplinary, drawing from sociology, education, and labor economics, as well as psychology, with important implications
for counseling.

Reports from organizations such as UNESCO, the International Labour Organization, the Nordic Council, the Council of Europe, and government agencies
provide statistical information on the roles of women and men in education,
work, and family. Another important body of knowledge has emerged in feminist
therapy, a political-ideological approach to therapy with the express purpose of
effecting change in society rather than getting individuals to adjust to the society.
Edna Rawlings and Diane Carter (1978) are among those who have formulated
a philosophy of feminist therapy. A monograph UNESCO commissioned me to
do for North American and Western European cultures identified sex stereotypes
in textbooks and instructional materials, teacher-pupil interactions, educational-
vocational guidance and counseling, and organizational structures and policies.
It also presented illustrative strategies and innovative programs to try to eliminate
stereotypes (Sundal-Hansen, in press b).

Issues Affecting Counseling

What are some of the topics important to counselors in relation to sex-role
issues across cultures?

1. *Sex-role stereotyping and socialization.* An abundance of literature exists
on this topic, with a recognition that each culture ascribes certain roles to men
and women, resulting in both a male and female stereotype that often limits
development.

2. *Individual goals versus family and societal goals.* The importance of sex-
role issues in a culture is related to issues of individual choice versus role
prescriptions. Cultures in which traditional family values and loyalties predominate are less likely to be concerned about gender issues than those that promote
the individual development and potential of all persons. Whether the goal is self-
actualization or self-subordination to the family or society will affect the priority
given to sex-role concerns.

3. *Literacy and educational options.* Promotion of literacy, especially of women,
has been a major goal of the Decade for Women. Figures on the distribution of
women and men in subjects and majors in schools and colleges offer powerful

evidence of the differential experience of women and men in education and of educational segregation that leads to occupational segregation.

4. *Sexual division of labor*. Data compiled in both Western and Third World nations indicate that a clear division of labor exists, with stereotypes of women's work and men's work. Numerous national and international documents reflect, however, that individuals within and across cultures are insisting on a greater share in public life and in economic, political, and social opportunities. A number of factors already cited contribute to the growing participation of women in paid work. However, women still tend to be distributed in a few occupations, such as agriculture, teaching, textiles, and service, and mostly at low levels of pay, skill, and responsibility. Percentages of women in professional occupations like physician, engineer, and executive and in the trades continue to be small (with some variation across cultures).

5. *Men's changing roles in family*. Although the emphasis of the 1970s was on the changing roles of women, the 1980s are witnessing the beginning recognition of both the negative effects of male socialization and of the impact of women's role changes on men. As women's lives have been defined by family, men's lives have been defined by work. The male stereotype includes an expectation that boys will be strong, rational, athletic, and vocationally successful. This has led to less involvement of men in parenting and nurturing activities within the family. The sharing of roles between the sexes both at home and work is a phenomenon that has been stimulated by women's increased participation in paid work, as well as by an emerging men's awareness of their restrictive socialization.

6. *Degree of commitment to equality*. Whether a society is authoritarian or democratic has much to do with its commitment to equality of the sexes. But even within Western democracies there is a tremendous range of beliefs and practice in commitment to egalitarian roles and relationships in education, work, and family.

7. *Freedom of choice versus selection and placement*. Democratic societies give a great deal of lip service to developing each person to his or her full potential and helping individuals make choices that are satisfying and self-actualizing. Newly developed countries with major tasks of creating food, shelter, roads, hospitals, communication, education, and the like are more likely to select the most talented to be educated and prepared for jobs to help develop the society. In many developing countries, it is the men who are selected and trained, with women's primary role in the family and fields. The few choices available to women (mostly teaching) in countries such as Nigeria and Qatar illustrate this. The level of employment and unemployment also affects how many options are available and to whom.

8. *The rate of societal change*. It is important for a counselor to know where a culture is on the continuum of change. All cultures change, some faster than others, and it is necessary to understand the forces both for and against change

in a given society. An essential part of this is the place religion and tradition play in influencing sex-role norms and values.

All of these points are examples of the types of factors that affect counseling in diverse cultures. Most of them relate to external factors in the society.

ASSUMPTIONS AND RATIONALE FOR GENDER-AWARE COUNSELING

A number of assumptions undergird attention to sex-role issues in counseling across cultures. A first is that there are differences in the career development of women and men of which counselors need to be aware. That this is so has been acknowledged in numerous publications during the past 20 years, particularly in the United States. Louise Fitzgerald and John Crites (1980) pointed this out and Rita Rapoza and I emphasized women's unique experience in our book of readings on counseling and career development of women (1978). I have argued for a systems approach that focuses on both women and men (in press a). In their extensive review of the literature, Louise Fitzgerald and Nancy Betz (1983) presented compelling evidence of this differentiation.

A second assumption is that sex-role issues affect both women and men and that both sexes need to work on reducing the negative effects of stereotyping. Although many still perceive this topic as "women's issues," a growing body of literature by male psychologists and researchers is providing ample evidence of how sex-role issues affect men. The inordinate emphasis on male occupational success, in the United States in particular, creates sex-role conflict and strain, sometimes resulting in physical deterioration (Skovholt & Morgan, 1981). James O'Neil (1981) clearly described men's role strain caused by their rigid, early role socialization. He conceptualized six patterns of gender role conflict and strain: (1) control, power, and competition issues; (2) restricted sexual and affectionate behavior; (3) obsession with achievement and success; (4) homophobia; (5) restrictive emotionality; and (6) health-care problems. This point of view has not yet had wide acceptance but is being disseminated by a small group of male scholars who dare to challenge norms.

A third assumption is that sex-role stereotyping pervades society and affects all aspects of the culture, including work, family, education, and leisure. As mentioned, sex stereotyping is a topic that has had considerable exposure and acceptance in the cross-cultural literature. J. Williams and D. Best (1982) tested both children and adults, and suggested research supports cross-cultural similarities over cross-cultural differences in many areas of human personality and behavior. The five psychological needs always more highly associated with men than women were dominance, autonomy, aggression, exhibition, and achievement. The four needs more frequently associated with women were abasement, deference, succorance, and nurturance. Other publications by researchers in Western Europe and North America reflect recognition of the problem of sex stereotyping and efforts in many sectors, including counseling psychology and education, to try to eliminate it (Safilios-Rothschild, 1980; Holland, 1980).

A fourth assumption is that gender is a major factor in determining life roles and options. Elsewhere I have suggested that gender is one of the most neglected variables in career guidance and counseling. It is strange that gender, one of the most obvious characteristics about us, has been so ignored until recent years. Much of the popular vocational-guidance and career-planning literature simply does not attend to sex-role issues in educational-vocational choices or diverse work-family patterns. This may be an awareness problem that is just beginning to gain attention (Wilgosh, 1983; Pleck, 1981).

A fifth assumption is that the study of human development over the life span requires us to look at the differential experiences and perceptions of women and men at different life stages. New knowledge about adult development indicates that "the seasons of a woman's life" may be different from the "seasons of a man's life" with important implications for counseling interventions. Carol Gilligan (1982) suggested, for example, that issues of identity and intimacy are different for women and men. For men, identity usually precedes intimacy, whereas for women, identity and intimacy are often viewed together. In career counseling, men start developing a vocational identity early in life, with marriage and family concerns coming later; women often think about responsibility and caring and how choice of an occupation or work participation at all will affect marriage and family roles.

A sixth assumption is that several variables besides aptitudes, interests, and values have to be taken into account while attending to sex-role issues in counseling. Although they may be important for men, too, they are especially important for a woman. They include locus of control or sense of agency, a feeling of self-direction in her life; self-concept and self-esteem (how she sees herself and values herself) and family esteem; her achievement motivation, including drive and energy; her risk-taking characteristics and willingness to try activities or make choices nontraditional for her sex; her sex-role orientation, whether traditional or feminist or androgynous; her economic status and the extent to which she is at survival or self-actualization need levels; her work orientation and the importance of work and family in her value system; and her planfulness, taking responsibility for her life versus leaving things to fate. These things provide a broader context for counseling women than some of the more traditional therapies.

EMERGING THEORETICAL FRAMEWORKS

Much criticism exists of traditional counseling theories and practices and their impact on women. In particular, they are criticized for keeping women in traditional stereotypic sex roles; sexist use of psychoanalytic concepts; treating women as sex objects, including seduction of female clients; and bias in expectations and devaluation of women. In the vocational-career area, just as there are no complete theories of men's career development, there are no full-blown theories of women's career development. However, there are partial theories that appear to hold promise as more adequate explanations of male and female behavior and development. Although space precludes full descriptions of them, a few are mentioned here.

Mary Sue Richardson (1981) has used role theory in a clear explication of the intersection of work and family. Joseph Pleck (1981), who reviewed research on the male sex role since the 1930s, analyzed traditional male sex-role identity and presented a new paradigm of male sex-role strain, challenging "the myth of masculinity." Pleck also described the work-family system in which men traditionally have carried the provider role and women the nurturer role. Now women are moving into the work role and men (albeit more slowly) into the family role, necessitating role renegotiation and some stress. He believes these changes will transform women's and men's lives and the structure of society as a whole. Gail Hackett and Nancy Betz (1981), building on socialization theory, offered a theory of self-efficacy, suggesting that women's socialization does not lead them to expectations of competence as does men's.

In approaching sex-role issues, it is useful to employ a systems perspective, as a theoretical framework, of human issues and not only women's issues. A systems framework allows us to examine the whole and determine how change in one part affects other parts. It suggests that we need to look at not only the development and education of girls and women but of boys and men; not only at work but how work relates to family, education, leisure, and existential questions about the meaning of life; not only at the individual but at the culture and ways in which it makes decisions both for individual development and societal need. Such a framework also helps increase awareness of the conscious and subtle barriers, internal and external, that limit expectations, aspirations, choices, and behavior.

Part of this context is what J. Chetwynd and D. Hartnett (1978) called a "sex-role system." To understand this system, it is necessary to distinguish among several terms:

Sex-role system	The network of attitudes, feelings, and behaviors resulting from the pervasiveness of sex-role stereotyping in a culture.
Socialization	The process by which behaviors, roles, attitudes, and beliefs are transmitted to the next generation (for example, through family, schools, churches, media, peers).
Stereotypes	The characteristics, habits, abilities, and expectations assigned to people solely on the basis of group membership, regardless of their attributes as individuals. *Sex-role stereotypes* are beliefs concerning the general appropriateness of various roles and activities for women and men. *Sex-trait stereotypes* are psychological characteristics or behavioral traits believed to characterize one sex with much greater frequency than the other.

Sex-role ideology   A normative view of appropriate behavior of females and males,
                           that is, a view of what females and males "should" do.

Three factors of importance to the sex-role system are (1) the assignment of
the masculine and feminine stereotype, the former associated with traits of dominance, aggressiveness, and rationality and the latter with passivity, dependence,
emotionality, and subjectivity; (2) the allocation of different activities based on
sex into a sexual division of labor; and (3) valuing male characteristics more
than female (Chetwynd & Hartnett, 1978). The long-range outcomes of socialization and stereotyping are the sex typing of occupations and the educational
paths leading to them and a sex-segregated labor force based on women's work
and men's work and women's roles and men's roles as prescribed by the culture.
It is important for counselors to be aware of the sex-role system and specifically
sex-role and sex-trait stereotypes in the culture. because they do affect individual
development, educational-occupational opinions, mental health, and achievement of societal goals. The BORN FREE program (Hansen & Keierleber, 1978),
a developmental, counseling-based intervention to reduce stereotyping and expand options for both women and men from kindergarten to adulthood, was
conceptualized in a systems framework linking sex-role stereotyping and socialization, an expanded concept of career, and effecting educational and social
change through collaboration of teachers, counselors, parents, and community.

FUTURE DIRECTIONS

Although the 1970s saw considerable progress in attention to issues of the
role and status of women and equal access and opportunity, we have just begun
the process of change. Worldwide trends toward global interdependency also
have implications for sex roles. New knowledge and perceptions described in
Marilyn Ferguson's *Aquarian Conspiracy* (1980) and Fritjof Capra's *Turning
Point* (1982) provide a view of the future that values connectedness, caring,
compassion, creativity, and collaboration, characteristics often associated with
women. On the basis of the present analysis it seems likely that the following
will happen:

1. The international women's movement will continue to expand, followed by a slowly
   emerging men's movement, with an eventual synergy of women and men stimulated
   by global awareness of the need for total talent utilization to solve world problems.
2. Using a variety of industrial, group, and organizational strategies, counselors will
   develop awareness and new counseling and consultation skills to help individuals,
   couples, families, and institutions cope with strains brought about by inability to
   manage changing roles in changing societies. Increased mobility will require skills in
   helping individuals cope with norms and values different from their own.
3. New knowledge about the psychology of women and men and new ways of knowing

will provide a better base for theory building, program development, and professional practice.

4. New forms of sex-role-related counseling will emerge, such as multiple role, dual career, single parent, and equal partnership counseling, along with feminist therapy and nonsexist or sex-fair counseling. They will emphasize human potentials, work-family linkages, and role integration.

5. The universality of sex stereotyping will be recognized, along with the negative effects on both women and men. Eventually, sex-role issues will be seen as not just "women's issues" but as human issues, and men will begin to "own the problem."

6. Equality of the sexes will become a more accepted goal in Western countries, and many new interventions to eliminate stereotypes and develop positive attitudes and programs will be created. They will include greater awareness of subtle biases in education and counseling and development of community, government, and educational programs to promote equality.

7. In an increasingly technological and global society dominated by computers, telecommunications, and space exploration, counselors will need to offer a "high touch" balance to maintain the human concern and insure that both girls and boys have equal access to technology, training, and emerging occupational and life options.

It should be clear from this abbreviated discussion that there are many individual, societal, and cultural factors a counselor must be aware of to integrate adequately sex-role considerations into counseling. If counselors are to facilitate human growth and development, they need to understand the power of gender and culture in determining life options. They also need to develop positive practices and programs to reduce the stereotypes and negative consequences of rigid sex-role socialization that keep both women and men from becoming their authentic selves.

REFERENCES

Capra, F. (1982) *The turning point: Science, society and the rising culture*. New York: Bantam Books.

Chetwynd, J., & Hartnett, D. (Eds.). (1978) *The sex-role system*. London: Routledge & Kegan Paul.

Council of Europe, Secretariat (Ed.). (1982) *Sex stereotyping in schools*. The Netherlands: Offsetdrukkerig Kanters BV, Alblasserdam.

Farmer, H. (1978) Why women choose careers below their potential. In Hansen, L. S., & Rapoza, R. (Eds.), *Career development and counseling of women*. Springfield, Ill.: Thomas, pp. 118–131.

Ferguson, M. (1980) *The aquarian conspiracy*. Boston: Houghton Mifflin.

Fitzgerald, L., & Betz, N. (1983) Issues in the vocational psychology of women. In Walsh, W. B., & Osipow, S. H. (Eds.), *Handbook of vocational psychology*, Vol. 1. Hillsdale, N.J.: Erlbaum.

Fitzgerald, L., & Crites, J. (1980) Towards a career psychology of women: What do we know? What do we need to know? *Journal of Counseling Psychology*, 27 (1), 44–62.

Gilligan, C. (1982) *In a different voice: Psychological theory and women's development.* Cambridge, Mass.: Harvard University Press.

Hackett, G., & Betz, N. (1981) A self-efficacy approach to career development of women. *Journal of Vocational Behavior, 18,* 326–339.

Hansen, L. S. & Keierleber, D. L. (1978). BORN FREE: A collaborative consultation model for career development and sex-role stereotyping. *Personnel and Guidance Journal, 56* (7), 395–399.

Hansen, L. S., & Rapoza, R. (1978). *Career development and counseling of women.* Springfield, Ill. Thomas.

Holland, J. (1980) *Women's occupational choice: The impact of sexual divisions in society.* Reports on Education and Psychology. Stockholm: Stockholm Institute of Education.

O'Neil, J. (1981) Male sex-role conflicts, sexism, and masculinity: Psychological implications for men, women, and the counseling psychologist. *The Counseling Psychologist, 9* (2), 61–80.

Pleck, J. (1981) *The myth of masculinity.* Cambridge, Mass.: MIT Press.

Rawlings, E., & Carter, D. (Eds.). (1978). *Psychotherapy for women: Treatment toward equality.* Springfield, Ill. Thomas.

Richardson, M. S. (1981) Occupational and family roles: A neglected intersection. *The Counseling Psychologist, 9* (4), 13–23.

Safilios-Rothschild, C. (1980) *Sex-role socialization.* Washington, D.C.: National Institute of Education.

Skovholt, T., & Morgan, J. (December 1981) Career development: An outline of issues for men. *Personnel and Guidance Journal,* pp. 231–237.

Sundal-Hansen, L. S. (in press a) Gender and career. In Gysbers, N. A. (Ed.), *Designing careers: Counseling and the quality of work-life.* San Francisco: Jossey-Bass.

———— (in press b) *Eliminating sex stereotyping in schools.* Paris: UNESCO.

Wilgosh, L. (1983) Beyond counselling women: Some contemporary issues. *International Journal for the Advancement of Counselling, 6* (2), 125–134.

Williams, J., & Best, D. (1982) *Measuring sex stereotypes.* A thirty-nation study. Beverly Hills, Calif.: Sage.

Counseling and Psychotherapy: East and West

CHIZUKO SAEKI AND HENRY BOROW

HISTORICAL AND PHILOSOPHICAL PERSPECTIVES

For purposes of this discussion, the terms *counseling* and *psychotherapy* are used interchangeably. Although some writers choose to distinguish between the two by asserting that psychotherapy follows a more clinical emphasis and is more directly concerned with changing personalities, distinctions blur upon close examination. Both designations are widely applied to systematic attempts to assist individuals with problems of life adjustment and interpersonal relations. That formal practices of helping those in psychological distress have not been limited to the Western world is abundantly clear in the social histories of virtually all ethnic and cultural groups. In many societies such helping systems have emerged over time from elaborate networks of mores in the form of folk therapies.

However disparate systems of counseling may appear in method, they seem to be bound by certain stable universals. Each focuses on human maladaptive behavior, each is premised on the belief that something can be done to help the troubled party, each has an apparatus or ritual for providing relief from besetting conditions or a refreshed manner of perceiving them, and each offers a qualified mediator or interventionist to facilitate desired change. Also common to counseling systems everywhere is the logical sequence of operations they follow in pursuit of solutions. In general, all attempt to identify the problem, to establish a hypothesis or to set an explanation, and, finally, to chart a course for change.

Beyond these similarities lie striking divergences in the specific aims and maneuvers of psychotherapeutic schemes that reflect the cultures from which they derive. As W. Tseng and J. F. McDermott (1975) have observed, each treatment system, to be effective in its particular setting, must define cultural norms for the client, reinforce the coping behaviors that are culturally approved, and frame some form of time-limited respite from regular cultural demands as, for example, catharsis or isolation from an intolerably stressful environment.

Since the Eastern and Western worlds differ markedly in such societal parameters of counseling, the traditionally dominant modes of intervention in the two worlds will themselves be shown to differ in significant and pervasive ways.

Historically, the earliest conceptions of Western psychotherapy were rooted in supernaturalism. The religio-magical model of mental disorder that prevailed during ancient and medieval times interpreted this group of aberrations as spiritual sickness. The soul was believed to be afflicted through its possession by Satan or other evil spirits, and exorcism and other magical rites were commonly employed to rid the disturbed persons of unwelcome guests and, by so doing, to effect a "cure." Gradually, the shift from mysticism and the occult to naturalism as a means of accounting for events in the physical world expanded its influence to the psychological realm and adherence to demonology waned. However, resistance was tenacious to the adoption of naturalistic explanations of behavior and its anomalies, since human beings, unlike inanimate objects, were believed to be endowed with inscrutable spiritual properties that defied and even forbade mundane analysis. One is reminded that the Greek "psyche" carries the meanings both of soul and mind. Nonetheless, sweeping advances in the physical and life sciences, culminating in the emergence of the subscience of neurology, created a climate for an empirically based psychology that offered little place for supernatural conceptualizations of emotional disturbances and their treatment.

No comparable secularization of the psychotherapeutic process or detachment from its spiritual origins has occurred in Eastern societies. Enduring doctrinal disciplines, such as Hinduism and Taoism, are elaborate moral systems that set out the conditions of psychological and spiritual health and furnish detailed prescriptions for its attainment (Watts, 1961). The philosophy of Taoism, for instance, teaches that inner harmony requires acceptance of the axiom that human existence is an inseparable part of the universe. Similarly, the ascetic and meditative practices of Yoga are designed to consummate the soul's union with the Universal Spirit. The folk therapies so prominent in the cultural histories of northern Asia are associated with primitive religions that commonly postulate the existence of controlling spirits that can be influenced alone by the shaman or medicine man, someone endowed with special magical powers to traffic in the supernatural. Although shamanism has been found in many forms and in virtually all regions of the globe, its firm hold on the mental-health dogmata and practices of Eastern groups finds no close parallel in contemporary Western Europe or North America.

An examination of Asian personality theory offers useful insights into the Eastern conceptions of personal adjustment and its attainment through counseling. P. B. Pedersen (1977) identified a number of Asian precepts of personality development and maintenance that constitute the rationale for treatment approaches. Among them are the beliefs that the newborn infant brings with it certain traits from its previous lives and will subsequently carry them with it into its next existence; that proper social relationships far outweigh free-rein individualism in moral importance; that continuous dependency relations in the

Hindu tradition are requisite to the attainment of personal maturity; that the Japanese parental posture of self-sacrifice and unconditional love of the child nourishes the growing child's strong sense of loyalty to family honor; and that a strict authority relationship within the extended family may actually foster achievement-oriented personality development rather than hinder it as might be expected in Western nations.

Still other contrasts between Eastern and Western philosophical tenets contribute to an understanding of comparative counseling approaches. Whereas Western positions emphasize the uniqueness of the individual, self-assertion, and the strengthening of the ego, Eastern views champion interdependence, play down individuality, and teach the negation of self, the losing of oneself in the totality of the cosmos. Whereas Western philosophy encourages the learning of rational means to resolve emotional conflicts, Asian spiritual disciplines espouse the virtues of accommodating a harmonious union with the environment and of transcending conflict. Whereas the Western position advocates the strategy of changing objective reality to improve one's lot, Eastern philosophy promulgates a more passive acceptance of reality and the modification of one's perceptions of it and attitudes toward it (Reynolds, 1976).

THE ENDS OF PERSONAL COUNSELING: EAST AND WEST

The avowed objectives of Eastern and Western psychotherapies bear a predictable correspondence to the prevailing moral philosophies and life views of the cultures in which they are anchored. Thus although they appear to embrace certain universal elements of sound mental health, some goals of counseling can be shown to be culture-specific (Pedersen, 1981). American psychology and psychiatry emphasize outcomes associated with improved assertive coping, including changing the environment, changing one's own mastery behavior, and the reduction and management of stress. Asian counseling disciplines, on the other hand, more typically mirror the life values associated with the enlightenment of inner experience, interdependence, and acceptance of and harmony with one's environment (Murphy & Murphy, 1968). The aims of treatment in both worlds are linked to the attainment of the good life as defined in the respective dominant cultures. Eastern and Western systems both address the nature and control of intrapersonal conflict but do so in different ways.

The importance of fitting into society and fulfilling one's obligations are more commonly and pointedly identified with the psychotherapies of Asia, and one is unlikely to find among them any close agreement with the gestalt prayer that in part asserts, "I do my thing, and you do your thing. I am not in this world to live up to your expectations and you are not in this world to live up to mine" (Perls, 1969). Still, the improvement of interpersonal relations is an important goal of most, if not all, counseling systems in the Western as well as the Eastern hemisphere. An American position on mental health first published by the National Association of Mental Health in 1951, and since then widely circulated and cited, characterized people in good mental health as individuals who have personal relationships that are both satisfying and lasting, as respecting the many differences they find in others, as being able to feel part of a group, and as being motivated by a sense of responsibility toward their neighbors and fellow humans. Adlerian psychotherapy is consistent with the Asian emphasis in viewing man as a whole and in helping troubled clients refocus their competitive striving for superiority as a humanely based altruism. A contemporary American treatment system, reality therapy, likewise stresses the aims of social commitment, connectedness, and improved interpersonal relationships.

Morita therapy, a prominent treatment mode of Japanese origin, illustrates how counseling aims may flow from religious and moral philosophy. Rooted in the spiritual discipline of Zen Buddhism, Morita therapy emphasizes the passivity-oriented goal of *arugamama*, that is, learning to accept reality and to take it as it is. Naikan therapy, in pursuing the aim of deepening the client's sense of gratitude for the succor and sacrifice of significant others, draws heavily on a value system that affirms the preemptive importance of family attachments and obligations. Other examples of culture-specific-treatment aims in Eastern societies are provided by shamanism, divination, and the folk therapies that frequently dwell on liberating the tormented seeker of help from hostile supernatural forces or interpreting to the client the meaning of occult signs so that he or she might better know what course to follow.

COMPARATIVE TREATMENT STRATEGIES-ORIENTATIONS

Not only the purposes of counseling but its methods as well are to be understood only within the particular sociocultural settings in which it is practiced. In the Western world psychology was the last empirical-knowledge discipline to detach itself from the mother science of philosophy. It did so with self-conscious determination and zeal, bent on finding acceptance among the family of well-established and respected physical and life sciences. Clinical-counseling psychology, as an emergent applied branch of the knowledge field, was heavily influenced by the medical model of mental illness and, over time, adopted the scientist-practitioner paradigm in dealing with its distressed clients. Psychotherapy, like other segments of basic and applied psychology, proclaimed its allegiance to objective observation and the quantification of data, and it devised standardized psychometric instruments to implement this pledge. Although diverse assumptions underlie the broad spectrum of Western psychotherapies, they may in general be described as rational-empirical in approach, concerned with diagnosis and classification of disorders and wedded to the conviction that the understanding and treatment of psychological problems are best served by resort to a useful theory of behavior.

By contrast to the treatment modes of Western-styled counseling, traditional Eastern methods, particularly those identified with religious systems and the folk therapies, tend to rely on intuitive, magically revealed explanations of disordered conduct and not on naturalistic, cause-effect accounts. They draw more upon holistic, molar views of the person and eschew analytical, atomistic approaches and preoccupations with behavior typologies. Notably absent on the Eastern scene are instances of established psychotherapies linked to sophisticated personality theory, such as social-learning theory. Given this lack, one does not expect to find among Asian methods the routine use of milieu therapy, deliberate social modeling, or the assignment of practice exercises as client homework of the type seen in Western cognitive-behavioral counseling and rational-emotive therapy. Furthermore, candidates for counseling in Asian settings are more likely to accord high authoritarian status to their therapists and are disposed to anticipate fairly direct and conclusive advice for handling their personal difficulties. The shamans and prophets of the folk therapies are often ascribed certain specified occult powers and an omniscience or infallibility rarely if ever identified with Western healing practitioners. In Korea, Taiwan, and Singapore, where the family clan system is dominant, a shaman may attempt to free an emotionally troubled client from the haunted attention of a deceased relative's spirit by magically arranging himself to be possessed by that afflicting spirit. The shaman may also decide to dispose of a problem by arranging a "ghost marriage" between his distressed male client and the spirit of an unmarried deceased female relative. In the primitive traditional psychotherapies of the East, the burden falls principally upon the healer to find solutions. His client is the more passive recipient of counsel and cure.

W. Tseng and J. F. McDermott (1975) noted the presence of certain core elements of psychotherapy in all counseling systems and settings irrespective of differences in orientation and technique. These elements include the client's prior expectations about the treatment process, the therapist's personality, and the ambience of the therapeutic operation. What seems clear is that any counseling proceeds more effectively when its methods are compatible with the expectations and beliefs that stem from the client's sociocultural experience; when the personal style and bearing of the therapist are conducive to the client's feelings of comfort, trust, and confidence; and when the surroundings and atmosphere are appropriate to the purpose of the encounter. Examples of the third condition are the shaman's distinctive raiment, which betokens his special powers and the psychologist's office accouterments and the framed license adorning his wall.

ASSESSING COUNSELING OUTCOMES

Puzzling to pragmatic contemporary Western psychotherapists is the seeming indifference of Eastern practitioners to testing the efficacy of their product. Yoga, Naikan therapy, Morita therapy, and, in their own way, the folk therapies are internally consistent logical systems that are self-validating. If one accepts their postulates, usually untestable, about the metaphysics of existence, and if one can be assured that the treatment ritual has been carried out in stringent conformity with the prescribed formula, it may then be said that each such system possesses an a priori validity and that it produces the results claimed for it. Despite this line of reasoning, Western-initiated insistence of proof of effectiveness has stimulated a few attempts at evaluation studies, particularly with Naikan therapy. Such research has been marked by soft data, inadequate experimental controls, and excessive reliance on clients' subjective reports of behavior change (Tanaka-Matsumi, 1979). Similarly, claims made about the hygienic effects of transcendental meditation upon physiological functioning, that is, lowered blood pressure, appear to have been based on studies with insufficient control over confounding variables. However, Western-oriented research on the validation of psychotherapy has also been controversial. Although recent summaries of published outcome studies have concluded that the average client shows greater improvement than untreated neurotics, numerous questions remain about which methods work best with which clienteles and for what reasons.

CAN NATIVE PSYCHOTHERAPIES BE TRANSPLANTED?

Owing in part to their vastly different philosophical bases, Asian and Western systems of psychotherapy operated for decades in almost mutually exclusive spheres of influence. Jungian analysis, unlike classical Freudian psychoanalysis, regarded the unconscious, particularly the collective or racial unconscious, as creative and trustworthy, and in this sense Jung's position was close to the Eastern notion of the individual's union with humanity, past, and present. Eric Fromm and D. T. Suzuki collaborated on a comparative treatise of Zen Buddhism and psychoanalysis. With these exceptions, few serious attempts were made to find common ground between East and West. Since midcentury, however, modern Western counseling approaches have been introduced into Japan, South Korea, Taiwan, and other Eastern countries, and concurrently, Eastern therapies have attracted increased attention in the United States and Western Europe.

How thoroughly have these movements been assimilated into their new cultural settings? There may be cause for skepticism. Although psychoanalysis, client-centered counseling, certain group therapies, and the diagnostic techniques of contemporary clinical psychiatry and clinical psychology have been adopted by some professional practitioners in the hospitals and clinics of technologically developed Asian nations, and although their professional journals publish Western-oriented theory and research papers, it is doubtful whether Western approaches fit the existing value structures. They have yet to achieve widespread acceptance or to make significant inroads upon indigenous conceptual systems.

In the United States existential forms of counseling have enjoyed a notable growth in interest, in part because they appear more relevant to the needs of individuals who experience social alienation and search for new life meanings. Zen, transcendental meditation, and the so-called human-potential movement are examples of adoptive approaches that emphasize inner experience and expanded self-awareness. But here, too, some writers have doubts about the genuineness of the new attachments. H. Cox (1977) found that young Americans who are part of the neo-oriental religious revival are generally disenchanted middle-class and upper-middle-class, educated, urban whites who are looking uncritically for authority and who "seek a kind of immediacy they have been unable to find elsewhere" (p. 39). Cox interpreted the conversion decision as being more a symptom of a societal malaise than a remedy for troubled minds.

What of the future? It seems reasonable to anticipate that transactions between East and West, as they explore one another's counseling forms, will continue and that a selective sorting and adopting of principles and techniques appropriate to the respective cultures will occur. Should that happen, the psychotherapies of both East and West will have attained a new maturity.

REFERENCES

Cox, H. (1977) "Why young Americans are buying oriental religions." *Psychology Today*, *11*, 36–42.

Murphy, G., & Murphy, L. B. (1968) *Asian psychology*. New York: Basic Books.

Pedersen, P. B. (1977) Asian personality theory. In Corsini, R. J. (Ed.), *Current personality theories*. Itasca, Ill: Peacock.

——— (1981) The cultural inclusiveness of counseling. In Pedersen, P. B., et al. (Eds), *Counseling across cultures*, rev. ed. Honolulu: University Press of Hawaii.

Perls, F. S. (1969) *Gestalt therapy verbatim*. New York: Bantam Books.

Reynolds, D. (1976) *Morita psychotherapy*. Berkeley: University of California Press.

Reynolds, D. K. (1980) *The quiet therapies*. Honolulu: University Press of Hawaii.

Tanaka-Matsumi, J. (1979) Cultural factors and social influence techniques in Naikan therapy. *Psychotherapy: Theory, research, and practice*, *16*, 385–390.

Tseng, W., & McDermott, J. F. (1975) Psychotherapy: Historical roots, universal elements, and cultural variations. *American Journal of Psychiatry*, *132*, 378–384.

Watts, A. W. (1961) *Psychotherapy East and West*. New York: Pantheon Books.

Cross-Cultural Counseling with Afro-Americans

GERALD G. JACKSON

The categorization of Homo sapiens by racial, rather than cultural, differences is a psychological mindset that has obfuscated a cross-cultural perspective of counseling Afro-Americans. Historically, Africans and then Afro-Americans, as the history of American psychiatry and social work confirms, were ostracized on the basis of a classification system that dichotomized groups into civilized and uncivilized categories. Defined as uncivilized, Afro-Americans were subsequently segregated from the Euro-American mentally ill, diagnosed according to social conventions, restricted to Euro-American therapists, and given eurocentric forms of mental-health treatment. As one consequence, "cross-cultural" has historically connoted for Afro-Americans the meaning of confrontation with and isolation from the Euro-American mental-health establishment.

During the Black Solidarity movement of the 1960s, a new connotation of "cross-cultural" emerged to challenge the assumptions of a eurocentric definition of counseling as color blind. Premier in this regard, Clemmont Vontress, through his germinal publications and provocative conference presentations, revealed the importance of cultural factors and racial attitudes to counseling visible minority groups. In retrospect, he was the father of a black perspective of counseling and instigator of intra-cultural counseling.

During the 1970s, stimulated by the Pan-African ideology of the 1960s, an africentric school of thought emerged to expand and consolidate the ideas promulgated by pioneers such as Vontress. My attendance at an Afro-American mental-health conference in 1974 stands out in my mind as the bedrock of this school and its cross-cultural denotation of counseling Afro-Americans. Most notable at this conference were the thoughts and theories of Na'im Akbar, Edward Nichols, Ivory Toldson, Frances Welsing, Robert Williams, and Bobby Wright. Where they departed in thinking from Afro-American conventional wisdom was in their affirmation of an African cultural connection in the design and implementation of counseling and psychotherapy.

Since then I have learned that there are several eurocentric beliefs and assumptions that have obviated the adoption of a cross-cultural outlook. These beliefs are that humankind consists of well-defined races, as opposed to cultural enclaves; that some races are superior to others; that superior races should rule over the inferior ones; and that attempts should be made to insure that racial-superiority beliefs are put into practice. The corollary of these beliefs are the following assumptions: (1) The world dominance of Europeans is the consequence of the evolution of the most fit to lead (social Darwinism). (2) Africans were an uncivilized group before Europeans enlightened them (colonialism). (3) The behaviors, beliefs, and attitudes of Afro-Americans are solely the consequence of an Euro-American cultural and philosophical tradition (dichotomism). (4) African culture and philosophy had no redeeming qualities upon which to base the solution of contemporary problems (ignominious past hypothesis). (5) The Western tradition of Cartesian logic is the only rational means for interpreting reality; therefore, it is the only basis upon which a system can be devised for counseling Afro-Americans.

Consistent with the preceding assumptions, the black perspective of counseling confined its analysis to Anglo-American history and focused its criticisms and recommendations on problems of immediate importance to Afro-Americans. Many Afro-American writers alleged that the source of the problem of counseling Afro-Americans was the basic orientation of counselors to focus on the individual, to the exclusion of environmental factors, and to rest their practices on racist beliefs about Afro-Americans. As a consequence, it was proposed that an environmentally focused model be used with Afro-Americans. Similarly, counselors and counselor-educators were instructed to change their culturally deprived definition of Afro-Americans, system-maintenance concept of counseling goals and objectives, Anglo-American way of interacting with Afro-Americans, and middle-class expectations and beliefs about intelligence, language, family, personality development, community, and American society.

Exponents of a black perspective of counseling reacted to the implicit assumption in the eurocentric outlook of white racial superiority and countered that they were superior to other racial groups in providing counseling and training for Afro-Americans, had a sub-culture upon which to predicate counseling theories and practices, and should, as a result of these sui generis factors, be in positions of authority.

Despite the claims made by a number of Afro-American writers, no encompassing theory of orientation emerged from their works to explain behavioral and cognitive differences among Afro-Americans and Euro-Americans, Hispanic Americans, and African and Caribbean immigrants. The trend has been to be either eclectic in the advocacy of counseling theories and techniques or, in the case of Afro-American behavior therapists, to endorse overtly the theory and techniques of behavior therapy and suggest covertly that the user employ an Afro-American cultural referent.

The overall failure of a black perspective to devise a counseling system that

included the Afro-American social experience and sub-culture was not a manifestation of deficit analytical skills but the result of the temporal framework used
and the consequent tendency to be reactive instead of proactive in thrust. In
short, the eurocentric approach and its black perspective derivative both lacked
a system that would allow for an appreciation of group differences, the centrifugal
force in counseling Afro-Americans.

As an alternative, in this chapter an attempt is made to illustrate how an
africentric framework facilitates an appreciation of group differences. Its assumptions are that cross-cultural counseling has not occurred with Afro-Americans, because Euro-Americans and a sizable proportion of Afro-American
counselors are unaware of the cross-cultural aspect of the process of counseling
Afro-Americans; that even when they are conscious of behavioral differences
between Afro-Americans and Euro-Americans, their racial socialization and academic training constrains them to perceive the physical attributes and cognitive
style of Afro-Americans in a negative, unefficacious, or romantic way; that there
is an Afro-American cognitive style, and it is based, in part, on the continuation
of an African ethos that must be recognized as legitimate; and that there is no
traditional Euro-American school of counseling or psychotherapy that can be
applied uniformly to all Afro-Americans.

In general, an africentric way of thinking went beyond the crystallization of
a black perspective of counseling (Jackson, 1976a). It opened the door to an
africentric psychology (Jackson, 1976b), upon which to sustain a theory of
counseling and psychotherapy (Jackson, 1976b), and provided a framework to
assess extant systems and approaches (Jackson, 1976b, 1979b). Correlatively,
it provided new interpretations and definitions of black self-concept, personality,
family, mental-health research, psychopathology (Jackson, 1976b, 1982), and
furnished alternative explanations for the success of certain approaches and
techniques with Afro-Americans (Jackson, 1972a, 1972b). Most central to the
underlying issue of racial difference in counseling, it provided a framework for
interpreting clashes between Afro-American and Euro-American professionals
along cultural rather than racial lines (Jackson, 1979c).

As a backdrop, several africentric theorists have made the following observations of differences between Afro-Americans and Euro-Americans. They noted
that Afro-Americans tended to perceive events as a whole visual picture (symbolic
imagery), whereas Euro-Americans tended to perceive reality through a theoretical statement that broke down things and people into parts (discursive reasoning). Afro-Americans tended to prefer inferential reasoning, based upon
contextual, interpersonal, and historical factors; and Euro-Americans preferred
either inductive or deductive reasoning, based upon a belief in the permanency
of the stimuli. Afro-Americans preferred to approximate space, numbers, and
time, based upon an affectively based dialectical system, which was in contrast
to Euro-Americans, who tended to prefer precision, based upon a concept of
one-dimensional time and objective space between individuals. Afro-Americans
preferred to focus on people and their activities, based upon a nature-centric

orientation and human-nature norm, as opposed to Euro-Americans, who showed a propensity toward things, based upon a eurocentric orientation and middle-class, male, Caucasian norms. Afro-Americans, based upon an axiology of cooperation, preservation of life, affiliation, and collective responsibility, had a comparatively keener sense of justice and were quicker to analyze it and perceive injustice than were Euro-Americans, based upon their valuation of competition, conflict, control of life, ownership, and individual rights. Afro-Americans were viewed as relatively more altruistic and concerned about the next person, based upon an ontology of spiritual essence, collectivism, interdependence, and oneness of being, than were Euro-Americans, based upon their belief in material essence, individualism, independence, and control of nature. Afro-Americans, based upon an epistemology of affect, immersion in experience, flexibility, and comple-mentarity of differences, preferred novelty, freedom, and personal distinctiveness to a greater degree than did Euro-Americans, based upon their belief in object-measure, observation of experiences, rigidity, and duality of differences. Finally, Afro-Americans, based upon a multimodal definition of the communication proc-ess, were more proficient in nonverbal communications and were less word dependent than were Euro-Americans (ebonics versus standard English).

The genesis of the preceding group differences is revealed in C. Diop's (1974) "Two Cradle Theory" of cultural differences between Aryans and Africans. He theorized that each group had distinguishable cultural differences based upon climatic and physical environment factors. Aryans evolved a patriarchal system that consisted of the suppression of women, materialist religion, sin and guilt, xenophobia, the tragic drama, city-state, individualism, pessimism, and a pro-pensity for war. In contrast, Africans had a less harsh climate, and it fostered a matriarchal system that consisted of the freedom of women, religious idealism, the tale as a literary form, no concept of sin, xenophilia, the territorial state, social collectivism, optimism, and a desire for peace.

Rather than accept the cultural differences, J. Kovel's (1970) research revealed that Europeans rejected African culture and the physical characteristics of Af-ricans. J. Hodge, D. Struckmann, and L. Trost (1975) took the notion of white racism a step further and showed how it was the consequence of a Western philosophical system. Mental-health theoreticians and practitioners, as the work by C. Willie, B. Kramer, and B. Brown (1973) documents, endorsed, supported, and advanced the supposition that Afro-Americans had no culture other than that which they gained from exposure to Europeans. The field of counseling, the black backlash in mental health, and the emergence of a black perspective of counseling illustrate and attest to the extension of the non-European cultural-antecedent hypothesis to their theories, perceptions, and practices with Afro-Americans (Jackson, 1977, 1979a).

Relatedly, the *raison d'être* and development of multimodal-behavior therapy illustrate why traditional counseling and psychotherapy missed the cultural mark. Arnold Lazarus started as a behavior therapist, subsequently devised a structure he termed *technical eclecticism*, and ultimately created a conceptual framework to dovetail with the multiple modalities he perceived in the conduct of counseling and psychotherapy. Traditional systems, he demonstrated, focused either on the cognitive or behavioral modalities, sometimes both, but seldomed encompassed behavior, affect, sensation, imagery, cognition, interpersonal relationship, and drugs (Lazarus, 1976).

To illustrate further, J. Berman (1979) conducted a study to determine if racial and sex-gender factors influenced the diagnosis of counseling problems. To assess the two variables, she used an individual-societal continuum and videotapes of culturally varied client vignettes. No sex-gender difference was found; however, in terms of racial difference, the Euro-Americans' diagnoses were almost exclusively individual, and the Afro-Americans' were a more equal distribution of individually and societally focused responses. Similarly, H. Gilliam and S. Van Den Berg (1980) sought to determine if a cultural difference existed between Afro-American and Euro-American college students in the interpretation of eye contact. He found that both groups reported that they felt comfortable with the confederate when he maintained normal eye contact and rated him attentive; however, when the confederate avoided eye contact, the Euro-American subjects rated the confederate lower in attentiveness and indicated that they felt less comfortable. The researcher concluded that the Afro-American low eye-contact protocol might result in Afro-American students being perceived as inattentive and job applicants as uninterested.

What is noteworthy is that in both studies the Euro-Americans dichotomized situations that did not have to be defined in either/or terms. More telling, in the second study the researcher reconstructed the data to conform to a dichotomy. The Afro-American mode that they interpreted to mean low eye contact, in actuality, consisted of a similar rating for the low and high eye-contact situations.

The capacity to define external events and people in a complementary rather than dichotomous fashion has been termed *diunital* logic and has been said to be a characteristic mode of Afro-American thinking that emanates from their West African cultural roots. For example, I. Van Sertima (1976) documented how Africans preceded Columbus's journey to America, and history revealed how no massive invasion ensued. M. Bradley (1978) chronicled, on the other hand, the uniquely aggressive tendency of Europeans to visit foreign lands and establish dominance. The key, as the behavior of Africans in the diaspora reveals, was the use of syncretism as an adaptational mode.

Some theorists have proposed that the behavioral and cognitive differences between Afro-Americans and Euro-Americans is bio-genetically based. Such individuals have a degree of kinship with sociobiologists; however, the more popular outlook is based upon a cerebral-dominance theory. One argument posited that Afro-Americans were conditioned, through a form of social engineering, to use only the right hemisphere of their brain (for example, intuitive, abstractive, nonverbal, creative, passive, less accessible to scientific inquiry); whereas Euro-Americans were socialized by their culture and its institutions to use their left (for example, linear, verbal, mathematical reasoning, aggressive, nonwholistic).

Another argument postulated that the use of the right hemisphere was based upon African cultural tradition. In reality, the cerebral dominance construct simply strengthened conceptualizations already advanced by social scientists, philosophers, and humanists. From these sources it can be gleaned that the Afro-American culture is associative, aesthetically oriented, oral, nonverbally oriented, polychronic, and affective. In contrast, Euro-American culture has been characterized as abstractive, theoretically oriented, literate, verb oriented, monochronic, and cognitive. Using diunital logic, I concluded, after reviewing and analyzing the works of Afro-American social scientists and humanists, that, if anything, the evidence suggested that Afro-Americans used both hemispheres (Jackson, 1979c).

Carried a step further, it is advanced that diunital thinking permeates the counseling process with Afro-Americans and explains the ambivalence in the literature on the race of the counselor, techniques, schedules, physical setting, objectives, and goals. One can describe diunitality, but really to fathom it, one must be familiar with the African language structure, philosophy, and culture that supported its use.

To illustrate its practice further, I am both optimistic and pessimistic about the future. Several trends give some indication of convergence between africanity and traditional approaches to research, counseling, and psychotherapy. The movement toward contextualism in the field of developmental psychology, the emergence and expansion of the field of environmental psychology, the theory of "dialectical time," and the elaboration of Lazarus's multimodal therapy system portend conceptual advances that are in concert with africanity. Relatedly, the cross-cultural research and training paradigm emerging from the work of Paul Pedersen and the Cross-Cultural Training Institute in Miami heralds a way of putting concepts and theories of africanity into practice.

My pessimism stems from the following realities. First, the cognitive style governing Afro-American behavior does not lend itself to full comprehension through the written word, the cornerstone of traditional counseling. Second, Western indices that result in the classification of an individual as Afro-American and the acquisition by such individuals of professional degrees do not, in the mind of the average Afro-American, qualify such persons to be cross-cultural brokers, and traditional guidelines for selection have not emerged. Third, there is more face validity for the beliefs and assumptions of the eurocentric perspective; therefore, even though an africentric cognitive style may have demonstrable utility, its adherents do not control the reinforcement contingencies that could result in cross-cultural communication and counseling.

REFERENCES

Berman, J. (1979) Individual versus societal focus: Problem diagnoses of black and white male and female counselors. *Journal of Cross-Cultural Psychology, 10*, 497–507.
Berry, J. (1976) *Human ecology and cognitive style*. New York: Russell Sage Foundation.

Bradley, M. (1978) *The iceman inheritance*. New York: Warner.

Diop, C. (1974) *The African origin of civilization* (M. Cook, trans.). Westport, Conn.: Lawrence Hill. (Original work published 1955).

Gilliam, H., & Van Den Berg, S. (1980) Different levels of eye contact. *Urban Education, 15*, 83–92.

Goldsby, R. (1971) *Race and races*. New York: Macmillan.

Hodge, J., Struckmann, D., & Trost, L. (Eds). (1975) *Cultural bases of racism and group oppression*. Chestnut Hill, Mass.: Two Riders.

Jackson, G. (1972a) Black youth as peer counselors. *Personnel and Guidance Journal, 51*, 280–285.

———— (1972b) The use of roleplaying job interviews with job corps females. *Journal of Employment Counseling, 9*, 130–139.

———— (1976a) The African genesis of the black perspective in helping. *Professional Psychology, 7*, 292–308.

———— (1976b) Is behavior therapy a threat to black clients? *Journal of the National Medical Association, 68*, 362–367.

———— (1977) The emergence of a black perspective in counseling. *Journal of Negro Education, 46*, 230–253.

———— (1979a) *Community mental health, behavior therapy, and the Afro-American community*. ERIC Document Reproduction Service No. ED 159 501.

———— (1979b) The origin and development of black psychology: Implications for black studies and human behavior. *Studia Africana, 1*, 270–293.

———— (1979c) The roots of the backlash theory in mental health. *Journal of Black Psychology, 6*, 17–45.

———— (1982) Black psychology: An avenue to the study of Afro-Americans. *Journal of Black Studies, 12*, 241–260.

Kovel, J. (1970) *White racism: A psychohistory*. New York: Vintage.

Lazarus, A. (Ed.). (1976) *Multimodal behavior therapy*. New York: Springer.

Van Sertima, I. (1976) *They came before Columbus*. New York: Random House.

Willie, C., Kramer, B., & Brown, B. (Eds.). (1973) *Racism and mental health*. Pittsburgh: University of Pittsburgh.

Cultural Identity in the Treatment Process

JANET E. HELMS

Since the early 1970s, discussants and researchers have called into question the use of traditional psychological theories for predicting the responses to personal counseling of Asian-American, black American, Hispanic American, and Native American clients. Underlying their arguments is the contention that traditional theories do not adequately take into account those unique cultural experiences of these groups that are likely to influence group members' personal adjustment. Nevertheless, alternative culture-specific theoretical perspectives have been slow to develop, and as a consequence, mental-health practitioners are left with little direction for their interventions.

One component of treatment planning is *diagnosis*, the delineation of the characteristics and etiology of the client's problem for the purpose of providing prescriptive treatment. Although efforts to integrate cultural variables into the diagnostic process have been varied, one of the more interesting and controversial approaches involves those models that attempt to use the client's cultural or racial identity for diagnostic purposes. In general, these models propose that, in response to discrimination and/or racism in American society, members of minority groups develop strategies for coping with their minority-group status, and the manner in which they come to cope becomes an important part of their personal identity.

It is difficult to talk about theoretical ancestors of the cultural identification models because present-day theorists seem to have developed their conceptual schemata independently of one another and with no awareness that the others existed. Nevertheless, Gordon Allport (1958) can probably be credited for contributing to an intellectual atmosphere in which it became somewhat acceptable to theorize about the effects of racism and prejudice on their victims. The civil rights movements of the 1960s can be acknowledged for awakening mental-health professionals to the possibility that cultural issues that had been ignored in society in general had also been ignored in the counseling process.

Based on anthropological observations, clinical impressions, and personal life experiences, Clemmont Vontress (1971), Stanley and Derald Sue (1971), and José Szapocznik and his associates (1980) independently developed similar typologies for describing the adaptation of black Americans, Asian-Americans, and Hispanic Americans, respectively. Vontress's model stressed the effects of different types of cultural identification on the therapeutic alliance; Sue and Sue's and Szapocznik's models stressed the effects of cultural identification on the identifier's symptoms and behavioral styles. William Cross (1971) and Charles Thomas (1971), also working independently, developed models in which they postulated a stagewise progression of identity development instead of a categorical classification system.

The cultural-identification models seem to generate highly emotional responses from reactants. The various points and counterpoints (for example, Abbott, 1973; Tong, 1972) raised in response to the Sues' original description of Chinese personality patterns illustrate the kind of controversy surrounding such approaches.

One criticism of the models is that they "blame the victim" by placing too much emphasis on the minority individual's responses to racism and too little emphasis on Anglo-American society's responsibility for perpetuating institutional racism. Proponents of this view contend that it encourages the counselor to focus on changing the minority individual rather than the system in which the individual is trying to survive. Still other reactants argue that the discrimination that existed in American society when these models were developed no longer exists, and as a consequence, such models are no longer functional.

Implicit in all of the models is some notion of biculturality, adaptation to one's culture of birth as well as Anglo culture. Most of the theorists view the bicultural alternative as the healthiest identity resolution in the United States. However, critics of the models view this type of adaptation as an abandonment of one's cultural roots; supporters view it as the addition of functional characteristics to one's original roots. Each of the models has a category whose members are purported to dislike their cultural group and ipso facto to have poor self-esteem. Some critics (for example, Banks, 1976) have questioned the inevitability of the link between reference-group orientation and personal identity. That is, they suggest that it might be conceivable that a person dislikes the cultural group into which he or she was born but likes himself or herself nonetheless.

The most important questions being asked about minority personality concern the *process* by which cultural identity develops. Classification systems do not seem to account for the individual who shifts from one manner of adaptation to another. On the other hand, stage models (my preference) do not seem to allow for the possibility that identity development may not follow a linear and continuous course; that is, it seems reasonable not to conclude that all individuals must start at the first stage in order to develop an integrated identity or that recycling back through previous stages is impossible. Be that as it may, questions about the process of identity development are important, because the answers should provide the counselor with information about when and how to intervene to promote healthy development.

FUNDAMENTAL ASSUMPTIONS

Several assumptions seem to be shared by the various models, although not necessarily to the same extent:

Assumption 1: Minority groups develop modal personality patterns in response to white racism. Much of the evidence used to support this assumption consists of between-group comparisons of minority and white profiles used standard personality inventories (for example, Gynther, 1972; Sue & Sue, 1974). These studies consistently demonstrate differences between racial groups, but whether these differences reflect real differences rather than psychometric deficiencies in the measures is still being debated. Also, whether such differences are attributable to white racism seems to be a moot question.

Assumption 2: Some styles of identity resolution are healthier than others. Evidence for this assumption is largely inferential; clinicians have observed that certain identity issues seem to characterize their clientele (for example, Butler, 1975; Sue & Sue, 1971) and other issues do not. However, Thomas Parham and I found that less-healthy affective states were correlated with attitudes derived from certain of W. E. Cross's stages. J. Szapocznik, W. M. Kurtines, and T. Fernandez (1980) found better levels of adjustment among bicultural adolescents.

Assumption 3: Cultural-identity development involves shifts in attitudes involving cognitive, affective, and conative components. The research necessary to address this assumption definitively has not been conducted, because no author has manipulated variables representative of each of the three components in a single study. However, some studies have shown a relationship among cultural identification and other attitudes (Parham & Helms, 1981; Sanchez & Atkinson, 1983), behaviors (Davidson, 1974), and affective states (Parham & Helms, 1984).

Assumption 4: Styles of identity resolution are distinguishable and can be assessed. At least three culture-specific measures have been developed to investigate this assumption: (a) J. Milliones's (1980) Developmental Inventory of Black Consciousness; (b) T. A. Parham and J. E. Helms's (1981) Racial Identity Attitude Scale; and (c) J. Szapocznik and colleagues' Bicultural Involvement Questionnaire. Studies using these measures have been useful in delineating relevant measurement issues, one of the primary issues being the difficulty in assessing transitional and undifferentiated identity resolutions, particularly if categorical rather than continuous methods of assessing individuals are used.

Assumption 5: Intracultural and intercultural interactions are influenced by the manner of cultural identification of the participants. No study has measured both cultural identity and intracultural or intercultural behavior simultaneously as a means of addressing the assumption. The closest approximation to such a study was A. R. Sanchez and D. R. Atkinson's (1983) use of a "behavioriod" measure (self-reported willingness to disclose in counseling) with which they found less willingness to disclose for those of their subjects with a mono-cultural (Mexican-American) identification.

FUNDAMENTAL THEORIES

It is useful to talk about cultural identification as a process in which a person can move from one set of characteristics to another, depending, at least partially, upon what is occurring in his or her psychosocial environment. This is essentially the perspective taken by stage theorists (for example, Cross, 1971; Thomas, 1971), and although other writers tend to discuss identification as though it were a fixed state, they do so more for the convenience of discussion than because of the basic belief that exclusive categories best explain individuals' development. It is also useful to note that all of the models propose an ongoing conflict between one's internal views of two cultural groups, white and relevant minority.

The identity models postulate from three to five stages or patterns of development and are meant to explain an aspect of adolescent-to-adult development rather than the entire evolution of identity from birth to death. In fact, most of these models assume that the identity-transformation process is triggered by some social movement that makes it possible for minority-group members to rebel against traditional socialization experiences and to seek new ways of being. It is not always clear whether the "social movement" must be institutional, that is, involve major societal changes, or whether it can be personal, that is, involve individual maturation as seems to have been the case for Malcolm X. Nevertheless, these new ways of being eventually become a part of the minority group's culture and offer alternative personality styles for upcoming members of the cultural group.

Most of the models begin at a phase before the individual's cultural awakening, a period during which he or she is enmeshed in viewing the world from a Euro-American perspective. Called by various names (including *preencounter, traditional, negromachy*), this stage is described as one in which the individual idealizes white culture and denigrates that of his or her own culture of birth. The primary affective condition associated with this stage is poor self-esteem and group esteem. Behavioral interactions are primarily with whites, since one's own group members are considered undesirable companions. The first stage or type is generally considered to be the least healthy, and counselors are frequently warned against unwittingly reinforcing this form of identity resolution (for example, Butler, 1975).

Due to lack of acceptance by the white world and/or because of a personally meaningful life experience, stage theorists propose, the person enters a *transitional stage*. The specifics of this stage are ambiguous. C. Thomas (1971) described it as a period of withdrawal and cultural reassessment; W. E. Cross (1971) described it as a period of decision in which the person decides to become a member of one's own cultural group. The affect associated with this stage is hypothesized to be a mixture of euphoria similar to a religious rebirth and confusion caused by the loss of one's former cultural identity.

The next form of identity resolution has been called *immersion-emersion* by Cross and Asian-American by the Sues. Although this form of identity resolution apparently can be very complex, acknowledgment of racism appears to be a significant aspect. The primary affect during the peak of this stage is anger. Behavior tends to be "militant," and one's interpersonal relationships are likely to be limited to other cultural-group members.

The final stage is one of internalization of one's cultural identity or biculturality and is described as a *transcendent phase*. In other words, the person uses his or her experiences with both cultural groups to shape a perspective that best fits her or his own life circumstances. No longer is it necessary to use cultural-group membership (be that race, sex, language, or something else) to judge what is "truth." No single affect should be associated with this type of resolution, except perhaps self-esteem; interpersonal relationships are not restricted by race or cultural group membership.

Although it is not always apparent from the presentations of the stage and type theories of cultural-identity development, they are in fact, cognitive theories in much the same sense that Jean Piaget's (1970) theory is a cognitive theory. That is, individuals have varied worldviews that lead to certain attitudes, cognitions, and perceptions, depending upon the person's form of identity resolution. As a consequence, it is not possible for someone else (as for example a counselor) to shift someone else's identity resolution. Nor are there particular developmental tasks that one must accomplish to be able to move on to the next stage. Rather, identity transformation seems to involve a combination of personal readiness, prior cultural-socialization experiences, and educational experiences. Therefore, exposing clients (and counselors) to situations demanding cultural flexibility may accelerate identity transitions but only if the person is ready.

FUTURE DIRECTIONS

Interest in the cultural-identification models seems to wax and wane, depending perhaps on what is happening in the sociopolitical arena. Theoretical formulations reached their zenith during the late 1960s and early 1970s; published empirical investigations began to appear only in the late 1970s and early 1980s. One would expect that as these models obtain increasing visibility in traditional psychological journals, the empirical evidence necessary to substantiate or elaborate on them will also increase.

Generalized models of minority-group-identity development may be coming in the future. It is probably more than coincidence that each time a new "minority" group is discovered, typologies similar to those discussed here are also discovered (see R. A. Ruiz & A. M. Padilla [1977] and H. A. Bulhan [1980] for further examples). Once investigators begin to investigate these models empirically, especially in clinical situations, it will be possible to determine which aspects are functionally equivalent across cultural groups.

A cultural-identification process occurs for all people, regardless of ethnicity or race, although the content of that process may differ. Thus I expect to see greater attention given to the issue of how the identification process works for whites, an issue that I raised in a recent paper (Helms, in press). Finally, for the identification construct to be useful for predicting the quality of the therapeutic alliance, it will be necessary for us to begin to ask questions about the effects of different combinations of resolutions or dyadic interactions.

REFERENCES

Abbott, E. (1973) Letter to the editor. *Amerasia Journal, 2*, 180–182.

Allport, G. W. (1958) *The Nature of Prejudice*. New York: Doubleday.

Banks, W. C. (1976) White preference in blacks: A paradigm in search of a phenomenon. *Psychological Bulletin, 83*, 1179–1186.

Bulhan, H. A. (1980) Dynamics of cultural in-betweenity: An empirical study. *International Journal of Psychology, 15*, 105–112.

Butler, R. O. (1975) Psychotherapy: Implications of a black-consciousness process model. *Psychotherapy: Theory, Research, and Practice, 12*, 407–411.

Cross, W. E., Jr. (1971) The Negro-to-black conversion experience: Toward a psychology of black liberation. *Black World, 20* (9), 12–37.

Davidson, J. P. (1974) Empirical development of a measure of black student identity. Ph.D. dissertation, University of Maryland.

Gynther, M. D. (1972) White norms and black MMPI's: A prescription for discrimination? *Psychological Bulletin, 78*, 386–402.

Helms, J. E. (in press) Toward a theoretical explanation of the effects of race on counseling: A black and white model. *The Counseling Psychologist*.

Milliones, J. (1980) Construction of a black consciousness measure: Psychotherapeutic implications. *Psychotherapy: Theory, Research, and Practice, 17*, 175–182.

Parham, T. A., & Helms, J. E. (1981) The influence of black students' racial identity attitudes on preference for counselor's race. *Journal of Counseling Psychology, 28*, 250–257.

——— (in preparation) The relationship of racial identity attitudes to black students' mental health.

Piaget, J. (1970) *Structuralism*. New York: Basic Books.

Ruiz, R. A., Casas, J. M., & Padilla, A. M. (1977) *Culturally relevant behavioristic counseling*. Los Angeles: University of California, Spanish Speaking Mental Health Research Center.

Ruiz, R. A., & Padilla, A. M. (1977) Counseling latinos. *The Personnel and Guidance Journal, 55*, 401–408.

Sanchez, A. R., & Atkinson, D. R. (1983) Mexican-American cultural commitment, preference for counselor ethnicity, and willingness to use counseling. *Journal of Counseling Psychology, 30*, 215–220.

Sue, S., & Sue, D. W. (1971) Chinese-American personality and mental health. *Amerasia Journal, 1*, 36–49.

——— (1974) MMPI comparisons between Asian-American and non-Asian students utilizing a student health psychiatric clinic. *Journal of Counseling Psychology*, *21*, 423–427.

Szapocznik, J., Kurtines, W. M., & Fernandez, T. (1980) Bicultural involvement and adjustment in Hispanic-American youths. *International Journal of Intercultural Relations*, *4*, 353–365.

Thomas, C. (1971). *Boys no more*. Beverly Hills, Calif.: Glencoe Press.

Tong, B. R. (1972) Reply to Sues. *Amerasia Journal*, *1*, 65–67.

Vontress, C. E. (1971) Racial differences: Impediments to rapport. *Journal of Counseling Psychology*, *18*, 7–13.

Projected Social Distances as an Indicator of Attitudes

LEONORE LOEB ADLER

HISTORY

In recent years much interest has focused on *proxemics*, the study of spatial arrangements, including personal space and interpersonal distance. *Personal space* was defined by Kenneth B. Little as "the area immediately surrounding the individual in which the majority of his interactions with others takes place" (1968, p. 237). It corresponded to Edward T. Hall's (1966) concept, which described it as a "bubble" that persons carry around with them, similar to a buffer zone in interpersonal interactions. The size and shape could vary, though, depending on the person's gender, age, personality, and ethnic and cultural background. The term *individual distance* in one of its earliest uses by Heini Hediger (1937) referred to the spacing that animals maintained between themselves and other conspecifics. Later studies explored the existence of schemata to determine social distances, or closeness, between a person or a physical object. In this connection Robert Sommer (1967) divided the spatial arrangements or social distances of individuals into two categories: relational space and sociofugal space. The concept of *sociofugal space* requires knowledge of how people arrange themselves to minimize contact or to discourage interaction. For example, in seating arrangements, being seated corner to corner is less satisfactory than being seated at opposite ends. *Relational space* applies to the way people orient to and position themselves relative to other persons in small social groups.

Investigators use a variety of techniques and measures to assess interpersonal spacing: analyses by tests, either verbal or nonverbal; and observations of naturally occurring interactions. The first category includes verbal rating scales such as the Bogardus Social Distance Scale, which derives from the premise that a person's ethnic attitudes (including prejudice) determine the individual, personal, and psychological distances that they choose in relating to members of various ethnic groups. Another measuring procedure in this category is the figure-placement task (test), in which respondents position symbols, depending on the ascriptions of the stimulus items. The procedures vary greatly and use, among other materials, gum-backed, human silhouettes; a felt and tape technique; and black rectangular stickers, which are modified to colored, round stickers; other projective techniques use gray, plastic, stylized 6'' (male) and 5.4'' (female) dolls. All of these symbols could be placed easily. The nonverbal methods provide a good tool to measure projected interpersonal distances. They are obtained by the respondents' manipulation of symbols that represent either persons in different social situations or objects. The projective techniques measure attitudes without being articulated or being recognized by the subjects or clients. It can therefore tap attitudes at variance with the respondents' verbally stated beliefs. It is deservedly a favorite method for investigations of social schemata.

The second category includes observation and measurement of physical distances between members of dyads or larger groups, as well as objects either in the laboratory or in social settings in the field. In this connection interpersonal distance is found to be systematically related to a number of variables, such as eye contact between the interactants, same or opposite sex of the target person, and social status of the stimulus person or objects.

PRESENT STATUS

Robert Kleck, Peter L. Buck, William L. Goller, Ronald S. London, John R. Pfeiffer, and Douglas P. Vukcevic (1968) reported differences between verbally and spatially expressed attitudes toward a stigmatized population. However, they found correspondence in their comparison between the physical and the projected interpersonal distance that subjects established from stigmatized stimulus persons (for example, ascribed epileptics). Following a similar method, Marvin A. Iverson and I also found close agreement between physical interpersonal distances among same-sex dyads in the laboratory (Adler & Iverson, 1974) when compared to projected interpersonal spacing by means of a figure-placement task (Adler & Iverson, 1975). The ascriptions of the test items paralleled the same social situations that were tested in the laboratory study.

The clear consistency of the results in either of the methods used—physical or projected social distances—could imply that people possess an underlying social schema that has a generalized effect on both their projected and actual interpersonal spacing.

Social schemata was referred to by James L. Kuethe (1962) and J.L. Kuethe and George Stricker (1963) as the tendency by individuals to group persons representing stimulus figures together. This grouping is generally consistent with regard to distance or closeness and pattern of arrangements among members of the same ethnic or cultural background. It has been suggested, however, that the modal response is determined by common social experiences, and idiosyncratic factors, including personality dynamics, are responsible for the deviations from it. On the other hand, David W. Lewit and Virginia D. Joy (1967) counter-proposed that the groupings may result from factors that are learned, although independent of the social experience of the individual.

Although proxemics may generate great interest and curiosity among psychologists, the greater challenge is found in discovering the underlying social schemata and reaching out beyond our own social environment to see whether such spacing or grouping has some universal bases. This means: do people in other cultures or geographical areas respond in similar manner?

The current trend is to focus on social spacing, interpret the prevailing attitudes, and predict the respondents' future behavior. Another use for interpersonal spacing, in terms of nonverbal communication, has been to teach and/or train individuals in behaviors such as assertiveness, seating during job interviews, and interaction with a variety of people in different social situations.

FUNDAMENTAL ASSUMPTIONS

A growing literature showed that interpersonal spacing varied with the gender of the interactants. However, the findings of the investigations were inconsistent. This fact suggested that perhaps interpersonal spacing was less a function of the gender of the respondents than it was of the interaction context in which it occurred. Nevertheless it seems appropriate to make the following statement: Under normal conditions interpersonal distances between female-female dyads are smaller than those between male-male pairs.

Social distances may vary in close or far spacing, depending on the stimulus items' effect. Generally, the following statement is typical: Stimulus items conveying "positive" or "neutral" effect result in closer interpersonal spacing than do items that project a "negative" effect and are "emotionally toned."

Among the earliest studies were those by Robert Kleck and associates (1968), who found that the "amputee," "epileptic," and "ex-mental patient" were responded to with greater projected interaction distances for interpersonal behavior; greater physical distancing occurred also from stigmatized persons than it did from stigma-free individuals. Other studies (Adler & Graubert, 1975); Graubert & Adler, 1982), although similar in results, used the ascription of "mental patient," both male and female. Comparisons of several student groups, both at college and high school levels, who followed different career programs, showed that students in volunteer programs did not perceive "retardate" or "mental patient," either male or female, to convey negative effects. The investigators concluded, based on their findings: The stimulus items that represent the respondents' professional commitment and environmental setting in which they offer their services in reality hold no "negative" emotional impact; therefore the responses to such stimulus items are similar as those are to "positive" or to "neutral" items.

The "retardate" and "mental patient," regardless of gender, did not hold a stigma for the student volunteers. However, in general, these items carry a stigma. Discussing social interaction, Erwin Goffman (1963) proposed that the presence of a stigmatizing characteristic resulted in avoidance of the stigmatized person by stigma-free others. The expression of attitudes of avoiding any contact with the stigmatized person resulted in the greatest social distances.

Two questions arose: Does a mental patient bear the brunt of stigma in other countries and cultures also? Are individuals displaying negative demeanor or inappropriate emotional behavior avoided by others in social settings in other parts of the world? To find the answers, two cross-national and cross-cultural parallel studies (Adler, 1978; Graubert & Adler, 1982), tested at the same time, were undertaken in eight countries: Australia, Great Britain, South Africa, the United States, Canada, Hong Kong, Israel, and the Philippines. These groups included both monolingual (English) and bilingual men and women college students; all were tested in English with the figure-placement task. In all of these countries the college students responded with large projected social distances to stigma-laden items (male and female "mental patients") and those conveying negative demeanor (losing control over his or her emotions). On the other hand, the stigma-free items (volunteer) and the positive demeanor (calm behavior) elicited close interactions. The clearest finding of these two studies was the impressive similarity of the responses across countries and cultures. Even though the means varied somewhat, the overall schemata were the same in each country. The investigators speculated about the background for such uniformity, suggesting that manifold causes contributed to this outcome. On hand of these findings, one can make the following statement: Despite the cultural and historical diversity of the countries that were included in the studies, the projected social schemata were similar in all groups of participating college students. The stigmatized items and those conveying bad demeanor elicited the largest social distances cross-culturally, and stigma-free stimuli and those representing good demeanor resulted in close interactional distances.

Cross-cultural research by Kenneth Little (1968) in five countries (Greece, Italy, Scotland, Sweden, and the United States) revealed similar schemata, although his little dolls were ascribed, among others, different degrees of acquaintanceship from friend to acquaintance to stranger. In all countries men and women responded with much closer spacing to "#1. Two good friends talking about a pleasant topic" than they did to "#9. Two strangers talking about an unpleasant topic" (p. 3). The same pattern emerged with status and authority interaction items, such as the closer distance, "#10. A policeman questioning a person about some burglaries that have occurred in the neighborhood," versus the greater distance, "#15. A shop owner discussing the weather with his assistant." Although Little concentrated on the mean projected interpersonal spacing of each national group, the underlying schemata were basically the same.

This was also the case when the mean projected social distances of groups of Native Japanese, Hawaiian-Japanese, and American Caucasians were compared. Darold Engebretson and Daniel Fullmer (1970) reported that of the three groups the student-friend dyads received closest spacing. However, it was interesting to note that the Hawaiian-Japanese group was well enculturated, since there were no significant differences between them and the American Caucasian group.

Another important aspect, in this instance pertaining to age group, was investigated by Reuben R. Rusch and James L. Kuethe (1979). The investigators found that preschool children were able to respond with projected social distance to several stimulus items-drawings that represented "school," "teacher," "desk," "friends," by placing the self-stamp (figure) on a sheet of paper. Supported by the results of these studies the following statement can be presented: Techniques for measuring social schemata with preschool and school-age children are appropriate for research and evaluation, since projected social spacing is highly correlated with actual interpersonal behavior.

THEORIES

One of the earliest theories on interaction distances was proposed by Edward T. Hall (1966). He derived three zones from observation of natural interactions ranging from what he termed *intimate*, *casual-personal*, and *social-consultative*. With these observations he emphasized the functional significance of interpersonal spacing in social responding.

Since the interest in social spacing has only a short history of less than a half-century, and most of the relevant national and cross-cultural research was generated during the past quarter-century, there exists a paucity of theoretical discussions. Much of the research seems to be piecemeal and opportunistic. The effect of these conditions was that many data were produced, but they did not yield many new universal theories of social distance. Each study analyzed its individual results and then progressed to compare the findings to other investigations. The emphasis concentrated on the means of the interpersonal distances of national or ethnic groups, which were at times not replicated by other research, thereby providing unstable bases for the evaluations. However, from a molar or an overall point of view, analyses and interpretations of the results of both physical and projected techniques show that the underlying social schemata are similar. For many years I believed that the discoveries of similarities in cross-cultural research were more meaningful than the findings of differences (Adler, 1977, 1978, & 1983). Therefore, it can be said that these studies indicate that interpersonal spacing is reliable behavior.

Another approach in the interpretation of distancing effects is to view experimental conditions from the standpoint of "frustration theory." Based on Abraham Amsel's research on the Frustration Effect, James H. McHose (1963) gave differential food reinforcement to rats in Goal Box 1, while rats received reinforcements 100 percent of the time in Goal Box 2. The three groups of subjects received either 100 percent reinforcement (every time they reached Goal Box 1), 0 (zero) percent reinforcement (no food in Goal Box 1), and 50 percent reinforcement (half of the time—in random order—when they reached Goal Box

1). The results showed that rats in the 50 percent reinforcement group ran faster from Goal Box 1 to Goal Box 2 than did the rats in either of the other two groups. He attributed the increased speed (ft./sec.) to the Frustration Effect. On the other hand, I reasoned (1972) that when organisms move faster away from a frustrating or an aversive stimulus, the respondents also put more distance between themselves and the unpleasant stimulus. In my anagram-solving tasks with college students I found a parallel. The subjects' interpersonal distances were closest after solving "easy" anagrams, and an intermediary distance was used by students with "difficult" lists, which they could not solve. However, the farthest distances were recorded from students in the "mixed" anagrams group. They quickly solved the "easy" words but were stuck with the "difficult" words, which was a frustrating experience for them. I therefore concluded that *distance* (in. or cm) can be thought of as being the equivalent to *speed* (ft./sec.) in terms of the precise distance covered during a fraction of a second in the rats' runway.

Another approach to the study of interpersonal spacing was undertaken by Darhl M. Pedersen and Loyda M. Shears (1973). They formulated a general systems theory that related personal space to social interactions. This team identified two systems: One was a *person system* that involved the individual with people, things, and the environment to which the responses were emotional and physiological. Another was a *group system* in which the group interacted with people, things, and space, which in turn yielded information about their movements and their interaction patterns. In both cases the desirable goal was to maintain a *steady state* of social relationships.

Still another theory was formulated by Michael Argyle and Janet Dean (1965) and was confirmed by Ralph V. Exline, David Gray, and Dorothy Schuette (1965). Their Affiliative-Conflict Theory stated that eye contact served the function of obtaining feedback during social interaction and of promoting intimacy without changing physical proximity. They observed that persons placed themselves closer to another individual or a picture of a person with closed eyes, or looking down, rather than when the eyes were open. Relying on such empirical principles, I (1972) successfully applied these findings in research on social spacing: my confederates avoided eye contact with the subjects before they were seated in an empty room in the laboratory.

FUTURE DIRECTIONS

Applying the findings of research with projected social distances to clinical counseling and guidance therapy, we realize that, like other projective techniques that have clinical application, this "pencil and paper method" is a good diagnostic tool. (It does not necessarily require a pencil but instead places little figures, dolls, or some type of stickers anywhere on the page or board. These procedures rely on projected interactions with a stimulus item that is identified in the instructions.) Not only can adults be tested in this manner, but it is suitable for children, who may not be able to verbalize their feelings and emotions. Attitudes can easily be identified by measuring the social distance, for example, toward "mother," "father," "friend," and "teacher-professor," as well as from "school" and "mental hospital." Using projected social schemata is an appropriate diagnostic measure when the responses are not random but are highly correlated with equivalent actual interpersonal behavior.

Identification of prejudiced attitudes toward any stigmatized population would be helpful to re-educate the persons involved. R. Kleck and associates (1968) observed greater social distances during interpersonal interactions from stigmatized individuals, whether they were "ex-mental patients," "epileptics," "amputees," or persons with any other stigma or handicap. They raised the question with regard to stigmatized individuals who constantly interact with people at greater than average distances. "What are the effects on their own behaviors, and their attitudes toward others?" (p. 11)

The question of nature versus nurture still seems strained at times. Robert Ardrey (1966) suggested that human territorial behavior was innate. On the other hand, the dispute involved the topic of personal space and whether such behavior could be modified to a great extent by learning. No adequate answers have been advanced so far.

The topic of prejudice will have to be dealt with currently and in the future. Here social-distance research, in terms of physical and projected spacing will prove to be a good diagnostic method. Prejudice has been studied for a long time, though. Although not dealing with actual social distance, it brings the following account to mind: Otto Klineberg (1954) described a research of one of his master-degree candidates, Eugene Hartley, who used a social-distance test, a Bogardus-type scale, that measured ethnic attitudes in terms of psychological distance. The students who were participating in Hartley's study attended eight colleges. They were told to indicate the degree of acceptance or rejection of 35 ethnic groups. They included fictitious groups such as the *Danerians*, the *Pirenians*, and the *Walonians*. Although some students did not answer any questions about the groups they had never heard about, a great many students responded with greater psychological distances from these fictitious groups than from a majority of the actual groups that were included in the study. Would such a prejudiced behavior still occur today? Future trends will move in the direction of greater application of projective social distance techniques as an indicator of attitudes. For example, if prejudice can be recognized early in childhood, measures can be taken to reduce or alleviate such negative attitudes and behavior.

The counselor who has a practice in a cross-cultural and cross-ethnic setting will probably deal with clients who try to adjust to new environments and deal with negative attitudes toward their ethnic or national minority groups. However, based on projective social distance behavior, the counselor will guide the client toward complete adjustment and eventual acculturation.

Supported by past research, future directions in counseling will rely on information and findings that can be applied cross-culturally, cross-ethnically, and within the same community. Projected social distance will provide the cues for analyzing attitudes and act as an indicator of a well-adjusted personality.

REFERENCES

Adler, Leonore Loeb (1972) Interpersonal distance as a function of task difficulty and praise from high or low status partners of the same or the opposite sex. Ph.D. dissertation, Adelphi University, Garden City, N.Y.

────── (1977) A plea for interdisciplinary cross-cultural research: Some introductory remarks. In Adler, L. L. (Ed.), *Issues in cross-cultural research*. New York: Annals of the New York Academy of Sciences, *285*, 1–2.

────── (1978) The effects of calm and emotional behavior on projected social distances: A cross-cultural comparison. *International Journal of Group Tensions*, *8* (I, 2), 49–63.

────── (1983) Cross-cultural psychology. In Wolman, B. B. (Ed.), *Progress, Volume 1: International Encyclopedia of Psychiatry, Psychology, Psychoanalysis & Neurology*. New York: Aesculapius Publishers, pp. 75–79.

Adler, Leonore Loeb, & Graubert, Jean G. (1975) Projected social distances from mental patient related items by male and female volunteers and non-volunteers. *Psychological Reports*, *37*, 515–521.

Adler, Leonore Loeb, & Iverson, Marvin A. (1974) Interpersonal distance as a function of task difficulty, praise, status orientation, and sex of partner. *Perceptual and Motor Skills*, *39*, 683–692.

────── (1975) Projected social distance as a function of praise conditions and status orientation: A comparison with physical interpersonal spacing in the laboratory. *Perceptual and Motor Skills*, *41*, 659–664.

Ardrey, Robert (1966) *The territorial imperative*. New York: Dell.

Argyle, Michael, & Dean, Janet (1965) Eye-contact, distance and affiliation. *Sociometry*, *28*, 289–304.

Duke, Michael P., & Nowicki, Stephen (1972) A new measure of social learning model for interpersonal distance. *Journal of Experimental Research in Personality*, *6*, 119–132.

Engebretson, Darold, & Fullmer, Daniel (1970) Cross-cultural differences in territoriality: Interaction distances of native Japanese, Hawaiian-Japanese, and American Caucasians. *Journal of Cross-Cultural Psychology*, *1* (3), 261–269.

Evans, Gary W., & Howard, Robert B. (1973) Personal space. *Psychological Bulletin*, *80*, (4), 334–344.

Exline, Ralph V., Gray, David, & Schuette, Dorothy (1965) Visual behavior in a dyad as affected by interview content and sex of respondent. *Journal of Personality and Social Psychology*, *1*, 201–209.

Goffman, Erwin (1963) *Stigma: Notes on the management of spoiled identity*. Englewood Cliffs, N.J.: Prentice-Hall.

Graubert, Jean G., & Adler, Leonore Loeb (1982) Attitudes toward stigma-related and stigma-free stimuli: A cross-national perspective. In Adler, Leonore Loeb (Ed.), *Cross-Cultural Research at Issue*. New York: Academic Press, pp. 335–347.

Hall, Edward T. (1966) *The hidden dimension*. Garden City, N.Y.: Doubleday.

Hediger, H. (1937) Die bedeuteng der flucht im leben des tieres und in der beurteilung tierischen verhaltens im experiment. *Naturwissenschaften, 25* (12), 1–14.

Kleck, Robert, Buck, Peter L., Goller, William L., London, Ronald S., Pfeiffer, John R., & Vukcevic, Douglas P. (1968) Effect of stigmatizing conditions on the use of personal space. *Psychological Reports, 23*, 111–118.

Klineberg, Otto (1954) *Social Psychology*, rev. ed. New York: Henry Holt & Co.

Kuethe, James L. (1962) Pervasive influence of social schemata. *Journal of Abnormal and Social Psychology, 68*, 248–254.

Kuethe, J. L., & Stricker, G. (1963) Man and woman: Social schemata of males and females. *Psychological Reports, 13*, 655–661.

Lewit, D. W., & Joy, V. D. (1967) Kinetic versus social schemas in figure grouping. *Journal of Personality and Social Psychology, 7*, 63–72.

Little, Kenneth B. (1968) Cultural variations in social schemata. *Journal of Personality and Social Psychology, 10* (1), 1–7.

McHose, James H. (1963) Effect of continued non-reinforcement on the Frustration Effect. *Journal of Experimental Psychology, 65*, 440–450.

Pedersen, Darhl M., & Shears, Loyda M. (1973) A review of personal space research in the framework of General System Theory. *Psychological Bulletin, 80*, (5), 367–368.

Rusch, Reuben R., & Kuethe, James L. (1979) Measuring the social schemata of preschool children. *Psychological Reports, 44*, 265–266.

Russo, Nancy Felipe (1971) Eye contact and distance relations in children. *Dissertation Abstracts International*, Order No. 71–14, 590, p. 123.

Sommer, R. (1959) Studies in personal space. *Sociometry, 22*, 247–260.

V

EDUCATION AND TRAINING

The ultimate goal of education and training in cross-cultural differences is not to develop a new "cross-cultural" specialty but to increase the excellence of *all* counselors and therapists, regardless of their clientele. By now it will be obvious to the readers that *all* counseling and therapy must attend to cultural differences in order to influence the client's behavior. There are several alternative models for introducing cultural material into the education and training process.

Harriet Lefley provides a valuable overview of the most visible cross-cultural training programs in the United States. J. Manuel Casas points out the importance of incentives for developing racial and ethnic-minority counseling opportunities. Stanley Sue, Philip Akutsu, and Cindy Higashi describe training issues in working with ethnic-minority clients, and Patricia Arredondo likewise looks at educational issues in training counselors. Victor Drapela broadens the educational focus to a global perspective. Richard Pearson offers a perspective of natural support systems that relates to the wide variety of counseling modes in other cultures. Frank Hull describes the special problems foreign students have in educational settings where counseling or therapy might be appropriate. In conclusion, Paul Pedersen examines the inadequacy of intercultural counseling and therapy.

Through education and training we stand on the shoulders of our mentors to see ahead into the future of a multicultural world that will not allow the luxury of conflict between cultures. We need to find out how to create harmony and get along with persons who see things differently from ourselves. The afterword by C. Gilbert Wrenn reviews progress since he first coined the phrase "culturally encapsulated counselor." This handbook is a glimpse of the widely diverse fields, professions, disciplines, and perspectives seeking the answer to that question.

Mental-Health Training across Cultures

HARRIET P. LEFLEY

Cross-cultural training for mental-health professionals is presently a growing area of interest in search of standardization and subdisciplinary status. The study of culture and mental-health has a long history in anthropology, stimulated by infusions from cultural psychiatry and cross-cultural psychology. With the exception of a few programs, the influence of this literature on professional training has been barely perceptible.

Recent years, however, have seen the publication of at least a dozen books focusing on cross-cultural-counseling issues (for example, Acosta, Yamamoto, & Evans, 1982; Marsella & Pedersen, 1981; McGoldrick, Pearce, & Giordano, 1982; Pedersen, Draguns, Lonner, & Trimble, 1981; D. Sue, 1981). Organizations such as the Institute on Pluralism and Group Identity of the American Jewish Committee and the Spanish Speaking Mental Health Research Center at the University of California, Los Angeles, have issued bibliographies, papers, and monographs oriented toward counseling specific populations.

Despite this interest, systematic training efforts are variegated, experimental, and relatively scarce. A recent survey of the status of ethnic-minority issues in clinical-psychology training programs (Bernal & Padilla, 1982) indicated that of 76 institutions returning questionnaires (106 were polled), most minority-related courses were taught by only 16 programs.

Three major training projects supported by the National Institute of Mental Health have been Brandeis University's Training Program in Ethnicity and Mental Health (Spiegel & Papajohn, 1983), the University of Hawaii's Developing Interculturally Skilled Counselors (DISC) program (Pedersen, 1981a), and the University of Miami's Cross-Cultural Training Institute for Mental Health Professionals (Lefley & Urrutia, 1982). Like most efforts, these programs have focused on different ethnic groups, contingent on locale; and different types of trainees (the former two on graduate students and post-doctoral trainees, the latter on practitioners); and they have differed in duration, emphasis, and format. Training approaches in cross-cultural counseling range in time and intensity from a full psychology graduate program, such as the cross-cultural-counseling specialty offered at Western Washington University, to summer seminars such as those conducted at Syracuse University, to one- or two-day workshops offered at professional meetings and at various U.S. colleges. Structured training models such as P. B. Pedersen's (1981b) Triad Training Model and the Bicultural Contextualizer developed at San Francisco's Chinatown Housing and Health Research Project (Loo, 1980) offer techniques for addressing the more substantive aspects of therapeutic interventions.

MAJOR ISSUES IN TRAINING

1. *Is cross-cultural training additive or substitutive?* The first major question relates to the basic conceptualization of cultural training, which is perceived by some as involving a total educational restructuring to impart a transcultural perspective and by others as adding cognitive and sensitivity skills to an existing technology. The latter position assumes that the psychodynamic, behavioral, cognitive, or systems approaches that are taught in most counseling-clinical curricula may be adapted to cultural context. An innovative addition, developed by F. X Acosta, J. Yamamoto, and L. A. Evans (1982), also trains the patient in role expectancies. Orientation sessions for low-income minority patients on the culture of psychotherapy is a creative example of the additive model, enabling client and counselor to meet on commonly understood grounds.

These authors, however, as well as many of those cited earlier, give guidelines on working with culturally different patients that in effect require modifications of theoretical orientation. Many report that experience with clients from ethnically diverse or Third World backgrounds indicates a selective kind of therapy: short term, ahistorical, directive, relational, authoritative, problem focused, and action oriented (see Lefley & Bestman, 1984). If true, does this exclude practitioners who believe that only long-term psychodynamic therapy is really effective? Do therapists then feel they are shortchanging patients who are culturally different? If a therapist must learn to touch or fraternally embrace a patient, to self-disclose, or otherwise to relate in culturally expected ways in order to keep the patient coming for treatment, in what ways does this violation of psychoanalytic taboos affect transference and countertransference? How does one deal with our mainstream American values of autonomy, separation, and individuation from the family system and with self-assertiveness as important therapeutic goals, when these things may be maladaptive in the patient's communally oriented culture? Can supernatural beliefs and alternative healing be integrated with a worldview that favors internal locus of control? Essentially, educational restructuring forces acknowledgment of cultural relativism. The old anthropological dilemma has vital relevance for mental-health providers, whose relationship with their key informants is one of considerable power, with the potential for alienating them from their supportive cultural matrix.

2. *How do we overcome theoretical and conceptual barriers to cross-cultural training?* In the M. E. Bernal and A. M. Padilla (1982) survey, clinical-psychology training directors reported great variability of faculty opinion on the importance of educating students on minority issues. Culturally specific topics, when dealt with, were inserted into standard courses such as social psychology, abnormal psychology, assessment, and personality. Minority issues are usually recognized as having sociological and political implications that impinge on mental health, but in clinical programs the notion of culture as an intervening variable is frequently perceived as negating a universalistic concept of mental disorder. The perception is based on two disputable premises: (a) the psychodynamics underlying all human behavior and relationships, individually, in families and in groups, is lawful and culturally exclusive, and (b) if major mental disorders are biologically based, they must share a universal etiology and symptomatology. Some theoreticians believe that introduction of cultural issues ipso facto imposes a sociogenic theory of disorder. Yet cultural variance and invariance in psychopathology and the etic-emic dilemma in assessment and therapy remain crucial theoretical questions. A major issue is how and to what extent they may become standard discursive elements of all professional training, regardless of locale or ethnic focus.

3. *How do we overcome institutional barriers to training?* This question is related not only to theoretical barriers but to issues of money and time. Clinical-training curricula are already packed full, and cross-cultural training is viewed as ancillary, particularly by those who do not see themselves as spending many years delivering services to clients of other cultures. Yet clinical training that is even partially supported by public funds requires attention to strategies for developing culturally appropriate service delivery for low-income and minority patients.

Institutional barriers are bilateral, however, and the issue of culturally appropriate therapies that may be more effective than existing models remains an ideologically and politically sensitive question in many communities, particularly if "culturally appropriate" is perceived as "inferior." This issue is a ramification of what has been discussed earlier with respect to brief, here-and-now therapies. A number of minority theoreticians believe that long-term psychoanalytic or personality-restructuring therapies, perceived as superior modalities, are appropriate for all patients regardless of background or socioeconomic status. The issue is not one of culture but of finances, time, and therapist commitment. This viewpoint does not, however, address the issue of an elitist investment of scarce resources in a small number of patients.

4. *Who is to be trained and at what level?* Empirically, cross-cultural training has taken place at four levels—undergraduate, graduate, post-doctoral, and in continuing education for clinicians. S. Sue (1983) argued that application of cultural knowledge is tenuous unless it is developed while actually working with ethnic-minority groups. Moreover, practitioners who already have experience with critical incidents can offer input that will enhance the direction and content

of training curricula as well as use the training for immediate application in the field. In contrast, emphasis on a contextual and relativist perspective may pose special problems at the earlier levels of clinical training, primarily involving stimulus bombardment and cognitive dissonance. When cultural information involves modification of theories, assessment procedures, and therapeutic techniques just being learned, students have to make constant conceptual adjustments while they are still in the early stages of absorbing knowledge, without experiential reference points. The dangers of overload and contradictory perceptions in training must thus be counterbalanced by the need to provide adequate preparation for questioning, reinterpreting, and adapting learned techniques when problems are encountered in the field.

5. *What is to be taught*? There are numerous approaches to cross-cultural training—unicultural, multi-cultural, and transcultural—involving variations in emphasis, content, and methodology. A *theoretical academic approach*, oriented toward epistemology and research, addresses issues such as normality-abnormality, classifications of mental disorder, psychiatric, epidemiology, and culture-bound syndromes. Within this framework, more profound questions are explored: symbolic structuring of health and illness constructs, conceptions of the person, causality, deviancy, power relationships and labeling, stigma and suffering, madness and badness, that is, the relationship between the ways in which cultural collectivities order reality and their perception of the origin and treatment of mental disorder (Marsella & White, 1982).

An *applied approach* may focus on particular ethnic or cultural groups, exploring behavioral norms, worldview and value systems, family structure and interactions, age and sex roles, supernatural beliefs and alternative healing practices, adaptive mechanism, stress points, coping styles, and normative support systems.

Since there is often a press for applied training, curriculum questions immediately arise. What is the proper mix of didactic and experiential components? Is cultural immersion necessary? Should general sociological and anthropological courses be required but perhaps adapted to a community mental-health perspective? If between-group differences are addressed, how do we deal with the vast range of within-group variation, for example, age, sex, socioeconomic status, regional-geographic differences? This is an old dilemma in modal personality research, exacerbated today by the large numbers of immigrants at varying stages of acculturation, who may make it untenable to use a specialized ethnic perspective.

Additionally, the ethnic-focused approach does not always provide adequate criteria for analyzing the interplay of culture and psychopathology in individual cases. Cultural input always has the built-in danger of stereotyping and inappropriate application. An ancillary question, then, is whether courses on culture must also be tempered by training on how to use an implicit feedback loop for applying or discarding cultural information in particular cases.

Curricula emphasizing a *transcultural perspective* might focus on a model for multi-variate synthesis, such as Hines & Pedersen's (1980) "cultural grid," which matches role behavior, expectation, and value meaning with social-system variables. Implicit is a person-environment context for observer and observed. The essential aspect of the transcultural perspective, according to H. H. Weidman (1979), is an objective or equidistant stance at a cultural interface. In counseling, however, it should also involve a particular kind of conceptual openness and an armamentarium of cognitive and interactional skills that are generalizable across cultures. In this respect, it may be necessary for trainees to explore their own self-cultural awareness, particularly any identity problems regarding their own cultural background as well as ethnocentric perception of the patient.

An integral component of the transcultural perspective, according to Weidman's view, is the notion of value parity. S. Sue (1983) suggested that cultural pluralism issues are "analogous to antinomies, in which cherished values and principles are pitted against one another," and this is nowhere more evident than in counseling the culturally different client (p. 583). A critical question in adopting the transcultural perspective is whether counselors can or *should* work against the grain, particularly in suppressing their own cherished values. Questions of genuineness must be balanced against role-modeling effects in developing with the client therapeutic goals that are adaptive and culturally syntonic and at the same time optimally growth enhancing for that particular individual.

6. *How do we distinguish the domains of socioeconomic, minority, migrant, and acculturative statuses from that which is purely ethnocultural?* Should cross-cultural curricula address the "culture of poverty," the "culture of migrants," or the "culture of minority status"? The notion of status or social groups that share commonalities across ethnocultural boundaries has long concerned anthropologists and sociologists. In training mental-health-service providers, however, the issue is important in deciding whether one takes a generalized community mental-health–human-services approach and extends it to all minority clients, regardless of ethnicity, or whether one focuses on specific cultural variables—commonalities in African, Asian, or Hispanic heritage, use of folk-healing modalities, and the like. The question is even more critical in deciding, for example, whether racism and its profound psychological sequelae or the trauma of being uprooted and transplanted in a foreign land are more salient variables in counseling than ethnic variation in psychosocial adaptation.

This discussion highlights the need to evaluate any given problem with a multi-variate grid such as that proposed by Hines and Pedersen. The essential issue is whether counselors can be trained to weigh the relative contributions of these multiple components, all of which come under the rubric of culture.

7. *Can the usefulness of cross-cultural training be demonstrated empirically? How do we evaluate its relevance to positive outcome in the field?* Although the issue of efficacy is certainly not limited to cross-cultural training, it is essential to pose this question when recommending modifications of existing disciplines. There have been a number of different models for evaluating cross-cultural training (for example, Triandis, 1977), and contributors to the "Evaluation" section of A. J. Marsella & P. B. Pedersen (1981) discussed discrete approaches

to evaluating expectancy effects, process, and outcome variables in cross-cultural counseling and psychotherapy. In the main, however, these contributions provide models rather than findings on efficacy. Some hard data are available from the Cross-Cultural Training Institute for Mental Health Professionals (Lefley & Urrutia, 1982), which demonstrated that knowledge acquisition and changes in social distance, attitudes, and values were accompanied by significant improvement in therapeutic skills with a client of contrasting culture. A major objective indicator was a significant reduction in patient dropout rates following cross-cultural training. More of these types of evaluation findings are needed to demonstrate that cultural education is not merely an elective addition to one's existing corpus of skills but indeed may be the most vital component in developing the truly effective counselor or psychotherapist.

FUTURE DIRECTIONS

Because of growing interest, it is likely that cultural issues will constitute an important addition to professional curricula within the next few decades. This may well generate significant contributions to theory and practice. First, training for culturally sensitive interventions will require further discussion and clarification of general issues such as short-term versus long-term therapies, nondirective versus directive techniques, therapist self-disclosure, systems analysis, and methods for contextualizing the individual case. Correction of deficits in norming procedures for scales widely used in psychological and psychiatric evaluation, standardization of new diagnostic instruments, or construction of normative profiles for major ethnic groups are potential developments.

Many cultural-awareness issues that strongly affect professional competence have rarely been addressed in traditional training. The primary techniques involve comprehension of one's own cognitive and value system in assessing others' behavior. Sensitive counselors require the ability to recognize other culturally related parameters: the uses of power in the patient-therapist relationship; diagnoses and prognoses as artifacts of labeling, role definitions, and cultural expectations; the strengths of family networks in the therapeutic process; and the role of belief systems in healing.

An important aspect of cross-cultural training is its potential for cross-fertilization. The transcultural approach, for example, forces reconsideration of Western-formulated theoretical axioms and diagnostic features that do not fit a universal grid. However, it also highlights non-Western therapeutic modalities that are empirically useful in other cultural contexts. Examples are deinstitutionalization models such as the African ARO villages (Lambo, 1978) and Asian therapies (Reynolds, 1980) that are increasingly being adapted for Western uses in stress management.

Cross-cultural training also looks at those elements of human variability that may be biologically based, such as differential response to medication (Lin & Finder, 1983). The International Pilot Study of Schizophrenia's findings of more benign prognosis for schizophrenia in the developing as opposed to the developed countries highlights the importance of high social support-low stress as a bio-cultural factor and also raises the possibility of a genetic-cultural link (Leff, 1981). For future directions, the most important aspect of cultural training may be its potential for directing students toward pathways for ultimate synthesis of the components and axes of mental health in biopsychosocial human beings.

REFERENCES

Acosta, F. X., Yamamoto, J., & Evans, L. A. (Eds.). (1982) *Effective psychotherapy for low-income and minority patients*. New York: Plenum.

Bernal, M. E., & Padilla, A. M. (1982) Status of minority curricula and training in clinical psychology. *American Psychologist, 37*, 780–787.

Hines, A., & Pedersen, P. (October 1980). The cultural grid: Matching social system variables and cognitive perspectives. Manuscript, East-West Culture Learning Institute, Honolulu.

Lambo, T. A. (1978). Psychotherapy in Africa. *Human Nature, 1*, 32–39.

Leff, J. (1981). *Psychiatry around the globe: A transcultural view*. New York: Marcel Dekker.

Lefley, H. P., & Bestman, E. W. (1984) Community mental health and minorities: A multi-ethnic approach. In Sue, S., & Moore, T., (Eds.), *Community mental health in a pluralistic society*. New York: Human Sciences Press.

Lefley, H. P., & Urrutia, R. (1982) Cross-cultural training for mental health personnel. Final Report. Report, NIMH Training Grant No. 5-T24-MH15429, University of Miami School of Medicine.

Lin, K-M, & Finder, E. (1983) Neuroleptic dosage for Asians. *American Journal of Psychiatry, 140* 490–491.

Loo, C. (1980) Bicultural contextualizer model for cultural sensitivity in counseling. Manuscript, Chinatown Research Center and the University of California, Santa Cruz.

Marsella, A. J., & Pedersen, P. B. (1981) *Cross-cultural counseling and psychotherapy*. New York: Pergamon Press.

Marsella, A. J., & White, G. M. (1982) *Cultural conceptions of mental health and therapy*. Dordrecht, Holland: Reidel.

McGoldrick, M., Pearce, J., & Giordano, J. (Eds.). (1982) *Ethnicity and family therapy*. New York: Guilford Press.

Pedersen, P. B. (1981a) Developing interculturally skilled counselors. Final Report. Report, NIMH Training Grant No. 1-T24-MH15552, Institute of Behavioral Sciences, Honolulu.

——— (1981b) Triad counseling. In Corsini, R. J. (Ed.), *Handbook of innovative psychotherapies*. New York: Wiley, pp. 840–854.

Pedersen, P., Draguns, J. G., Lonner, W. J., & Trimble, J. (Eds.). (1981) *Counseling across cultures*, 2nd ed. Honolulu: University Press of Hawaii.

Reynolds, D. K. (1980) *The quiet therapies: Japanese pathways to personal growth*. Honolulu: University Press of Hawaii.

Spiegel, J. P., & Papajohn, J. (1983) Training program in ethnicity and mental health.

Final Report. NIMH Training Grant No. 5-T24-MH14962. Brandeis University, The Florence Heller School, Waltham, Mass.

Sue, D. W. (1981) *Counseling the culturally different*. New York: Wiley.

Sue, S. (1983) Ethnic minority issues in psychology: A reexamination. *American Psychologist, 38*, 583–592.

Triandis, H. C. (1977). Theoretical framework for evaluation of cross-cultural training effectiveness. *International Journal of Intercultural Relations, 1*, 19–45.

Weidman, H. H. (1979). The transcultural view: Prerequisite to interethnic (intercultural) communication in medicine. *Social Science & Medicine, 13B* (2), 85–87.

The Status of Racial- and Ethnic-Minority Counseling: A Training Perspective

J. MANUEL CASAS

Until recently, *racial- and ethnic-minority counseling* was simplistically defined as any counseling relationship in which the client is a member of a racial- or ethnic-minority group and the counselor a member of the majority group (that is, white, middle class, and English speaking). Although accurately reflecting a social, political, and economic reality prevalent in the United States at the time, the definition, from a social science perspective, was limited in scope and in retrospect was inaccurate.

With the advent of the sixties, the growing attention posited on racial- and ethnic-minority groups by the society at large provided an incentive for social scientists to take steps via their research to extend the definition of *racial- and ethnic-minority counseling* to encompass more accurately and comprehensively the relationships between *counselors* and *clients* who are of a different racial, ethnic, and/or social-cultural background. Complementing the efforts of the social scientists were the socio-political efforts on the part of the two major professional associations (American Psychological Association [APA] and American Association for Counseling and Development [AACD]) to make racial- and ethnic-minority counseling in the broadest sense a reality by formulating policies and establishing organizational committees and boards to direct and/or oversee efforts to reach and work with racial- and ethnic-minority groups more effectively. From a policy perspective, the Vail Conference held in 1973 under the auspices of both the American Psychological Association and the National Institute of Mental Health (NIMH) set a serious tone for making such counseling a reality. More specifically, this conference put forth the recommendation that conducting therapy or counseling without cultural sensitivity would be declared unethical. The intention of this recommendation was that knowledge of culture related to therapy would cease being an esoteric field and become a matter of direct and practical concern for the vast majority of practicing clinical—and, by implication, counseling—psychologists.

Within the APA varied committees and boards were established, including the Committee on Equality of Opportunity in Psychology, the Board of Social and Ethical Responsibility in Psychology, the Minority Affairs Office, and the Board of Minority Affairs. In a similar vein, AACD established the Association of Non-White Concerns. Working through these newly created committees and boards or already established divisions and associations, objectives, guidelines, and recommendations were formulated to improve the responsiveness of the profession to the training, research, and service needs of racial- and ethnic-minority groups. For a more detailed account of the professional associations' efforts relative to these groups, refer to J. M. Casas (in press).

In light of these professional efforts, the purpose of this chapter is to evaluate, from the training perspective, the status of racial-ethnic persons in the clinical and counseling areas of psychology and to make brief and specific recommendations to serve as an impetus for the professional to strengthen and expedite additional efforts to make racial- and ethnic-minority counseling a reality.

Racial- and ethnic-minority counseling is in line with what other writers call "cross-cultural counseling." But the term *cross-cultural counseling* is open to a variety of interpretations that could include all differences (for example, sex, age, role, life-style, socioeconomic status). Furthermore, this term also encompasses works conducted on foreign-born persons living in countries other than the United States. In contrast, the term *racial- and ethnic-minority counseling* directs specific attention to those variables—race, ethnicity, and minority status— that have been consistently used to single out, categorize, and even explain blacks, Hispanics, Asian-Americans, and/or Native Americans, who, living within the United States, have most recently been the focus of so-called cross-cultural-counseling efforts.

THE STATUS QUO

Although the actions taken by organizations such as APA and AACD were well intentioned and exemplary, the impact of such actions relative to racial-ethnic minorities appears to have been much weaker than what was originally desired. Racial-ethnic minorities continue to be underrepresented in fields of applied psychology. For example, between 1971 and 1979 N. N. Wagner and his associates (Kennedy & Wagner, 1979) consistently found Native Americans, Asian-Americans, blacks, and Hispanics to be underrepresented seriously both as students and faculty in clinical-psychology programs. W. Parham and J. R. Moreland (1981) conducted a survey of APA and non-APA approved programs and also found blacks and Hispanics underrepresented as students in counseling psychology.

In a very comprehensive study, N. F. Russo, E. L. Olmedo, J. Stapp, and R. Fulcher (1981) found that members of racial- and ethnic-minority groups comprise 1,284 or 3.1 percent of all APA members. More specifically, blacks (1.2 percent) are the largest group, followed by Asians (1.05 percent), Hispanics

(0.7 percent), and American Indians (0.2 percent). Furthermore, although clinical psychology is the largest subfield and has the largest number (511), it does not have the largest percentage of racial- and ethnic-minority-group members. Examining representation of racial- and ethnic-minority members across employment settings, the prevailing pattern shows that minority doctorate holders are least represented in independent practice and academic settings and most represented in four-year colleges and human-service settings. The employment pattern for master's level members is much the same as that of doctoral-level members.

Using the statistics from the 1980–81 Survey of Graduate Departments of Psychology, N. F. Russo and colleagues (1981) provided a closer look at the representativeness of racial- and ethnic-minority persons in academic settings (that is, graduate departments of psychology). Inspecting doctoral and master's departments, they found that approximately 5.0 percent of the graduate faculty in both types of departments are racial-ethnic minorities. Furthermore, racial- and ethnic-minority persons were more often jointly appointed and part-time faculty than full-time faculty, and only 3.1 percent of the tenured faculty in doctoral departments and 3.8 percent in master's departments were racial- and ethnic-minority-group members. Examining the most prestigious position in academia—full professorship—the statistics showed that of 2,073 full professors in doctoral-level graduate departments of psychology, 57 (2.7 percent) were from racial- and ethnic-minority groups. From this total, 8 (14.0 percent) were women. These data compare with 1,050 assistant professors, of whom 88 (8.4 percent) were members of minorities, and of this total 40 (45.9 percent) were women.

Addressing the fact that with the exception of L. K. Jones (1976) no comprehensive survey of ethnic-minority representation in counselor education had been published in the professional counseling literature, D. R. Atkinson (1983) conducted a survey of all counselor-education programs in the United States. From his survey Atkinson found that relative to population statistics blacks and Hispanics were underrepresented as students. In addition, racial-ethnic minorities were more likely to be enrolled in part-time and master's degree programs and less likely to be enrolled in full-time and doctoral-degree programs.

Although the accuracy of findings presented in the various studies attempting to assess the representativeness of racial- and ethnic-minority persons within psychology is open to question for a variety of reasons (Atkinson, 1983), the preponderance of evidence supports the conclusions reached by most researchers that racial-ethnic minorities have been and are underrepresented in psychology, and that such underrepresentation is particularly high in applied psychology.

Optimistically, there is evidence that the number of racial-ethnic minorities enrolled as students and actually completing a doctorate in psychology is slowly increasing. For instance, Russo and associates (1981), using data from the National Research Council and the 1980–81 Survey of Graduate Departments of Psychology, showed that the percentage of racial-ethnic minorities increased from 6.7 percent in 1977 to 8.0 percent in 1980, and although the increase has been slow, there were actually higher percentages of racial-ethnic minorities among new doctorate recipients than there were among doctoral APA members or faculty in graduate departments of psychology. Whether such an incremental trend will continue is questionable. In fact, several authors have expressed the concern that minority admissions have "peaked" and are actually on a downward trend. Others have contended that if the downward trend has not yet begun, it soon will begin, given the existing political climate of the social and behavioral sciences. M. E. Bernal (1980) further contended that the incremental trends appear to be so weak that they are almost meaningless, given the mental-health needs of the rapidly growing racial- and ethnic-minority groups.

There are many reasons for the fact that the profession has fallen short in its efforts to improve the representation of racial-ethnic minorities within psychology. In particular, institutional changes in the area of recruitment and admission policies, curricula, and training that could contribute to substantial increases in the number of racial- and ethnic-minority psychologists have not been made (Bernal, 1980). Support for this contention relative to recruitment was provided by D. R. Atkinson and B. Wampold (1981), who found that counselor-education programs seem to be making only limited efforts to recruit, admit, and support minority students.

In terms of graduate admission policies, the tendency has been to adhere to the use of traditional criteria (that is, graduate aptitude tests and undergraduate grade point averages [GPAs]) to identify students who can successfully complete clinical and counseling graduate programs (Bernal, 1980). This practice continues despite the fact that reviews of research related to trainee selection have shown little evidence of a strong relationship between these criteria and successful completion of graduate training in psychology. In the area of clinical psychology, there is evidence that students admitted into programs largely on the basis of nontraditional criteria (for example, peer and admission-committee assessments, letters of recommendation, undergraduate curricular and extra-curricular achievements, definitions of interest in psychology, and statements of career aims) did as well as majority students who scored substantially higher on traditional admission criteria (Heine, 1976).

Within counseling psychology, numerous studies and reviews have also examined a number of variables (for example, personality characteristics, social intelligence, cognitive flexibility, communication skills, and performance on pseudo-counseling situations, as well as undergraduate GPA and graduate aptitude tests) as predictors of future success in counseling (Rowe, Murphy, & De Csipkes, 1975). Interestingly, not one of these studies has offered conclusive evidence that any of these variables, singly or combined, predict counseling effectiveness much better than chance. Accordingly, D. R. Atkinson, D. Stasso, and R. Hosford (1978) concluded that a variety of theoretical, philosophical, and intuitively based criteria may well be as good or better than that which has been researched to date.

Despite the available evidence that nontraditional admission procedures can be as effective as the traditional ones, there is a hesitancy to adopt such procedures. The hesitancy appears to result from the unproven belief that the adoption of such procedures would result in a lowering of admission standards for racial-ethnic minorities. At this time, it would appear that having alternative procedures would provide the opportunity to assess whether differential selection criteria have differential validity for separate groups.

With respect to curricula, efforts have resulted in a marked increase in the number of articles that provide conceptual frameworks for integration of racial- and ethnic-minority curricula and practica in training psychologists. In addition, varied researchers have not only proposed but implemented training modules to better prepare counselors and clinicians to work with racial- and ethnic-minority persons (see Arredondo's chapter in this book). On a national scale, several conferences and workshops have been organized to address the training of minority mental-health professionals.

Until recently, it has been impossible to gauge the success of these efforts, because the actual inclusion of minority content in psychology graduate-training programs had not been investigated. However, recently M. E. Bernal and A. M. Padilla (1982) conducted a survey to determine the current status of minority curricula and training in clinical psychology. Their findings largely reflected a reluctance on the part of training programs to include course work on mental-health and socio-cultural issues relative to minority groups. Furthermore, although the findings indicated that the preparation of clinical psychologists to work with minorities is regarded as "somewhat important," they also provided ample evidence that such preparation actually receives minor attention.

CONCLUSION AND RECOMMENDATIONS

The professional associations have taken action at the organizational and policy-making levels; however, available evidence shows that efforts have fallen short of meeting their mark, and much has yet to be done to improve the general status of racial- and ethnic-minority persons relative to training and subsequently to make racial- and ethnic-minority counseling a substantive reality. If efforts have fallen short, it is not from a lack of good intentions and prescriptive recommendations that have been proposed by groups within the associations (for example, APA's Board of Minority Affairs and the Division of Counseling Psychology and AACD's Association for Counselor Education and Supervision) and by concerned individuals (for example, Bernal, 1980; Bernal & Padilla, 1982; Sue, Bernier, Durran, Feinberg, Pedersen, Smith, & Vasquez-Nuttal, 1982) but from a failure to provide strong incentives to encourage the profession to act on the good intentions by following through on selective recommendations. Working from this perspective, in this section no additional prescriptive or "how to" recommendations are made; instead, attention is solely focused on recommendations relative to incentives.

From a theoretical perspective, it should be noted that incentives serve to motivate individuals to take specific action to obtain certain rewards or avoid certain punishers. Furthermore, given past learning experiences and/or present situational conditions, that which is rewarding to one individual may be perceived as negative by another. With this in mind, the following brief recommendations are put forth knowing that some individuals, especially those already actively involved in racial- and ethnic-minority counseling, will see them as necessary and positive, and others will see them only from a negative perspective:

1. Accreditations of training programs should be contingent on (a) demonstrated efforts to recruit, admit, and retain racial- and ethnic-minority students and faculty; and (b) the provision of racial- and ethnic-minority curricula and training, course content, and training procedures should be subject to review and approval by an informed and sensitive office or committee (for example, in APA, the Office of Minority Affairs).
2. Funding agencies (for example, NIMH) should make eligibility for awards by institutions contingent on meeting the same criteria as that suggested for accreditation.
3. Preparation for licensing should require course work pertinent to racial- and ethnic-minority persons. Such course work should emphasize socio-cultural variables in understanding human behavior. The licensing exams should contain a significant amount of relevant questions dealing with racial- and ethnic-minority groups and concerns.
4. As with individuals who specialize in the use of special techniques (for example, hypnotherapists, sex therapists), certification should also be required of any individual whose position requires extensive interactions with persons from racial- and ethnic-minority groups.

As evident, these recommendations do not provide a "how to" component based on the belief that the professional associations—the members—know exactly how to get things done when they want them done. The trick is to get them to want to do that something, thus the emphasis on incentives. With respect to making racial- and ethnic-minority counseling a reality, the profession knows what it ethically should do, knows the incentives that will facilitate the "how to." All that's necessary at this time is for it sensitively and realistically to want to do something about it.

REFERENCES

Atkinson, D. R. (1983) Ethnic minority representation in counselor education. *Counselor Education and Supervision, 23*, 7–19.
Atkinson, D. R., Stasso, D., & Hosford, R. (1978) Selecting counselor trainees with multicultural strengths: A solution to the Bakke decision crisis. *The Personnel and Guidance Journal, 56*, 546–549.
Atkinson, D. R., & Wampold, B. (1981) Affirmative action efforts of counselor education programs. *Counselor Education and Supervision, 6*, 262–272.
Bernal, M. E. (1980) Hispanic issues in psychology: Curricula and training. *Hispanic Journal of Behavioral Sciences, 2*, 129–146.

Bernal, M. E., & Padilla, A. M. (1982) Status of minority curricula and training in clinical psychology. *American Psychologist, 37*, 780–787.

Casas, J. M. (in press). Policy, training, and research in counseling psychology: The racial/ethnic minority perspective. In Brown, S., & Lent, R. (Eds.), *Handbook of counseling psychology*. New York: Wiley.

Heine, R.W. (1976) Comparative performance of doctoral students admitted on the basis of traditional and nontraditional criteria. Manuscript, University of Michigan, Ann Arbor.

Jones, L. K. (1976) A national survey of the program and enrollment characteristics of counselor education programs. *Counselor Education and Supervision, 15*, 166–176.

Kennedy, C. D., & Wagner, N. N. (1979) Psychology and affirmative action: 1977. *Professional Psychology, 10*, 234–243.

Parham, W., & Moreland, J. R. (1981) Nonwhite students in counseling psychology: A closer look. *Professional psychology, 12*, 499–507.

Rowe, W., Murphy, H. B., & De Csipkes, R. A. (1975) The relationship of counselor characteristics and counseling effectiveness. *Review of Educational Research, 45*, 231–246.

Russo, N. F., Olmedo, E. L., Stapp, J., & Fulcher, R. (1981) Women and minorities in psychology. *American Psychologist, 36*, 1315–1363.

Sue, D. W., Bernier, J. E., Durran, A., Feinberg, L., Pedersen, P., Smith, E. J., & Vasquez-Nuttal, E. (1982) Position paper: Cross-cultural counseling competencies. *The Counseling Psychologist, 10*(2), 45–52.

Training Issues in Conducting Therapy with Ethnic-Minority-Group Clients

STANLEY SUE, PHILLIP D. AKUTSU, AND CINDY HIGASHI

For several reasons, national interest in the mental-health needs of ethnic minorities has steadily grown in the past decade. First, the ethnic-minority population (particularly American Indians, Asian-Americans, blacks, and Hispanics) has grown to represent roughly 17 percent of the nation's total population. Second, the available evidence suggests that ethnic-minority groups are under particular stress, involving problems such as immigrant status, poverty, culture shock, prejudice, and discrimination (President's Commission on Mental Health, 1978). Third, the kinds of mental-health services available to ethnic minorities have traditionally been ineffective or unresponsive to their particular needs, and few opportunities exist to become more adequately trained for work with these groups. Martha Bernal and Amado Padilla (1982) revealed that few programs have actually provided training experiences relevant to ethnic groups. Finally, the issues surrounding ethnic-minority groups can no longer be viewed as minor or peripheral to the concerns of the nation. As noted by H. Hodgkinson (1983), whites are motivated to work with minority students and workers more by enlightened self-interest than political liberalism or noblesse oblige.

Some attempts have been made to address these issues by recruiting ethnic minorities into the mental-health field, by training individuals to work with ethnic-minority clients, and by altering psychotherapeutic services and programs to meet better the needs of these clients, but results of these efforts are still unclear. They have not been systematically applied and planned. The purpose of this chapter is to offer some suggestions on how to train individuals, especially non-minorities, to work with ethnic-minority groups. Although our examples may deal specifically with Asian-Americans, the basic training elements are also applicable to work with other ethnic-minority groups.

MATCH OR FIT

Our underlying assumption is that intervention or treatment is more likely to be effective when it matches or fits the cognitive map, life-style, or cultural background of clients. That is, ideally the intervention strategy is culturally consistent with the expectations and background of the clients. When treatment approaches are culturally inconsistent with the background and expectations of clients, many clients fail to use psychotherapeutic services, prematurely terminate treatment, or fail to show positive outcomes (Sue & Morishima, 1982).

A client-therapist cultural match may also result in positive therapeutic outcomes. Matches are important, because they presumably facilitate certain processes or conditions. First, the therapist is better able to understand, assess, or diagnose the problems and situation of the client in a sensitive manner. Second, the therapist can use a language or concepts that are within the worldview or background of the client. Hence therapy is more comprehensible and acceptable to the client. Third, intervention techniques can be geared toward the personal or environmental supports or limitations that the client has. Other conditions can be listed. The main point is that although client-systems matches do not guarantee positive outcomes, they enhance the probability of favorable change. There are many unresolved issues given that the "fit" is important. For example, how far do we go in matching? Can't a client be sometimes helped by therapists or by systems that are radically different from the client? On what key variables should matching occur? These questions should really be examined through empirical research. If we have erred in therapeutic intervention, it has probably been in the direction of ignoring relevant cultural and situational variables in ethnic populations.

To increase the responsiveness of mental-health services to minority groups, we must find the right service for the person, change the person to fit the service, or change the service to fit the person. The first alternative is based upon the assumption that appropriate services are somewhere available. The task is to have the services accessible. Clients who have special needs, for example, a Chinese-speaking client who is located in a non-Chinese community, may not have access to bilingual therapists because of physical distance from these therapists, because of catchment-area boundaries, because of lack of knowledge of the service, and so on. By solving these problems, the client can obtain responsive services. The second approach is to change the person to fit the service. Preparing clients for services (for example, explaining the services, giving information on the process of treatment, correcting stereotypes of treatment, or other forms of pretherapy intervention) may facilitate a better person–mental-health-service match. This method can also be hazardous if it is carried to the extreme of robbing persons of their cultural values and of implying that there is but one single standard (for example, one must change to meet requirements for therapy) to which all persons should conform. Finally, services themselves can be changed to accommodate diverse cultures and persons. This direction is the most innovative and responsive and yet the most complicated and difficult. It implies flexibility, attention to individual differences, multiethnic and multilingual mental-health personnel, a structure dictated by human needs rather than by bureaucratic roles, knowledge and experiences relevant to ethnic groups, and the integration of new forms of intervention.

TRAINING IMPLICATIONS

Assuming that the match between therapist and client is important, how do we go about training therapists to provide culturally consistent forms of treatment? We believe that three elements are particularly important: Knowledge of clients' culture and status, actual experiences with these clients, and the ability to devise innovative treatment strategies. These elements are important regardless of whether therapists refer clients elsewhere, try to change clients to fit the service, or change the service to fit the client.

Knowledge of Culture and Status

In training students or mental-health professionals to work with ethnic-minority groups, the notion is often argued that the culture of these groups be examined. Implicit in this notion is the assumption that one's cultural background influences perceptions, expectations, expression of symptoms, nature of stressors and resources available, and so on. Therefore, to work effectively with clients, the therapist needs to take cultural factors into consideration.

We do not want to question this assumption. However, simply understanding the culture of clients is insufficient when dealing with ethnic-minority groups. Here we want to distinguish between a cultural-determinism perspective and an ethnic-minority-group approach. The former uses culture as an *independent* variable in explaining similarities and differences in the values, perceptions, and behaviors of ethnic-minority groups. The latter views the perceptions and behaviors of ethnic-minority groups as a function of the *interaction* of cultural patterns and institutions in the United States. The status of ethnic-minority groups in this country has been influenced not only by the cultural values of these groups but also by the values, reactions, and institutions of the larger society. In addition to acquiring knowledge of culture, one must also develop awareness of interethnic relationships, racism, and the historical-political-social and psychological context in which these groups have functioned.

How can this knowledge be obtained? There are several means to learn more about the culture and background of minority groups:

1. Have courses and curricula focusing on ethnic-minority groups and issues. Specific courses on ethnic minorities, race relations, and so on could be offered, or ethnic content could be included in existing clinical-counseling courses.
2. Make reading lists of literature available. There is now a growing body of literature on ethnic-minority groups, and training programs should have this literature available for students.

3. Expose students to seminars, workshops, guest lectures, and so on that focus on ethnic issues in culture, mental health, treatment, and personality. Programs should provide students with these experiences.

4. Make use of available films, videotapes, and other media. For example, the National Asian American Psychology Training Center, an APA-approved clinical psychology internship program in San Francisco, has developed a series of videotapes concerning Asian-American issues discussed by mental-health professionals and community leaders.

Actual Experience

Many training programs do not expose students to ethnic-minority-group issues to any substantial degree. The few programs that do include minority-group issues rely primarily upon course work and lectures. Knowledge acquired through these didactic means is important. However, at another level of analysis, these techniques are perhaps necessary but not sufficient in facilitating skills in working with ethnic-minority-group clients. Knowledge of ethnic-minority groups along with actual experience (for example, seeing a large number of such clients or working in ethnic communities) is needed. Typically, information contained in the literature or in courses tends to be abstract. That is, when one discusses culture, reference is made to the socially transmitted behavioral patterns, values, beliefs, and institutions that are *characteristic* of a group or community. By characterizing a group, individual differences within that group are likely to be deemphasized. Donald Campbell (1967) warned that the finding of actual differences between cultural groups often leads to exaggerated stereotypes of these differences.

Another example of the potential problem is based upon a study by Donald Atkinson and his colleagues (1978). As part of that study the investigators hypothesized that Asian-Americans would prefer counselors who engaged in logical, structured, and directive approaches rather than in affective, reflective, and ambiguous approaches. It was thought that the preference could be attributed to Asian cultural values and experiences that emphasized restraint of emotional displays and interactions in the context of structured roles. By varying counseling approaches, the investigators found a clear preference among Asian-Americans for a structured and directive counselor. The problem lies not in the findings themselves but in the misuse of the results. After reading the published study, many therapists and counselors may believe that they are "culturally responsive" if they now treat Asian-American clients in a directive and authoritarian manner, even though many of these clients are highly assimilated and no longer hold traditional Asian values. Knowledge about the culture of ethnic-minority groups should not be applied without consideration of the particular ethnic client. Otherwise, the cultural context for a group is confounded with the particular individual from that group.

It is through experience with members of an ethnic-minority group that within-group heterogeneity is fully appreciated. One can then see the total range of behaviors and values within the ethnic community. If therapists and counselors want to work effectively with ethnic clients, they should see as many ethnic clients as possible or they should immerse themselves in ethnic communities or activities. Obviously, training programs often have difficulty providing students with access to ethnic clients or communities, especially when the individuals of a particular ethnic group are few or are not found in that area. Such programs may have to make special arrangements to find more ethnic clients for students or at least give students the opportunity to spend time in settings where ethnic individuals are located.

Innovative Strategies

In addition to having knowledge and experience, trainees should be innovative when working with ethnic-minority clients. Because of cultural differences or minority-group status, traditional forms of treatment or counseling may not be effective. By distinguishing between innovative and traditional forms of treatment, we are not implying that there is a clear demarcation between these forms of therapy; nor is it being suggested that it is possible to identify clearly traditional therapeutic practice. Rather, our assertion is based upon several working hypotheses:

1. Counseling and therapeutic practices in this country are primarily designed for work with mainstream Americans.
2. Training programs provide trainees with skills in these (traditional) practices.
3. Oftentimes, these practices are not consistent with the cultural values or life-styles of ethnic-minority-group clients. The greater the difference between treatment tactics and client's life-style or culture, the greater the need for innovative (less traditional) forms of treatment.

Innovative approaches should be considered especially if more traditional therapeutic strategies are likely to be ineffective. These innovative approaches should be based upon cultural considerations. It is one thing to advocate innovation but a different matter to suggest the means for acquiring the skills in finding non-traditional tactics. How do training programs go about inculcating these skills in trainees? Several key points are important:

1. In working with ethnic-minority groups, therapeutic approaches should be assessed for their effectiveness and potential side effects.
2. Innovative strategies should be devised if it is likely that the cost (for example, side effects) of traditional approaches are high and the benefits (therapeutic outcomes) are low.
3. Those innovative or alternative strategies that better match the culture or life-style of clients should be considered.

4. Trainees should be taught to be flexible and willing to assume roles that are not typically associated with therapists or counselors.

5. In devising non-traditional strategies, knowledge of culture, experience with members of an ethnic group, and the advice of supervisors or consultants knowledgeable about the client's culture or life-style are important.

SUMMARY

It was not possible to provide here an in-depth or elaborate analysis of the procedures to use in training those not familiar with ethnic-minority groups. Nevertheless, we have tried to outline the central issues in training. Evidence suggests that training programs are not sufficiently preparing trainees to work with ethnic-minority groups. Consequently, mental-health services are not adequately addressing the multitude of problems encountered by minority groups.

We believe the directions for more adequate training must be based upon an appreciation of the concept of match or fit between service delivery and client background or life-style. To increase this match, trainees need to acquire knowledge, experience, and ability to devise innovative intervention approaches.

Although the problems in training and in-service delivery can be easily documented, the real task is not simply to reiterate the problems. Rather, we must specify what directions to take, in view of the problems, and begin to implement solutions. Once this occurs, the mental-health professions will gain increasing credibility and effectiveness in dealing with the needs of all Americans.

REFERENCES

Atkinson, D. R., Maruyama, M., & Matsui, S. (1978) The effects of counselor race and counseling approach on Asian Americans' perceptions of counselor credibility and utility. *Journal of Counseling Psychology, 25,* 76–83.

Bernal, M. E., & Padilla, A. M. (1982) Status of minority curricula and training in clinical psychology. *American psychologist, 37,* 780–787.

Campbell, D. T. (1967) Stereotypes and the perception of group differences. *American Psychologist, 22,* 817–829.

Hodgkinson, H. L. (1983) Guess who's coming to college. *Academe, 69,* 13–20.

President's Commission on Mental Health (1978) *Report to the President.* Washington, D.C.: U.S. Government Printing Office.

Sue, S., & Morishima, J. K. (1982) *The mental health of Asian Americans.* San Francisco: Jossey-Bass.

Cross-Cultural Counselor Education and Training

PATRICIA ARREDONDO

The professional origins of cross-cultural counselor education can be traced to the emergence and popularity of ethnic awareness and judicial mandates on behalf of minority groups. With the passage of the Civil Rights Act of 1964 and the black movement of the late sixties, previously disenfranchised groups such as women and minorities gained greater recognition as "equals" under the law. Affirmative-action guidelines became the password that would insure accessibility to university study and to equal-employment opportunities. Both are areas relevant to cross-cultural education.

Within the American Psychological Association (APA), there have been ongoing efforts by psychologists concerned about appropriate training to work with underserved cultural groups. The 1973 Vail Conference (Korman, 1974), the Austin Conference (1975), and the Dulles Conference (1978) cited the failure of clinical and counseling psychology to meet the mental-health needs of ethnic-minority groups. It was further suggested that all professional psychologists require training and continuing education in the special issues of different religious, ethnic, sexual, and economic groups.

The increased sensitivity and awareness around ethnic-minority issues has generated consideration of gender, sex, age, life-style, physical handicap, and physical-disability factors. These concerns are being addressed comprehensively by the Human Rights Committee of the Association for Counselor Education and Supervision (Arredondo, 1983b). A human-rights annotated bibliography (Arredondo & Okoawo, 1983) and a training manual (Arredondo & Gawalek, 1982) have been published for use on pre-service and in-service levels.

The Ethical Standards of Psychologists (1979) Revision adopted by the American Psychological Association also addresses the need for cultural sensitivity. Principle 2—Competence—maintains that psychologists must recognize differences among people, such as those that may be associated with age, sex, socioeconomic and ethnic backgrounds (p. 2). The Standards for Providers of

Psychological Services (1977), in their statement of personnel qualifications skills, cite "language, cultural and experiential background, race and sex" as directly relevant to the needs and characteristics of the users served (p. 5).

Although standards exist, there is still a disparity between cultural knowledge and skills development in training due "to the lack of institutional support beyond the theoretical level" (Sue et al., 1982, p. 51).

To address the cross-cultural competency-training void comprehensively, the Education and Training Committee of Division 17, Counseling Psychology, has developed a position paper outlining cross-cultural counseling competencies (Sue et al., 1982). This is a professional milestone, because for the first time culture-based differences are recognized as inherent in psychological training and practice. In effect, this chapter asserts for all psychologists the centrality of culture to one's work and everyday encounters and provides tangible means (the competencies) by which one can become culturally skilled and effective. Furthermore, the Education and Training Committee recommends that the specific competencies be adopted by APA "to be used as a guideline for accreditation" (Sue et al., 1982, p. 45). Response to this recommendation has far-ranging implications for psychological training as well as licensing criteria. Regardless of the outcome, there are counselor educators, such as myself, who have been and will continue to be engaged in cross-cultural training activities.

The contextual-background information is important to this chapter to assess better the status quo of cross-cultural counselor education and training in the United States. A cross-cultural emphasis in counselor education and training has received increasing attention in the past decade. Courses, conferences, seminars, degree specializations, research studies, assessment and evaluation procedures and instrumentation, and professional organizations in the name of cross-cultural counselor education are reported in the literature and at national conventions with greater frequency. This development occurs within a sociopolitical and historical context in the United States that is visibly culturally pluralistic and growing, with the continuous arrival of immigrants and refugees.

This is a constructive presentation, one that describes training from both theoretical models and practical implemented applications. The latter serve as demonstration projects, replicable in diverse institutional settings. The former provide conceptual, competency-based perspectives for cross-cultural counselor training.

CROSS-CULTURAL TRAINING MODELS

Conceptual Frameworks

Theoretical models to understand persons better in terms of cultural life experiences, societal forces, and individual psychodynamics have been proposed by psychologists (Arredondo, 1981, 1983b; LeVine & Padilla, 1980; Pedersen, 1978; Sue, 1977, 1978). In general, they draw from the fields of anthropology, sociology, cross-cultural psychology, ethnic studies, social-learning theory, and political science and present a more comprehensive approach to understanding persons as individuals and as members of the group. These cross-cultural frameworks complement those introduced in other areas, for example, human development, personality, and psychodynamic theories, suggesting a whole rather than a fragmented view of persons. Although ethnic-minority persons have been the subjects of these models, a generic relevance exists as will be evident in the following examples.

Derald Wing Sue et al. (1982) proposed a general theory of worldviews as a means of identifying differences in the perspective held by minority groups and all people in general. He defined a *worldview* as how a person perceives her or his relationship to the world (nature, institutions, other people, things, etc.). Worldviews are highly correlated with a person's upbringing and life experiences. Additional components are economic and social class, religion, and sex. All bear on the individual's identity development. According to Sue, the formation of worldviews incorporates the two psychological orientations of locus of control and locus of responsibility. He conceptualized four worldview categories reflecting the individual's degree of internality and externality on the two constructs. The views are internal locus of control-internal locus of responsibility; external locus of control-external locus of responsibility; external locus of control-internal locus of responsibility; and internal locus of control-external locus of responsibility.

Another model proposed by Sue (1977) considers the appropriateness or inappropriateness of counseling approaches. This requires a knowledge of minority-group cultures and experiences, that is, cultural and class values, language factors, and unique and common experiences. This information would assist in the consideration of potential counseling strategies and techniques and the counselor's ability to effect them.

A model of pluralistic counseling particularly in reference to Hispanics (LeVine & Padilla, 1980) has application with other groups, because it is based on the Personality Mediation Approach ($C^1 \blacklozenge P \blacklozenge C^2$). This posits a chain reaction in which culture creates individual personality, and the individual in turn embellishes and changes the culture (p. 5). Both individual and cultural dynamics are important, requiring the clinician "to integrate an understanding of the dual cultural experience into the therapeutic process" (p. 14). I propose a psychohistorical approach (Arredondo, 1983a) as another means to understanding immigrants and people in general. To this end, I have designed a Multi-Factor Needs Assessment that looks at biographical and clinical data from the perspective of contextual factors such as history, politics, family systems, and cultural factors; and from individual factors including age, sex, and entry status (immigrant, refugee, illegal entrant). For example, knowledge about a woman's home country, its political climate, and its historical evolution may explain why she left, what occupation she held, and the cultural expectations of women. This information allows one to see beyond her immigrant status, with its inherent limitations, to her strengths and resources. As a result, more appropriate and relevant interventions can be planned.

Summary

This is far from a thorough presentation of cross-cultural theoretical models and reflects only those developed with United States minority groups. There are other non-Western approaches such as *Ho'oponopono*, a Hawaiian problem-solving approach (Nishihara, 1978), Naikan and Morita therapy, Arab folk-healing approaches, and *espiritismo*, a form of folk healing among some Latino groups. For counselor educators, these models offer alternative perspectives that could be introduced in counseling theory and practicum and other courses. They broaden the trainee's knowledge base and demonstrate the generic value of cross-cultural models. A. Roark (1974) suggested that "counseling minority group members is no different from counseling other people," because in all cases, personal effectiveness is the goal (p. 172).

Competency-Based Training

A number of competency-based training models have also been proposed (Ivey, 1977; Arredondo-Dowd & Gonsalves, 1980; Copeland, 1983; Casas, 1982). A. E. Ivey's (1977) Taxonomy stresses cultural skills with communication skills. "One who has cultural expertise is able to relate with self, others and society" (p. 279). The P. Arredondo-Dowd and J. Gonsalves (1980) schema stresses multiple competencies—counseling, cultural, linguistic, and pedagogical—as a means of preparing culturally effective counselors. A competency-based, cross-cultural-counseling model for the eighties has been outlined by Manuel Casas (1982). He included courses, practicum, and workshops within a cross-cultural-counseling specialization. Content-area courses are drawn from anthropology, sociology, psychology, psycholinguistics, and sociolinguistics. Simultaneously, trainees would take core counseling courses of a theoretical and skill-building nature. Elaine Copeland (1983) also outlined the types of competencies that should be developed in skills-building areas. The focus is particularly on the trainees as the facilitators of the client's growth and development from culturally informed perspectives.

GRADUATE-TRAINING PROJECTS

At the same time that the committee was developing the competencies, there were cross-cultural-training efforts underway at American universities. These efforts have taken different formats:

1. As specially funded projects (the DISC Project at the University of Hawaii)
2. As specializations integral to existing counseling psychology programs (at Boston

University; Teachers College, Columbia University; the University of California, Santa Barbara; California State University, Northridge; Syracuse University; the University of Massachusetts at Amherst; and Western Washington University at Bellingham)

3. As continuing-education conferences (the Winter Roundtable on Cross Cultural Counseling and Psychotherapy, Teachers College, and the Bilingual Counseling Conferences, Boston University)

The projects to be described have common features worth noting: they are designed with existing institutional-programmatic fabric; cross-cultural courses are required of all students, not just those in the specialization; the cross-cultural specialization is not isolated; the practicum provides relevant cross-cultural-counseling experiences; there is visible leadership by the faculty that is, in most cases, minority; there is an effort to attract a culturally diverse graduate-student population; and the training approaches are replicable. Due to space limitations, one or two projects are described below for each format.

Developing Interculturally Skilled Counselors: A Training Program

This project was designed and directed by Paul Pedersen with associate director Anthony Marsella at the University of Hawaii and the East-West Center. The project was funded through the Institute of Behavioral Sciences (TIBS) near the university for the years 1978–1981.

"The DISC project was directed toward a better understanding of ways in which cultural differences affect counseling" (Pedersen, 1983, p. 6). It combined an emphasis on intercultural *awareness* of cultural bias, *knowledge* about culturally different dynamics of mental health, and *skills* to make culturally appropriate interventions. With its interdisciplinary approach, the project provided "one possible basis for a comprehensive training, research and development program" (Pedersen, 1983, p. 26). Participants were all graduate students from a range of disciplines related to mental health such as psychology, anthropology, public health, education, communication, and social work. Recommendations for future programs focus on three primary goals: to encourage work by mental-health specialists in culturally diverse areas and settings, to broaden the culturally encapsulated mental-health point of view, and to increase the number of culturally effective mental-health personnel beyond the boundaries of ethnicity and race awareness. There must be a sensitivity to other human rights concerns also.

The Bilingual Cross-Cultural-Counseling Specialization

The primary objective of this training is to prepare culturally effective counselors to work with bilingual-multicultural populations (Arredondo-Dowd & Gonsalves, 1980). This approach is grounded in counselor-training principles and bilingual education providing a means to understand better the problems and advantages of working with linguistic-minority groups. I originated the project at Boston University in 1979, and it is an integral part of the master's program in counseling. This has led to acceptability, recognition, and integration "in-house" and has contributed to the rationale for federal support through Title VII, Bilingual Education Act. These monies were earmarked for student train-eeships from 1979 to 1983. Doctoral students also participated.

A typical program requires course work in the Counseling and Bilingual Education Program involving summer study and two semesters of full-time at-tendance. There is a two-semester, 20-hour-per-week practicum in an approved bilingual placement. To date, schools, mental-health centers, social-service agen-cies, vocational-training centers, court clinics, and hospital outpatient units have been used as training sites. Supervision is provided by a qualified bilingual clinician.

The heart of the specialization is the bilingual emphasis. Since 1979 there have been 30 graduates representing these language groups: Cape Verdean (Cre-ole), Chinese, Haitian (Creole French), Italian, Portuguese, Spanish, and Vi-etnamese. Project products include the *Activities Workbook for Linguistic Minority Groups* (1983) and videotapes that demonstrate counseling with a specific lin-guistic-minority group.

Other Programs

At the University of Massachusetts, Amherst, there is a strong emphasis on cross-cultural and minority issues, urban education, and oppression in School of Education (SED) curricula. Within the Counseling and Human Services pro-grams, at both the masters and doctoral level, there are specialized course work and practicum experiences. There are cooperative efforts between the Bilingual Education and Counseling programs, and as at Boston University, the cross-cultural-counseling course is required of all students.

Cross-cultural counseling is one of six specializations in the Counseling Pro-gram at Teachers College, Columbia University. All students take the required generic courses and then select among courses in six content areas, such as social organizations, to complement their area of specialization. Within the Counseling Program, there are four courses with a cross-cultural and minority emphasis. The practicum is on campus, at the Psychological Consultation Center, open to the public. Additionally, students have a field-work component in a setting relevant to their specialization.

Cross-Cultural Continuing Education

Teachers College was also the site of the Winter Roundtables on Cross Cultural Counseling and Psychotherapy (February 1983 and 1984). Coordinated by Sam Johnson, Jr., the conference presentors addressed practical dilemmas in cross-cultural practice, research, and training from their perspectives in psychiatry, psychology, social work, and education. The weekend Roundtable is available on a graduate-level credit and non-credit basis. A Certificate Program in Cross Cultural Training and Development is also available during summer terms.

The Bilingual Counseling conferences at Boston University have emphasized work with specific linguistic- and ethnic-minority groups, such as Cape Verdean, Chinese, Haitian, Portuguese, Puerto Rican, and Vietnamese. Presentations are made by local psychologists of the specific background assisted by program graduate students. The conferences are geared to particular groups such as mental-health workers, hospital staff, and personnel in the business sector.

FUTURE DIRECTIONS

Planning for the future suggests building from the past, taking the workable training efforts and maximizing them through diverse applications. More specifically, however, I recommend an outline that may assist in the planning of a cross-cultural education program of studies:

1. Articulate objectives that can be effected through existing curricula and practicum experiences.
2. Identify institutional and community-based resources.
3. Specify competency areas to be addressed through training, for example, consciousness raising, cognitive and experiential learning, interpersonal skills, assessment, and research.
4. Articulate enabling activities by which these competency areas will be addressed in existing courses, seminars, or through new course work.
5. Identify settings where these skills and knowledge can be exercised with culturally and linguistically diverse clients.
6. Design an evaluation procedure that corresponds to the objectives, competency areas, and enabling activities.
7. Work in cooperation with another colleague, not alone.

The growth of ethnic- and linguistic-minority populations in the United States is predicted, necessitating bilingual skills more than ever before. Fluency in English and a second language, particularly Spanish, is already a criterion for many counseling roles. Future demographic trends suggest greater linguistic diversity and an increase in international relations. It behooves counselors to consider the acquisition or restudying of a non-English language.

The underrepresentation of ethnic-minority persons in counseling-psychology training is a responsibility that must be assumed by all, not just a few, to make training relevant and appropriate (Atkinson, Morten, & Sue, 1983). There must be active recruitment of qualified candidates to insure greater representation and choice among future counseling psychologists. Our thinking must be long term and in anticipation of our potential global interactions.

Given these future trends, I foresee cross-cultural counselor training as central to counseling psychology. The models described are heuristic rather than ethno-specific, providing relevance across cultures. Counselor-educators must learn from these models now and apply them to course work and practica. It is our responsibility to trainees and the public alike. I urge this as a means of reminding my colleagues that we are in an enviable position of bringing about change, provided we are willing to look through multiple cultural lenses.

REFERENCES

American Psychological Association (1977) Standards for Providers of Psychological Services. Washington, D.C.

———— (1979) Ethical Standards of Psychologists, rev., Washington, D.C.

Arredondo, P. (1983a) Professional responsibility in a culturally pluralistic society. In Walz, G., & Benjamin, L. (Eds.), *Shaping counselor education programs in the next five years: An experimental prototype for the counselor of tomorrow*. ERIC/CAPS, pp. 91–106.

———— (1983b) A psycho-historical approach for understanding immigrants. Paper.

———— (1984) Identity themes for immigrant young adults. Paper.

Arredondo-Dowd, P. M. (1981) Personal loss and grief as a result of immigration. *The Personnel & Guidance Journal, 59* (6), 376–378.

Arredondo-Dowd, P., & Gawalek, M. (Eds.). (1982) *Human rights training manual*. Washington, D.C.: Association for Counselor Education & Supervision.

Arredondo-Dowd, P., & Gonsalves, J. (1980) Preparing culturally effective counselors. *The Personnel & Guidance Journal, 59*, 376–378.

Arredondo, P., & Okoawo, R. (Eds.). (1983) *Annotated bibliography*. Washington, D.C.: Association for Counselor Education & Supervision.

Atkinson, D. R., Morten, G. & Sue, D. W. (1979) *Counseling American minorities: A cross cultural perspective*. Dubuque, Ia.: Brown.

Casas, J. M. (1982) Complementary cross cultural counseling model for the '80s. Paper.

Copeland, E. J. (1983) Cross cultural counseling and psychotherapy: A historical perspective, implications for research and training. *The Personnel and Guidance Journal, 62*, 10–15.

Ivey, A. E. (1977) Cultural expertise: Toward a systematic outcome criteria in counseling and psychological education. *The Personnel & Guidance Journal, 55*, 296–302.

Korman, M. (1974) National conference on levels and patterns of professional training in psychology: Major themes. *American Psychologist, 29*, 441–449.

LeVine, E. S., & Padilla, A. M. (1980) *Crossing cultures in therapy: Pluralistic counseling for the Hispanics*. Monterey, Calif.: Brooks/Cole.

Nishihara, D. (1978) Culture, counseling, and ho-oponopono: An ancient model in a modern context. *The Personnel & Guidance Journal, 56*, 562–566.

Pedersen, P. (1978) Four dimensions of cross cultural skill in counselor training. *The Personnel & Guidance Journal, 56*, 480–484.

———— (1983) Developing interculturally skilled counselors: A training program. Paper presented at the American Psychological Association, Anaheim, Calif.

Roark, A. (1974) A tentative model for helping relationships with minorities. *Counseling & Values, 18*, 172–173.

Sue, D. W. (1977) Barriers to effective cross-cultural counseling. *Journal of Counseling Psychology, 24* (5), 420–429.

——— (1978) Eliminating cultural oppression in counseling: Towards a general theory. *Journal of Counseling Psychology, 25*, 419–428.

Sue, D. W., et al. (1982) Position paper: Cross-cultural counseling competencies. *The Counseling Psychologist, 10* (2), 45–52.

International and Comparative Perspectives in Counselor Education

VICTOR J. DRAPELA

Events of the past decades have dramatized the increasing interdependence of nations large and small. As Shirley Hufstedler (1980) observed, "today the effects of an event on one side of the world are likely to ripple all the way around the globe. . . . There is no longer a country on the face of this shrunken planet that can go it alone" (p. 8). This reality is being recognized by politicians, social scientists, economists, and industrial planners alike. In fact, educated persons in all walks of life are expected to become familiar with the international scene and to view events at home and abroad in global rather than parochial terms.

Counselors should pay particular attention to the life-styles and coping behaviors of people in other countries, especially if they want to engage in cross-cultural counseling and therapy. Familiarity with foreign socio-cultural milieus forms an attitudinal basis that will blunt cultural biases, promote cross-cultural sensitivity, and foster a healthy appreciation of ethnic traditions and values.

HISTORICAL BACKGROUND

Although Frank Parsons is generally acclaimed as the founder of American guidance, one important aspect of his legacy has been virtually forgotten—his strong commitment to international liaison among guidance professionals. He studied the social, economic, and educational systems abroad, particularly in Europe and in New Zealand (Davis, 1969), and his social philosophy was significantly influenced by like-minded humanitarian innovators abroad.

Unfortunately, the trauma of the Great Depression and the isolationist movement, which affected American society before World War II, hampered most international outreach efforts within the counseling community. Yet as the social climate of America changed in the 1940s, counselors did show new signs of interest in international affairs. The founding of the UNESCO-sponsored International Association for Educational and Vocational Guidance and the subsequent establishment of the International Round Table for the Advancement of Counselling served as powerful stimuli.

The American Personnel and Guidance Association (APGA) formed an International Education Committee, and in 1966 its Executive Council adopted a policy statement urging counselor-educators "to emphasize appropriate international perspectives in professional preparation programs" (*APGA International Courier*, 1966, p. 2). A survey conducted ten years later uncovered a surprisingly high level of interest among APGA members in international issues. The association created in 1977 the permanent International Relations Committee and has since increased the number of international programs at its conventions. APGA Press has published several special issues of its journals devoted to international topics—the *Vocational Guidance Quarterly* in 1976 and the *Personnel and Guidance Journal* in 1978 and 1983. One of the APGA divisions, the Association for Counselor Education and Supervision (ACES), established in 1983 its own task force to lend support to international studies in counselor-preparation programs.

Such studies are widely accepted in Europe, where counselor-educators recognize the need for learning from the experiences of other countries. The three-volume work by Kurt Heller (1975, 1976) and the textbook by Jozef Koščo, Dušan Fabián, Marta Hargašová, and Vladimír Hlavenka (1980) serve as examples of international guidance studies in German-speaking countries and in Soviet-bloc countries, respectively. In contrast to the European practice, most American counselor-education curricula do not contain clearly structured international-studies components. Some guest lectures, occasional seminars, and isolated academic courses are available at major universities, but any systematic introduction to cross-cultural analysis and to comparative methodology is missing in most American counselor-education programs.

THE COMPARATIVE FORMAT OF INTERNATIONAL STUDIES

The model of international studies for counselors that is proposed here reflects the comparative thrust that has proven its merits in other academic fields such as education, sociology, psychology, or anthropology. In this perspective, counseling and guidance are perceived as worldwide human services that help individuals attain self-awareness, psychological maturity, social responsibility, and an appropriate repertoire of problem-solving and coping skills.

In this broad, generic sense, guidance and counseling have a common denominator and can be found in all societies from impoverished Third World nations to affluent, technologically advanced world powers. Helping people, particularly youth, come to terms with their social environment is the generic goal shared by all nations and ethnic subcultures. How this generic goal is to be attained, however, and what is meant by coming to terms with one's social environment differ from country to country. To understand the common ground of guidance and counseling and the high degree of variability in their applications is the principal outcome of the comparative process in international studies.

There are some regions of the world, for example, in the Middle East or Africa, where formal counseling services are virtually unknown, and yet the socialization and adjustment processes are facilitated through spontaneous, informal guidance functions within the extended family (Moracco, 1979) or through interventions by therapeutic figures in the tribal system (Makinde, 1980). Such informal guidance exists also in countries with well-established, professionally staffed counseling services. In every nation, powerful societal forces are constantly at work molding values and ethical standards of the population and having a major impact on the format and orientation of human services for growth and adjustment.

To be comprehensive, international studies in counselor education need to cover not only the existing formal and informal guidance and counseling but should place major emphasis on the all-important social and cultural climate of the country. By implication, it seems unrealistic to label guidance and counseling services in various cultures as ''superior'' and ''deficient.'' More useful dimensions for comparing such services are their priorities and format, for example, guidance for manpower use versus assistance for personal development; information-giving versus counseling; or unstructured lay guidance versus professionally staffed services (Super, 1974).

METHODS FOR COMPARATIVE STUDIES

As I have discussed elsewhere (Drapela, 1979), methods applicable to international studies

can be placed on a continuum between two extreme positions. On one end are loosely structured learning experiences that expose students to various aspects of life in a foreign country. . . . On the other end is the pure research model that is concerned with relationships of specific variables but is oblivious of potential cultural experiences by the researchers. (p. 15)

One of the reasons for the slow acceptance of international studies in American counselor education may have been their image—a research specialty of limited value to counseling practitioners. Although in some cases this image may have been accurate, international studies do not have to adhere to such a restricted format. The model proposed here has been developed with typical graduate students in mind, most of whom want to become involved in counseling practice.

This approach does not use the traditional research methodology concerned with building or testing theories, which in the view of Leo Goldman (1978) generally makes little contribution to counseling practice. On the other hand, international studies should also avoid the devious trap of amateurism that lacks in direction and purpose (Noah & Eckstein, 1969). The method proposed here charts a middle course between the two extremes. It has a research component that can best be described as a combination of historical and naturalistic research through participant observation (Smith, 1981). But it places strong emphasis on experiential and participatory strategies that help students experience the impact of foreign cultures. The didactic process is personalized and interactional in which "learning results from the interaction between the teacher and the student, between the student and his content, and between his thought and his life" (Lapp, Bender, Ellenwood, & John, 1975).

The method proposed here parallels the approach of area studies, for example, Slavic or Scandinavian, used by social sciences, with an added coverage of formal and informal guidance services in the geographical area. "Soft data" related to social attitudes, cultural values, or stated objectives and client expectations in counseling form a broad framework and help interpret available "hard data" such as statistical figures on school counseling services, vocational-guidance systems, or the preferred counseling orientation by therapists of a country (Khan, 1983; Small, 1979).

There are regular class lectures—preferably by speakers who have firsthand knowledge of the foreign country under study—and audio-visual presentations. However, active student involvement is of utmost importance. Class members are required to do their own research through reading, while searching for samples of folk art, dress, and food items typical of the country under study and to share their findings with fellow students. The participatory learning format lends itself to class discussions, to role playing of situations one would likely encounter in the foreign country, and to the use of mental imagery (Richardson, 1969), for example, trying to cope with a hypothetical problem according to foreign mores and values rather than one's own.

In this context, one may wonder whether instructors of international and comparative-guidance courses would not have to be persons who lived for a considerable time abroad. There is no doubt that such firsthand experience is a major asset. But even instructors who have acquired a wide range of professional experiences overseas may not have gained sufficient expertise on every country they want to cover in their courses. When dealing with culturally distant issues, many instructors engage the assistance of competent resource persons from other departments of the college or university (including foreign students) or from the professional or business community. In every instance, the involvement of such resource persons broadens the scope of relevant information, helps clarify complex cultural attitudes or national prejudices, and adds authenticity to the learning experience.

THE LEARNING PROCESS FOR COMPARATIVE STUDIES

The success of international and comparative studies in academic settings depends largely on an appropriate selection of guidance and counseling models that are to be analyzed and compared and the structure of the learning process that is to be used for facilitating both cognitive and emotive growth of students.

When deciding on the geographical areas to be covered in an academic course, it is preferable to study a limited territory in sufficient depth rather than cover a much larger area less thoroughly. The study of three geographical regions is about the maximum that students can adequately absorb in a three- or four-credit course during an academic term. Additionally, the guidance and counseling models to be discussed should have a sufficient degree of contrast, for example, in terms of their social philosophy, expressed priorities, and methodology.

While exploring the foreign guidance models, students need at first a point of reference that is familiar to them—the guidance and counseling services in their own country. In the latter phases of the course they will have acquired the skill to compare foreign guidance models with one another without necessarily referring to their own.

The learning process proposed here incorporates principles of the earlier explained methodology that combines historical and naturalistic research with experiential and participatory learning strategies. Its structure involves a sequence of stages that resemble the stages typically used in comparative education. George Bereday (1964) developed a four-stage sequence consisting of (1) description (gathering of data), (2) interpretation (evalution of data), (3) juxtaposition (establishing similarities and differences), and (4) comparison (simultaneously evaluating and forming conclusions).

The structure of the learning process proposed here for comparative guidance and counseling builds on Bereday's model but expands the sequence to six stages to maximize the cultural impact on students and to facilitate their personal and professional values clarification.

Six-Stage Sequence

1. *Assembling general information on the country under study.* This information should include geographic, historical, demographic, socio-economic, and value-related data. Primary sources that originated in the foreign country should be used whenever possible. Because of language barriers, however, well-documented secondary sources must often suffice. The cultural climate should be explored in some detail by acquiring not only theoretical knowledge but also tangible samples of folk art, dress, food, and so on that would shed light on typical life-styles and career patterns, family structures, social customs and values, leisure activities, and other relevant areas. At first the plethora of heterogeneous pieces of a mosaic may overwhelm the students, but eventually, with the help of the instructor and resource person, a vivid, realistic image of daily life in the country emerges.

2. *Assembling data on education, guidance, and counseling in the country.* Information on the public school system and private educational institutions is usually available. It is more difficult to obtain data on guidance and counseling:

For instance, are professional counseling services available in the country, and if so, are they primarily linked to the school system, to vocational and social-service agencies, or are they delivered by private practitioners for a fee? This is also the time to determine the nature of informal guidance functions exercised by family and other social institutions. Are the top priorities of guidance and counseling in the area of personal development or career planning to satisfy the needs of national economy? Additional questions will emerge in the process of collecting data.

3. *Assessment of the foreign guidance model by its own standards*. Students examine the country's human services from the vantage point of foreign professionals. What are the views of practitioners, administrators, and consumers regarding the effectiveness of guidance and counseling in their country? In this stage, students should assume the perceptual frame of reference and view issues from the vantage point of those whose behavior they observe (Combs & Snygg, 1959). It is up to the instructor to foster this tolerant attitude and make students aware of their cultural biases that may affect the assessment process.

4. *Non-evaluation juxtaposition of the foreign and the American (or any selected) guidance model*. In the fourth stage students explore what the two guidance models have in common and how they differ from each other: How are these similarities and differences related to the distinct cultures of the two countries? Can one expect convergence or divergence of these guidance models in the near future? (Later in the course this process is used for juxtaposing two foreign guidance models.)

5. *Evaluation of the foreign model according to our own standards*. At this stage students consciously assert their philosophical preferences and cultural biases while evaluating the effectiveness of the foreign guidance model according to their standards. They may identify foreign strategies that would prove useful in this country, perhaps in modified form. They may also conclude that certain other foreign approaches would be clearly counterproductive here and may ask: does the foreign guidance model do for its consumers what we consider to be an appropriate aim of counseling and guidance?

6. *Clarification of personal values and professional commitments*. The insights provided by the five preceding steps help students form a new or modified perspective of their personal values and the role they want to assume as counselors in our society. This final stage of the learning process usually stimulates personal disclosures and sharing of feelings—dynamics typical of a growth group—deepening the students' self-awareness and social perspectives.

INITIATING INTERNATIONAL STUDIES IN COUNSELOR-EDUCATION PROGRAMS

The following hints are based on my own professional experiences acquired during the past 14 years—since I started teaching courses on comparative guidance and counseling. A good opportunity for initiating such studies presents itself in counselor-education seminars, where the central topic can be selected by the instructor. It is advisable to do preparatory work by discussing one's plan with colleagues in the department and by contacting prospective students individually and through class announcements.

If such seminars are well prepared and well received by students, the groundwork has been laid for the administrative approval of a new course on comparative guidance and counseling. There may be need for additional publicity, but most of the recruiting is done by word of mouth, if students had good experiences in the seminars. Unlike comparative education, international-guidance studies have not yet produced an adequate volume of literature; nevertheless, there are sufficient resources available in book and journal-article format. After the course has been successfuly offered as an elective at the master's level, it can be incorporated—with proper modifications—in the Ed.S., Ed.D., or Ph.D. curricula.

At present, international studies are still at a pioneering stage in counselor education. Their instructors, who also serve as their promoters, have to maintain a high degree of professional motivation to succeed. There are, however, indications of a more favorable climate developing in the counselor-education community: the decision by ACES to form its own task force for international affairs; the increasing participation of American counselor-educators in international meetings; the more numerous international programs at our professional conventions; and the forecasts in literature that international issues will be among the major thrusts to influence counselor preparation in the 1980s (Sweeney, 1979).

REFERENCES

APGA International Courier (May 1966).

Bereday, G.Z.F. (1964) *Comparative methods in education.* New York: Holt, Rinehart & Winston.

Combs, A. W., & Snygg, D. (1959) *Individual behavior.* New York: Harper & Row.

Davis, H. V. (1969) *Frank Parsons: Prophet, innovator, counselor.* Carbondale: Southern Illinois University Press.

Drapela, V. J. (Ed.). (1979) *Guidance and counseling around the world.* Washington, D.C.: University Press of America.

Goldman, L. (Ed.). (1978) *Research methods for counselors: Practical approaches in field settings.* New York: Wiley.

Heller, K. (Ed.). (1975, 1976) *Handbuch der Bildungsberatung.* Stuttgart: Klett, 3 vols.

Hufstedler, S. M. (1980) A world in transition. In *Educating for the world view.* New Rochelle, N.Y.: Council of Learning.

Khan, J. A. (1983) The evolution of counseling and guidance in Australia; or, As yet no counseling kangaroos? *Personnel and Guidance Journal, 61,* 469–472.

Koščo, J., Fabián, D., Hargašová, M., & Hlavenka, V. (1980) *Teória a prax poradenskej psychológie.* Bratislava: Slovenské pedagogické nakladatel'stvo.

Lapp, D., Bender, H., Ellenwood, S., John, M. (1975) *Teaching and learning: Philosophical, psychological, curricular applications.* New York: Macmillan.

Makinde, O. (1980) Indigenous counselling techniques among the Yoruba and Igala people of Nigeria. *International Journal for the Advancement of Counselling, 3*, 171–184.

Moracco, J. (1979) Arab countries. In Drapela, V. J. (Ed.), *Guidance and counseling around the world*. Washington, D.C.: University Press of America.

Noah, H. J., & Eckstein, M. A. (1969) *Toward a science of comparative education*. New York: Macmillan.

Richardson, A. (1969). *Mental imagery*. New York: Springer.

Small, J. J. (1979) New Zealand. In Drapela, V. J. (Ed.), *Guidance and counseling around the world*. Washington, D.C.: University Press of America.

Smith, M. L. (1981) Naturalistic research. *Personnel and Guidance Journal, 59*, 585–589.

Super, D. E. (1974) The broader context of career development and vocational guidance: American trends in world perspective. In Herr, E. L. (Ed.), *Vocational guidance and human development*. Boston: Houghton Mifflin.

Sweeney, T. J. (1979) Trends that will influence counselor preparation in the 1980s. *Counselor Education and Supervision, 18*, 181–189.

The Recognition and Use of Natural Support Systems in Cross-Cultural Counseling

RICHARD E. PEARSON

For counselors and other mental-health workers, the importance of informal assistance from what Gerald Caplan (1974) called "kith and Kin" support systems is that even in societies with extensively developed systems for delivering mental-health assistance, help from family, friends, neighbors, and other peers continues to be the preferred source of assistance for many (perhaps most) of the ordinary and extraordinary issues of development (Gurin et al., 1960). Thus the natural support system (NSS) is positioned to exert an important influence in confirming or disconfirming the importance of an individual's problems, in providing assistance, and in recommending which health-seeking or health-restoring activities are appropriate for the individual.

As counselors and other mental-health workers come into contact with cultural groups different from their own, the inability to recognize the contributions and style of operation of clients' NSS, when combined with a common clinical tendency to see family and peer groups as sources of pathology (Heller, 1979), may create formidable barriers to effective collaboration with clients' NSS. Specifically, in cross-cultural contexts, counselors may overlook, misinterpret, or devalue the positive role that NSS can play in preventing and ameliorating personal difficulties and thus be prone to overlook the possibilities for furthering clients' growth by reinforcing, strengthening, or collaborating with those systems.

PRESENT STATUS

Descriptions of families, peer relationships, neighborhoods, and communities across human groups of many times and places indicate that although the particular form may vary, the fact of intra-group assistance and cooperation is a basic element of human association. In the last decade this broad recognition has been focused, especially by the work of Gerard Caplan (1974), into a recognition that assistance from family, friends, neighbors, co-workers, and other members of one's NSS stands as a major influence in the prevention and re-mediation of psychological disfunction. Within the context of the NSS, individuals are known as unique persons; their background and characteristics are appreciated and taken into account as others respond to them. Also, the symbol systems and worldviews that guide activities are familiar to the individuals who are being "supported." For these reasons NSS are, typically, not only the most easily accessed sources of assistance, but often the most preferred.

Clearly, literature from anthropology, psychology, and sociology in which the nature and role of social support is explored is related to those aspects of cross-cultural counseling that recognize the important influence of families, peer groups, and other informal relationships. However, in spite of the clear relevance of social-support theory and research to cross-cultural counseling, only scattered studies (for example, Escobar & Randolph, 1982; Vaux, 1983) have specifically examined social support and support systems from cross-cultural perspectives. Also, although the terms *support* and *support systems* are commonly found in the cross-cultural-counseling literature, their use seems to reflect general, commonsense perspectives rather than the more specific, differentiated use that the literature of social support now allows.

For example, building upon James House's (1981) view that supportive activities can be considered to fall into four categories (emotional support, appraisal support, informational support, material support), one might note that persons in a particular group tend to emphasize material support (for example, relieving the individual of chores, loaning money, giving needed tools or other objects) in supporting bereaved persons. Concerning another group, one might observe that there are strong differences between sex groups in terms of the types of support that can be given and received. Both observations, made possible by a differentiated view of social support and natural systems, would have relevance for the design and implementation of counseling interventions for members of those cultural groups.

Recent developments elaborate network analytical methods based on techniques originally developed by anthropologists to organize and analyze field data (Mitchell, 1974) can provide ways of more precisely identifying the composition of NSS in particular human groupings than has previously been true. Using such techniques (for example, measures of density or communication pathways), it is possible to move, for example, beyond general statements about the important role of the extended family in helping individuals deal with marital difficulties to a specification of the fact that same-sex, closely related persons of the individuals' age cohort are most active in supporting (offering feedback and other types of appraisal) to persons in that group having family problems.

In sum, the current situation with regard to the recognition of the use of NSS in cross-cultural counseling is that there is a literature (for example, family therapy; ethnographic descriptions of the characteristics of different cultural groups; articles, chapters, and books on "how to counsel ———s") in which the role of social support from NSS is recognized. However, although such work often implicitly examines the way in which persons in those groups conceptualize and deliver informal support, an integration of concepts and methods from the recent and continuing social-support-focused research and practice in fields not directly related to human services has enormous potential in clarifying the precise nature of social support and its delivery in different cultural settings.

Specific questions relevant to cross-cultural counseling that can be generated by drawing upon existing theoretical and research literature are: (1) Across cultural groups, what types of social support are considered to be appropriate for particular life issues? (2) How do the particular actions through which social support is delivered vary? (3) From whom, among the people in their natural systems, do particular individuals receive support for specific concerns? (4) How can counselors strengthen and cooperate with (rather than weaken, interfere with, or displace) the NSS of clients?

FUNDAMENTAL ASSUMPTIONS

Attention, by counselors and other mental-health workers, to the presence and influence of NSS in cross-cultural contexts rests upon several assumptions: (1) The impact of NSS has significance to the work of counselors. (2) The operation of these systems can be recognized and understood. (3) It is possible to form collaborative relationships with clients' NSS as a strategy in pursuing counseling objectives.

Impact of NSS

The caseloads of mental-health workers bear testimony to the reality that families, peer groups, and informal community helpers can affect individuals in harmful ways. Although this situation leads some practitioners to view families and the peer groups as sources of pathology (Heller, 1979), it is important to recognize that such caseloads are usually atypical of the broader population being served. If the work of Gerald Gurin and his colleagues (1960), who studied patterns in the use of mental-health services in the United States, has generalizability to other contexts, it may be pointed out that it is only *after* the natural system has proven non-responsive or inadequate that persons seek the assistance of formal helpers. For most persons the family, friends, co-workers, and other informally available persons who make up their NSS stand as the primary resource, a "first line" of assistance when the demands of ordinary and extraordinary life concerns exceed their own self-help resources.

Although the ability of NSS to "buffer" the negative impact of physical and psychological stressors has received extensive attention (Cobb, 1976; House, 1981), day-to-day contributions that they make to individuals' general health has great significance for those concerned with issues of normal development and for primary prevention-oriented practitioners. The very ability of the individual to survive and mature into an adequate member of the group rests heavily upon assistance from the NSS; it is typically only when such assistance is limited or negative that disfunctionality results.

Understanding NSS

Accounts that examine various aspects of the social organization and analyze the psychological experience of particular groups are common in scholarly and popular literature. To some degree these ethnographies comment upon the issue of interpersonal support and thus can provide a basis for developing an understanding of the manner in which the particular group conceptualizes and delivers social support. However, such accounts usually lack the sort of specificity that can be obtained by examining support phenomena in light of the conceptual and assessment refinements now available. Therefore, the counseling practitioner will often have to move beyond general descriptions of supportive behavior to determine exactly *what* type of support is provided *to whom, by whom*, for *what types* of concerns.

Interfacing with NSS

One general approach to counseling involves an emphasis upon the social context as both the source of and remedy for personal concerns. Family counseling stands as an example of this "context-based" approach. Also, a variety of "network therapies" (for example, Reuveni, 1979; Speck & Attneave, 1973) have been developed that proceed by gathering any persons in clients' social networks who might be contributive to the cause or cure of the difficulties. Although formats may vary, all emphasize opening up communication among network members so that information concerning the causes and consequences of the problem can be exchanged. Mobilizing the resources of the network to ameliorate the client's concerns thus becomes possible.

It seems natural to suggest that the use of system-involving strategies has great relevance when working with clients from cultural groups in which family and community ties play an important part in shaping attitudes and behavior. Such groups may already have mechanisms for "gathering the clan" that can be adapted (Evernham & Maretzki, 1982) or used directly (Attneave, 1969) by counselors.

RELEVANT THEORY AND PRACTICE

Three areas of theory and practice can be identified that may serve as a basis for understanding the nature and role of social support in cross-cultural counseling: (1) sociobiological views concerning the role that intra-familial and intra-group cooperation have played in the evolution of species; (2) the ability of social support to act as a buffer against physical and psychological stressors;

and (3) treatment approaches that emphasize the inclusion of individuals' social network.

These three categories are broad, generic areas that, although they do not focus specifically upon cross-cultural counseling, provide rich theoretical perspectives for recognizing, understanding, and interfacing with the natural support structures of cultural groups.

Sociobiology

Although the role of conflict and aggression is often stressed in discussions of the evolutionary process, some theorists (for example, Wilson, 1974) have noted that intra-familial cooperation and mutual aid are recurring patterns in the functioning of many species. Sociobiological theory calls attention to the fact that contributing to the survival of one's kin increases the likelihood that one's own "gene pool" will survive, even if one, as an individual, does not (Barkow, 1977). Thus mature individuals of many species are often seen to postpone their own reproductive activities to contribute to the survival of younger siblings in conditions of food scarcity.

Whether or not one accepts as fact that patterns such as "kin selection" are imprinted upon individuals at the biological level, sociobiological perspectives serve the useful purpose of sensitizing the counselor to the extent to which intra-familial cooperation and mutual aid are a part of the human experience. As a result of dealing with the casualties of pathogenic families, it is, perhaps, understandable that counselors and other mental-health professionals might lose sight of the reality that for most persons, in most cultures, the NSS does an excellent job of nourishing its members.

Social Support as a Buffer

The work of John C. Cassel (1974), an epidemiologist, can be identified as a major impetus for research exploring the ability of social support to shield persons from the harmful effects of environmental stress. His "buffering" hypothesis suggested that individuals' heightened susceptibility to physical and psychological illness, observed in situations of overcrowding, social disruption, and rapid change, results from the interference that such conditions cause to the feedback they receive about the appropriateness of their behavior. Cassel hypothesized that when individuals are cut off from a sense of "where they are at" and how they are doing, they are apt to experience chronic stress and thus become subject to a wide range of ills. Social support, he asserted, can serve to buffer persons from stress by offering direct and indirect guidelines that provide direction and assurance as they respond to life situations. G. Caplan (1974) extended Cassel's view to include a broader picture of the supportive potential of interpersonal relations. He suggested that the buffering effect of social ties stems not only from the feedback and information they provide but from the assistance they provide in the form of sharing tasks and other responsibilities, and in the provision of needed material resources (for example, money, objects, implements).

Although the buffering hypothesis is not without its critics, it has served as a point of departure for an enormous body of research that explores the nature and impact of social support. In an overview of this research, House (1981) noted that in addition to having buffering properties, the NSS enhances individuals' well being by contributing to overall health and robustness and by reducing the presence of pathogenic factors in individuals' surroundings.

System-Involving Interventions

E. Mansell Pattison (1973) suggested that a distinction can be made among treatment strategies on the basis of their view of the appropriate relationship between individuals and the primary social group to which they belong. In "closed" approaches individuals are considered as autonomous entities, and the goals of treatment involve contributing to their ability to be self-directed and independent. In contrast, "open" approaches stress the importance of viewing individuals in terms of their group membership. Goals for treatment in open strategies focus upon confirming and strengthening the reciprocal benefits that accrue when individuals and their groups are in harmony.

Although Western cultures are often described as encouraging the development of rugged individualism, it should be recognized that as with any broad generalization wide variation exists among subcultures and individuals in the extent to which a consideration for, or the actual intervention of, the NSS guides decisions and behavior. As counselors move into practice that involves clients from non-Western cultures (for example, Southeast Asian, Native American, African) in which identities of clients may be inseparably tied to familial and community obligations, interventions based on a "closed" model are apt to be seen as irrelevant at best and harmful at worst. The ability to understand the manner in which individual-group relationships are structured is an important skill in cross-cultural counseling. Moreover, the ability to design interventions that are compatible with such conceptualizations (perhaps even incorporating traditional forms and procedures) may be central to counseling effectiveness.

FUTURE DIRECTIONS

The need for counselors who can operate effectively in cross-cultural settings is apt to be heightened by factors such as immigration, increased acceptance of the benefits of cultural diversity, and the extension of Western-oriented models for mental-health services into new cultural contexts. Moreover, a more specific need for counselors who can recognize and collaborate with clients' NSS is apt to be further strengthened as primary, prevention-oriented approaches to mental-health services are pursued. Such approaches stress the importance of reducing the incidence of psychological disfunction by directing preventive interventions to "at risk" individuals. It has been widely recognized that NSS stand as the first source of assistance that individuals turn to when self-help efforts fail. Therefore, counselors who can recognize and initiate appropriate collaboration with culturally different clients' NSS are in a position to strengthen a source of readily available, primary-prevention-significant assistance.

To the extent that a recognition of the importance of NSS becomes an important focus in cross-cultural practice, it may be expected that there will be important implications for counseling practice and counselor education.

With regard to counseling practice, there will be a need for the development of heuristic perspectives and diagnostic techniques that can aid practitioners as they deal with the problems of understanding, describing, and assessing the support relationships of their culturally diverse clients. Once having developed such understandings, counselors will be faced with the necessity of designing interventions to which clients and their significant others will be receptive. Certainly, current family and network-oriented intervention strategies will provide some direction in the design of such interventions. However, a promising area from which counselors may be able to draw ideas is the indigenous helping procedures of the groups themselves. Thus L. Evernham and T. Maretzki (1981) described the manner in which family therapists in Hawaii examined a traditional means of resolving family conflict (*ho'oponopono*) as a guide for developing culturally relevant approaches.

Concerning counselor education, it seems apparent that the development of practitioners who can recognize and collaborate with clients' NSS in cross-cultural contexts will require additions to current preparation approaches. One of the most general changes will involve a willingness to incorporate concepts and materials from anthropology and sociology. Not only do these two fields focus upon material concerning the characteristics of particular groups and subgroups that may be of concern to counselors, they also focus upon group phenomena in a way that can provide counselors with perspectives and techniques for understanding the social contexts within which their clients are embedded.

REFERENCES

Attneave, C. (1969) Therapy in tribal settings and urban network intervention. *Family Process, 8*, 192–210.

Barkow, J. H. (1977) Human ethology and intra-individual systems. *Social Science Information, 16*, 133–145.

Caplan, G. (1974) *Support systems and mental health: Lectures on concept development.* New York: Behavioral Publications.

Cassel, J. (1974) Psychosocial processes and stress: Theoretical formulations. *International Journal of Health Services, 4*, 471–482.

Cobb, S. (1976) Social support as a moderator of life stress. *Psychosomatic Medicine, 38*, 300–314.

Escobar, J. T., & Randolph, E. T. (1982) The Hispanic and social networks. In Recerra,

R. M., Karno, M., Escobar, J. (Eds.), *Mental health and Hispanic Americans*. New York: Grune & Stratton.

Evernham, L., & Maretzki, T. (1982) Anthropological and psychiatric issues in ethnic social support systems. Paper presented at the 32d Annual International Communication Conference, Boson, Mass.

Gurin, G., et al. (1960) *Americans review their mental health: A nationwide interview survey*. New York: Basic Books.

Heller, K. (1979) The effects of social support: Prevention and treatment implications. In Goldstein, A. P., & Kanfer, F. H. (eds.), *Maximizing treatment gains: Transfer enhancement in psychotherapy*. New York: Academic Press.

House, J. S. (1981) *Work, stress and social support*. Reading, Mass.: Addison-Wesley.

Mitchell, J. C. (1974) Social networks. *Annual Review of Anthropology, 3*, 279–300.

Pattison, E. Mansell (1973) Social system psychotherapy. *American Journal of Psychotherapy, 27*, 396–409.

Reuveni, U. (1979) *Networking families in crisis*. New York: Human Services Press.

Speck, R., & Attneave, C. (1973) *Family networks*. New York: Pantheon.

Vaux, A. (1983) Social support: Variation across subpopulations. Paper presented at the American Psychological Association Convention, Anaheim, Calif.

Wilson, O. E. (1974) Social networks. In Siegal, B., et al. (Eds.,), *Annual Review of Anthropology*. Palo Alto, Calif.: Annual Reviews Inc.

Counseling and Therapy with the Nonimmigrant in the Educational Environment

W. FRANK HULL IV

> I'm not doing anything but sitting in my room drinking coffee and smoking cigarettes. None of this has any meaning. Sometimes I think I should just kill myself. My roommate thinks it is because I have no parents, no country, and no religion. The psychiatrist keeps giving me pills but they aren't helping. Why do I feel like this? What should I do? My grades are O.K.
>
> —Kabul

Although certainly not typical sentiments, the thoughts in this letter from Kabul convey the desperation that some struggle with during educational sojourns. In this case Kabul is finishing an initial engineering degree at a midwestern university well known for its international students and academic program. Calls to the international student advisor elicit an "I-don't-know-what-to-suggest" response, without any offer to check it through. Calls to the psychiatrist in the student health center elicit an "I-don't-know-what's-left-to-try" response, again with no offer to call the student. There he sits, alone in a walk-up room. What is the responsibility of the university and its officers, faculty, and staff for the mental well being of a lonely international student? How can we facilitate cross-cultural counseling and therapy within an educational environment?

The nonimmigrant (as determined by passport regulations for the country in question)—be that person student, faculty, staff, or official guest—poses a unique challenge to the counselor or therapist regardless of the cultural backgrounds of either the therapist or client. Each of these students or scholars is in the host country for a specific purpose, somehow related to education or to the production of a scholarly-scientific project. Yet each is in the foreign educational institution for a limited time. Each is expected by the educational institution and, indeed, by the home and host countries as well, to return "home" at the end of the sojourn.

Cross-cultural counselors and therapists continually need to remember specific issues that bear upon the international client when that client is within an educational institution: (1) The goal of the sojourn has an impact on what the therapist can do. (2) The fact that it is a sojourn itself has an impact on helping techniques that might be used. (3) Collateral issues inside or outside of the institution impact upon both the therapy and the client. (4) The institution's considered role in the international realm affects the client and is reflected in the environment in which the client copes. Yet beyond these more theoretical issues, the realization has to be that a skilled and cross-culturally sensitive therapist must weigh all of this and apply it with helping care and concern to each individual client, like Kabul.

THE IMPACT OF THE SOJOURN'S GOALS

The nonimmigrant student or scholar may be at the educational institution for many reasons—some conscious, some unconscious. For example, most students come with the stated goal of securing a degree or certification. However, the degree itself means many different things—attaining prestige, fulfilling a family's goal, ultimately living in another country, attaining financial and material gains, opting for further degrees, and so on. If underlying assumptions change—a sudden shift in the home country's politics, loss of a parent or parents, falling in love, and so on—a crisis can occur. Similarly, if grades slip or written language is inadequate for academic purposes, the sojourn's entire goal can suddenly be threatened or become unattainable.

Understanding the individual's sojourn goals is imperative to the therapist. The meaning of the sojourn is often intertwined in another culture's values and modes of expressions. The short-term or long-term goals, at home or elsewhere, add variables that make the counseling situation even more complex.

In this context of the sojourn's goals, the surfacing issue has seen little research or academic attention. Is the goal of therapy in this situation limited to assisting the client in coping with the process of securing the degree or certification, or does it extend to helping the client delve into deeper, more personal issues in that client's life or home culture? It is one thing to assist a client with adjustment in a host culture for a temporary period so that re-entry into the home culture is facilitated and another thing to assist a client into considering ultimate life meanings and adaptations, possibly those different from the home culture. Although variables that influence the goal of therapy within the educational sojourn are discussed throughout this handbook, the goal of the sojourn with the sojourn's anticipated length, expectations, hopes, assumptions, and so on is a factor that is not adequately considered in the therapeutic literature, nor has it been researched cross-culturally.

THE FACT OF THE SOJOURN AND COUNSELING-THERAPY TECHNIQUES

It is well established that not only do methods of personal assisting vary from culture to culture, but expectations of the nature of the helping process and the patterns of interactions with the helper also vary. Others in this handbook have already discussed methods and techniques. One piece of research that begins to illustrate the initial approach problem within the context of the Western clinic is that of Sue and colleagues (1974). In considering Native Americans, Chicanos, blacks, and Asian-Americans with Anglo clients, Sue pointed out that approximately 50 percent of the non-Anglo clients did not return to therapy after one contact. For Anglos, the figure was 30 percent. Sue suggested that part of the cause may have been inappropriate interpersonal interactions. If this finding can be generalized to any degree from a Western community mental-health facility to an intercultural situation, fragility from interpersonal interactions on the international student or scholar who enters a student health clinic for an initial contact must be carefully considered.

Questions abound. How does role identification (especially in terms of identification with a *student* image) influence the interaction of the therapist with an international client? How is that further complicated by a "student" who is considerably older? What about when this student is accustomed to being perceived as an influential person in the home culture? Furthermore, how does the question of how the client perceives the stratification or importance of the home country-culture in the eyes of the host country-culture or therapist impact upon the therapy? These issues are uniquely related to an educational sojourn.

If methods of helping vary by culture, how can the therapist be attuned enough to consider *all* of the possible variables within an international client? Must we have an indigenous therapist? Assumptions, values, and even the norms and ideological patterns of a client's culture often follow specific interactional procedures. How are these matters considered initially as well as throughout the therapy process? What about credibility? Is the counselor perceived as credible, or is it just that the internal pain, possibly loneliness, is *so* intense that the international student or scholar would be pleased to talk to anyone? What constitutes "successful" therapy and in which set of cultural assumptions, the home or the host?

Although studies on international students abound, research within the educational sojourn on effective counseling-therapy techniques remains in its infancy. Although one can extrapolate from other studies and writings, we do not have clear answers in this area.

Multicultural-multinational investigations are imperative. Consider the work of Otto Klineberg and myself (1978, 1979) in fifteen countries. Personal depression was a problem reported by a large number of international students. On the other hand, positive and meaningful social contact in that study appeared as a complex variable within the educational environment that seemed to generalize as a positive or negative experience throughout the whole sojourn.

We earlier raised (Hull, 1978; Klineberg & Hull, 1979) a modified culture-contact hypothesis arguing that "foreign students satisfied and comfortable with their interactions with local people and with local culture during their sojourn will report not only broader and more frequent contact, in general, as could be expected, but will also indicate more general satisfaction with their sojourn experience both academically and nonacademically'' (Hull, 1978, p. 104). Such students should require less counseling and therapy. When such attention is necessary, these clients should more easily re-enter the educational environment. But is it the culture contact with a meaningful local person, as indicated in that investigation, or is it a predisposed psychological type that seems to make some individuals basically happy and easily adaptable to almost anything that comes their way? More research of a clinical nature is necessary.

Can educational institutions build that element of positive contact into their environments in new ways, possibly through more effective involvement of community individuals and groups? Few educational institutions are addressing this question and its preventative mental-health implications. Those who are addressing it are doing so only in the most rudimentary ways.

Given these questions, it could be argued that within an educational institution with its specific, limited mission and goals, the most appropriate technique of all is careful listening by a professional capable of a positive gut reaction to an international client (C. Rogers, 1951). But that ''gut reaction'' must be not only positive but genuine and thus the need for a staff. One person simply cannot do it all.

The need for a staff, then, takes us to the issue of training personnel to deal with international populations within the educational institution. Here, unfortunately, it can be noted that there is little standardization in the professional backgrounds of most professionals charged with meeting the needs of international students and scholars on campuses throughout the world, including the United States.

INSTITUTIONAL ISSUES THAT IMPACT UPON THERAPY

The issues that the educational institution itself is considering, in some cases within the context of discussions at local, regional, or national levels, must also be taken into consideration by the therapist. Although these issues have a history of having come and gone, some with periods of high intensity, clear and agreed-upon answers have not yet emerged.

There is little agreement on how international persons should be treated strictly as a matter of policy, considering the interests of both sending and receiving countries. Here the British have started some consideration of the ''British interests,'' focusing on long-term and short-term economic considerations (Williams, 1981). Among the variables considered were cost-benefits, foreign policy, development policy, commercial concerns, and international perspectives. There is a paucity of national policy implications from data-based studies.

Although at first glance such economic studies may seem unrelated to counseling and therapy, the way an educational institution views an international student or scholar does influence the treatment that the international individual receives and does influence greatly the context in which the mental-health professional is expected to treat the international client. It makes a difference whether the international person is considered a valued part of the educational community and is encouraged to make personal as well as professional contributions from the home culture, or whether that individual is viewed as usurping space from a citizen and a burden on institutional, in some cases, tax, resources. What about a student from a country that becomes unpopular? The client may face assumptions in local attitudes on the part of faculty, students, and staff that imply "you adjust to us"; or, on the other extreme, "we must, of course, adjust everything to you."

The therapist must be aware of what the client is encountering within the particular educational environment. The client may be trying to cope with, for example, a faculty member who will never for conscious or unconscious reasons value, or be open to, or give an earned grade to a student from a culture or group that is disliked. In such cases the most effective "therapy" may be to insure that the international student is not in that particular class or to remove the student from that section immediately.

The problem is that few helping professionals, especially at large educational institutions, have the privilege of that detailed a view of the institution or the authority to take such swift action. When direct administrative intervention is required, where does that fit into our theories and perspectives, even ethics, in cross-cultural counseling and therapy?

It is an understatement to point out that all is not as it should be within the United States. A committee for the American Council on Education (1982) reported that a sketchy level of service and consistency in dealing with international students exists; the committee also noted that the support and cooperation of the faculty are essential in making these students feel welcome. Are faculty prepared to give support and participation in these days of limited resources and stepped-up pressures for research and publications? Faculty who do support and participate may well do so to the neglect of other responsibilities and to their ultimate lack of professional success at the institution. Few institutions reward faculty for this involvement, even when it is recognized as necessary and within the institution's overall interests.

In 1983 the Institute of International Education did another report: *Absence of Decision: Foreign Students in American Colleges and Universities—A report on policy formation and lack thereof.* The title describes too many educational institutions in the United States, and unfortunately, the situation is not necessarily better elsewhere. In reality, there are very few educational institutions worldwide where international students and scholars are a meaningful priority, with the possible exception of some institutions in which political or religious considerations are primary.

Counselors and therapists have to work with international clients in the context of today's educational institutions but with the hope and active participation toward an improved future.

SUMMARY

Counseling and therapy with a nonimmigrant in an educational environment must be viewed within a context, a *gestalt*, if you will. Here I have raised issues related to more personal counseling and treatment of clients within educational institutions worldwide. The proposition has been raised that the educational institution's view of international students and scholars, as well as its view of itself in an international context, has an impact on the pressures and stress encountered by the international student. I have suggested that the counselor and therapist need to be aware acutely of the institution in which the helping relationship occurs. The sojourn itself (stated and unstated goals and expectations) will influence the type of counseling and therapy that is appropriate. The client's goals for the sojourn, not always overt, cannot be overlooked. Although preventative mental health is important, the issue of positive social contact has been raised here.

In short, in educational institutions procedures and processes often work against the international person and build in stress and unnecessary pressure. International contributions with students and scholars are rarely priorities. Clearly, more research and clinical investigations are indicated, but they must be multinational. Rarely do they occur.

In the meantime, we return to the case of Kabul, bringing us back to the individual. Although we consider issues and await more pertinent multinational research, most of us will continue to bear that awesome responsibility of responding to our own professional Kabul. Impressively, at least to me, educational institutions throughout the world do contain a large number of host faculty, staff, students, community groups, and individuals who do respond positively and genuinely to their international students and scholars.

REFERENCES

American Council on Education (1982) *Foreign students and institutional policy: Toward an agenda for action.* New York, N.Y.

Arkoff, Abe, Thaver, Falak, & Elkind, Leonard (1966) Mental health and counseling ideas of Asian and American students. *Journal of Counseling Psychology, 13,* 219–223.

Coelho-Oudegeest, Maria de Lourdes Ivonne (1961) Cross-cultural counseling: A study of some variables in the counseling of foreign students. Ph.D. dissertation, University of Wisconsin.

Cole, M. B., & Bruner, J. S. (1972) Cultural differences and inferences about psychological process. *American Psychologist, 32,* 867–876.

Goodwin, Craufurd D., & Nacht, Michael (1983) *Absence of decision: Foreign students in American colleges and universities—A report of policy formation and the lack thereof.* New York, N.Y.: Institute of International Education.

Hull, W. Frank (1978) *Foreign students in the United States of America: Coping behavior within the educational environment.* New York: Praeger.

Klineberg, Otto, & Hull, W. Frank (1979) *At a foreign university: An international study of adaptation and coping*. New York: Praeger.

McFayden, M., & Winikur, G. (1956) Cross-cultural psychotherapy. *Journal of Nervous and Mental Disorders, 123*, 369–375.

Rogers, C. R. (1951) *Client-centered therapy*. Boston: Houghton Mifflin.

Sue, S., & McKinney, H. (1974) Asian Americans in the community mental health care system. *American Journal of Orthopsychiatry, 45*, 111–118.

Sue, S., Allen, D., & Conaway, L. (1975) The responsiveness and equality of mental health care to Chicano and Native Americans. *American Journal of Community Psychology, 6*, 137–146.

Sue, S., McKinney, H, Allen, D, & Hall, J. (1974) Delivery of community mental health service to black and white clients. *Journal of Consulting and Clinical Psychology, 42*, 594.

Vontress, C. D. (1969) Cultural barriers in the counseling relationship. *Personnel and Guidance Journal, 48*, 11–17.

Williams, P. (Ed.). (1981) *The overseas student question: Studies for a policy*. London: Heinemann Educational Books.

Intercultural Criteria for Mental-Health Training

PAUL PEDERSEN

We are at the starting point in the development of criteria for cross-cultural counseling and therapy. The next step will either result in a separate specialization or a diffusion of cultural competencies toward all counseling relationships. In either case the criteria of intercultural expertise have been too loosely defined. Research on criteria development needs to emphasize intentionality (asking the right questions), complexity (getting the right answers), and balance (taking the right action). Increased intentionality allows counselors to increase their awareness for matching an appropriate intervention with the appropriate context. Complexity is both good and necessary to an accurate description of an individual's personal cultural orientation. Balance describes the force field of positive and negative elements in a culture. Maintaining and facilitating that value-balance are important criteria for cross-cultural counseling and therapy.

Persons who have learned to relate to their client's host culture will function more effectively and intentionally. Furthermore, persons who have adapted to any one cultural environment will need to re-adapt themselves for each subsequent, culturally different environment. To the extent that the counselor or therapist is finely tuned to the nuances of one culture, he or she may even have a more difficult time adapting to a different culture. Training can facilitate that adaptation through a transfer of learning. This transfer of learning can be improved by training through both decreasing stimulus generalization and at the same time increasing stimulus differentiation so that two persons from different cultures will be more likely to accurately attribute the same cause or explanation for events and situations.

HISTORY

During the 1970s general systems philosophy provided the most popular framework for designing training programs. These systems emphasized instructional objectives, precisely controlled learning experiences, and measured performance on evaluation criteria. There was emphasis on immediate feedback and continuous modification of the training input, researching the measured achievements of training, and designing a within-systems framework to facilitate interaction between components of the system. Finally, there was a framework for interaction between the training program and its environment. One of the difficulties with intercultural training programs, or any training that includes the intercultural dimension, is that the variables are so complex that accurate measurement or even identification of variables is almost impossible.

PRESENT STATUS

Defining the criteria for intercultural training is complicated by conflicting findings in research on the special qualifications of intercultural adjustment. Since available research uses a variety of criteria to measure success, most methodologies are not comparable and are usually limited to variables for a single measure of analysis. There is no comprehensive theory of intercultural training (Ruben & Kealey, 1979).

There are several approaches for intercultural training that promise to develop measurable criteria. The Canadian International Development Agency advocates training objectives that combine technical and communication competencies (Ruben & Kealey, 1979), emphasizing both the "how" and the "what" of training as important. They emphasize the capacity (1) to communicate respect, (2) to be non-judgmental, (3) to personalize knowledge and perceptions, (4) to display empathy, (5) to demonstrate reciprocal concern, and (6) to tolerate ambiguity. An interesting aspect of their findings is that in at least some cases persons who have undergone intensive culture shock during transition were ultimately more effective. This may be because persons most aware of their subjective perceptions experience more shock. Persons who expressed "respect" for persons within their own culture were more likely to be tolerant and respectful toward and comfortable with persons from other cultures. Persons who were excessively task oriented toward problem solving and interpersonal interaction tended to be less effective than the less consistently task oriented. Advisors who were non-judgmental, respectful, relativistic in their orientations to knowledge, and more tolerant of ambiguity were also more effective.

Much Peace Corps research between 1952 and 1970 unsuccessfully attempted to identify appropriate intercultural training and assessment measures for training and selecting volunteers for service in foreign countries. Clinical interviews by psychologists and psychiatrists, personality inventories and aptitude tests, peer assessment, self-ratings, background assessment, and situational tests were all used, but results were inconclusive with no success in predicting adjustment or success of volunteers overseas (Pedersen, 1983).

FUNDAMENTAL ASSUMPTIONS

A basic controversy for intercultural criteria is the question of whether behavior is a function of inherent personality traits or a response to situational contingencies. The relation between measured personality traits and behaviors is very low, and most Peace Corps-funded research has supported a conclusion that measured traits are not a good predictor of success in adjusting to another culture. However, it is necessary to some extent to consider both traits and situational factors in intercultural training and assessment.

Several traits have been suggested. Some people are better at social relations and completing tasks competently. In situations of stress, people become more rigid and repetitive and tend to think more narrowly in categories (Brislin, 1981). A capacity for empathy, however, contributes to the ability for establishing warm and cordial relations with host cultures. Strength of personality, described through a positive self-concept and high levels of self-esteem, is also frequently associated with success in another culture. Intelligence, or the ability to solve problems in unfamiliar settings, is frequently cited as an important inherent capability (Brislin, 1981). A high task orientation can interfere with interpersonal relations when the individual is willing to sacrifice other's feelings to accomplish the task just as a high tolerance of ambiguity can contribute to success.

P. Adler (1977) described the "multicultural person" as someone who is adaptive, continually in transition, and can see his or her culture from the outside, which contributes to intercultural success. Likewise, however, Adler cited negative consequences of multiculturalism, including the inability to differentiate important cultural elements from unimportant elements, identity diffusion, loss of personal authenticity, superficiality, and lack of tolerance for monocultural persons. One clear conclusion is that the greater the number of prejudicial stereotypes, the greater the difficulties in cross-cultural situations.

One frequently used approach to training is to develop a "culture assimilator" to help trainees accurately analyze situations, make appropriate attributions about persons involved in those situations, compare patterns of attributions, and become skilled in anticipating the attributions ascribed to a behavior by host-culture residents. These patterns of attribution are most evident in the form of stereotypes about how different persons are expected to act, taught primarily through the family and school as part of our socialization, and reinforced through the mass media as social truth. Individuals are taught that some people should be avoided because of their color, religion, social status, or some other personal characteristic that divides into "in-groups" and "out-groups" (Brewer & Campbell, 1976).

FUNDAMENTAL THEORIES

Although personality traits will resist change, it is possible to learn new styles of situational coping. There appear to be several types of skill that can be expected to contribute to intercultural competence. These skills include knowledge of subject matter, language, communication skills, taking advantage of opportunities, ability to use traits in a given culture, and ability to complete one's task.

L. Lee (1979) described social and cultural competence as a dynamic process that draws on individual, cognitive, linguistic, and social capabilities. When these capabilities are translated into functionally appropriate interpersonal strategies in specific intercultural context, competence is said to increase. The more alternatives of action or strategies an individual possesses, the more choices for dealing with the environment and the greater flexibility for responding through increasingly complex strategies. Other outcomes of learning include increased world mindedness, less authoritarian tendencies, increased internal control and humanitarian tendencies. Even if we were able to define the criteria of intercultural competence, we would have difficulty training persons to meet that criteria.

In planning orientation programs a wide range of approaches have been tried. Most orientation programs develop categories that cut across cultural boundaries. If people can learn to work in more than one culture they are more likely to develop an "intercultural perspective." Many persons are sent to another culture with little or no preparation other than information about the task they are expected to complete and with very little preparation for cross-cultural problems they will need to solve. The basic resource for cross-cultural adjustment is not information, however, but the support and acceptance by others in the host culture.

People who are most successful in adjusting to a new culture are often not completely successful later in readjusting to their home culture. There are even some studies that suggest that anxiety about intercultural interaction *increases* after orientation programs and that some host cultures prefer untrained sojourners (Bochner, 1977). The difficulty for intercultural training obviously arises when people move out of the controlled-training classroom setting and attempt to apply what they have learned to the real outside world.

The importance of interculturally skilled counseling and therapy is widely recognized in the priorities of the National Institute of Mental Health, the American Psychological Association's accreditation criteria, the 1979 President's Commission on Mental Health needs assessment, and numerous other professional and public organizations at the national as well as the international level (Pedersen, 1981). There are still, however, few degree-oriented academic programs at the university level to train counselors in cross-cultural skills, there are few articles in the major professional mental-health journals on cross-cultural counseling (Sundberg, 1981), and there are few programs scheduled in the area of cross-cultural counseling at professional meetings of counselors and therapists (Pedersen & Inouye, 1984).

Most counselors or therapists with an interest in cross-cultural counseling have had to develop their own programs in the area from courses scattered throughout the curricula. Many of these pre-service courses have emphasized the specialized perspective of one or another ethnic group in relation to the dominant culture.

There is less emphasis on the skill required for working in a multicultural population where age, sex role, life-style, socio-economic status, *as well as or combined with* ethnicity and nationality, may determine a person's "cultural" point of view. Many of the in-service or pre-service training programs have emphasized *either* awareness, knowledge, or skill to the exclusion of the other two elements, rather than balancing the emphasis of each component *with* one another interactively. Many of the training programs emphasize one disciplinary point of view, rather than the complementary viewpoints of different disciplines viewing the same cultural issue. Many of the training programs emphasize either classwork or field experience, with less involvement of resource persons from cultures being discussed. In the teaching of knowledge, awareness, or skill from an indigenous cultural perspective, a balanced emphasis on both the classroom and the field work is important.

CRITIQUE OF THEORIES

Although a variety of training approaches have been developed to prepare counselors to work with culturally different clients, there has been no systematic development of methods toward a theoretical basis, no comparisons of training outcomes, and no agreed-upon outcome criteria (Pedersen, 1981). It is not surprising therefore that skills-training models adapted for preparing counselors to work effectively in any one culture are likely to fail in a multicultural setting. Training approaches can be divided into those emphasizing culturally specific knowledge or skills related to the unique values of a particular culture and those emphasizing culturally generalized aspects that would apply in any contrasting culture. Although there is a quantity of materials that emphasize the guidelines for working within a specific cultural group, there are very few approaches that successfully generalize from one culture to another (Pedersen, 1983).

Human-relations training emphasizes genuineness, warmth, and empathy as primary and universally appropriate therapy skills. Personal growth and self-exploration in a culturally inappropriate setting have, however, led to increased adaptational difficulties when clients become more dissatisfied with their own cultures. By treating the person as an isolated individual, human-relations training has often placed the responsibility for mental health on the individual rather than the social unit and has assumed the generalized value of openness and direct communication. Empathy, warmth, and genuineness are values specific to some middle-class Westernized dominant cultures, but not all cultures, and any attempt to enforce their universal acceptance would be inappropriate.

Microtraining introduced a single skill at a time through expert modeling of that skill and the opportunity to rehearse the skill up to a criterion of competence. A. E. Ivey (1980), the primary architect of microtraining for counselors, suggested that "attending" and "influencing" microskills are still presented in the context of middle-class, verbally oriented approaches. Although Ivey readily acknowledged the importance of cultural differences, there are as yet no guidelines for how each microskill might be adapted to different cultures.

Life-development training emphasizes increased understanding of yourself through some knowledge of helping skills and experience in applying those skills. Here again we find an emphasis on the individual rather than the social context. The linear series of development stages toward the goal of "adulthood" as a symbolic goal has institutionalized the importance of self-reliance, achievement, and independence from others, contrary to the value of many non-Western societies. In many cultures independency longings are themselves neurotic, and dependency does not have the negative connotations of immaturity (Pedersen, 1979).

Structured Learning emphasizes social-reinforcement feedback through modeling, role playing, and the transfer of training skills through learning theory (Goldstein, 1981). A. Goldstein's approach is sensitive to the importance of a client's cultural expectations and emphasizes reformulating skills to fit a client's perspective rather than expecting the client to conform. It is difficult to locate appropriate rewards for each culturally different context that can reinforce a behavior in a culturally or socially appropriate manner.

Interpersonal Process Recall (IPR) has developed training methods that combine response modes, stimulus effect, reviewing interviews, debriefing from an inquirer, mutual recall, and processing feedback from the client (Kagan & McQuellon, 1981). There is abundant evidence for IPR's effectiveness since it was first used in 1962. There is, however, an assumption that insight will result in changed behavior and that direct approaches are more appropriate than indirect teaching of skills toward an outcome of greater trainee independence and autonomy. IPR assumes high levels of self disclosure, which would be difficult for more private cultures and may increase rather than decrease the stress levels or problematic aspects of their situation.

I developed a training model (1981, 1983) where the counselor and client are accompanied by an *anticounselor* (whose task it is to make the differences of expectations and values between the counselor and client explicit) and a *procounselor* (whose task it is to make the similarities of expectations and values between the counselor and client explicit). Immediate and continuous feedback from the client, anticounselor, and procounselor to the *culturally different* counselor provides an opportunity for the counselor to increase skill in (1) perceiving the problem from the client's viewpoint, (2) recognizing specific sources of resistance, (3) reducing counselor defensiveness, and (4) rehearsing recovery skills for getting out of trouble. The Triad Model attempts to create a safe context for counselors to learn about a culture by direct contact.

Intercultural training must be adaptive to the variety of specific contrasting cultures where it is applied. To a large extent the benefit of training will be measured by its relevance to real-life situations in their complexity. In many cases the goals of training will include not only outside individuals in the role of counselor or therapists doing "talk therapy" but natural support systems indigenous to the culture itself with a minimum of outside intervention.

REFERENCES

Adler, P. (1977) Beyond cultural identity: Reflections upon cultural and multicultural man. In Brislin, R. (Ed.), *Culture learning: Concepts, applications, and research.* Honolulu: University Press of Hawaii.

Bochner, S. (1977) The mediating man and cultural diversity. In Brislin, R. (Ed.), *Culture learning: Concepts, applications, and research.* Honolulu: University Press of Hawaii.

Brewer, M., & Campbell, D. (1976) *Ethnocentrism and intergroup attitudes: East African evidence.* New York: Wiley/Halsted.

Brislin, R. (1981) *Cross cultural encounters: Face to face interaction.* Elmsford, N.Y.: Pergamon Press.

Goldstein, A. (1981) Expectancy effects in cross-cultural counseling. In Marsella, A. J., & Pedersen, P. (Eds.), *Cross-cultural counseling and psychotherapy.* Elmsford, N.Y.: Pergamon Press.

Ivey, A. E. (1980) *Counseling and psychotherapy: Connections and applications.* New York: Prentice-Hall.

Kagan, N., & McQuellon, R. (1981) *Interpersonal process recall.* In Corsini, R., *Innovative psychotherapies.* New York: Wiley.

Lee, L. (1979) Is social competence independent of cultural context? *American Psychologist, 34,* 795–796.

Pedersen, P. (1979) Non-western psychologies: The search for alternatives. In Marsella, A., Tharp, R., & Ciborowski, T. (Eds.), *Perspectives in cross-cultural psychology.* New York: Academic Press.

——— (1981) Triad counseling. In Corsini, R. (Ed.), *Innovative psychotherapies.* New York: Wiley.

——— (1983) Cross-cultural training of mental health providers. In Brislin, R., & Landis, D., *Handbook of intercultural training.* Elmsford, N.Y.: Pergamon Press.

Pedersen, P., & Inouye, K. (1984) The international/intercultural perspective of the APA, *American Psychologist, 39* (5), 560–561.

Ruben, B. D., & Kealey, D. J. (1979) Behavioral assessment of communication competency and the prediction of cross cultural adaptation. *International Journal of Intercultural Relations, 3* (1), 15–47.

Sundberg, N. (1981) Cross-cultural counseling and psychotherapy: A research overview. In Marsella, A. & Pedersen, P. (Eds.), *Cross-cultural counseling and psychotherapy.* Elmsford, N.Y.: Pergamon Press, pp. 28–63.

Afterword: The Culturally Encapsulated Counselor Revisited

C. GILBERT WRENN

Once, as a young man, I "revisited" my childhood. I returned to the village where I had spent the first few years of my life and was sorely disillusioned. The houses and yards were all smaller—and dingier—than I remembered them to be, the streets were narrower, my "swimming hole" was a puddle—and only ten years had elapsed. I regretted the return.

So the request of Paul Pedersen to update an article of twenty-one years ago (Wrenn, 1962) aroused some apprehension. Would I be disillusioned again, find that my ideas were as shrunken in size as had been the houses and streets of my childhood town? In the article I had outlined some anticipated changes that might threaten a counselor's equanimity, examined types of cultural encapsulation, and suggested some preventive measures that could be taken. Would this structure hold up?

SOME EARLIER PROJECTIONS OF CHANGE

Some of these earlier projections have been so well accepted and discussed that they are by now almost shopworn. Very briefly, they are changing family patterns, involvement of government in our lives, appearance and disappearance of occupations, and new types of post-secondary education. Still current and expanding is the intricate economic and military interdependence of the various nations of the world (the United States will never again be an island) and the vast implications of my now very tame 1962 statement that "space flight is near reality." We have arrived at a new feeling of the vastness of space and the awesomeness of a pulsing, ever-changing universe. We are now no longer shocked even by the concept of a universe containing hundreds of millions of planets suitable for the creation and maintenance of various forms of life.

A FEW OTHER AREAS OF CONCERN ABOUT CHANGE THAT THREATEN COMPLACENCY

There are changes in every dimension of life; change is a dimension of living. The selection of a few demonstrate the threat.

A Few Situations That Are Threatening to Survival

1. The nuclear threat to the survival of civilization. It does not matter who starts such a war or why; the slaughter of hundreds of millions with centuries of aftermath horrors will be the same.

2. The use of alcohol and mind-altering drugs is pandemic, starting with both kinds during childhood; high usage during the critical mind- and character-forming period of adolescence; the cowardly habituation of otherwise responsible adults; the encouragement of drug usage as a political and social weapon to weaken entire populations (see *Reader's Digest*, October 1983)—the illness spreads too fast for the treatment to keep pace.

3. Lawlessness or deliberate defiance of the law; personal, business, and government corruption; violence; personal danger; widespread fear.

Situations Threatening to One's Ability to "Keep Up" or to Feel in Control

1. The rapidity of the development of computers and robotics, both of which are confusing in terms of the stability of both skilled labor and middle management. They are confusing also in terms of one's ability to keep up with developments that become personal competitors for the integrity of one's cognitive self.

2. The struggle to relate each news item from some unknown part of the world to the rest of the world, only to realize the vagueness of one's idea of the exact location of that country in the world. "Syria must be next door to Israel, for they're so worried about it—but then *where* are the Marines in relation to Syria?" "Where *is* El Salvador (or is it San Salvador?), and why is it so important?" There is confusion about the part the United States has in the World Bank and why so many nations are deeply in debt to *our* banks—and on and on.

3. The pleas for help that come in every mail delivery leave us confused and frustrated. You cannot help them all; how to decide? To be reminded of starvation; the torture of political prisoners; the brutality and complete denial of human rights in some countries; and the hunger, injustice, and discrimination in our own country tears at the heart. My wife, Kathleen, and I let the letters pile up for a month and then sort them into categories such as meeting hunger directly; providing wells, tools, and seed; education for the poor but willing to work; care for the salvation from death and education of orphans; improvement of government; fighting discrimination and injustice; conservation measures to

maintain quality of life. We then decide how much we can give to at least one agency in each category, once or twice a year.

We cannot dig wells, feed orphans, or fight the Klan—one person is puny. But with our money added to that of 2,000 or 10,000 others we are a force that can do much. But even here, it is never enough, and it is still frustrating because of the unevenness of life among the peoples of the world. This monthly accounting with the love in my checkbook constantly raises the question, "Is my checkbook as big as my heart—is my *heart* big enough?"

So it is easy to give up, to retreat inside, to spin around oneself a cocoon of pretended reality that will protect one against the harshness, the fears, the decisions, to be made concerning the world outside.

SOME KINDS OF ENCAPSULATIONS

Two common reactions to the problems of our world, our nation, that lead to encapsulation are (a) a sense of *hopelessness* about the world—"It's too big for one person to do anything about it—too far advanced to stop it—it's too complex"; and (b) a *denial* of the reality of the change or the situation—"It just can't be true—I don't believe it's real—it is highly exaggerated—give it time, it will get better."

1. These two barriers to the acceptance of apparent reality are useful—they are comfortable. Holding them in mind, one can eliminate from immediate awareness anything that is too stressful to accept. The weaving of the cocoon begins with the creation of rationalizations, which, when dealt with strenuously or frequently enough, become one's personally valid substitutes for reality.

Facing a client's wishfulness with reality is one of the counselor's most important functions. This does not have to be harsh; the counselor has many ways of facing reality but saving face—"Yes, I see what you mean. There are other possibilities which have some evidence back of them"—"You've made a point; let me try something else on you." There are many ways of helping a client face reality, but none of them are particularly effective if the client senses that you are ducking reality yourself and speaking from within your cocoon.

2. Counselors can unconsciously find themselves operating within the cocoon of their own work setting. The conditions of work, of the daily realities, of the kinds of clients, of the kinds of colleagues, can lull a counselor into seeing that small world as synonymous with the larger world. It is your real world, but it is a limited one, perhaps an unreal one, to your clients. Another kind of encapsulation is when you see your particular sampling of clients as representative of people in general. They seldom are. It is most risky when a counselor sees clients who are outside the counselor's cultural or sub-cultural cocoon. These clients are real but not to the counselor.

Counselors in any agency of society suffer from this limitation of reality—workers in hospitals, prisons, mental-health clinics, and so on. The counselor in private practice is equally restricted in his or her sense of what people are generally like. Such a counselor sees only clients who *choose* to see a counselor, have the money to do so, have a crisis situation that forces them to see someone. The client, furthermore, will try to see the counselor whose reputation for a certain point of view or way of behavior is comfortable for the client. A Carl Rogers client would seldom seek out Albert Ellis, and a Gilbert Wrenn client would be one who likes what he or she has heard about Gilbert Wrenn. I will never see some kinds of people as clients.

3. A third type of dangerous thinking for a counselor is to interpret the world to the client from within the counselor's particular and unique life experience. The cocoon woven here comes from a kind of conceit in assuming that the counselor's experience is of value to the client even though that client is younger, was reared in a different world, and has a unique family background, school experience, job experience, and value structure. How *can* the counselor be so smug as to assume that his or her world bears any but the slightest resemblance to that of the client?

PREVENTION AND TREATMENT OF ENCAPSULATION

1. Let us engage in long-ranging thinking, at least once a day. We are exposed to the short-range views every day by the news media, an unending procession of sad and negative events. To balance this daily thrust of thought that the world is rapidly unraveling, we need to consider what the futurists are saying, for theirs is a very different story. They are students of long-range trends in social behavior; students of the trends in social, scientific, and philosophical thought; collectors of the reflections of leading thinkers in all parts of the world—their view is very positive (Ferguson, 1980; Capra, 1981; Naisbitt, 1982; Cetron and O'Toole, 1982). I challenge anyone to read any one of the four books cited (and there are others) and not feel more positive about self and the future.

Exciting in particular is the movement of leading scientists toward the inclusion of transcendental and spiritual realities in their thinking. Here is physicist Fritjof Capra, who sees a trend away from our sole dependence upon scientific empiricism and logic, with their mechanistic and reductionistic limitations, toward the reality also of mysticism and spirituality, the interdependence of all phenomena, the brotherhood of all people (Capra, 1982, 1981). Here are two eminent brain scientists, both Nobel Prize winners, one saying that his lifelong studies convince him that the mind is more than the functioning of the brain, that above both is something that might be called a soul (Eccles & Potter, 1977). The other wrote that the survival of humankind is not dependent upon more brain research but upon a restructuring of our values. He proposed the assumption of a religious commitment to the importance of values such as population planning, respect for the beauty of the land, the development of renewable energy (Sperry, 1983).

Our future is *possible* and appears to be *good*. Let us ponder these things and take heart.

2. Develop a habit of unlearning something every day—make way for the new truth by discarding what is no longer true. Each day we should take some "fact" that is no longer a fact and drop it from our vocabulary: examine some situation that is very familiar to us but is no longer present in our society; question something that we believe in but that other people of integrity—of another culture or sub-culture—may reject. Carl Jung once wrote that the serious problems of life are never really solved, that the meaning of a problem is not its solution but in constantly working at it. It is only this process of constant examination that saves one from a sense of futility.

3. We must trust other people to have solutions for situations for which we can see no light ahead. As we observe our troubled world, remember that many people are worrying about these same situations and are finding solutions, are trying out options, are engaging in appropriate studies. We are not alone in the world. We must rid ourselves of the conceit that if we see no way that that is the end of it, that our thinking cannot be improved upon.

In particular, I feel that we who are middle-aged or over must trust our young people and their ingeniousness, inventiveness, and courage. They often do not know enough to be afraid and back off, so they forge ahead and get something done. Our image of the young is badly warped, for again the media portrayal is often of the young who are emotionally unbalanced, antisocial, amoral, personally vicious, and without respect for human life. These examples are only a small fraction of the whole body of young people; yet they get the headlines. Believe in the youth that you know—tell them so. Help them over their growing pains, their trial and error mistakes that are a part of learning. Give them confidence in themselves, and you will contribute to the solutions that they will develop during the next few decades.

4. Risk something every day—a new idea, a new approach to anything, a new trust in a person. If you risk, you cannot cower. Cocoons are not woven very quickly or tightly when you take a risk, when you say to life, "I don't know the outcome, but I'll try." Nor do you need to expect all successes—far from it. A batting average of 0.700 or 0.800 is unheard of in baseball, but in life you might attain it. Expect some failures, and you will not be overcome by them.

There is a risk in trusting others, for sometimes you will be hurt. But there is a greater risk in not trusting, for then you may hurt another who desperately needs your trust.

There is risk in *accepting* another's love and trust, for he or she in offering love may expect something in return. However, not accepting an offer of help or love may seriously wound the giver, for in not accepting you are saying, "I do not trust the sincerity of your offer. I do not want to be under obligation to you." Also, in not accepting you are denying the other the pleasure of giving, a pleasure that you experience when *you* give.

I risk myself when I *do* something to correct a situation, for it may be the wrong thing to have done. Is it worse to extinguish a fire awkwardly than to do nothing at all and let it burn? I risk myself when I ask a question out of my ignorance. Which is better, to learn or to preserve my personal pride?

This recital of risks could be extended, as I did in a recent chapter (Wrenn, 1984), but the point here is that taking risks is a powerful way to avoid the risk of weaving your cocoon.

I am optimistic, but I think it is an informed optimism after more than half a century of working with people. People can avoid encapsulation by looking at threats rather than looking around them; by working out a personal solution to a frustration such as "So many people and situations need help; how can I, one person, make a difference?" by taking the long view and then trusting a mighty army of others, particularly the young, to make the long view come to pass; by purging ourselves almost daily of ideas and relationships that were once valid but no longer are.

I am also optimistic about the world, and I refuse to let current crises blind me to the long wave of learning by the human race. Consider a statement from the "Values and Lifestyle Study" made by SRI (formerly Stanford Research Institute), a three-year, one-million-dollar study for eighty-five corporate clients who wanted to know—for product planning and production purposes—"What will be important to people in the next decade or two?" In the report of the study is a small excerpt entitled "The Evolution of Symbols of Success": from quantity toward quality, from the group toward the individual, from abundance toward sufficiency, and from waste toward conservation.

Past symbols: fame, being in *Who's Who*, five-figure salary, college degree, splendid home, executive position, live-in servants, new car every year, club membership.
Present symbols: unlisted number, Swiss bank account, connections with celebrities, deskless office, second and third homes, rare foreign car, being a vice-president, being published.
Future symbols: free time any time, recognition as a creative person, oneness of work and play, rewarded less by money than by honor and affection, major societal commitments, easy laughter and unembarrassed tears, wide-ranging interests and actions, philosophical independence, loving others, being in touch with oneself. (SRI, 1981)

If this is to be the future, and some of it is in sight now, I am willing to stretch my present age of 81 to at least 100!

REFERENCES

Capra, Fritjof (1981) *The turning point: Science, society, and the rising culture*. New York: Simon and Schuster.

——— (1982) Spirituality and social values: An interview by Renee Weber. *The American Theosophist, 70*, 325–333.

Cetron, Marvin, & O'Toole, Thomas (1982) *Encounters with the future: Forecast of life in the 21st century*. New York: McGraw-Hill.

Eccles, John C., & Potter, Karl (1977) *The self and its brain.* New York: Springer International.

Ferguson, Marilyn (1980) *The aquarian conspiracy: Personal and social transformation in the 1980's.* Boston: Tarcher/Houghton Mifflin.

Naisbitt, John (1982) *Megatrends: Ten new directions transforming our lives.* New York: Warner Books.

Sperry, Roger (1983) Interview by Yvonne Baskin. *Omni, 5,* 69–75, 98, 100.

SRI (formerly Stanford Research Institute) (1981) Values and lifestyle study. *Leading Edge Bulletin, 1, 1.* (See also *Leading Edge Bulletin 3,* 1983, 1–2. Complete study available in Mitchell, Arnold (1983) *Nine American Lifestyles.* New York: Macmillan.

Villoldo, Alberto, & Dychtwold, Ken (Eds.). (1981) *Millennium: Glimpses into the 21st century.* Boston: Tarcher/Houghton Mifflin.

Wrenn, C. Gilbert (1962) The culturally encapsulated counselor. *Harvard Educational Review, 32,* 444–449. Reprinted in Mosher, R. L., et al. (Eds.). (1965) *Guidance: An examination.* New York: Harcourt, Brace and Company.

——— (in press) Personal reflections on my experiences in counseling psychology and in life. In Whiteley, John M., et al. (Eds.), *The Counseling Psychologist.*

Index

About the Contributors

LEONORE LOEB ADLER received a Ph.D. in experimental social psychology from Adelphi University. She is affiliated with the Department of Psychology at Malloy College, Rockville Centre, New York, where she is the Director of the Institute for Cross-Cultural and Cross-Ethnic Studies. Adler is currently President of the Division of Social Psychology of the New York State Psychological Association.

PHILLIP D. AKUTSU is a graduate student in the Clinical Psychology Program at the University of California, Los Angeles.

PATRICIA ARREDONDO, Assistant Professor of Education at Boston University, directs the Bilingual Cross-Cultural Counseling Specialization. She has conducted longitudinal research investigating identity and career development for immigrant young adults and developed the *Human Rights Training Manual for AACD*.

DONALD R. ATKINSON is Professor of Education and Director of Training in the Counseling Psychology Program at the University of California, Santa Barbara. He is coauthor of *Counseling American Minorities: A Cross-Cultural Perspective* (1983) and the author or coauthor of more than sixty professional journal articles, many of which deal with cross-cultural issues. He has also written a number of articles about the recruitment, selection, training, and retention of ethnic-minority-counselor trainees.

CAROLYN L. ATTNEAVE, Ph.D., Sci.D., is Professor of Psychology and Adjunct Professor of Psychiatry and Behavioral Sciences at the University of Washington. Of Delaware heritage, she has worked as a lecturer and research associate at the Harvard School of Public Health, on the Minority Affairs and

American Indian Panels of the President's Commission on Mental Health and the White House Conference on the Family, and as an officer board member of the original Planning Committees and the first Board for Minority Affairs of the American Psychological Association.

HENRY BOROW is Professor of Psychological Studies and Counselor Educator at the University of Minnesota. He is the former chairperson of the International Relations Committee, American Personnel and Guidance Association and the past president of the National Vocational Guidance Association and the Division of Counseling Psychology, American Psychological Association. He received the Eminent Career Award, National Vocational Guidance Association, and is author or editor of four books and more than one hundred published papers.

LAWRENCE M. BRAMMER is Professor of Educational Psychology and Counseling at the University of Washington. He has published five books on counseling and adult development as well as more than sixty articles on counseling, testing, and human development. He is a fellow of the American Psychological Association and a diplomate of the American Board for Professional Psychology.

J. MANUEL CASAS is an Assistant Professor in Counseling Psychology at the Graduate School of Education, University of California, Santa Barbara. He is cofounder of JMC & Associates, a leading Hispanic-owned and -oriented business- and educational-consulting firm. His special interests focus on the development of effective counseling-communication skills among persons of different cultures and management of job-related stress. He has researched and published works in these areas.

NATHAN DEEN is Head of the Department of Counseling Studies at the University of Utrecht, the Netherlands, and Managing Editor of the *International Journal for the Advancement of Counseling*. He developed counselor education in the Netherlands and contributed to the introduction of counseling services in Dutch schools.

WYNETTA DEVORE is Associate Professor of Social Work at Syracuse University. She taught at Rutgers Graduate School of Social Work and Kean College of New Jersey. Her teaching has been primarily in areas of direct practice, human behavior, and health care. Her publications have been related to ethnicity as a factor in practice, and her major work is *Ethnic Sensitive Social Work Practice* (1981), coauthored with Elfriede G. Schlesinger.

JURIS G. DRAGUNS was born in Latvia, completed his high school education in Germany, and obtained college and doctoral degrees in the United States. He has held clinical and research positions at the Rochester (N.Y.) State Hospital and Worcester (Mass.) State Hospital, respectively. He is Professor of Psychology at Pennsylvania State University, where he teaches courses in psycho-pathology, personality theory, clinical assessment, and cross-cultural psychology. He is coeditor of *Counseling across Cultures* (1981) and *Handbook of Cross-Cultural Psychology*, Vol. 6, *Psychopathology* (1980) and has written extensively on the relationship of culture to personality, mental disorder, and modes of psychological intervention.

VICTOR J. DRAPELA, Ph.D., is Professor and Chair of the Counselor Education Department at the University of South Florida in Tampa. In addition to international guidance studies, his interests lie in the areas of personality and counseling theories, consultation, and supervision of counselors. He is the editor of a textbook for comparative studies in guidance and counseling, *Guidance and Counseling around the World* (1979), and the author of two books, *Youth Guidance in the Soviet Bloc* (1970) and *The Counselor as Consultant and Supervisor* (1983).

OLIVA M. ESPIN teaches counseling psychology at Boston University. She has chaired the Hispanic Task Force, Division 35 (Psychology of Women), of the American Psychological Association and is active in other professional organizations, including the National Hispanic Psychological Association. She was National Institute of Mental Health fellow at Harvard University while doing a study of Hispanic women healers.

JONATHAN A. FREEDMAN is Director of Education and Training at Hutchings Psychiatric Center. He is coauthor (with Barry Glassner) of *Clinical Sociology* (1979), the first text in the field. Freedman is the current President of the Clinical Sociology Association. He serves on the faculties of Syracuse University, Upstate Medical Center, and the New School for Social Research. He has worked on several levels of focus: individual, organizational, occupational, community, ethnic, and religious concerns, both directly and as a consultant.

N. JANE GERSHAW is a Clinical Psychologist who has worked at Norristown State Hospital and Hahnemann Medical College and Community Mental Health Center. She currently serves as Chief of the Syracuse Veterans Administration Mental Hygiene Clinic with a faculty appointment to Syracuse University and SUNY Upstate Medical Center. She is coauthor (with Robert Sprafkin and Arnold Goldstein) of *Skill Training for Community Living* (1976), *I Know What's Wrong but I Don't Know What to Do about It* (1979), and *Skillstreaming the Adolescent* (1980).

ARNOLD P. GOLDSTEIN is a Professor of Psychology at Syracuse University, where he directs the Center for Research on Aggression. He is the author or editor of twenty books and more than sixty articles on active therapeutic ingredients, research methods, behavior-change procedures, aggression control, and the teaching of prosocial skills. His books include *Therapist-Patient Expectancies in Psychotherapy* (1963), *Psychotherapy and the Psychology of Behavior Change* (1966), *Psychotherapeutic Attraction: The Lonely Teacher* (1971), *Police Crisis Intervention* (1979), *Hostage* (1979), *Structured Learning Therapy* (1973), *Skill Training for Community Living* (1976), and *Psychological Skill Training* (1981).

JANET E. HELMS is Associate Professor of Psychology at the University of Maryland. Her teaching and research interests include measurement and the psychology of women, minorities, and immigrant populations. She has published one book and approximately fifteen journal articles.

EDWIN L. HERR was President of the American Association for Counseling and Development and is Professor and Head of the Division of Counseling and Educational Psychology at Pennsylvania State University. He has authored some twenty books and monographs and more than two hundred articles on counseling and guidance. At present he serves as a member of the Executive Council of the International Round Table for the Advancement of Counseling. He has also served as a visiting fellow at the National Institutes for Careers, Education and Counseling, Cambridge, England; and as an Asian Foundation lecturer, Yashida International Education fellow, and research fellow in the Japan Society for the Promotion of Science in Japan.

CINDY HIGASHI, an American Psychological Association Minority Fellowship recipient, is a graduate student in clinical psychology at the University of California, Los Angeles.

W. FRANK HULL IV is Director of International Programs at the Office of the Vice President for Academic Affairs at Arizona State University. He is also Adjunct Resident Professor of Intercultural Communication in the College of Public Programs. His most recent book, *At a Foreign University* (1979), was coauthored with Otto Klineberg.

GERALD G. JACKSON is currently President of New Arena Consultants, Visiting Lecturer at Cornell University, and Research Associate at the Center for Human Environments, Graduate School of the City University of New York. His several publications on the black perspective in counseling have been published in various books on counseling American minorities.

ENRICO E. JONES, Associate Professor of Psychology at the University of California, Berkeley, has published in the areas of cross-cultural psychology and clinical intervention and is coauthor of *Minority Mental Health* (1982).

OTTO KLINEBERG is the Robert Johnston Niven Professor Emeritus of Social Psychology at Columbia University and has recently returned to New York after twenty years as visiting professor at the University of Paris (The Sorbonne). His publications include *Negro Intelligence and Selective Migration* (1935), *Race Differences* (1935), *Social Psychology* (1940, 1954), and *The Human Dimension in International Relations* (1964).

TERESA LAFROMBOISE (Ph.D., University of Oklahoma), a Visiting Scholar at Stanford University, is an Assistant Professor of Counseling Psychology at the University of Nebraska–Lincoln. She has authored studies on the social influence process in cross-cultural counseling with American Indian clients and has designed and evaluated social-skills training interventions with American Indian groups.

HARRIET P. LEFLEY, Associate Professor of Psychiatry at the University of Miami School of Medicine, directed the Cross-Cultural Training Institute for Mental Health Professionals and has been involved in cross-cultural research and service delivery for the past fifteen years.

MADELEINE M. LEININGER, R.N., Ph.D., Lh.D., F.A.A.N., is Professor of Nursing and Anthropology and Director of the Center for Health Research, College of Nursing, Wayne State University. She is the author of 12 books and 220 articles on the subjects of transcultural nursing, mental health, administration, and counseling. Leininger was dean of schools of nursing at the Universities of Washington and Utah and served as distinguished visiting professor at several universities.

WALTER J. LONNER is Professor of Psychology at Western Washington University, Bellingham, Washington. The founding editor of the *Journal of Cross-Cultural Psychology*, his main area of activity in teaching, writing, and research involves the growing focus on cross-cultural issues and problems. He has been involved as editor or author with a number of books, including *Counseling across Cultures* (1981, with Paul Pedersen, Juris Draguns, and Joseph Trimble) and volume 3 of the *Handbook of Cross-Cultural Psychology* (1980, with H. C. Triandis).

RAYMOND P. LORION, Ph.D., is Professor and Director of Community Psychology at the University of Tennessee. From 1982 to 1984 he served as visiting scientist at the National Institute of Mental Health and then as acting associate administrator for prevention in the Alcohol, Drug Abuse, and Mental Health Administration. He has written two review papers on psychotherapeutic treatment, which appeared in *Psychological Bulletin* (1973, 1974), and a major review appearing in the *Handbook of Psychotherapy and Behavior Change*, Vol. 11 (1978).

LUDWIG F. LOWENSTEIN, M.A., Dip. Psych., Ph.D., is a Founder and Director of Allington Manor School in Hampshire, England, following years of experience as Chief Educational Psychologist of Hampshire. His background includes work in mental hospitals, child-guidance clinics, and residential centers for maladjusted adolescents in New York City. He is Chief Examiner in Educational Psychology at the College of Preceptors, London, and Visiting Professor to the University of Khartoum (Sudan). More recently his appointments have included a directorship of the International Council of Psychologists, and he is editor-in-chief of the journal *School Psychology International*.

NOREEN MOKUAU, D.S.W., is Assistant Professor in the School of Social Work at the University of Hawaii. Her primary interests in intercultural counseling relate to the identification and impact of culture-specific and culture-general values on therapeutic process and outcome. She recently conducted an empirical study for the Pacific Asian Mental Health Research Project, which broadly addressed this area, and is currently engaged in similar conceptual and empirical projects.

AMADO M. PADILLA is Professor of Psychology at the University of California, Los Angeles. He is also Director of the Spanish Speaking Mental Health Research Center, which is funded by the National Institute of Mental Health. He has published extensively in the area of Hispanic mental health. His current research interests include acculturative stress among immigrants and child bilingualism.

DELORES L. PARRON, Ph.D., is Associate Director for Minority Concerns of the National Institute of Mental Health. Before that she served as the associate director of the Division of Mental Health and Behavioral Medicine at the Institute of Medicine, National Academy of Sciences. As a staff member of the 1978 President's Commission on Mental Health, Parron coordinated the panel on special populations.

RICHARD E. PEARSON is Associate Professor of Education in the Counselor Education Program at Syracuse University. The author of more than twenty-five articles and chapters, his interests have focused particularly upon group work in counseling. Recently, his research has examined the nature and impact of social support and the natural systems through which it is delivered. He has collaborated with former students and other researchers to examine natural support-system issues in English- and-French-speaking Canada, Puerto Rico, and Ecuador.

PAUL PEDERSEN is Chairman of the Counseling and Guidance Program and Professor of Education at Syracuse University. He is coauthor or editor of thirteen books, twenty-six chapters in books, and thirty-nine articles, mostly on counseling across cultures. He was director of the National Institute of Mental Health–

funded DISC (Developing Interculturally Skilled Counselors) four-year project at the University of Hawaii and the East West Center. He taught and conducted psychological research in Indonesia, Malaysia, and Taiwan for six years.

CHIZUKO SAEKI was born in Manchuria in 1946, raised in Japan, and received a B.A. in literature and English from Tokyo University through the Foreign Studies Program in 1968. She received an M.A. in education from Keio University, Tokyo, in 1978. Currently, she is a Ph.D. candidate in educational psychology from the Counseling and Student Personnel Psychology Program at the University of Minnesota.

NELLY SALGADO DE SNYDER is Associate Director of the Spanish Speaking Mental Health Research Center. Trained as a clinical psychologist at the National University of Mexico, she has been interested in mental-illness and substance-abuse prevention and treatment programs. Currently pursuing a doctorate in social policy at the University of California, Los Angeles, she is also conducting research on the topic of Hispanic interethnic marriages and children of such unions.

ELSIE M. J. SMITH is a consultant in private practice. She is a member of the editorial boards of *The Counseling Psychologist* and *The Journal of Counseling Psychology* and has authored *Counseling the Culturally Different Black Youth* (1973) and coauthored (with James Hansen & Richard Warner) *Group Counseling Theory and Process* (1980).

ROBERT P. SPRAFKIN directs the Day Treatment Center and serves as Director of Psychology Training for the Syracuse Veterans Administration Medical Center. He is coauthor of *Working with Police Agencies* (1976) and coauthor (with Arnold P. Goldstein and N. Jane Gershaw) of *Skill Training for Community Living: Applying Structured Learning Therapy* (1976), *I Know What's Wrong but I Don't Know What to Do about It* (1979), and *Skillstreaming the Adolescent* (1980).

DAVID SUE is Associate Professor of Psychology at the University of Michigan–Dearborn. He has research and writing interests in Asian-Americans, behavioral approaches to counseling, and human sexuality. He has coauthored a text on abnormal psychology with his brothers, Derald and Stanley.

DERALD WING SUE is Professor of Counseling Psychology at California State University, Hayward, and President of Psychological Corporation in California. He served as the first president of the Association of Asian-American Psychologists and is the author of numerous publications and books, including *Counseling the Culturally Different: Theory and Practice* (1981) and *Counseling American Minorities*, 2nd ed. (1983).

STANLEY SUE is Professor of Psychology at the University of California, Los Angeles. He was formerly a faculty member at the University of Washington and director of training at the National Asian American Psychology Training Center. He coauthored (with J. K. Morishima) *The Mental Health of Asian Americans* (1982).

L. SUNNY SUNDAL-HANSEN is Professor of Counseling and Student Personnel Psychology in the Educational Psychology Department at the University of Minnesota and Director of BORN FREE, a federally funded program to reduce stereotyping in career options for women and men. She is the editor of *Career Development and Counseling of Women* and author of several articles on sex roles across cultures, a chapter on gender and career for the National Vocational Guidance Association decennial volume (1984), and the UNESCO monograph *Eliminating Sex Stereotypes in Schools* (1983).

NORMAN D. SUNDBERG is Professor of Clinical and Community Psychology with the Department of Psychology at the University of Oregon in Eugene, Oregon. He has done research and taught in India, Australia, Spain, and Germany. Many of his cross-cultural research publications are about adolescent interests, values, time perspectives, and family perceptions. His teaching and research activities include clinical assessment at both the graduate and undergraduate level. Professor Sundberg's most recent book is *Introduction to Clinical Psychology* (1983, with Julian Taplin and Leona Tyler).

DONALD SUPER is Adjunct Research Professor at the University of Florida and International Coordinator of the Work Importance Study and Professor Emeritus of Psychology and Education at Teachers College, Columbia University. He is a fellow of the National Institute for Careers Education and Counseling, Cambridge, England, and Visiting Professor of Psychology at the University of Paris. Super served as president of the American Personnel and Guidance Association, National Vocational Guidance Association, and the Division of Counseling Psychology of the American Psychological Association. He has published widely in the area of counseling psychology.

HARRY TRIANDIS is Professor of Psychology at the University of Illinois in Urbana-Champaign. His books include *Attitude and Attitude Change* (1971), *The Analysis of Subjective Culture* (1972), *Variations in Black and White Perceptions of the Social Environment* (1976), and *Interpersonal Behavior* (1977). He edited the six-volume *Handbook of Cross-Cultural Psychology* (1980–1981). He is past president of the International Association of Cross-Cultural Psychology, the Society of the Psychological Study of Social Issues (Division 9 of the American Psychological Association), and the Society for Personality and Social Psychology (Division 8 of the American Psychological Association); vice-president of the International Association of Applied Psychology; and recipient of awards by several international psychological associations.

JOSEPH E. TRIMBLE is Associate Professor of Psychology at Western Washington University, Bellingham, Washington. He has served on a number of agencies and committees of the National Institute of Mental Health, National Institute of Alcohol Abuse and Alcoholism, National Institute of Drug Abuse, and American Psychological Association.

CLEMMONT E. VONTRESS is Professor of Education at George Washington University, Washington, D.C., and is best known for his more than seventy articles, chapters, and papers on the ways in which ethnicity affects the counseling process. An exponent of existentialism as a counseling modality, he is a frequent consultant to universities, organizations, and agencies in the United States and abroad.

KAREN WATSON-GEGEO, Associate Professor of Education at Harvard University, is an anthropologist who has done applied research in linguistics, education, and the human services in cross-cultural context.

BEA WEHRLY, Professor of Education at Western Illinois University, is a counselor-educator with special interests in cross-cultural counseling and international guidance and counseling.

AARON WOLFGANG, Associate Professor at the Ontario Institute for Studies in Education and the University of Toronto, has edited and coedited several books in the areas of intercultural counseling and nonverbal behavior as well as contributed chapters to these books and others. His most notable book is *Nonverbal Behavior: Applications and Cultural Implications* (1979).

C. GILBERT WRENN is Professor Emeritus in Counseling Psychology at Arizona State University and was formerly a professor at the University of Minnesota and Stanford University. He is author of *The Counselor in a Changing World* (1962), *The World of the Contemporary Counselor* (1973), *College Student Personnel Work* ( ), and some four hundred other books, chapters, and articles. Wrenn was also consulting editor for the forty-two-volume series *Student Personnel and Counseling* (1961–1974) and was editor of the *Journal of Counseling Psychology* (1953–1964).